BAUHAUS CULTURE

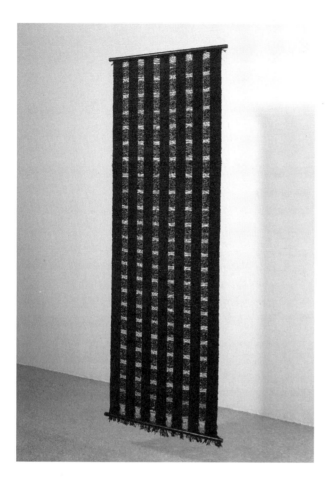

BAUHAUS CULTURE

FROM WEIMAR TO THE COLD WAR

Kathleen James-Chakraborty, Editor

UNIVERSITY OF MINNESOTA PRESS
MINNEAPOLIS · LONDON

The University of Minnesota Press gratefully acknowledges the work of Edward Dimendberg, editorial consultant, on this project.

Chapter 5 was first published in slightly different form in *The Art Bulletin* 75, no. 4 (2003); reprinted courtesy of the College Art Association. Chapter 7 was originally published in German with more extensive illustrations as "Bauhaus-Architekten im 'Dritten Reich,'" in *Bauhaus-Moderne im Nationalsozialismus: Zwischen Anbiederung und Verfolgung,* edited by Winfried Nerdinger in collaboration with the Bauhaus-Archiv, Berlin (Munich: Prestel Verlag, 1993); copyright 1993 by Prestel Verlag; reprinted with permission.

Published by the **University of Minnesota Press**
111 Third Avenue South, Suite 290
Minneapolis, MN 55401-2520
http://www.upress.umn.edu

LIBRARY OF CONGRESS CATALOGING-IN-PUBLICATION DATA
Bauhaus culture : from Weimar to the cold war / Kathleen James-Chakraborty, editor.
    p.   cm.
Includes bibliographical references and index.
ISBN-13: 978-0-8166-4687-6 (hc : alk. paper)
ISBN-10: 0-8166-4687-2 (hc : alk. paper)
ISBN-13: 978-0-8166-4688-3 (pb : alk. paper)
ISBN-10: 0-8166-4688-0 (pb : alk. paper)
1. Bauhaus. 2. Bauhaus—Influence. 3. Art—Study and teaching—Germany—History—20th century. 4. Art schools—Social aspects—Germany. I. James, Kathleen, 1960–
N332.G33B4263 2006
709.43'09041—dc22
                                                                              2006006953

Printed in the United States of America on acid-free paper

The University of Minnesota is an equal-opportunity educator and employer.

12 11 10 09 08 07 06   **10 9 8 7 6 5 4 3 2 1**

CONTENTS

ILLUSTRATIONS

ACKNOWLEDGMENTS

This book has had an exceptionally long gestation, and I want to begin by thanking the authors, in particular, for their extraordinary patience.

Beatrice Rehl initiated this project by asking if I would be interested in editing a collection of essays on the Bauhaus. Excited by the opportunity to consider this august institution from new points of view, I assembled my team, keeping a particular eye out for people who had done excellent work on the history of modern German art, architecture, and design, but who had not necessarily worked on the Bauhaus. In addition, Winfried Nerdinger graciously gave me permission to translate the pathbreaking essay on Bauhaus architecture during the Third Reich that he had already published in his own collected volume.

I am extremely grateful to Edward Dimendberg for shepherding the collection to a safe harbor at the University of Minnesota Press. Pieter Martin has proved an exemplary editor, and it has been an unalloyed delight to work with him. My research assistants, Noga Wizansky, Don Choi, Elihu Rubin, and Peter Allen, were also invaluable; Noga assembled most of the bibliography, and Peter completed the onerous tasks of collecting the illustrations and necessary permissions. The Committee on Research at the University of California supported their efforts and funded the illustrations for my own essays here.

Finally, I thank my parallel project during these years, my family, Sumit and Shomik Chakraborty, who sustained me throughout.

INTRODUCTION

Kathleen James-Chakraborty

The Bauhaus was the site of the twentieth century's most influential experiment in artistic education. It gave institutional form to instruction in the avant-garde painting and architecture for which many of its faculty were already famous at the same time that it prompted their continuing transformation (Figure I.1). In Weimar, where it was founded in 1919, Dessau, where it reopened in 1926, and Berlin, where it finally closed in 1933, a concrete alternative to the state-sponsored fine arts academies that had flourished during the nineteenth century finally took definitive shape. Here the Arts and Crafts project of injecting art into daily life through the redesign of objects of daily use directly confronted the reality of mass production. Here a rich student life encompassing festivals, jazz bands, and sexual experimentation set a legendary and perhaps unsurpassable standard for communal dedication to the new.

Two other aspects of the Bauhaus account for much of its enduring impact. One is the degree to which the abstraction characteristic of the objects and works of art created by those who taught and studied at the Bauhaus still appear to represent a central fact of modernity: the rationalization implicit in industrialization (Figure I.2). Only in 1923 did the school decisively orient itself toward industrial rather than craft production. Nonetheless, its entire history can be described as a series of attempts to come to terms with the ways in which machine production had transformed the relationship between an object and its maker and between those who made and those who used such objects. Whether the result of nostalgic, quasi-spiritual experiments with handwork or of rigorous attempts to resist commercial spectacle, Bauhaus designs developed in relation to an awareness of these realities. The scope of this engagement with the machine created the compelling impression that a particular approach to design was as inevitable as the technological progress to which it was so closely linked.

The Bauhaus is also central to any discussion of the relationship in the twentieth century between politics and art. Walter Gropius founded the Bauhaus in the literal shadow of the constitutional convention being held in Weimar to establish the first German republic (Figure I.3). The school continues to be the visual standard-bearer for the Weimar Republic, to which Hitler dealt a deathblow just months before his rise to power finally forced the school's third director, Ludwig Mies van der Rohe, to shut its

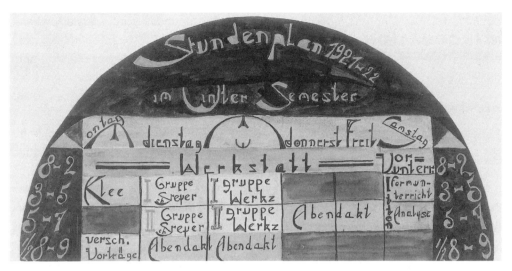

Figure I.1. Lothar Schreyer, timetable for winter semester at the Weimar Bauhaus, 1921/22. Pen and India ink, red tempera, watercolor over pencil. Bauhaus-Archiv, Berlin.

doors (Figure I.4). Scholars continue to argue over the degree to which the Bauhaus was a "cathedral of socialism," preserving the revolutionary spirit that in the wake of the country's defeat in World War I had swept away the monarchy and introduced the hope of a more egalitarian society.[1] What is certain is that that was always its public reputation.[2] Engendering continual controversy that prevented the school from ever gaining a secure financial or institutional footing, its utopian ideals also contributed enormously to the influence its faculty, its students, and their ideas have had ever since.

The purpose of this introduction and of the essays that follow is to describe the scope of the reforms that occurred at the Bauhaus, while calling into question the degree to which the school should continue to symbolize an uncomplicated relationship between art, modern technology, and progressive politics. Because of the Bauhaus's centrality to any account of modern art, architecture, or design, accounts of its history are often hagiographic or highly hostile in tone, depending on whether the writer shares his or her subject's goals.[3] Most serious scholars of the Bauhaus have remained loyal to its ideals. In consequence, they have often been reluctant to avail themselves of approaches to art, architectural, and design history detached from the belief in a universal formalism that was key to the thinking of many of those associated with the school. Those who pioneered such approaches have, on the other hand, not always used them to gain deeper insight into what they have superseded and have instead focused on other topics.[4]

This book differs from many others on the Bauhaus in the degree to which its authors are self-conscious about their relationship to the historiography of their subject. It does not offer a comprehensive survey history of the Bauhaus. That exists elsewhere, above all in the useful account offered by Magdalena Droste.[5] Instead, it suggests new ways of understanding the school's position in the history of Weimar German and, more broadly, twentieth-century culture.

TEACHING AND LEARNING AT THE BAUHAUS

Gropius originally intended the Bauhaus to be a place where art and craft would be joined in a new unity. From the beginning this effort spawned new methods of instruction in the visual arts. During the second third of the twentieth century, reforms associated with the Bauhaus almost entirely replaced earlier academic practices.

Throughout its short history, the Bauhaus was an institution in flux. The first fundamental shift in direction occurred in 1923, when Gropius reoriented the school away from craft and toward industrial design. Others followed with the appointments of new directors: Hannes Meyer in 1928 and Mies van der Rohe in 1930. Nonetheless, several important features of the school remained relatively constant. These included the preliminary course, the workshop-based approach to design instruction, and the presence on the faculty of both prominent artists and architects.[6]

The preliminary course (*Vorkurs*), originally taught by Johannes Itten and later by László Moholy-Nagy and Josef Albers, was perhaps the most crucial. Although Itten's almost cultlike teaching differed very much from the more "objective" approach favored by Moholy-Nagy, all of the course's instructors made the then radical assumption that students should be schooled in the principles of abstraction before proceeding to more individualized study. The Bauhaus replaced traditional instruction in drawing

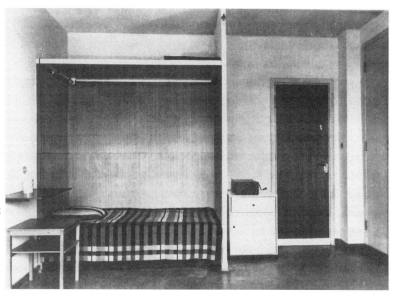

Figure I.2. Walter Peterhans, photograph of student room at the Dessau Bauhaus, 1925/26. The blanket was designed by Gunta Stözl and made in the weaving workshop. Bauhaus-Archiv, Berlin.

Figure I.3. Walter Gropius, "Manifesto and Program of the State Bauhaus in Weimar," 1919. Woodcut by Lyonel Feininger. Bauhaus-Archiv, Berlin. Copyright 2005 Artists Rights Society (ARS), New York / VG Bild-Kunst, Bonn.

from casts of Greek and Roman sculpture or from the life model with exercises that developed skills in formal composition and encouraged students to respect the inherent qualities of their materials. These exercises formed the foundation not only of later instruction at the Bauhaus but also of new art, architecture, and design curricula around the world. Far from being confined to universities and academies of fine arts, their impact extends today even to the instruction offered to small children.

Once a student had completed the preliminary course, he or she proceeded to an individual workshop. As the first two essays in this collection make clear, the idea that designers should understand the way in which their designs would be fabricated was not new. Nor was Gropius's pairing of form masters—fine artists without experience in a particular craft—with technical experts. The results were nonetheless both radical and impressive. Whether working as craftspeople or industrial designers, Bauhaus students synthesized lessons learned from the abstract art taught in the preliminary course and by the form masters with an awareness of how objects were actually constructed. Although workshop instruction would never become as universal as variants upon the exercises featured in the preliminary course, its impact upon design itself was equally far-reaching.

Many of the students who came to the Bauhaus were not novices. Especially in the school's early years, most had already studied art, usually painting, in a more conventional setting. They were attracted first to Weimar and then to Dessau above all by the presence of some of Europe's leading abstract artists. Wassily Kandinsky's prominent position in the history of art was already assured when he arrived in Weimar in 1922;

Figure I.4. Iwao Yamawaki, *The Attack on the Bauhaus,* 1932. Photocollage. From *Kokusai-Kenchiku* 8, no. 12 (December 1932): 272. Bauhaus-Archiv, Berlin.

by the end of the decade, Paul Klee's would equal it. No other school in the world, with the possible exception of the architecture department of Vkhutemas in Moscow, shared the commitment to the new espoused at the Bauhaus. Although, as Rose-Carol Washton Long's essay demonstrates, photography came to supplant painting as the medium of choice among the school's students, it was the caliber of the painters that provided the original inspiration for most of the experiments unleashed there.

The Bauhaus remains even more strongly associated, however, with architecture. All three of its directors were architects. In her essay, Wallis Miller charts the school's progression from offering no formal instruction in architecture to becoming, under Mies's leadership, dominated by the subject of building. From the beginning, architecture contributed to the public face of the institution. With its equation of the studio classrooms with the glazed concrete frame of an American daylight factory, the purpose-designed structure in which the school reopened in Dessau in 1926 continues to be the most compelling manifestation of the school's intention to marry industry and art. Finally, the role that Gropius and Mies later had in reforming American architectural instruction assured the school's prominence in that field for decades to come.

Much of the excitement of studying at the Bauhaus came from the way in which Gropius fused prewar reforms in design instruction with the frisson of even newer developments in avant-garde art to create what became across the course of the century an institutional apparatus for consolidating the latter. For the students, however, as numerous interviews and memoirs make clear, the sense of liberation was not confined to the release from academic conventions of artistic production.[7] Their loyalty to the school, which in most cases remained one of the most cherished experiences of their lives, was buoyed by something at least as effervescent as it was earnest. This playfulness, which Gropius cleverly reinforced through elaborately staged festivals, lifted student spirits and, as Juliet Koss persuasively shows, saved the school's eventual famed alliance between art and the machine from ever becoming merely mechanical.

DESIGN LABORATORY

At the time and since, many objects produced at the Bauhaus, particularly after 1923, whether or not they were themselves machine made, have often appeared to embody an "objective" relationship to modern industrial production. Although criticism of this position was often voiced during the heyday of postmodern historicism, the more recent vogue for neomodernist design has reinforced popular understanding of Bauhaus designs as uncomplicated and even "timeless" manifestations of an enduringly valid equation between form and fabrication.[8]

For a generation, however, scholars of Weimar German culture have focused their attention upon the ways in which issues of consumption as well as production influenced the period's art, literature, and music, not to mention film.[9] They have been inspired by the example of many of the period's own cultural critics, especially those associated with the Frankfurt school.[10] Descriptions of the Bauhaus as exclusively pre-occupied with mass production ignore its active engagement with consumerism as well as the degree to which many German artists, architects, and designers, including Bauhaus faculty and students, welcomed and manipulated capitalist mass culture's erasure of bourgeois cultural forms.[11]

The apparent objectivity of Bauhaus photography, drama, and design regains its representational status in the essays by Rose-Carol Washton Long, Juliet Koss, and Frederic J. Schwartz. The shift from painting to photography as the school's two-dimensional medium of choice, and the fascination many at the Bauhaus had with bodies reconfigured as dolls or automata, dramatized the parallel shift from individual to collective consciousness prompted by the emergence of a mass public. New forms of popular culture, including illustrated newspapers, radio, film, and records, earned profits because they were targeted at a broad spectrum of the middle and working classes rather than an educated elite. As Germany's own history would quickly demonstrate, however, there was nothing inherently emancipatory about a development that had only a coincidental relationship to the almost simultaneous establishment of democratic government.

German mass culture was distinctive during the Weimar Republic in the degree to which abstraction's apparent universality replaced the specific appeals to class identity (or mobility) common elsewhere.[12] Also remarkable were the ways in which the industrial origins of the commodity were displayed and celebrated rather than masked.[13] It is in this context that the Bauhaus's "rational" fusion of abstract art and industrial technology must be understood, even as the school resisted many of the forms of spectacle manifested in metropolitan centers such as Berlin. Unlike the commercial counterparts with which it was frequently compared, for instance, the Dessau Bauhaus was almost never shown in night views.[14]

The Bauhaus's goals were overwhelmingly aesthetic and utopian, but they did not necessarily exist in opposition to the marketplace. Moreover, that marketplace traded, as Gropius was very well aware, in ideas and reputations as well as products. Publicity at the school took a variety of forms from Gropius's often skillfully orchestrated defense of its state subsidies to the posters and kiosks designed by the advertising workshop.[15] As Schwartz repeatedly demonstrates, its faculty and students proved incapable of controlling the way in which their designs were received and absorbed. Many, including certainly Gropius himself, were more successful, however, when political as well as artistic shifts forced them to write their own history.

BAUHAUS POLITICS

The history of the Bauhaus as written during the last two-thirds of the twentieth century was inextricably intertwined with the political events that forced its closure. Many of the essays in this collection take a critical view of how that history was originally fashioned in relationship to fascism, exile, and the cold war. The Bauhaus was the first and re-mains Nazism's most notable cultural victim. The centrality of this fact to its enduring influence has, however, remained relatively unexamined. It has also overshadowed the institution's complex relationship with nationalist politics before and after the Weimar Republic.

The origins of the Bauhaus, for example, did not lie exclusively or perhaps even pre-dominately in the politically progressive resistance to capitalism launched by the Arts and Crafts movement in Britain and temporarily reinvigorated in Germany following the revolution of November 1918.[16] As John V. Maciuika's opening chapter makes clear, many early-twentieth-century advocates of design reform in Germany sought to stimu-late the economy and restore a relatively conservative social consensus rather than to alter society radically. In the last years before World War I, German grand dukes, civil servants, and industrialists alike championed the extreme simplification of architecture and design as a rational response to the country's recent and rapid industrialization.[17] The Bauhaus inherited considerably more from these efforts than from the German left's far more modest engagement with design reform.[18]

In the heady aftermath of the November Revolution, there was little reason for any-one to draw attention to these precedents. At home and abroad, Wilhelmine Germany now seemed dangerously nationalist rather than culturally progressive.[19] The German Werkbund's lasting impact upon German design remained clear, but the degree to which the organization's definition of "good design" was originally driven by political and economic, as well as cultural, considerations was suppressed.[20] Instead, the right-wing hostility that repeatedly threatened the school's existence gave credence to its progressive political image. Of its three directors, however, although Gropius was cer-tainly an ardent supporter of the November Revolution, only Meyer was a fully commit-ted socialist. Mies proved more tolerant of Nazi than of Communist students, a number of whom he immediately expelled.[21]

Although Adolf Hitler favored monumental neoclassicism and the Nazis dismissed expressionist art as degenerate, as Paul Betts has shown, "the Nazi assumption of power hardly disturbed the commercial production and distribution of design wares."[22] Bauhaus designs not only continued to be manufactured but also were exhibited at home and abroad as examples of outstanding German design. There were, of course, many affiliated with the school who suffered terribly during the Nazi dictatorship in Germany and across Europe during World War II. Jewish alumni paid for their reli-gious heritage with their lives. However, as Winfried Nerdinger makes clear in his es-say, which was originally published as part of a groundbreaking reconsideration of the fate of Bauhaus modernism during the Third Reich, Gropius and Mies, as well as many of their students and their employees, served the Nazis with varying degrees of willingness.[23] Even after he left Germany, first for Britain and then the United States, Gropius remained careful for many years not to speak out publicly against Hitler or his government. Mies enjoyed substantial support within the Nazi regime in its early years; only Hitler's personal taste for neoclassicism prevented him from becoming its leading architect.[24] Bauhaus-trained architects faced little discrimination during the Third Reich, especially if they were willing to assist in the design of the factories crucial to arms production. The formal vocabulary they had learned at the Bauhaus now glorified Nazi technological and military prowess.

After the Bauhaus's demise, however, many of those who had been affiliated with it, as well as their most ardent supporters, turned to politics to defend an experiment that appeared in danger of being extinguished by the turn away from geometrical abstraction toward surrealism and regionalism. By the mid-1930s, the particular modernism associated with the school now appeared simply unfashionable to many. Equating these forms with democracy, as Alfred Barr did in 1938 in his introduction to the catalog of the Museum of Modern Art's Bauhaus exhibit, and/or socialism helped sustain the impact of the aesthetic experiments the school had supported.[25]

The Bauhaus legend proved particularly convenient, as Gropius was among the first to realize, to cold war efforts to bolster liberal democracy by casting it as the protector of abstract art. Modern architecture and design's postwar ascendancy was predicated in part upon the assumed contrast between authoritarian and democratic architecture.[26] Greg Castillo demonstrates the degree to which the attention given to a battle between styles drew attention away from architects' complicity with fascism.

Later, during the 1960s, when modernism slowly shifted from being a contemporary to a historical phenomenon, its goals of transforming society if not art largely unachieved, a new generation found in the idealism of its original expressionism promising precedents for resisting the institutionalized practices spawned by the mature Bauhaus.[27] Although this effort was initially confined to the capitalist West, by the 1980s the Bauhaus became a cherished model for civic society in Eastern Europe as well.[28]

It is difficult not to romanticize the Bauhaus, but the legacy of this impressive institution has surely now proved robust enough to withstand rigorous scholarly scrutiny. That it is possible to exaggerate its independence from mass culture and its political purity does not mean that those affiliated with it and the art they produced were not often original, critical, committed, and influential. Such exaggeration does, however, drain their personal and communal struggles of much of the vitality that so animated the school itself, as well as set a standard for uncomplicated moral behavior that is dangerously naive.

BAUHAUS CULTURE

WILHELMINE PRECEDENTS FOR THE BAUHAUS

HERMANN MUTHESIUS, THE PRUSSIAN STATE, AND THE GERMAN WERKBUND

John V. Maciuika

The Bauhaus, an educational experiment undertaken at a revolutionary time, has an obscure prehistory. Founded in Weimar in 1919 by the Thuringian state initially to revive the crafts, the school, led by Walter Gropius, quickly broadened its mission to promote a radical fusion of the fine arts, the decorative arts, and architecture. As the standard-bearer of a reformed artistic culture, the Bauhaus, Gropius proclaimed, would lead postwar German society in a process of social, economic, and cultural renewal.[1]

Direct precedents to the Bauhaus did not exist before World War I. Yet many of the school's organizational principles, innovative curricular features, and aesthetic theories originated during the reign of Kaiser Wilhelm II between 1888 and 1918. After the world war swept away the Wilhelmine era's dynastic imperial rule and replaced it with the Weimar Republic's divisive, fragile democracy, Gropius's school emerged at the center of heated ideological debates about its value to the new nation. Heralded as art's cosmopolitan avant-garde and castigated by nationalist detractors as a menace to traditional German culture, the Bauhaus fought for survival in a process that shrouded the school's origins in numerous, often self-serving myths. As other contributions to this volume demonstrate, Gropius worked equally avidly to shape perceptions of Bauhaus modernism in contexts as varied as Nazi Germany and the cold war United States.

After World War II and until his death in 1969, Gropius nurtured an image of the Bauhaus as a unique artifact of Weimar-era democracy. Casting the school as an antipode to Nazism with no debts to such significant pre–World War I institutions as the Prussian state, Gropius reflected a widespread post–World War II tendency to condemn Wilhelmine Prussia as a militant and retrograde precursor to Hitler's Germany. Art and architectural historians also subscribed to Gropius's notion of Bauhaus cultural reform as a bridge from the Weimar Republic to a postwar democracy, choosing to overlook the school's relationship to reforms sponsored by various German states. In fact, a variety of Wilhelmine developments in fields as varied as architecture, art, design, politics, economics, and social reform helped prepare the way for the Bauhaus.

A key Wilhelmine contribution to the prehistory of the Bauhaus was the gradual redefinition of the relationship between architecture, the decorative arts, and the role of artists as makers and interpreters of form. The closer integration of the fine and applied arts not only became an aesthetic end in itself but also came to be understood as a means of encouraging social unity and economic development. All over Europe in the late nineteenth century, progressive artists and designers exhibited a new determination to develop styles and working methods that no longer mimicked the historical forms typically absorbed through nineteenth-century academic training. Like their colleagues in the fine arts, progressive designers increasingly sought to develop working methods whose products could be regarded as appropriate responses to a modern age.[2]

Adherents of the Arts and Crafts movement, for example, revived old crafts techniques from the Middle Ages, while their art nouveau counterparts borrowed from industry to produce new forms inspired by plants and nature. Accompanying social theories and reform programs, owing much to the writings of Augustus Pugin and John Ruskin, raised the status of artists, artisans, and designers, even as they promoted a general belief that art and the design of people's environments could play a role in improving the lives of the general populace. Rapidly exposing more readers than ever before to new images, ideas, and currents of thought, countless new arts journals arose in the 1890s to disseminate this message across international borders.

Against this backdrop there were three major overlapping prewar developments, all emerging out of the Wilhelmine empire's radically changing political, social, and economic landscape, that prepared the way for the postwar Bauhaus. The first of these precedents, the British Arts and Crafts movement of the late nineteenth century, caught the attention of Germans and other Continental Europeans interested in the potential offered by the movement for a rebirth of design and artistic quality. Britain's apparent shift in artistic sensibilities and revival of superior craft production—exemplified by such figures as William Morris, Charles R. Ashbee, William Lethaby, and numerous others—inspired countless European artists, craftsmen, architects, and patrons. This shift pointed to new possibilities for the fusion of old and new, recasting, so to speak, ancient artistic techniques for use under modern commercial and industrial conditions.[3] Experiments in art nouveau and its German counterpart, the Jugendstil or "youth style," were just the first in a number of developments inspired by the Arts and Crafts movement and its promise of national renewal in the artistic, economic, and cultural sectors.[4]

A second key Bauhaus precedent arose from the specific ways in which Prussian state government reworked Arts and Crafts ideas in the opening years of the twentieth century. Institutionalizing key Arts and Crafts principles between 1903 and 1907 to place a reformed system of design education at the service of a modern economy, it coordinated an elaborate organizational effort to improve the quality of consumer products through artistic intervention. Unlike many British reformers—who bemoaned machine production—forward-thinking German artists and their official counterparts embraced mechanization as a tool to spur design innovation, increase commercial production, and enable Germany to catch up and compete effectively with neighboring powers.[5]

Following the Prussian state's lead in the autumn of 1907, proponents of the "new movement" in design reproduced the main elements of Prussia's system in the private sector and, at a national scale, in the third most important Bauhaus precedent: the German Werkbund. A private association formed by two dozen architects, artists, craftsmen, and manufacturers, the Werkbund grew quickly to become the leading representative of modern tendencies in German design before World War I. Its leaders enlisted a diverse yet like-minded membership from various artistic and intellectual backgrounds. Although not itself a school, the Werkbund combined an educational and economic mission. Through publications, public lectures, exhibitions, and other positive "propaganda organs," the Werkbund worked to educate consumers in matters of modern taste, improve the quality of German products through artistic intervention, and establish a model for Germany's cultural renewal through a synthetic approach to economic, aesthetic, social, and technological questions. Its purposeful investigation of the role artists should play in an age of burgeoning technology and factory production endured, as we shall see, as the most important and direct precedent to the Bauhaus and to twentieth-century German design culture generally.[6]

THE INGREDIENTS OF CHANGE:
GERMANY AND INTERNATIONAL INFLUENCES

Spurred by an economic boom and supported by a wide range of patrons that included prominent nobility, leading industrialists and merchants, and state and local governments, Germany around 1900 was rife with fresh artistic enterprises and experimentation.[7] As the British case confirmed, the promotion of such applied arts as furniture making, ceramics, and interior decoration made good economic sense: improved quality in crafts production commanded higher prices, reinforced demand for talented craftsmen, and boosted the reputation of an entire region. For this reason, culturally and economically minded German patrons engaged in an array of efforts to educate the public in matters of taste, hoping to distinguish their city or region as one of Germany's leading modern artistic centers.

In pursuit of these goals, many patrons sponsored talented foreign architects and artists willing to bring their fresh ideas to Germany. At the same time, because regional identity remained strong in Germany after unification in 1871, reform efforts undertaken by different patrons often reflected the particular local or regional character of German cities and states. This might well have been expected in a Wilhelmine Empire in which four separate kings continued to rule in the respective kingdoms of Prussia, Bavaria, Saxony, and Württemberg, with Prussia's king simultaneously reigning as German emperor. Beyond these kingdoms, five grand duchies, thirteen duchies and principalities, and three "free cities" filled out the complex political map of the Second

Reich.[8] Rivalries lingered, reflecting a combination of local pride in the "homeland" (*Heimat*) and an unwillingness to relinquish too much influence to the dominant state of Prussia, many of whose state ministries doubled as imperial ministries.[9] The federal constitution, which made the areas of culture and education the responsibility of individual state governments, helped preserve a measure of state autonomy while feeding a lingering sense of competition among the federated states.[10] It also meant that the character of individual royal houses and regional governments influenced the internal dynamics of design reform. This fact was not lost on Charles-Edouard Jeanneret (Le Corbusier after 1920) during his extensive study tour of Germany in 1910–11, which included a period of employment with Peter Behrens in Berlin.[11]

Perhaps the most lavish of early experiments undertaken to elevate modern German taste occurred in the central German town of Darmstadt, home to the region's wealthiest artistic patron, Grand Duke Ernst Ludwig of Hesse. In 1899 the grand duke invited Joseph Maria Olbrich, the gifted young Austrian architect who had recently completed the Secession building and gallery in Vienna, to design a grand communal studio building called the Ernst Ludwig House (Figure 1.1). Situated atop the Matildenhöhe, a hill above the town, this cultlike "temple of work" became the monumental center for an elite colony of artists, who were housed in additional Olbrich-designed private residences.[12] The German painter Peter Behrens also designed a house for himself, the artist's first complete building. In so doing Behrens exemplified a popular trend, dating to the economic boom of the late 1890s, in which numerous painters (among them Hermann Obrist, Richard Riemerschmid, Bruno Paul, and Otto Eckmann) expanded their repertoires to include the design of furniture, rooms, and eventually entire buildings.

With much fanfare and religious-mystical ritual choreographed according to the philosopher Friedrich Nietzsche's notions of cultural rebirth, the entire Darmstadt architectural ensemble opened in the summer of 1901 as a public exhibition titled "A Document of German Art." The exhibit served as a platform for the Jugendstil and the young generation's ongoing rebellion against nineteenth-century academic doctrines, and successfully promoted increased collaboration between Hesse's artists and commercial firms. Praised by some critics for the spirited demonstration of bright colors, bold sculptural massing, and classical and vernacular forms, the exhibition was panned by others who regarded the Jugendstil as inflated, self-important, and culturally irrelevant. The exhibition failed financially and came to be regarded by many as an artistic dead end. Two further exhibitions in 1904 and 1908, while introducing other important individual Jugendstil works by Olbrich, did not significantly alter the situation. Moreover, the young Austrian architect's untimely death in 1908 put a halt to the growth of the Darmstadt Colony and its fame.

Henry van de Velde, a painter of Belgian origin who also embraced design and architecture in the 1890s, was a second important foreign influence on German de-

Figure 1.1. Joseph Maria Olbrich, Ernst Ludwig House, Darmstadt Artists Colony, Darmstadt, 1901. From *Deutsche Kunst und Dekoration* 8 (1901).

velopments. Inspired by the values of William Morris, John Ruskin, and other founding figures of the British Arts and Crafts movement, van de Velde captured the imaginations of patrons and critics alike, among them the Berlin-based connoisseurs Harry Graf Kessler and Julius Meier-Graefe. Relocating to Berlin in 1900 as one of the best-known practitioners of a *Gesamtkunstwerk* approach—creating a "total work of art" out of a room, its contents, and even the clothing to be worn by its occupants—van de Velde carried with him the heritage of his Belgian predecessor, Victor Horta. However, van de Velde's emphasis on abstraction moved beyond the purely naturalistic, botanically inspired designs of Horta and his French counterpart, Hector Guimard.[13]

With his fame growing, van de Velde accepted a court invitation to work for another powerful member of Wilhelmine Germany's nobility, the Grand Duke Wilhelm Ernst of Saxony-Weimar. Like his counterpart in Hessen, Wilhelm Ernst sought a revival of the arts, culture, and the local crafts economy, and appointed van de Velde to lead a crafts seminar in Weimar in 1902. Commissioned to build new buildings for the Grand Ducal School of Arts and Crafts between 1904 and 1911, van de Velde also became the school's founding director in 1907. The Weimar school's structures eventually served as the first home to the Bauhaus in 1919, a consequence of van de Velde's recommendation that Walter Gropius succeed him as school director after war-related pressures prompted the Belgian artist's resignation and departure from Germany in 1915.[14]

By interpreting for themselves the lessons of the British Arts and Crafts movement and art nouveau, major foreign talents such as Olbrich and van de Velde injected fresh energy into early-twentieth-century German arts and design. Within Germany, too, artists and craftsmen took up the call for enhanced craft quality and design creativity. In 1897, the artists August Endell, Hermann Obrist, Bruno Paul, and Richard Riemerschmid, inspired by Morris, united to found their own company in Munich, the United Workshops for Art in Handicraft. Similarly, the Dresden-based master woodworker and furniture maker Karl Schmidt opened his own entrepreneurial furniture design company, the Dresden Workshops for the Applied Arts, one year later. A spate of new arts journals appeared in the 1890s to back the new movement and heralded the new paths being explored in design. Among the new titles were *German Art and Decoration* (1897), *The Architect* (1895), *Decorative Art* (1897), and *The Youth* (1896), with the latter inspiring the name Jugendstil.

Sponsorship of influential foreign artists in the late 1890s, coupled with individual initiatives toward artistic, cultural, and economic renewal, confirms that Germany's overall turn-of-the-century artistic climate was shifting radically to accommodate international currents and tastes. At the same time, a growing network of progressive journals, design firms, artists colonies, and schools formed the basis for a new German cultural awareness of the contribution that modern design could make to economic development, social reform, and cultural renewal. Yet to achieve more widespread and lasting influence, systematic changes were needed. The architect Hermann Muthesius oversaw a governmental reworking of the Arts and Crafts movement that became the core of a distinctively German modern movement whose values and goals, expressed first in the German Werkbund, would later directly influence design thinking at the Bauhaus.

ART, COMMERCE, AND THE MACHINE:
REWORKING ARTS AND CRAFTS IDEAS

While new artistic and design experiments could be seen in many parts of Germany around 1900, the impetus for penetrating, lasting change in design culture originated in the gigantic state of Prussia. Covering more than two-thirds of German territory and employing a vast modern bureaucracy, Prussia was slow in recognizing the importance to its economy of reforms in the arts and crafts. Yet once officials acted to set the lumbering Prussian bureaucratic machine in motion, its policies proved decisive.

The government body most closely associated with issues affecting the crafts, product design, and the applied arts generally was Prussia's Ministry of Commerce and Trade. As the de facto trade ministry for the whole German Empire (which, due to long-standing disputes with the influential Prussian state, never succeeded in establishing a trade ministry of its own), the Commerce Ministry had a direct interest in managing all sectors of the economy, from agriculture and heavy industry to commercial trade and the individual arts, crafts, and trades. The applied arts were only one sector of Germany's growing economy, but since manufacturing and exports of finished goods had long been on the rise, they naturally interested the ministry.[15]

As the twentieth century approached, Commerce Minister Theodor Möller, a National Liberal politician and successful Westphalian industrialist, faced several dilemmas. On one hand, Möller and his circle of advisers joined other Germans in celebrating the forces of industrial and commercial expansion during the 1890s, as all signs seemed to indicate that Germany stood a good chance of one day rivaling Britain as Europe's leading industrial and commercial power. On the other hand, however, these forces of expansion, although responsible for the proliferation of new commissions for artists and architects in this decade, raised several warning flags. First, the rising concentration of power among large businesses and industrial manufacturers was proving detrimental to the far older sector of traditional arts, crafts, and trades producers, many of whom were being put out of business by these larger, more sophisticated competitors. Compounding this problem during the 1890s was the surge in popularity of the Socialist Party: since 1890, when a twelve-year ban imposed on the party by Chancellor Otto von Bismarck had been lifted, the socialists had campaigned with phenomenal success among embattled workers, craftsmen, and tradesmen convinced that Germany's expanding "new economy" was leaving them behind.[16]

Alongside this dilemma, ministry officials were acutely aware that for decades, German export products had been faring extremely poorly in international markets. As long as export revenues to Britain, France, and the United States remained comparatively low, Germany's economic expansion would be hindered, as would the nation's prospect of becoming Europe's foremost industrial power. Thus, as the Prussian Commerce Ministry saw it, something had to be done both to shore up the troubled crafts and trades sector, and to raise the overall quality of German product design and manufacturing. Failure to do so would, at best, keep Germany from becoming a serious competitor in international export markets, and could at worst lead to levels of revolutionary unrest of the sort that plagued Russia in 1905.

The Commerce Ministry responded by taking a familiar step: it sent someone to study the problem. As far back as 1826, the ministry had dispatched the renowned architect Karl Friedrich Schinkel on a study tour to report on English developments.[17] Exactly seventy years later, it assigned Muthesius, another of its architects, to the German embassy in London to report on a variety of English technical, industrial, and artistic matters. Over the next seven years during Muthesius's time in England, and then for another decade back on German soil, what evolved under the ministry's guidance was a wholesale redirection of Prussia's program for arts and crafts education, training, and production. Guided by the findings and recommendations of Muthesius, but in reality the product of a multilayered state apparatus affecting dozens of schools and industries in Prussia's larger towns and cities, the transformation of the state's arts, crafts, and trades education system represented the first systemwide, government-led reforms subordination of design to economic development policy.[18]

The first step in this transformation began as a veritable flood of cogent articles and critical analyses, correspondence, and government reports issuing from Muthesius in England. More than 100 articles, seven books (some multivolume), and more than 1,000 pieces of correspondence combined to spark the shift in official Prussian policy. The architect's thinking—informed by university studies in philosophy, art history, and architecture, and preceded by a two-year teenage apprenticeship in masonry and the building trades—seemed well suited to untangling the complex connections between industrial production, design quality, applied arts education, and economic policy.[19]

Muthesius's mission in England, moreover, embodied a particular current of feeling in turn-of-the-century Germany that mingled admiration and envy, rivalry and a sense of inferiority. To the visiting architect, the specific appeal of British architects and designers lay in their reaction to decades of industrialization and scientific progress—a reaction he believed led them to produce tasteful, artistic home furnishings and comfortable, well-lit, hygienic modern homes for the doctors, lawyers, businessmen, and professors who comprised the nineteenth century's newly ascendant bourgeoisie (Figure 1.2). Addressing the calls for modern cultural renewal being issued by many Germans, Muthesius's publications and specific policy recommendations analyzed the British scene for clues that would aid his government in improving the quality of export products and thus raise Germany's international status.[20]

In early articles the visiting German architect accurately characterized the British Arts and Crafts movement less as a single style than an approach to design. Some, like Morris, founded a firm and became active in socialist politics; others, like Lethaby, became teachers. Still others, like Ashbee, established guilds in opposition to the training of the nineteenth-century art academies. All were concerned in one way or another with the effects of industrialization and its accompanying degradation of English working conditions, living standards, production quality, and even the simple (if idealized) values of village life. Reworking British ideas in accordance with the official Prusso-German bureaucratic reform mentality, Muthesius's articles and books downplayed such left-leaning Arts and Crafts values as guild idealism, collective citizen action, and, of course, socialist activism. His best-remembered books, such as *Style-Architecture and Building-Art* of 1902, argued instead that in order to raise production quality and reground modern German culture, the preoccupation of the traditional crafts with obsolete historical forms had to be abandoned. These forms, the architect reasoned, needed to give way not just to Arts and Crafts designs emphasizing fitness of form to functional purpose, but even more to scientifically objective, machined forms. Engineering design in the late nineteenth century, after all, had already provided such modern design breakthroughs as the bicycle, the suspension bridge, and the battleship

Figure 1.2. Philip Webb, Red House, Bexleyheath, Kent, 1859–60. From Hermann Muthesius, *Das englische Haus: Entwicklung, Bedingungen, Anlage, Einrichtung, und Innenraum* (Berlin: Ernst Wasmuth, 1904–5).

(Figure 1.3). He believed contemporary applied artists needed to learn the material and constructional lessons embodied by such modern forms.[21]

The proper goal of the twentieth century, Muthesius concluded, was not for designers to seek a distinct style or look—such as art nouveau and its proponents had claimed—but instead to develop an approach to design and manufacturing that grew out of a thorough understanding of the tectonic possibilities of modern machine tools, materials, and production techniques. By *tectonic,* Muthesius referred to the degree of technical and artistic mastery achievable in the application of constructional principles to specific materials. Once German applied artists and industry had mastered modern machines to the same sophisticated degree that Arts and Crafts practitioners understood their hand tools, then the resulting forms—true products of their time—were guaranteed to have high quality and would therefore be competitive.

London-based arguments such as these were music to the ears of Minister Möller, who by 1904 would express the wish that Muthesius be empowered to exercise "the greatest influence in the largest possible number of fields" at the Commerce Ministry.[22] Muthesius began writing his recommendations for the reform of the Commerce

Figure 1.3. Sir Benjamin Baker and Sir John Fowler, with construction engineer William Arrol, the Forth Bridge, spanning between North and South Queensferry, Edinburgh, 1883–90. From W. Westhofen, *The Forth Bridge* (London: Engineering Journal Reprint, 28 February 1890), Plate 4.

Ministry's schools for arts, crafts, and trades when he returned to Berlin in the summer of 1903, producing a steadily widening scope of influential policy changes. When he began to direct more than three dozen Prussian arts, crafts, and trades schools away from the copying of historical ornaments and toward design methods based on the qualities of particular materials, he was laying important groundwork for later twentieth-century practices. And when, in 1904, he authored a ministerial decree requiring design students to get up from their drafting tables and actually build their designs in newly instituted, mandatory instructional workshops, he was implementing a change that would become a cornerstone of Bauhaus pedagogy. By encouraging schools to emphasize product functionality and at the same time requiring greater contact with local crafts industries, Muthesius aroused vehement opposition among traditional crafts practitioners and trade unions—as would the Bauhaus. Muthesius argued that raising taste, quality, and the competitiveness of German goods was part of a more general cultural renewal for which Germany was long overdue. According to him, the educated middle classes would lead this renewal of culture, and their interest in "good design" would become one of the defining features of German bourgeois culture. Under the Commerce Ministry's reforms, meanwhile, applied arts students were meant to become designers of useful modern products, and no longer mere reproducers of historical styles.

In late 1902, Möller persuaded the thirty-four-year-old Peter Behrens to direct the Commerce Ministry's flagship Arts and Crafts school in Dusseldorf. Whereas some schools in the Prussian system concentrated on a single trade like ceramics or metal-work, larger schools like the Arts and Crafts schools in Dusseldorf, Krefeld, and Mag-deburg offered a full spectrum of design, crafts, and architectural studies. Their cur-ricula included painting, graphics, textile design, furniture making, interior design, and architecture, but could also range from fine metals and jewelry work to book design, ce-ramics, or sophisticated joinery. Under Behrens's leadership the school would achieve remarkable results.[23]

In his recommendations Muthesius followed lessons most closely derived from new British schools like Lethaby's Central Schools of Arts and Crafts, founded in London in 1896 through a bill initiated by the Fabian Socialist Sidney Webb. Ignoring the socialist origins of the school, Muthesius instead held it up as an example of effec-tive reform. Publishing a detailed article about the school in an 1898 issue of *Dec-orative Art*, he noted that Lethaby and his partner, the sculptor George Frampton, had developed instructional workshop-based curricula for "no less than ninety-eight" government-supported Arts and Crafts schools.[24] In his last English assignment in June 1903, he evaluated this and twenty-six other British arts, crafts, and technical training schools in a study tour organized for Behrens and three top Prussian officials from the Commerce and Finance ministries. Arriving in Berlin the following month, Muthesius embarked immediately on an analogous tour of ten top Prussian applied arts schools. In a detailed report to the Commerce minister, he harshly criticized a traditional peda-gogy that emphasized teaching students to draw Gothic or classical ornaments for application to isolated objects with almost total disregard for materials or methods of assembly or for the design of integrated interiors.[25]

The Arts and Crafts movement's influence on Muthesius and the Prussian system prompted the issuing of an "Instructional Workshops Decree" on 4 December 1904. This decree introduced practical workshops where students would develop their de-sign projects in tandem with a hands-on, materials- and construction-oriented design process. It established sixty-one new trial and instruction workshops in Prussian ap-plied arts schools.[26] Van de Velde used the Prussian Workshops Decree as his model when he applied for funding to establish his own instructional workshops in Weimar.[27] The impetus for the reforms was economic as well as aesthetic, as it would later be for Gropius when he called for "a proliferation of the crafts and industry in the state of Weimar as a result of the re-molding of the schools in accordance with a craft-oriented, practical approach."[28] In creating the Bauhaus, Gropius also gathered literature and advice from such respected applied arts school directors as Rudolf Bosselt of Magde-burg and Richard Riemerschmid of Munich, both of whom had been key players in the Prussian state's prewar reform efforts.[29]

Instructional workshops were not new. Many European schools had followed the example originally set by London's South Kensington Museum and School of Design where, beginning in 1853, Henry Cole had been appointed to teach ornamental art, design, and, as Cole wrote, "the practical application of such knowledge to the improvement of Manufactures."[30] Just over a decade later, the Viennese followed the British example and founded the Austrian Museum of Art and Industry in 1864, which added a school of applied arts in 1868, while in Berlin the Prussian government founded the Berlin Museum of Applied Arts in 1867.[31] By the opening years of the twentieth century, individual schools in Vienna, Stuttgart, and Breslau had instituted instructional workshops, inspired in part by such English examples as Ashbee's Guild and School of Handicraft in London, and by the successful entrepreneurial crafts workshops already operating in Dresden, Munich, and Vienna. However, Möller's push to enable Prussia to catch up with these individual schools assured one thing: that its reforms would affect dozens of schools and industries at a single stroke, and would provide models beyond Prussia's borders for such institutions as van de Velde's Grand Ducal School of Arts and Crafts.

Lethaby's Central School model elicited Muthesius's admiration on several counts: it advocated "teaching crafts through practical examples"; the study of nature and abstract drawing to replace historical copying; the encouragement of students' "own artistic thinking process" to set them "on the path to an artistically independent handling of a particular craft"; and, finally, the enabling of the student to "embody his thinking in his work [by] bringing the limits of materials to consciousness."[32]

Muthesius crystallized these thoughts in the Commerce Ministry's Workshops Decree. Its language swept aside decades of historicist pedagogical methods, concepts, and long-accepted definitions in the areas of drawing, design, and execution of student work. The following excerpt explains the new mission of the Prussian workshops as de facto centers of the schools:

> Teaching in instructional workshops will make it possible to bring the essential relationships between material and form to the express consciousness of the student, and thereby teach him to develop his design more objectively, economically, and purposefully. This involvement with materials will further rid the student of the mistaken notion that producing outwardly pleasing drawings—which take no account of materials and their character—is a goal worth striving for. The workshops will also convey new worthwhile artistic impulses; instead of being based on outwardly transmitted forms, these will be grounded in the insights into the working possibilities of the material that have been gained through the student's own activities. . . . The essence of the Applied Arts School implies that artistic and technical instruction in the workshops go hand in hand.[33]

Under old methods from the 1870s, 1880s, and 1890s, students' ornamented designs were executed in workshops by craftspeople who had not participated in developing the drawing, but who had to figure out how to construct the object to match the drawn forms. The old methods, the decree explained, were a symptom of overspecialization that had led to "the one-sided training of arts and crafts draftsmen, who know nothing of materials and who are alienated from the activity of the craftsman."[34]

Both English and German school reform efforts regarded the workshops as "a supplement and not a replacement to instruction from master teachers." A further goal of both nations was for schools to "orient to industry."[35] Here, however, a major difference between typical English schools' mission statements and the 1904 Prussian decree emerged: by its very nature, arts and crafts education in England remained on a path separate from that of industry. The London County Council expressed the wish to see the crafts made "useful to industry" and so promoted their study, but a specific English policy incorporating industry failed to materialize before World War I. Tradition, materials, and hand craftsmanship in the English arts and crafts remained evidence of the search for honesty and ethics in the industrial age.

Prussian policies, by contrast, sought in the most direct way possible to exploit the commercial potential of the Arts and Crafts movement in order to further Prussia's economic development priorities. Ashbee roundly criticized Muthesius for embodying the Prussian "commercial spirit," and for lacking the moral idealism that lent the British movement its largely anti-industrial tone.[36]

The Prussian workshops decree, for its part, articulated exactly where the instructional workshops were to stand with respect to industry. For example, schools establishing workshops were advised "in the first place to consider local industries, following those working techniques in which artistic value will rest primarily on the work of the artist."[37] This local emphasis enabled schools to develop individualized curricula matching the economic profile of their city and region. The decree also supported having workshops led by master craftsmen as long as these had demonstrated the "artistic capabilities" to teach equally the "artistic and the technical" sides of workshop courses. In cases where this was not so, teaching was "to be divided between an artist and a technician, in which the technician works under the direction of the artist."[38] Betraying the Prussian bureaucracy's deeply ingrained regard for nineteenth-century hierarchical traditions and social deference, Muthesius observed:

> Doubts concerning any conflicts between artist and technician appear to me unfounded because, while the technician in such cases would be a common master craftsman, from the outset his social standing requires a recognition of the authority of the full teacher who is the institution's retained artist. The division between artist and technician in the described fashion is followed at the arts and crafts school in Vienna.[39]

Although in official settings the Commerce Ministry cultivated the appearance that it wished to avoid conflict with traditional arts, crafts, and trades producers, it could hardly conceal the fact that academically trained artists were to remold the arts and crafts through their expertise and, by reconfiguring the crafts workshops, improve the artistic and economic value of their products.[40] The Bauhaus, too, would in 1922 abandon its idealistic proclamations of an egalitarian artistic community in favor of a remarkably similar hierarchical arrangement. Denying equal status and voting rights to teaching craftsmen at meetings of the Bauhaus's council of "Form Masters," Gropius rescinded an earlier promise assuring equality among teaching artists and craftsmen.[41]

As Muthesius was completing the final draft of the Workshops Decree, Commerce Minister Möller further expanded the architect's influence by founding a special department within the ministry to enlarge the scope of activities in arts, crafts, and trades reform. In January 1905, this department took its final form as the State Trades Board, with Muthesius, as one of five founding members, responsible for crafts and trades exhibitions, continuing education, and broadening the ongoing reform of Prussia's arts, crafts, and trades schools.[42] The State Trades Board's charter documents nationalistically asserted that the new agency would enable Germany to emerge victorious in the "trades competition of the peoples."[43]

The State Trade Board's Standing Committee on Trades Policy, created in 1905, furnished a ministerial blueprint for the later private, national German Werkbund. In addition to Muthesius, the Commerce minister, and four other ministerial members, the Standing Committee comprised leading representatives of the applied arts in their individual branches, heads of trades associations, executives from Prussian industry, directors of arts and crafts schools, mayors of several important Prussian cities, and delegates from the Prussian legislature. Members of this committee, who held their posts for five years, met on a biannual basis in Berlin.[44] Serving as a government tool to reeducate the public about taste and quality through professional and student exhibits that bore the stamp of the new design thinking, the State Trades Board introduced organizational principles and a design philosophy that directly anticipated the Werkbund's stated mission of educating national taste and improving exports through the cooperation of artists, artisans, and manufacturers.

To conservative trades associations like the Association for the Economic Interests of the Crafts, the creation of the State Trades Board and its Standing Committee on Trades Policy, coupled with further increases in state subventions for arts and crafts schools that followed the new direction in design, represented a clear call to arms. Muthesius responded in kind. In early 1907, his inaugural lecture as the first chair of the applied arts at the new Berlin College of Commerce, "The Significance of the Applied Arts," aggressively denounced all those who refused to abandon traditional crafts practices in favor of an objective functionalism.[45] Holding old design techniques and shoddy material practices accountable for having made the words "'German' and 'tasteless' into practically identical concepts," he announced that the "future belongs to those producers who subscribe to the new movement."[46] Linking the education of consumers about the integrity of products and materials to the moral integrity of the masses and the nation, Muthesius argued that any unwillingness among manufacturers to subscribe to this outlook represented a mortal threat to Germany's national progress and health.

The Association for the Economic Interests of the Crafts responded by angrily demanding that Clemens Delbrück, who replaced Möller in late 1905, dismiss Muthesius from his ministerial post. The resulting "Muthesius Case" proved a focal point for Wilhelmine debates about "traditional" versus "modern" crafts practices. In a reply to the association, Delbrück wrote that Muthesius had been acting "as an academic instructor . . . and independent from his activity as a member of the State Trades Board," and refused to fire him.[47] When the matter arose for debate in the Prussian Chamber of Deputies, Delbrück defended Muthesius as "an expert colleague" whom he considered an "indispensable public servant."[48]

At the height of the controversy, and to demonstrate their support for Muthesius, twelve artists and twelve crafts manufacturers formally withdrew from the association to form the Werkbund in October 1907. Although Muthesius prepared a speech for the founding meeting and would go on to be one of the Werkbund's leading theorists of artist-designed industrial "types," he did not attend its inaugural meeting in Munich. The furor surrounding the Association for the Economic Interests of the Crafts and the "Muthesius Case" was still too fresh in people's minds. Moreover, his presence would only have lent credence to the association's argument that the government backed manufacturers to the exclusion of crafts practitioners.

The aggressive provocation contained in Muthesius's College of Commerce opening address was undeniably an extension, and in many ways a culmination, of policies he had helped to develop in the Commerce Ministry. Indeed, since the college's bylaws showed that its trustees were accountable to the Commerce minister for such major decisions as appointing the school's director, there was a degree of disingenuousness in Delbrück's assertion that Muthesius was acting as an independent academic.[49] By broadening his focus on the applied arts and challenging German manufacturers explicitly to embrace what he believed to be rational principles, Muthesius was following several years of ministerial economic development policies to their logical conclusion. Kept out of the spotlight for the moment by his government employers, he nonetheless quickly became one of the Werkbund's chief officers. Never abandoning his government post, he gained prominence in the Werkbund over the next several years as the advocate of rationalized production of "types" controlled by designers.[50]

PETER BEHRENS:
DESIGN REFORM PEDAGOGY IN THE MODERN MARKETPLACE

If Muthesius's rise had been gradual, Behrens's was meteoric. The same month in which the Werkbund was formed, Behrens left his post as director of the flagship Dusseldorf Applied Arts School to accept a position that easily made him the association's leading practitioner: he became chief artistic designer and architect for the AEG,

Figure 1.4. Peter Behrens, exterior of the exhibition pavilion for the Delmenhorst Linoleum Company at the Third German Applied Arts Exhibition in Dresden, 1906. From *Dekorative Kunst* 15 (1907).

Germany's General Electric Company, in Berlin.[51] Behrens's numerous commissions from German industry, obtained in accordance with Prussian state directives during his four-year term as the Dusseldorf school director, had prepared him well for his work with the AEG. As early as 1904, numerous exhibits of Dusseldorf students' work from courses taught by Behrens and such talented design colleagues as Rudolf Bosselt, Fritz Ehmcke, and Johannes Lauweriks revealed a fundamental shift away from earlier Jugendstil design and the Darmstadt legacy. As Behrens wrote during his years as director, "The arts and crafts school of today must reconcile the demands of craft and the needs of industry in accordance with aesthetic directives and artistic impulses."[52]

Best known among Behrens's works of this period is the templelike Delmenhorst Linoleum Company exhibition pavilion, built for the Third German Applied Arts Exhibition in Dresden in 1906 (Figure 1.4). Executing the company's posters, brochures, linoleum flooring and wall patterns, and several exhibition buildings, Behrens rapidly consolidated his position as the acknowledged star of the German design world with dazzling displays of versatility and flexibility that dignified the commodities manufactured by his clients and the advertising through which they were marketed. His adaptation of a monumental yet abstracted classicism struck a chord with business executives, art critics, and the public alike. Tapping the roots of classical tradition while remaining sensitive to the dramatic—even theatrical—possibilities of contemporary materials like linoleum, steel, concrete, and glass, Behrens embodied a modern artistic spirit that exceeded the highest hopes of the reform-minded Commerce Ministry.[53]

As the nation's first modern industrial and corporate image designer, Behrens set an example that was by no means lost on three of his young AEG office trainees in Berlin: Ludwig Mies van der Rohe, Walter Gropius, and the Dusseldorf graduate Adolf Meyer. These future leading figures of twentieth-century German architecture assisted Behrens when, in 1908–9, he designed the instantly iconic AEG Turbine Factory. The consummate image of an industrial "temple of work" erected in the industrial Moabit section of Berlin, the Turbine Factory was admired by Le Corbusier during his visit to Behrens's office in 1910 (Figure 1.5). As Stanford Anderson has observed, the Turbine Factory epitomized the moment in Behrens's career when the architect most decisively subordinated such modern materials as glass, concrete, and iron to

Figure 1.5. Peter Behrens, general view of AEG Turbine Factory, Berlin-Moabit, 1909. From Walter Müller-Wulckow, *Deutsche Baukunst der Gegenwart: Bauten der Arbeit und des Verkehrs* (Königstein im Taunus and Leipzig, 1929).

the creation of an inspired industrial corporate image emphasizing "corporeality and classical expression."[54] Behrens worked with his engineer, Karl Bernhard, to imbue the AEG factory with an aura of substantiality and monumentality at variance with the kind of light-framed, open, airy edifice that one might otherwise expect from an iron structural frame with glass infill. Thus, concrete corner pylons with horizontal bands carried no structural load, although they appeared to anchor the structure and support the roof with their tapering, horizontally striated bulk. Similarly, what Anderson identifies as an impressive "corporate display-facade" required a concealed iron truss to support its main feature: a concrete pediment bearing Behrens's hexagonal-patterned AEG logo. Although supported from behind, the pediment appeared to rest on an iron beam that topped a window frame rising at an outward slant from below.[55] At each stage of the design process, Behrens subordinated the engineering practicality and the functional dictates of materials to the generation of the most powerful visual image possible for the factory as a temple: tapering pylons, slanted windows, and angular vertical truss supports maximized the dramatic potential of linearity, shadows, light, and elemental geometries. As Frederic Schwartz has pointed out, such deft combinations of architectural imagery, corporate symbolism, and commercial expedience lay at the heart of the Werkbund's claims to be Germany's leading force for renewing culture through the harmonization of commerce and art.[56] Strict functionality and sober objectivity yielded to monumentality of appearance and to the creation of compelling corporate images.

Gropius and Meyer, who formed a partnership in 1910, pushed such explorations even further in their factory designs. In their first major commission, the Fagus Shoe-Last Factory of 1911, they replaced the non-load-bearing concrete pylons of Behrens's AEG factory with their antithesis: seemingly dematerialized glass corners. In their model factory building for the 1914 Werkbund Exhibition in Cologne, the pair punctuated the non-load-bearing corners of the building with circular glass corner towers housing spiral staircases. In both instances, Gropius and Meyer, as trained architects, inverted some of the painterliness of Behrens's design by exploiting the architectonic potential of non-weight-bearing corners. With equally compelling visual impact, they chose to reveal, rather than hide, the manner in which their modern factory buildings stood.[57]

Architectural examples such as these accumulated in support of the Werkbund's aim to blend art, design, and commerce to promote Germany's political, economic, and cultural goals. Working closely with the Commerce Ministry and other branches of government, the Werkbund also strove to educate Germans about the value of what it understood as quality in design, and to disseminate information about the Werkbund and its member firms' products abroad. In Berlin, for example, the Werkbund joined the Commerce Ministry in 1910 in funding the Institute for Decorative Arts, or Höhere Fachschule für Dekorationskunst. The school's students and design faculty filled Berlin's department stores, shop windows, advertising kiosks, and exhibitions with posters and product displays that were by turns flashy and provocative or sober and subdued.[58] Beginning in April 1913, the German Foreign Ministry also took steps to support the Werkbund, directing German consulates and embassies around the world to distribute its brochures, posters, and advertisements to aid in the marketing and sales of German products in foreign markets.[59] This effort was complemented by a traveling exhibition of German posters, products, and architectural photographs from Karl Ernst Osthaus's German Museum for Art in Commerce and Trade, which toured the United States in 1913. By 1915, even the Prussian Chamber of Deputies had opened its legislative chambers to the Werkbund's "Fashion Division," which put on a show of the latest modern German dresses and accoutrements in a bid to challenge France as the world's fashion capital. Together this constellation of government ministries, private associations, exhibitions, and events increasingly gave modern German capitalist culture a distinctive shape.[60]

THE WERKBUND CONGRESS IN COLOGNE:
"AN ASSOCIATION OF THE MOST INTIMATE ENEMIES"

The first Werkbund exhibition, held in the summer of 1914, should have been Muthesius's finest hour. In many respects it represented the culmination of all that he had been working to achieve in aesthetic and applied arts reform, on the one hand, and the implementation of the Commerce Ministry's strategy for orderly and systematic German economic development, on the other. As had been the case since at least 1900, Muthesius served as a valuable bridge between the artistic community and government policy makers eager to translate innovations in design into a program for Prussia's and Germany's continued growth. Now the Werkbund offered the ministry an effective extragovernmental means to further its policy goals.

Yet by mid-1912 Muthesius would comment that the Werkbund, whose headquarters were moved from Karl Schmidt's factory town, the new Garden City of Dresden-Hellerau, to Berlin in April of the same year, needed to be "rescued and restored from its ash-heap existence . . . and developed into a German center of culture."[61] He wrote these bitter yet still hopeful words to the Werkbund's new executive secretary, Ernst Jäckh. Although the Werkbund's membership expanded from 970 to more than 1,800 through Jäckh's efforts, conflicts over self-definition, artistic direction, and leadership plagued the association until they boiled over at the Cologne Exhibition in July 1914.[62]

The Werkbund's conflicts revolved around a fundamental tension between positions within the organization—tensions the Bauhaus would inherit. Gropius fought to reconcile what the Werkbund apparently could not: the demands of industrial production versus designers' insistence on total artistic and creative independence. Yet the famous "Werkbund debate" of July 1914 represented less the opposition of irreconcilable philosophical positions than another struggle over direction and control of the organization. The way in which this conflict developed and played out would influence deeply both its participants and subsequent developments in Weimar Germany.

Muthesius, whom Gropius called "the black sheep" at the center of attention and hostility at Cologne, combined the Commerce Ministry's political agenda with impolitic tactics at the association's meeting during the exhibition in 1914.[63] As Angelika Thiekötter has shrewdly observed, the diverse and ambitious group of men who formed the Werkbund in 1907 worked in relative unison as long as they turned their energies toward goals perceived to advance the association's common interests. Once they had to reach decisions on matters of internal policy and organizational direction, however, consensus, already tenuous to begin with, was all too likely to collapse into intrigue and conflict.[64] This was especially true when it came to the planning of the exhibition, a process that triggered conflict as soon as it began in earnest in 1912.

Relocating the Werkbund central office to Berlin had been only the first step in giving the organization a new identity. Meeting in Vienna in June 1912, Werkbund members listened as Peter Bruckmann, the silverware manufacturer from Heilbronn, accompanied by Jäckh, explained the terms of the association's new orientation. In addition to seeking to double the organization's membership, the Werkbund was to concentrate on building the most direct relations possible with the German Empire's centers of economic and political power. Government officials, bureaucratic authorities, and their supporting associations would all assume unprecedented influence over the affairs of the organization.[65] In Jäckh's later estimation, Muthesius counted as by far the most decisive personality in the Werkbund, for "he alone had the accurate conception of politics . . . as a synthesis of all human relations, ranging from physical matters to the metaphysics of psychology, from 'material' to 'form.'"[66]

Such unqualified praise for Muthesius became a rarity as 1914 approached, for the architect took on a role—a personality, even—that pointed to a significant shift in attitude, a subordination of his previous valuation of architecture and artistic culture to an unbending emphasis on commerce and trade. Events leading up to 1914 strongly suggest that the government played a major role in planning the exhibition and was, perhaps, a decisive factor in prompting artistic individualists such as van de Velde, Gropius, Endell, and Bruno Taut to seek to topple Muthesius from the Werkbund leadership.

Contemporary documents suggest that Muthesius, appearing suddenly with an appointment as "second chair" to the exhibition planning committee in Cologne after the committee had already been formed, exerted considerable control over commissions for exhibition buildings and over the content of the exhibition in general. Thwarted if not hindered outright by the government architect in their efforts to build exhibition buildings, such designers as van de Velde, Endell, Gropius, and even Behrens voiced loud opposition to the bland, commercial direction pursued by exhibition planners.[67] Although Muthesius adopted a conservative stance that he deemed would be more appealing to potential new Werkbund industrial partners, it is significant that precisely those buildings he most opposed—Gropius's Model Factory and van de Velde's theater among them—won the greatest critical praise for their individualistic spirit and notable designs.

Muthesius's behavior also reflected another emerging pattern in his thinking that tended to eschew any overt individualism in design, and leaned strongly toward an emphasis on the "typical" in modern architecture and industrial production. What began as a meditation on the essence and importance of form in his 1911 Werkbund speech "Where Do We Stand?" evolved over the course of the planning phase of the exhibition into a firm commitment to the identification and reproduction of "types" in design.

In his contribution to the 1913 Werkbund yearbook, titled "The Problem of Form in Engineering Construction," Muthesius urged all Werkbund members to recognize that aspects of beauty and function interacted dynamically from the beginning of any design process, whether involving a household object or a building. The vital work for generations of artists in any period, he argued, was to accelerate the evolution of fitting aesthetic forms (in the Vitruvian sense of *commoditas,* or "fitness") for each newly invented object. This could be shown historically through an examination of the design efforts that had surrounded the first steamships (in which a steam engine was mounted on a sailing ship), the first railway wagons (which resembled earlier horse-drawn mail coaches), or early gas lights (whose forms resembled candles). Over time, designers learned to relate the forms of these objects to the expression of their capabilities and functional requirements.[68]

Muthesius's development of this new and unprecedented position regarding the "typical" coincided with the planning phase of the First Werkbund Exhibition between 1912 and 1914. His philosophical shift and his contemporaneous actions in the exhibition planning committee could hardly have been a coincidence, particularly since his notion of "types" so strongly favored new forms of production in the trades and industry. By *Typisierung* ("making of types"), Muthesius did not mean standardization or mass production, words he consciously avoided using in ten "theses" he distributed one week prior to the opening of the Werkbund's annual congress at the exhibition in early July. Instead, he advocated the recognition of tendencies toward the "typical," which he claimed could be identified through a look at any era known for the greatness of its architectural, artistic, or applied arts production. The identification and collective recognition of "types" of products and designs were the best way, he reasoned, for Werkbund artists and designers to aid German industry. "Productively capable and dependably tasteful large enterprises," Muthesius wrote in his ninth thesis, "are the precondition for such an export. [By contrast], the individually produced, artist-designed object cannot even begin to fulfill domestic demand."[69] Muthesius further contended that Germany's progress in arts and crafts design and production needed to be publicized widely through a propaganda campaign, and was a national matter of life and death. The world, he explained, would ask for German products once these goods possessed a "convincing expression of style," for which the German movement recently had provided the basis.[70]

Muthesius was again relying on the cachet of his privileged government position in an effort to impose the will of the Commerce Ministry on a newly inaugurated phase of Werkbund policy. This is most likely what made the Werkbund into a "monster" in the estimation of the architect Hans Poelzig and turned Muthesius into a conduit, as Osthaus ominously wrote, for "underground" and "subaltern" forces, by which he almost certainly meant the Prussian government and its economic policy makers.[71] All of these men battled for levels of artistic integrity, independence, and individuality that they saw evaporating from the Werkbund.

Seven years earlier, in 1907, it had been the traditional crafts practitioners of the Association for the Economic Interests of the Crafts who had opposed Muthesius's advancement of the Commerce Ministry's will. At the Werkbund Exhibition of 1914, it was the elite cadre of artists, architects, and supporters of "artistic individualism" whose ire was aroused. Spearheaded by van de Velde, the individualists rallied to draft and print ten "countertheses" the night before Muthesius gave his scheduled speech to the Werkbund assembly. These theses protested the introduction of types as well as "every suggestion of a canon" that Muthesius's types seemed to imply.[72] The core of the counterprotest, supported by many of the architects and artists aggrieved during the exhibition planning process, cannot be regarded as having been against only the principle of types per se, but also against the wanton, undiplomatic, and autocratic way in which Muthesius had imposed his (and the Commerce Ministry's) will on the Werkbund membership. Not only had many designers' talents been suppressed in the preparations for the exhibition, but there was also a palpable sense that the artists, who so valued their independence and creative freedom, were simply being drafted as part of an economic program in applied arts manufacturing over which they would have absolutely no control.

Van de Velde, for example, was no foe of industry or of the concept of serial production in itself, as he had made plain in the journal *Pan* as early as 1897. There he explained his desire "to avoid systematically everything in furniture that could not be realized by big industry. My ideal would be a thousand-fold multiplication of my creations."[73] Similarly Gropius, one of the "individualist" camp at the Werkbund debate of 1914, had written a proposal for the industrial production of prefabricated houses for farm workers as early as 1911, and as such had clearly anticipated an aspect of Muthesius's modern "types" in architectural terms.[74] By opposing Muthesius in 1914, van de Velde and Gropius clearly were rebelling against authoritarian efforts to commandeer their skills for a greater institutional and national agenda, for in principle Muthesius's ideas did not run contrary to beliefs they had expressed independently.

Knowing that van de Velde had prepared his countertheses, Muthesius toned down the address he gave before the entire assembly. Titled "The Future Work of the Werkbund," the speech was a diplomatic effort to appraise the exhibition and to advance the new Werkbund orientation as a positive step for all. Admitting that the exhibition suffered from "a certain stillness . . . not to say listlessness," Muthesius agreed that the fractious Werkbund, by staying together in spite of having been called "an association of the most intimate enemies," offered "the best proof of the greatness of the idea that moves us beyond all differences of opinion."[75]

Artistry had suffered at the hands of efforts to give the exhibition the broadest possible appeal, Muthesius acknowledged, but on the positive side, businesses had begun taking the Werkbund seriously—to the point that "today the whole merchant class and the great majority of industrial producers seek to work with us." Underlining this as the purpose of the whole exhibition, he continued: "It is of the greatest importance to establish this here. And this confirmation calls forth a certain reproach, that actual new [Werkbund] products are only to be seen in such small numbers. It raises the question, what does the German Werkbund want?"[76] The Werkbund, he argued, must in the end choose the direction of developing the "typical," for that was the direction of development during all great eras of art. By shunning the unusual and seeking the orderly, the typical nevertheless also managed to bear within it the paradoxical quality of retaining "the worthwhile particular, the personal, and the unique." He assured his audience that the call for the typical was not a demand for the artist to concentrate only on a single form: "The artist follows only his own inner drive. He enjoys complete freedom, because he can only work in this way."[77] Nevertheless, the character of the present day called for acknowledgment of unprecedented levels of international exchange, as well as developments in technology that "practically overcome the boundaries of time and space." With this international quality of contemporary life arose the tendency toward "a certain similarity to the architectonic forms over the entire globe."[78] Muthesius was not advocating standardization or mass production by machines as the basis for a new style, and did not discuss either of these industrial processes in his speech, but he was clearly speaking of a wish to put the Werkbund at the forefront of discovering what the style representative of contemporary life would be.

No collective decisions could be taken at the end of the congress, for the proceedings following Muthesius's address were drowned in a sea of debate. The arguments reflected not only a lack of clarity and specificity in Muthesius's speech but also the pent-up emotions of the individuals who had been slighted or thwarted in their various ambitions for the exhibition. It was evident that the power struggle over the leadership of the Werkbund was every bit as important as, indeed if not more important than, the confused arguments over artistry, aesthetics, and quality. Muthesius withdrew his ten theses by way of seeking conciliation with the individualist faction but assured his audience in his closing remarks that he stood by the content of his lecture.[79]

CONCLUSION

The split that occurred within the Werkbund in 1914 did not heal during the course of the First World War. By 1916, and perhaps out of disillusionment with the policies of the government he had strained to back, Muthesius gave way and withdrew from the Werkbund.[80] Although his name continued to appear as a Werkbund member until 1922, he was largely inactive, except for the appearance of an occasional excerpt from his writings in Werkbund publications. The architect's arguments for the development of types remained a lively topic of discussion among the members—particularly for Gropius, who was at the Western front during the fighting. As Thiekötter has observed, his letters to Osthaus reveal that the Werkbund battles seemed to agitate him more than the bullets whistling around his ears.[81]

The Werkbund crisis cast into sharp relief the defining issues of design in an industrially and technologically sophisticated century. The individual integrity of the artist, pressures from competitive governments and capitalist industries toward cost reduction and efficiency through the development of industrial product "types," and the implications of new materials, methods, and tools for design: all of these would survive the Werkbund conference and endure as burning questions long after Wilhelmine Germany's defeat in 1918.

Gropius's famous attempt to tackle these design issues saw its fruition, of course, in the Bauhaus. There, too, however, the unstable political situation frustrated efforts to unite major artistic, crafts, and architectural talents under the banners of architecture and workshop instruction. Instructional workshops were up and running by 1921, but were never fully integrated with the school's fine arts classes. The primacy of individual artistic creativity, taught with devotion to a cultlike following in the preliminary course developed by the Swiss painter Johannes Itten, conflicted with the resurgent industrial orientation of the 1923 Bauhaus exhibition. Whether clothed in the stylized monk's robes worn by Itten or rallying beneath the 1923 exhibition banner of "Art and Technology: A New Unity," Bauhaus students and faculty clearly wrestled in their own context with questions that had faced the prewar Werkbund. The issue of designers' orientation to industry and machine production demanded every bit as much attention from the three Bauhaus directors—Gropius, Hannes Meyer, and Mies van der Rohe—as it had from Commerce Minister Möller, the directors of Prussian applied arts schools, and the Wilhelmine Werkbund.

The political, economic, and social conditions underlying Wilhelmine precedents to the Bauhaus were totally unique, even if the issues introduced were not. Historians like Nikolaus Pevsner and Julius Posener, among the first and most authoritative voices to write about the modern movement's "pioneers," focused diligently on the contributions to design innovation of such individuals as Morris, van de Velde, Muthesius, and Gropius.[82] They sought to characterize an emergent modern movement as politically progressive, emancipatory, and potentially redemptive. However, their works severely downplayed attention to the influence exerted upon designers by Germany's political institutions and state economic priorities, a fact that hindered more complete understanding of twentieth-century design's origins for decades.

The story of pre-1914 Bauhaus precedents transforms as soon as the customary historical frame is widened to include Wilhelmine Germany's complex institutional and cultural contexts. The German government, as we have seen, was every bit as influential in inspiring the rise of the Werkbund as, say, the Arts and Crafts movement, even though the government's concerns regarding the arts and crafts differed considerably from those of most designers. A more complete understanding of twentieth-century German architecture and design must therefore take into account the ways that modern state interests, burgeoning consumer society, international competition, and globalization impinge on designers and design culture. From this perspective, commercial, industrial, and political forces are every bit as important as individual artistic inspirations in shaping modern design developments. Design may be primary, but it can only be understood historically after taking account of the numerous conditions that combine to create it.

HENRY VAN DE VELDE AND WALTER GROPIUS

BETWEEN AVOIDANCE AND IMITATION

Kathleen James-Chakraborty

In 1951, the Swiss architect Max Bill, himself a former student of the Bauhaus, wrote to the school's founding director Walter Gropius.[1] Bill was, with Gropius's approval, working to found a West German successor to the Bauhaus that would open outside Ulm in 1955 as the College for Form (Hochschule für Gestaltung). He hoped that Gropius would have some kind words for an elderly architect, fast approaching ninety, who was living in exile in Switzerland. The man in question, Henry van de Velde, had designed the buildings in which Gropius had first established the Bauhaus in 1919 (Figure 2.1). Moreover, van de Velde had founded the Grand Ducal Saxon School of Arts and Crafts, the original occupant of one of these structures, and had in 1915 recommended that Gropius succeed him as its director.

Four decades later, however, Gropius was not disposed to send even a few polite words, much less to share credit for the revolution in the visual arts unleashed in 1919 in Weimar. "It is not so that the Bauhaus is based upon his ideas. It is quite obvious that in his school small van de Veldes were educated, who were emulating the master. Consciously I put the basis of the Bauhaus on different ground, namely, to find a common denominator of approach which should be impersonal," he dismissively replied to Bill.[2] Why was Gropius, then at the peak of his power and fame, so threatened by a man whom the intervening decades had treated so unkindly? What indeed was the relationship between the institutions the two men had founded in Weimar? And what larger issues regarding the definition of modern architecture and design and the apportioning of credit for its invention were at stake here?

Unlike Hermann Muthesius, van de Velde was neither a German civil servant nor a German citizen. The answers to these questions thus tell a slightly different story than that set forth in the preceding chapter, albeit one that also focuses on institutional continuity between the Wilhelmine and Weimar eras rather than the rupture caused by World War I. Precisely because Muthesius and van de Velde represented the two poles of the German Werkbund, the stories of their individual impact upon the next generation complement each other. An account of the relationship between Gropius and van de Velde has the additional advantage of hinting at the fears that may have driven Gropius, not only in Weimar, but also in the years that followed.

Figure 2.1. Henry van de Velde, Grand Ducal Saxon School of Arts and Crafts, Weimar, 1905–6. Photograph by Louis Held. Bauhaus-Archiv, Berlin.

An understanding of the degree to which the memory of van de Velde haunted Gropius begins with biographical parallels. In Weimar, each struggled in frustration against a politically and aesthetically conservative bureaucracy that sought to constrict a vision of artistic married to social change. Each placed enormous importance upon ensuring his place in history, threatened in both cases by the dislocations of emigration and exile. Although van de Velde was a generation older, the ideas of the two men and the way in which they implemented them also often converged. Van de Velde and Gropius shared a commitment to an art of its time. Each believed in the importance of the machine to such an art. Their pedagogical methods also overlapped, as did their conception of architecture in relation to the other arts. Already in 1901, van de Velde had criticized the emphasis that European art academies placed upon painting and sculpture as independent forms of fine art. Instead, he believed, they should be taught in relation to architecture and the decorative arts. Such an approach, he claimed, would discourage a sentimental dependence upon narrative in favor of greater artistic harmony achieved through abstraction.[3] Thus, although Weimar lay outside Prussian control, he was quick to heed Muthesius's call for workshop-based instruction.

There were, however, important reasons for Gropius to want to distance himself from van de Velde. First, van de Velde had an extraordinary aptitude for political ineptness. He had alienated both Germans and his fellow Belgians during World War I, eventually fleeing Weimar for Switzerland. It had taken almost a decade for him to be welcomed back to Brussels, which he had to leave again after World War II, during which he had worked for the German occupation government.[4] Gropius, too, had plenty of experience with treacherous political situations. As Winfried Nerdinger demonstrates in a subsequent chapter, he had briefly sought work from the Nazis before leaving Germany in 1934 for London and then the United States. Like van de Velde, he would learn what it was like to live in a country that had gone to war against the one in which he had been born. Finally, in the fifties, van de Velde's supporters pointed out the socialist roots of the reforms he had helped launch, while Gropius distanced himself from descriptions of the Bauhaus that emphasized its left-wing leanings.[5]

Moreover, there was a kernel of truth at the core of Gropius's charges. Although there is no evidence that he imposed his own aesthetic as strongly upon his students as Gropius claimed, van de Velde had indeed defended artistic individuality at the contentious 1914 meeting of the Werkbund. That Gropius had originally attracted the older architect's attention by supporting a position that he would later reject as a deviation from the path toward a machine aesthetic was something he perhaps wished to forget.

Gropius's curt dismissal of van de Velde was nonetheless not entirely fair. The Bauhaus in general and Gropius in particular certainly owed a great deal to van de Velde and to the school he had founded.[6] Recovering the connections between the two institutions and their directors may slightly diminish Gropius's claims to originality, but it also assists us in understanding the Bauhaus and his own role in administering it. Gropius knew that in order to succeed he needed not only to radically revise van de Velde's intentions, but also to avoid imitating van de Velde's often prickly response to local authorities and the public they represented. He would have to be far more diplomatic than his predecessor; it was also crucial that he take an active role in trying to shape public opinion at the local, national, and international level.

This mission endured long after Gropius left the Bauhaus in 1928. Indeed, once he arrived in the United States, Gropius's reputation depended in part upon his ability to convince others of the importance of the Bauhaus and of his own centrality to it. Van de Velde was an inconvenient reminder that institution building was a collaborative process, something Gropius, much as he espoused collaborative architectural practice, was loath to acknowledge in the case of the Bauhaus. More to the point perhaps, van de Velde was by the 1950s exactly what Gropius feared becoming, a man whose commitment to the new had not ensured him as large a place in history as he craved.

Gropius's fear was real. Appreciation of van de Velde grew during the following decades, years in which admiration for Gropius would wane along with enthusiasm for modernism. The ways in which Gropius had redefined his accomplishment at the

Bauhaus in order to accord with postwar conditions on both sides of the Atlantic increasingly seemed at odds with the alienation many felt from an industrial aesthetic or simply "good form." Meanwhile, the frank sensuousness of van de Velde's work combined with his early commitment to socialism sparked revived respect for the somewhat sad and lonely figure Gropius had disparaged.[7]

A FINGER ON THE PULSE OF HIS AGE

Van de Velde achieved his initial renown as a leading proponent of art nouveau (or Jugendstil—"youth style"—as it was known in German). This international movement reached, as van de Velde himself did, across both artistic media and national borders. Van de Velde's early success was a result of his ability to integrate himself into a wide variety of different contexts. Trained as a painter, he achieved fame instead as a designer of graphics, metalwork, and furniture before focusing his attention upon architecture. A proud Fleming, he nonetheless thought in international rather than provincial terms, introducing British arts and crafts theory into Antwerp and Brussels, and Belgian art nouveau design into France and Germany. His position between cultures was not always a comfortable one, however. Throughout his life, van de Velde oscillated between being a sophisticate at home in northern Europe's principal cities and an alien unwelcome even in his native land.

Van de Velde was born in 1863 in Antwerp, where he studied painting at the Academy of Fine Arts.[8] From the beginning he was interested in experimentation, embracing first impressionism and then the pointillist technique developed by the French artist Georges Seurat. Even as a young man he was also interested in the institutional structures that supported stylistic change. In 1888, he joined Les XX (the Twenty), Belgium's leading art organization, whose concerns and example would help determine the course of his career.

Founded in 1883, Les XX set a number of key precedents for the various reform movements with which van de Velde would be associated. By offering a private, profit-oriented alternative to the official salon, Les XX provided a model for the later popularity throughout Europe of secessionist alternatives to government-sponsored exhibits.[9] Furthermore, its exhibits were organized with an eye to details of publicity and installation that foreshadowed the efforts of the Werkbund, where the objects on display were often mass-produced commodities rather than singular works of art. Even more important for van de Velde were the group's web of international connections and its association with socialist politics.

In the 1890s, van de Velde was one of Europe's most cosmopolitan artists, personally acquainted with many of the most important artists and critics in Belgium, France, the Netherlands, and Germany. Through his wife, he was also familiar with the British Arts and Crafts movement, whose example he repeatedly championed in his writings. His position at the crossroads of developments in the visual arts exposed him to a wide variety of artistic movements in different media and facilitated his role as someone who introduced and adapted foreign ideas for new audiences.

In 1893, van de Velde abandoned painting in favor of architecture and the decorative arts, because he believed that only in this way could he contribute to the revival of art as a vital force that beautified and ennobled daily life. The artistic reforms that swept through Brussels and the rest of Belgium in van de Velde's youth were inextricably tied for those engaged in them with attempts to reform Belgian society, which, like its counterparts across Europe, had been polarized by rapid industrialization and urbanization. Les XX was firmly allied with attempts to democratize society through such reforms as universal male suffrage, finally instituted in Belgium in 1893. Many members of the group and the circle of patrons gathered around them were sympathetic to the new Belgian Workers Party. Van de Velde delivered party-sponsored lectures on the Arts and Crafts movement to largely working-class audiences.[10]

As was the case for many Belgian intellectuals of his generation, van de Velde's condemnation of bourgeois materialism and the social inequalities upon which it was based were initially inseparable. It was sympathy for the plight of the working class that led him to the work of the men who would become his heroes, John Ruskin and William Morris. The two Englishmen had asserted that the status of the workers could be improved by restoring the dignity of handcraftsmanship. Although not able to stop the process of modernization, they did create something of a refuge from its impact in buildings and furnishings that revived medieval forms and helped keep more recent vernacular traditions alive.[11]

As impressed by Morris's designs as by the social goals that motivated him, van de Velde remained detached, however, from the nostalgic aspects of the British Arts and Crafts movement. While Ruskin and Morris were greatly influenced by the deep-seated piety characteristic of nineteenth-century middle-class British reformers, van de Velde was, as a member of the Continental left, profoundly anticlerical. Although he admired the Gothic, he never imitated it. For him the role of church, like that of the nobility, must be curtailed in order to create a society in which political power was shared equitably among at least the male members of the middle class and in which even workers had access to such institutions as parliaments.[12]

Divorcing Morris's work from medievalism left van de Velde free to focus upon its understatement. In Morris's directness he found a concrete alternative to what he regarded as the sentimentality of academic art's emphasis on narrative and the stifling claustrophobia of symbolism's self-absorption.[13] Morris's dedication to structure and purpose was a welcome shift away as well from the often allegorical figural ornament that encrusted almost every object in the homes of those who could afford such status symbols.

The year 1895 was a defining one in van de Velde's career. He began to plan his own dwelling, the Bloemenwerf, in the Brussels suburb of Uccle. Here he created a portrait of an artist deeply attached to late-nineteenth-century standards of bourgeois comfort and at the same time in rebellion against the ways in which that comfort was conventionally expressed. In the same year Siegfried Bing's gallery Maison de l'Art Nouveau opened in Paris. Van de Velde contributed three rooms to what quickly became the city's most controversial new gallery. His designs helped inaugurate a debate over contemporary design that bestowed international attention on the style that would become synonymous with Bing's gallery. Although Paris would soon become a center of art nouveau production, van de Velde was not easily integrated into France's explicitly aristocratic rococo heritage. Instead, he faced considerable hostility as a foreigner impinging upon its traditional expertise in the production of luxury goods.[14]

The display of the same rooms two years later in Dresden, however, proved more successful, bringing van de Velde to the attention of those Germans interested in developing their own counterpart to the British Arts and Crafts movement and to Belgian and French art nouveau. During the second half of the nineties, a steady procession of Germans interested in artistic reform visited the Bloemenwerf. One result was his work for the manufacturers of Tropon, a health food made from egg whites, which turned to him for both packaging and advertising (Figure 2.2). The company went bankrupt in 1901, cutting short an experiment in corporate imagery that nonetheless provided an important precedent for Peter Behrens's later work for the AEG. German enthusiasm for his work prompted van de Velde to move in 1900 to Berlin.

Van de Velde was seldom satisfied with his reception in Germany and many of his most ambitious projects failed to ripen, but the next fifteen years were certainly the most productive of his exceptionally long life. He continued to design a variety of decorative objects but increasingly worked at an architectural scale. His early projects in Berlin were crucial in making the Jugendstil fashionable throughout the country, while his collaboration with Karl Ernst Osthaus turned Hagen, a city in northwestern Germany's highly industrialized Ruhr region, into a notable center for modern art and design.[15] Of more importance to this story were his activities in Weimar and at the Werkbund exhibition in Cologne.

Van de Velde's German career was anchored in the reform of middle-class domesticity and civic life. During his formative years, the dividing line in Belgium was class. By the time he left for Berlin, language was replacing it in importance. Van de Velde's attachment to the Flemish cause may have helped him disengage from his earlier focus upon the welfare of the worker.[16] In Germany, where his clients were typically aristocrats and industrialists for whom artistic change was an alternative to more profound social disruption, his lingering attachment to socialism quickly waned.[17]

Van de Velde's efforts to fit into a German context were undermined, however, by his continued loyalty to the sinuous curves of art nouveau. Long after its brief popularity in German design circles gave way to contempt for what became seen as facile fashion, van de Velde refused to adopt the quasi-abstract, quasi-neoclassical rectilinearity

Figure 2.2. Henry van de Velde, advertising for Tropon Biscuits, circa 1898. Karl Ernst Osthaus-Museum, Hagen.

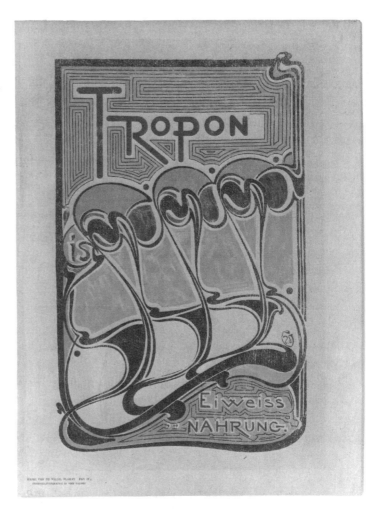

that became characteristic of Central European design as the new century took hold.[18] He instead upheld the fluid line as a means of artistic and emotional expression.[19] What had begun as an allegiance to an international style became in Germany the personal approach to form he would defend in Cologne (Figure 2.3).

VAN DE VELDE AND THE GRAND DUCAL SAXON SCHOOL OF ARTS AND CRAFTS

Van de Velde arrived in Weimar in 1902. He came to the small but fabled city with high hopes of inaugurating another golden age in its history, one that might rival that of the era in which Johann Wolfgang Goethe was its most famous resident. Like Goethe before him, he was dependent upon the patronage of the local court, which had grown even more provincial after being stripped of much of its political authority following

32 KATHLEEN JAMES-CHAKRABORTY

the unification of Germany in 1871. Over the course of the next thirteen years, van de Velde would watch many of his hopes for transforming the city fall victim to what he would always view as local narrow-mindedness. At the same time, however, he would also quite literally build the foundations upon which Gropius would construct the Bauhaus and once again briefly make the city one of Europe's leading intellectual centers.

From the beginning, van de Velde's mission was pedagogical. In 1903 he was named a professor; the following year he began to plan the building in which his School of Arts and Crafts opened in 1907. It, along with the neighboring School of Fine Arts, another of his designs, would later house the Bauhaus. Although his resources were relatively limited, van de Velde's school anticipated the Bauhaus in several crucial ways. He had received a conventional academic education, but had come to condemn the isolation of the minor from the fine arts. Art, van de Velde believed, benefited from its association with use, which should operate to limit its decoration to abstract ornament of an elegant simplicity. In Weimar he established workshops in goldsmithing and enameling, bookbinding, weaving and embroidery, carpentry, ceramics, and metalwork, where students learned to fabricate the objects they designed. These would stand in drastically revised form at the core of the Bauhaus curriculum. Like its successor, van de Velde's school was also intended to be a research laboratory for local industry, which it could assist by generating new designs and educating designers.[20]

By the time van de Velde's school actually opened, however, he was already often at loggerheads with the court. This meant that he lacked the budget to import the faculty of the caliber that Gropius would soon bring to the Bauhaus. The school remained

Figure 2.3. Henry van de Velde, silver tea service, circa 1905. Karl Ernst Osthaus-Museum, Hagen.

small and its impact on the general reform of design education and craft production in Germany slight. None of its alumni achieved the prominence accorded many of those who would study in the same building during the 1920s. Nonetheless, the school was more progressive than the Bauhaus in one crucial respect: the equal opportunities it accorded its female students. While Gropius attempted with some success to confine female students to the weaving workshop, van de Velde appears to have been comfortable with the composition of a student body in which women consistently outnumbered men.[21] Van de Velde offered many of his female students the opportunity, still relatively rare in Germany at this time, to train for careers as professionals.

Van de Velde's impact upon Weimar extended beyond his teaching. His physical imprint upon the city is far more discernible than that of the Bauhaus, which is confined to the presence of a single model house. In Weimar the former painter converted himself from a graphic artist and a designer of interiors and the objects that filled them into an architect with truly monumental ambitions. An apartment for Henry Graf Kessler and a house for himself were among the domestic commissions that enabled him to continue to develop his conception of the modern artistic dwelling, while the two art schools were the city's most prominent new civic buildings. His most ambitious projects for Weimar revolved, however, around the city's association with Friedrich Nietzsche, who had died there in 1900.

The philosopher's sister Elisabeth Förster-Nietzsche was initially one of van de Velde's greatest local supporters.[22] The designer of an ornate edition of Nietzsche's *Thus Spake Zarathustra,* published in 1908, van de Velde was one of the many architects in Germany who admired the philosopher for offering a way out of what he saw as the stifling bourgeois culture of the preceding generation.[23] Förster-Nietzsche commissioned van de Velde's renovation of an existing villa to house the philosopher's papers, but she eventually balked at his and Kessler's grandiose schemes for a Nietzsche temple and stadium, which were consequently never built.

One reason for the rejection of this scheme may have been the degree to which van de Velde's architectural forms were now out of sync with that of such important reform-minded contemporaries as Peter Behrens, Theodore Fischer, and Hans Poelzig. While these architects increasingly turned to history, whether the neoclassicism espoused by Behrens or the regional vernaculars invoked by Fischer and Poelzig, van de Velde remained committed to the invention of an entirely modern style. German criticism of the Jugendstil as unnecessarily arbitrary and thus little more than a capitulation to consumerism distanced van de Velde from the success of German design reform in the last years before World War I. He alone failed to offer an image of national, or at least regional, stability that served as a bulwark against the inroads of an international marketplace, in which he was instead deeply implicated.

Days before the outbreak of the war, van de Velde finally resigned from his position. Convinced that he could not overcome the increasing alienation from the court he had

Figure 2.4. Henry van de Velde, theater, Werkbund Exhibition, Cologne, 1914. From Gustav Adolf Platz, *Die Baukunst der Neuesten Zeit* (Berlin: Propyläen Verlag, 1930), 286.

sensed since his friend Kessler's disgrace in 1906, he sought instead to return to Belgium.[24] Although his position as an enemy national in Weimar marginalized him, in 1915 he had the opportunity to recommend that one of three men succeed him.[25] Two of the men whose names he gave, August Endell and Hermann Obrist, were, like van de Velde himself, well known in Germany as former pioneers of the Jugendstil, active in both architecture and the decorative arts since the turn of the century. The third was Gropius, a much younger man whose interest in American factories clearly distinguished him as a member of a new generation, although his established family connections (his great-uncle had been a prominent architect in Berlin) and nationalist rhetoric appeared to make him a relatively safe choice. Van de Velde's list corresponded almost exactly to that of the colleagues who had provided him with the most stalwart support when, also in July 1914, he had battled Muthesius, Germany's foremost critic of art nouveau.

DEFENDING INDIVIDUALITY

In July 1914, as detailed in the preceding chapter, Germans interested in modern design gathered in Cologne. The assassination on 28 June of Austro-Hungary's Crown Prince Franz Ferdinand cast a shadow over the assembly, but war had not yet been declared. The Werkbund's annual meeting was held in conjunction with the organization's most ambitious undertaking to date, a vast exposition held on fairgrounds on the east bank of the Rhine, whose buildings included a theater designed by van de Velde (Figure 2.4). Instead of celebrating its successes, however, the group's discussions mirrored the bellicose tone being taken by diplomats and the popular press. Just as Europe would soon divide into two warring camps, the Werkbund nearly split in half over Muthesius's advocacy of "types." Van de Velde countered:

> By his innermost essence the artist is a burning idealist, a free spontaneous creator. Of his own free will he will never subordinate himself to a discipline that imposes upon him a type, a canon. Instinctively he distrusts everything that might sterilize his actions, and everyone who preaches a rule that might prevent him from thinking his thoughts through to their own free end, or that attempts to drive him into a universally valid form, in which he sees only a mask that seeks to make a virtue out of incapacity.[26]

Although like Muthesius, he had not been present at its founding, van de Velde was among the Werkbund's leading members. The two were equally committed to its goal of taming the economic and social processes unleashed by industrialization by integrating art into the design and marketing of its products. Because they agreed that the quality of mass-produced goods could help restore cultural and social unity to a dangerously divided society, this debate over tactics was also one that implied contrasting social ideals.[27] Van de Velde's individualism could also be seen, as John V. Maciuika demonstrated in the preceding chapter, as a stand against Muthesius's nationalism. Certainly Muthesius deplored art nouveau as much because it was French as because it quickly became commercialized, commercialization itself associated in Germany with France and with America. Although he was no longer a socialist, van de Velde's continued belief in the possibility of dynamic artistic change did not exclude the possibility as well of political progress. This was expressed in spatial terms in the seating plan of the theater he contributed to the exhibition. He banished not only the box seats that distinguished wealthier members of the audience without necessarily giving them a better view of the stage but also the tiered seating at the rear of the house. Orchestra seating alone filled the rectangular hall.[28]

Van de Velde's position has been branded reactionary, a last gasp of art nouveau whimsy that denied the realities of machine production. This ignores the extent to which his own admiration for modern engineering had helped create the intellectual climate in which Muthesius could take such a positive view of industrialization within the context of design reform. In Germany van de Velde gained a greater understanding of the economic issues that governed the design and marketing of mass-produced products. Nonetheless, he repeatedly lamented their impact, deploring in particular the importance placed on the export market.[29]

Van de Velde's leadership of the opposition to Muthesius also demonstrated the stature he retained in Germany as a theorist. In Cologne he was able to command the support not only of his contemporaries Endell and Obrist but also of Gropius and Bruno Taut, whose pavilions there established them as the leaders of a new generation. Van de Velde's prolific career as a designer of everything from books to buildings has helped obscure his importance as a writer. His ideas were as fresh as, and more enduring than, the characteristically curvilinear lines with which he so successfully blurred the boundaries between form and ornament. Whereas van de Velde's designs from the first decade of the twentieth century remain closely linked to art nouveau, his essays form a key bridge between the Arts and Crafts movement and the International Style.

Although both van de Velde and Muthesius were inspired by the example of British Arts and Crafts architecture and design, they drew different lessons from it. Muthesius sought to revive what he believed to be the premodern connection between the artifacts of daily life and enduring cultural traditions.[30] Van de Velde called more explicitly for the creation of an entirely new style. If he himself never espoused the industrial aesthetic later commentators often assumed Muthesius had favored, he certainly prepared the way for those who did.

In Germany the socialist leanings that had encouraged van de Velde to uphold Ruskin and Morris as the precedent upon which design reform should be based gave way to a focus upon the invention of a new ornament and then a new style. He was not the first to recognize in modern engineering a precedent for a reinvigorated modern art and architecture, but he was the first to do so in the context of the reform of the decorative arts rather than architecture.[31] In particular, his formalist view of Morris narrowed the gap between Morris's own designs and the very machines he had loathed. For van de Velde, there was no contradiction between Morris's revival of the rush-seated chairs found in eighteenth-century farmhouses and such triumphs of modern engineering as the Firth of Forth Bridge.[32] Both were welcome models of simplicity and utility. This imaginative leap would become standard in accounts of the prehistory of interwar modernism. So would the tendency to elide Morris's critique of capitalism with an admiration for industrialization, at least when functionalist design made its products detachable from the taint of a consumerism defined in strictly aesthetic terms, that is, as representational or historicist ornament unrelated to structure, material, or purpose.

Van de Velde's continued dedication to the new, although neither original nor unique, was particularly important as by 1905 throughout Europe a corset of historicism increasingly restricted and smoothed the voluptuous experiments of the turn of the century. Although he himself quickly imposed considerable discipline upon the whiplash tendrils that had once enlivened almost everything he designed, he was not ready to relinquish an inventiveness that seemed to his opponents almost irrational. Ironically in view of his later criticism, Gropius was probably attracted to van de Velde's position in 1914 in part because it offered an alternative to the regimentation that he and other younger architects found stifling. Certainly van de Velde was alone of his generation in producing a building for the exhibition that offered an alternative to the increasingly monumental, even bombastic, constructions in which the distinction between architectural reform and reinforcing the status quo was quickly collapsing. Gropius, who, with Adolf Meyer, was the architect of another such structure, could not have failed to notice this.

IMPERSONAL AND INDUSTRIAL

In 1919, Gropius moved to Weimar to reorganize van de Velde's school and the neighboring Academy of Fine Arts into the Bauhaus. Without van de Velde, there would have been no institution to reform, no buildings already associated with artistic change, and no workshops in which to begin the new project of marrying fine art and craft education. The Bauhaus occupied the buildings van de Velde had designed for its predecessors for as long as it did the Dessau structure that gave architectural form to its institutional identity. It also inherited van de Velde's precarious relationship with conservative local authorities, who, after the revolution of November 1918, were even quicker than before to equate new art with the threat of social upheaval. Paradoxically, however, Gropius would achieve the fame he craved only by founding and sustaining an institution in which eventually the role of individual artists would apparently be subordinated in exactly the way van de Velde had deplored in 1914.

Gropius's star began to rise in late Wilhelmine Germany just as van de Velde's began to fall. Born in 1883 in Berlin, he studied architecture in Berlin and Munich. He chose the profession undoubtedly more out of respect for family tradition than because of artistic talent. Despite the freshness of his ideas, Gropius relied upon others to realize them; he was almost unable to draw.[33] Nonetheless, he secured a place with Behrens before forming a partnership with Adolf Meyer. With the help of his family connections, Gropius and Meyer secured several commissions, including most notably in 1911 the job of designing the facades of a shoe last factory in Alfeld.

In the last years before the war, Gropius traveled in circles that increasingly overlapped with van de Velde's without in any way coming under his spell. He lectured in Hagen, in Osthaus's museum, giving a speech there whose nationalist overtones echoed Muthesius. Gropius also supervised the construction of two Behrens-designed villas near the house van de Velde had built for Osthaus on the city's suburban outskirts. Their geometric massing and neoclassical detail contrasted with van de Velde's somewhat rustic essay. Even in Cologne, where Gropius and van de Velde were finally and temporarily to come together in support of an idea, the work of the younger architect was noticeably at odds with that of the man who would give him his greatest opportunity. Gropius and Meyer reprised their Alfeld performance in the public setting of the Werkbund exhibition, where their model factory established a delicate balance between abstract monumentality and a celebration of the almost feather-light facades made possible by steel and concrete frame construction (Figure 2.5). It was a very different view of concrete and of the future than that offered by van de Velde's theater, which seemed almost to slouch under the weight of its walls.

Figure 2.5. Walter Gropius and Adolf Meyer, model factory, Werkbund exhibition, Cologne, 1914. From Platz, *Die Baukunst der Neuesten Zeit*, 369.

Gropius saw active duty as an officer during the war and was decorated for his bravery. He became an enthusiastic revolutionary, however, helping to found the radical Working Council for Art (Arbeitsrat für Kunst) in the first days following the November Revolution in 1918.[34] Whatever his initial intentions for the Grand Ducal Saxon School had been, the Bauhaus never lost its association with the first flush of revolutionary optimism.

The circumstances that brought first van de Velde and then Gropius to Weimar were only roughly parallel. In 1919, Gropius could merely dream of being as well connected internationally as van de Velde had been already in 1902. While van de Velde's facility as a draftsman infused his work in a variety of media, Gropius had relatively little experience outside of architecture. Gropius was, however, eager to carry van de Velde's mission of marrying art and objects of daily use to a new generation, one whose aspiration to unite design and social change had been reawakened by the November Revolution.

This was a goal that van de Velde might well have shared had he been a German national experiencing the birth of the Weimar Republic from the inside. It was certainly one that he had anticipated, even if the products he designed had remained luxury items outside the reach of even most middle-class consumers. The form Bauhaus products took, however, quickly proved too radical for him. The Bauhaus masters and their students progressed from a somewhat roughhewn, craft-oriented expressionism to designs that married constructivist geometry to an industrial aesthetic in works that were intended to reflect the "objective" character of mass production (see Figure I.2). Furthermore, by 1926 Gropius explicitly supported standardization, writing, "The creation of standard types for all practical commodities of everyday use is a social necessity."[35] Although van de Velde by this time eschewed applied ornament, he refrained from machine age imagery. Furthermore, he chose during this period to construct almost all of his buildings out of exposed brick, a material whose rich texture resisted the flattening of facades in imitation of the two-dimensionality of painted canvases.

At the Bauhaus, Gropius launched an investigation into the production of art and design whose engagement with mass production and mass culture, although often romanticized by both participants and their chroniclers, was nonetheless far more direct than anything anticipated by van de Velde. Many of the results have been described as *sachlich,* a German adjective that means sober as well as objective. Any attempt to describe the art or the school from which it emanated as anonymous, however, runs aground on the shoals of the considerable role that strong personalities—Gropius's among them—played in the daily life of students and masters alike.[36] And if Gropius's tenure could be characterized as impersonal, then how was he to receive credit for what had happened during it?

WRITING HISTORY

Long after Ludwig Mies van der Rohe, its last director, closed its doors in 1933, the Bauhaus remained central to both van de Velde's and Gropius's view of their own contribution to the history of architecture and design. Neither offered anything approaching an objective view of the past. Although van de Velde was more apt to consult the archival sources in reconstructing his account, both men were—quite humanly—prone to distorting the historical record in their own favor. In the end the issue was not accuracy but the importance of standardization and the anonymity it implied, to the abstraction that both regarded as the paramount expression of modernism in the visual arts. Here there was no room for agreement.

In chronicling the accomplishments of himself and his Flemish friends Willy Finch and Georges Lemmen, van de Velde in *The Renaissance in the Modern Decorative Arts,* published in 1901, almost simultaneously established a genealogy of the modern movement in architecture and the decorative arts. His account of the importance of British precedents to later developments in Germany would be almost universally accepted, most notably in Nikolaus Pevsner's *Pioneers of the Modern Movement from William Morris to Walter Gropius.*[37] Pevsner mapped out a chronology that led from Philip Webb's Red House for Morris (see Figure 1.2) through van de Velde's chairs for the Bloemenwerf to Gropius and Meyer's Fagus Factory, which he identified as the most important precedent for the Bauhaus. Pevsner followed van de Velde's example, as well, in the way in which form, technology, and theory were intertwined without much attention to economic conditions, social structure, or issues of inhabitation and use. The story van de Velde presented of the birth of Belgian art nouveau was a highly partisan one, however. Almost no one would follow his example and give so much credit to Flemish painters. Instead, there is widespread agreement about the importance of architects from the country's French-speaking community, above all, Victor Horta.[38]

For van de Velde the principal accomplishment to celebrate was the break art nouveau artists and architects had made with historicism. The invention of a new style, one which was of its time in that its simplicity and attention to function matched those of modern engineering, was for him the key achievement in establishing an approach that he rightly understood would dominate these fields throughout the century. This achievement won him the respect of such leading postwar architects as Alvar Aalto, who described him in a eulogy as "the European continent's grand old man in terms of revitalizing the arts."[39]

Gropius insisted, however, that the breakthrough had come only a generation later. Objects of art and of daily use must display their machine origins through designs whose standardization reflected mass production processes rather than being an idealization of norms that encompassed historical precedent as well as modern engineering. Such designs would necessarily be impersonal, as for Gropius they represented an almost scientific response to social, economic, and especially technological facts. He noted in 1958 that the Bauhaus had not begun by making fashionable items, but had instead been a laboratory for research about form. This, he claimed, had produced homogeneity instead of stylishness. He insisted once again that this approach had imbued design with the character of a social art for the entire community.[40]

Had he wished to acknowledge the importance of the elder figure, Gropius could have described to Max Bill in 1951 the ways in which the Bauhaus had been indebted to van de Velde in particular and art nouveau in general. The search for a new style that would fit the character of the times and generate objects that were functional rather than allegorical or historicist was certainly not a new one in 1919, nor was the characterization of the times in terms of the machines that mass-produced functional goods. Van de Velde was scarcely the only figure who had voiced such ideas already, but he was certainly their principal exponent in late Wilhelmine Germany, not to mention Weimar itself. Similarly, van de Velde's ideas about the proper training of those who would develop this new style accorded with Gropius's own actions. Only when the "fine arts" of painting, sculpture, and architecture were integrated with the design of useful objects could art sustain the daily life of all members of society.[41]

Gropius hesitated to admit any of this in part because to reject convention is the purpose of any avant-garde. He was also afraid, however, of following van de Velde into seeming oblivion. Gropius must have been terrified that he would fail like his predecessor. Could he shield himself, as van de Velde had not, from the pettiness of local officials by taking his case to a larger public, in the process making the Bauhaus the emblem of liberal culture in the embattled republic?[42] Could he steer a course between the extremes of left and right that would preserve the historical importance of his achievements? Could he, despite his waning artistic powers, still find a place among the world's most respected architects long after leaving Weimar behind? By answering these questions in the affirmative, he found the success that had eluded van de Velde.

Sixteen years after responding to Bill, Gropius answered yet another query about van de Velde. Although he repeated many of the same points he had made before, he was now more generous: "Van de Velde's personal approach in art and architecture was strong and had its influence. I like particularly the comprehensiveness of his approach to buildings and all their contents. The unity, however, which I am striving for, is to find the common denominator for many individuals in order to help secure a form character, an image, which represents a whole region or country beyond any individual achievement."[43]

What Gropius intended to be an impersonal representation of Weimar Germany has come to stand for even more. Seven decades after the Bauhaus shut its doors, the image of modernity in architecture, advertising, design, and typography in particular continues to be defined in surprisingly stable terms that, if not always invented at the Bauhaus, were certainly popularized through their association with the school. Furthermore, these terms now transcend issues of national identity, as they have won acceptance, albeit for varying periods of time, in regions and countries on all six inhabited continents. Although both hesitated to acknowledge it, Gropius realized many of van de Velde's goals.

FROM METAPHYSICS TO MATERIAL CULTURE

PAINTING AND PHOTOGRAPHY AT THE BAUHAUS

Rose-Carol Washton Long

3

In the first years of the Bauhaus's existence, Walter Gropius, an architect, appointed primarily painters—seven of the first eight hired—to the faculty to help shape the direction of the new school and its impact upon the arts and society in Germany. Although he believed architecture could unite the visual arts with craft in order to effect cultural transformation and change, he viewed painting as critical for creativity in all the arts. By the time of Gropius's departure in 1928, photography, which had not even been mentioned when the school was founded, had been accepted as a stimulus for visual experimentation and was increasingly viewed as having great potential to carry out the Bauhaus mission of reaching a wide audience. Painters in the school, however, felt threatened by the developing interest in photography and viewed the situation as a battle between opposing forces.

László Moholy-Nagy, whom Gropius brought to the Bauhaus in 1923, and his wife, Lucia Moholy were the major force for the interest in the medium of photography. When his book *Malerei, Fotografie, Film* (Painting, Photography, Film) was published as the eighth Bauhaus book in 1925, painters at the Bauhaus complained that their medium was losing influence. Oskar Schlemmer vividly captured their anguish when he wrote to a friend in December 1925 about Moholy-Nagy's book: "But will you agree with the author of the book of photographs when he wipes the slate clean of anything that might be called painting? That is the crucial question at the Bauhaus, and in part of the art world as well; . . . Since at the moment he is also Gropius's prime minister, he possesses great, almost enormous, influence in the art world."[1] Even shortly after Moholy-Nagy's arrival at the Bauhaus, Schlemmer had expressed concern that the young Hungarian would replace the Russian painter Wassily Kandinsky, whom Gropius had hired in 1922 and put in charge of one of the basic classes, as a central influence on the director.[2] Despite Schlemmer's concerns, photography did not replace painting, and Kandinsky and his theories retained a critical hold on Bauhaus education. Nonetheless, photography gained respectability as a new and effective tool for reaching the public. Even though descriptions of the two men usually depict them as polar opposites, Kandinsky and Moholy-Nagy shared many values, values that in a curious way prepared numerous stuudents for the public role photography was to play at the

43

Bauhaus. Indeed, both Kandinsky and Moholy-Nagy drew sustenance from Russian constructivism and Dutch De Stijl as they struggled to dispel traces of their expressionist heritage from their work.

THE PRIMACY OF PAINTING

When Gropius was appointed director in 1919, he was very much affected by the young expressionist generation of artists and their association with the struggles of the new republic. Filled with a fervor to reshape society by reforming art education, he was determined to break down the artificial barriers between high and low art, that is, to place the applied artist—the craftsperson—on the same level as the so-called fine artist—the painter and the sculptor. Instead of separate schools for technical work, he believed the mixture of all levels of instruction would be enriching, and in the first Bauhaus manifesto, he called for all the arts to join together.[3] In keeping with the new Weimar constitution, Gropius promised equal status to women. But in practice neither women nor crafts achieved equality with men and painting. Male painters were the ones assigned to teach basic design courses about color and form and, even more important, the ones who sat on the governing council of the Bauhaus. Gropius associated painters with free will and creativity, feeling they were less dependent on costly material and less tied to the dictates of patrons than were applied artists or even members of his own profession. He did give the title of "master" to those who headed the practical workshops as well as to those who taught the preliminary design courses, and he hoped to admit an equal number of male and female students. By 1920, partly because of the great number of women who applied to the school, Gropius spoke about enforcing tougher restrictions for female applicants and encouraging them to move into craft workshops, especially the one devoted to weaving. As art historians Magdalena Droste and Anja Baumhoff have discussed, weaving at that time was more commonly thought of as a feminine craft, and it became the first predominately female workshop, albeit with a male painter in charge.[4] Nonetheless, Gropius's call for a new type of art education, which he believed could stimulate a regenerative collective unity among all level of artists, attracted numerous young men and women to Weimar.

During the early years of the Bauhaus, Gropius continued to advocate many of the ideas formulated during his association with utopian expressionist groups, such as the Arbeitsrat für Kunst, founded at the beginning of the new republic. The Bauhaus manifesto, with its Feininger cover alluding to a cathedral, and Gropius's July 1919 speech to Bauhaus students, with its metaphoric references to a crystalline sign of a new future emanating from a monument, owe a great debt to the expressionist poet and novelist Paul Scheerbart as well as to the architect Bruno Taut and the critic Adolf Behne, who along with Gropius comprised the leadership of the Arbeitsrat. The egalitarian emphasis on breaking down barriers between artistic groups, the commitment to innovation, and the comparison of architecture to religion have a visionary tone that contrasts with Gropius's writings before World War I. Gropius's experiences during the war had convinced him that a radical break with past structures and systems was necessary: "Capitalism and power politics have dulled the creativity of our generation and the . . . intellectual bourgeois society of the old regime—indifferent and dull, unimaginative, arrogant, and badly educated—has demonstrated its inability to be representative of German culture."[5] Taut's admonition to architects to study "the new painting" is reflected in Gropius's turning for his faculty in the early years to painters connected with the expressionist gallery of Sturm.[6] Choosing at first Johannes Itten and Lyonel Feininger, he soon after called upon Lothar Schreyer, Georg Muche, Oskar Schlemmer, Paul Klee, and Wassily Kandinsky, all of whom had exhibited in the Sturm Gallery or had been published in its periodical bearing the same name. The antinaturalism and antiacademicism of these painters seemed to represent a new and revolutionary artistic vision.

These instructors—especially Itten and Muche—shared Gropius's metaphysical, utopian vision of changing society through educational reform. Gropius was aware that his instructors would be criticized for their internationalism, their political views, their connection with expressionism, and the abstraction of their painting. When he wanted to appoint Klee and Schlemmer, Gropius had to write to the national minister of culture for assistance in dealing with the new government's fears that the two Swiss-born artists were "more wildly expressionistic than the artists already present."[7] But Gropius believed he was living in a catastrophic period of world history in which much misery and privation had to be endured before "spiritual and religious ideas" would find their "crystalline statement" in the "smallest things of everyday life."[8] In his speech of July 1919, Gropius reminded the students that they were part of "small, secret, secluded leagues" that would help work out a "new, great world idea."[9] Of all the painters whom Gropius invited to teach at the Bauhaus, no one has been more closely associated with mysticism and expressionism than Itten. Accounts of Itten's attempts to establish a Mazdaznan regime at the Bauhaus often obscure his achievement as an abstract painter and his originality in organizing the preliminary course that all students had to take as their introduction to the school. His insistence on meditation exercises before working, his urging students to feel a certain movement before they drew it, his exploration of free abstract drawing, and his emphasis on experimenting with unusual materials affected not only the instruction at the Bauhaus but much of art education since that period. But Itten created a crisis at the Bauhaus when he insisted that students follow the dietary and meditative principles of Mazdaznanism. Schlemmer wrote that it wasn't the conversion of the student cafeteria to vegetarianism but Itten's favoritism toward students who followed Mazdaznan ideology that split the Bauhaus into "two camps."[10] This along with his reluctance to sell work produced at the school were the major issues that eventually led to Itten's resignation in the fall of 1922. When Kandinsky arrived in June, Schlemmer prophesied that the Russian would fill Itten's place.[11]

Kandinsky, despite his return to Russia in 1914[12] after a lengthy stay in Germany, was the best known of the painters Gropius invited to teach at the Bauhaus. His manifesto, *On the Spiritual in Art,* published in Munich in late December 1911, which described abstract painting as a stimulus to a new world order, had captured the attention of artists and critics throughout Europe (the book had reached a third edition by the fall of 1912). This, along with the exhibition group and yearbook—*The Blue Rider*—that he helped to establish, had ensured the fame of his large-scale, vividly colored oils. Taut had specifically urged others in his field to study the "spirited compositions of Kandinsky."[13] Given his recognition in Germany in connection with the new development of abstract expressionism[14] and his role in art education and museum reform in the Soviet Union, it is not surprising that Kandinsky was invited to teach at the Bauhaus when he left Moscow for Berlin at the end of 1921. The European blockade of Soviet ports had not prevented him from learning about the new art school in Weimar, and he wrote favorably about Gropius's attempt to have painters, sculptors, architects, and applied artists work together. In a 1920 report on "international art politics" for the Moscow Department of Visual Arts, Kandinsky praised the Weimar school for being less mechanical than the Soviet institutes dedicated to art education.[15] By the fall of 1922, Kandinsky was deeply involved in the activities of the school, directing the wall-painting workshop and teaching the theory of form and color, along with Klee, for the basic design course.

Kandinsky's belief in the power of art to change humanity, his antimaterialism, his exploration of evocative color and form, and his synthetic experiments with applied art and theater design were part of his appeal to Gropius. By the time he arrived, Gropius had become especially concerned about the divisions within the Bauhaus. He was continually defending the Bauhaus against attacks from numerous directions, including assertions that all Bauhaus students were communists, foreigners supported by state money, mystical expressionists, or wild bohemians. The denouncements of the De Stijl proselytizer Theo van Doesburg, who blamed the school for "mixing expressionist hysteria with a half-baked religious mystique, and elevating it to a dogma (Mazdaznanism)," were of particular concern, since van Doesburg was living in Weimar and attracting Bauhaus students to his classes focusing on geometry and technology in the arts.[16] In a circular from February 1922, Gropius warned Bauhaus faculty about "wild romanticism" and stressed that they should not cut themselves off from the outside world and cultivate isolation.[17]

Kandinsky had also changed by the time he started to teach at the Bauhaus. Although he continued to view expressionism as a path to abstraction, his choice of forms was radically different from his works done in Germany before the war. Instead of the amorphous shapes and painterly textures of his prewar oils and watercolors, he now concentrated on utilizing precisely drawn geometric forms—circles, trapezoids, and rectangles—drawn with the aid of a compass and ruler (Figure 3.1). Exposure in

Figure 3.1. Wassily Kandinsky, *Circles in a Circle,* 1923. Oil on canvas. The Louis and Walter Arensberg Collection of the Philadelphia Museum of Art. Reproduced with permission of the Artists Rights Society (ARS)/ADAGP, Paris.

the Soviet Union to the theories and works of Alexander Rodchenko and other constructivists, as well as to the works of Kazimir Malevich, Ivan Kliun, and El Lissitzky, contributed to his growing belief that geometric forms could become a universal language for abstraction. The fear that he had expressed in his 1911 manifesto—that geometric forms would be viewed as decorative and hence meaningless—was alleviated by the conviction of these Soviet artists that geometric abstraction, because of its break from the academic styles supported by the czar, could be a political and cosmological metaphor for the new world order. Lissitzky, who left for Berlin about the same time as Kandinsky, frequently used red and black squares, circles, and rectangles against a white background in his works. His 1922 book *A Suprematist Tale of Two Squares in Six Constructions,* published in Berlin, used this geometric language to relate the story of the new utopian epoch.[18] Kandinsky was much more disenchanted with the Soviet regime than was Lissitzky, and he used numerous colors in addition to the red and black favored by Lissitzky and other Soviet constructivists. The bright primary colors of yellow and blue so favored by the less political but still socially and cosmologically oriented Dutch De Stijl group also appear in Kandinsky's works of this period.

Kandinsky may have turned away from the vague shapes associated with expressionist cosmic visions, but he did not abandon his underlying belief in the power of color and line to evoke transcendent states. In the preliminary Bauhaus course, he continued his earlier synesthetic experiments, relating color, form, and composition to universal emotional equivalents. He continued to maintain, as he had before the war, that contrasting colors and the play of thin versus thick lines and/or shapes could create the illusion of movement and space in his canvases.[19] Because he felt these concepts could be examined in a scientific manner, Kandinsky circulated questionnaires asking students and faculty to list their perceptions of color and form correspondences.[20] In his classes on color, he assigned his students the task of arranging colors in connection with geometric shapes. Such assignments affected many of the students. The primary colors and geometric shapes of the cradle designed by Peter Keler bear testament to the impact of Kandinsky's theories as well as to those of van Doesburg.[21] Kandinsky also emphasized that the placement of groups of forms could have universal implications. He explained that compositions leading the eye upward could seem light and those directing the eye downward could seem heavy and oppressive. He even went so far as to equate the upper portion of the canvas with heaven and the lower part with earth.[22] Although he warned that these explanations were metaphoric, his choice of words grew out of his firm conviction that painting could be "a stimulus for all the other arts."[23]

Although Kandinsky's continued belief in the power of easel painting distinguished him from Soviet constructivists such as Rodchenko, his association with the Soviet Union, as well as his dignified demeanor and his calm certainty, brought his pronouncements on color and form correspondences wider acceptance than Itten's. At the Bauhaus he continued to search for methods to communicate his metaphysical and utopian goals. Before the war he had begun to experiment with creating the illusion of cosmic infinity on the flat plane of the canvas by deploying his amorphous forms of contrasting colors against a light background; his exposure to Soviet artists reinforced his use of color, line, and compositional direction as a means to communicate the struggle for a utopian world. Malevich, Mikhail Matiushin, and others emphasized that the illusion of space and motion on the canvas could be a sign for the fourth dimension, one of their metaphors for the new, elevated consciousness necessary for the struggle toward utopia.[24] While Kandinsky did not refer to the fourth dimension in the title of any of his works, he did explain that "the circle of all the primary forms points most clearly to the fourth dimension."[25] In his 1926 treatise, *Punkt und Linie zur Flache* (Point and Line to Plane), he wrote that he wanted the spectator to experience in his work "extending the dimension of time."[26] He maintained that in order to achieve this, the artist needed to dematerialize the picture plane by creating a sensation of indefinable space on the canvas. In *Circles in a Circle* of 1923 (Figure 3.1), he played off one dimension against another by contrasting the central, large, flat, black circle with smaller, slightly modeled circles, placed at varying points along the picture plane. The diagonal rays of beige and gray, larger at the bottom and smaller at the top, further convey the sensation of depth. When the school moved from Weimar to Dessau, Kandinsky did not abandon these experiments. In *Several Circles* of 1926, he used a dark rather than a light background to create a sense of indefinable space.[27] The colors and sizes of the several circles create a tension and movement as the small purple orbs appear to drift forward and float against the black background, suggesting a chart of star clusters similar to the one Kandinsky included in his 1926 treatise. He continued to advocate in his classes and essays for "a synthetic point of view" in order to provide "a living organic link between fields that seem to be widely separated." He explained that art education had to offer "a philosophical foundation of the meaning of human activity."[28]

THE IMPACT OF MOHOLY-NAGY

When Moholy-Nagy arrived at the Bauhaus in the spring of 1923, he was also committed to the use of abstract forms in his work to communicate his utopian views. But his belief in progress through the use of technology and the machine differentiated him from most of the painters on the faculty. Although he had exhibited at the Sturm Gallery and was convinced that the creation of new forms could assist with the development of an improved world order, the twenty-seven-year-old Hungarian émigré was thought to represent an important new direction, that of Russian constructivism. In a review of his work, Lissitzky had praised his use of "clear geometry," contrasting it to "octopus-like German abstraction," and had noted his absorption of Russian revolutionary ideas.[29] His coauthorship in 1922 of the *Book of New Artists*,[30] with its visual celebration of the machine, and his participation in the Dada-Constructivist Congress in Weimar in the fall of 1922, must have impressed Gropius. By that point the he had become convinced that creative work had to be connected with industrial design if the school and reform were to survive. While Moholy-Nagy may not have had the international reputation of van Doesburg, he was not considered as dogmatic nor as authoritarian.[31] He called for a "collective art" for the "new communist culture,"[32] but unlike many Soviet constructivists, Moholy-Nagy did not insist on the abandonment of easel painting, explaining that "all the channels of intuition" should be opened so that the "maximum number of people" could be affected.[33] Yet for a number of years after he arrived, Bauhaus painters felt resentful about Moholy's enthusiasm for technology and his closeness to Gropius. Feininger complained in 1925, writing about a Moholy-Nagy essay: "Nothing but optics, mechanics, taking the 'old' static painting out of service. . . . [H]e talks of movies, optics, mechanics, projections, and movement, and even of mechanically produced 'optical slides,' multi-colored. . . . Actually it is a question of mass production . . . but why attach the name of art to this mechanization of all visual things[?] . . . [T]hese would never bother me were they not considered by Gropi to be the most important at the Bauhaus. And for him and for a technical institute . . . Moholy is the only person of practical importance."[34]

At the time he was appointed, Moholy-Nagy had experience in working with sculpture, book design, and photograms, but he still was deeply involved in the medium of painting. A comparison of one of his oils, *A II*[35] (Figure 3.2), with Kandinsky's *Circles in a Circle* reveals numerous similarities beyond their choice of circular geometric forms. Their use of transparent planes and of a light background, against which the geometric forms appear to float, signifies a common interest in space, light, and movement. Moholy-Nagy, like Kandinsky, was quite aware of the popular notions of the fourth dimension as a metaphor for a new consciousness. He was also quite cognizant of the popularity of Einstein's theory of relativity and the concept of dynamic energy as a universal entity. As he wrote in a 1922 essay, "We must therefore replace the *static* principle of *classical art* with the *dynamic principle of universal life* . . . dynamic construction (vital construction and *force relations*) must be evolved in which the material is employed only as *the carrier of forces*."[36] He used transparent planes arranged at angles to the

Figure 3.2. László Moholy-Nagy, *A II,* 1924. Oil on canvas. Solomon R. Guggenheim Museum, New York. Copyright 2005 Artists Rights Society (ARS), New York / VG Bild-Kunst, Bonn.

picture plane to dynamically construct the effect of light passing through both matter and time, the effect of movement through space. For Moholy-Nagy, light was both cosmological and scientific. In a study of Moholy-Nagy's sources, Eleanor Hight discusses the impact of Malevich's and Kandinsky's metaphysical understanding of light and space, as well as Gropius and Taut's discussion of light emanating from crystalline shapes, as significant forces affecting the direction of Moholy-Nagy's work.[37] Other art historians such as Oliver Botar stress that Moholy-Nagy's interest in communicating a universal vital force stemmed from his immersion in the philosophical concepts of "biocentricism," one of the many isms in the early twentieth century that tried to find the organic oneness in all things. For Botar, Moholy-Nagy's attempt to synthesize science and cosmology grew out of his adherence to the pseudo-scientific principles of biocentricism.[38]

In addition, most art historians agree that the contact Moholy-Nagy had in Vienna and Berlin with the theories and works of the Russian constructivists, and the Berlin Dadaists would have forced him to confront the issue of identifying a form and a medium most suitable to the new industrialized age. Soviet constructivists and Berlin Dadaist artists compared themselves to engineers as they envisioned utilizing technology and the machine to find forms related to their message. The act of painting in oil on an individual canvas was condemned as elitist. Among the most radical artists in the Soviet Union, painting and sculpture were justified if they were viewed as laboratory experiments for productive goods, that is, for goods designed for mass production. In Germany, radical left artists such as John Heartfield and George Grosz, determined to find a technological medium and form that could make their works more accessible to the masses, used montages cut from commercial photographs in mass-produced newspapers and journals to make their vision more understandable.

Moholy-Nagy's photographic experiments were a logical outgrowth of his interest in merging art and technology. As he and his wife, Lucia Moholy, explained in their famous 1922 essay "Production—Reproduction," familiar methods such as photographs, usually associated with ideas of reproduction, could be used in an innovative manner called "productive creation"[39] to stimulate and improve human consciousness. In other words, the technical apparatus of photography could be utilized in an unfamiliar way to provoke a new way of seeing, and hence a new vision of utopia, as art was one means of invigorating the mind. The two experimented with the placement of objects on light-sensitive surfaces, a process they called photograms, to achieve works that reflected the new interrelationship of art and technology. Lucia Moholy later recalled: "The beginning of the idea dated back to the pre-Bauhaus period. . . . During a stroll in the Rhon Mountains in the summer of 1922 we discussed the problems arising from the antithesis Productions versus Reproduction. This gradually led us to implement our conclusions by making photograms."[40] Although not actually called photograms until 1925, these experiments involved the technological because of the specially treated

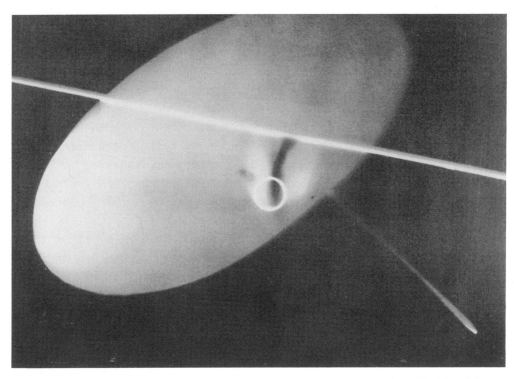

Figure 3.3. László Moholy-Nagy, *Cameraless Photo,* before 1925. Photogram. From László Moholy-Nagy, *Malerei, Fotographie, Film* (Munich: Albert Langen, 1927), 72. Copyright 2005 Artists Rights Society (ARS), New York / VG Bild-Kunst, Bonn.

surfaces. At the same time, they shared with the oils of the same period a use of transparent planes floating at angles in an ambiguous space (Figure 3.3). Graduations of light and dark instead of graduations of color created the nonstatic effect of dynamic movement. Moholy-Nagy later explained that the photographer could manipulate light the way the painter manipulated color, and he praised the constructivists for leading the way to "the highest level of reflected light composition."[41] Because he believed that color and light were "rooted in biological laws," he maintained that their effect in a visual work could transcend "climate, race, temperament, education."[42]

Until recently, critics and scholars did not recognize Lucia Schulz Moholy's contribution to her husband's experiments in photography.[43] Before they met in 1920, Moholy-Nagy had not experimented with or revealed an interest in the photographic medium. Lucia, on the other hand, had longed to be a photographer and had experience with the printing and publicity aspects of publishing. They had much in common, however. Both were from countries carved out of the old Austro-Hungarian Empire; she from the newly established Czechoslovakia, he from Hungary. Both had roots in

Judaism, although Moholy-Nagy, like many assimilated Hungarian Jews, converted to Protestantism in 1918. Both had been involved in activist politics with anarcho-communist leanings. During the revolutionary beginnings of the Weimar Republic, she had lived in Henrich Voegeler's Worpswede commune, with its emphasis on Kropotkinian anarchism and expressionist pacifism, and had helped care for wounded revolutionaries. He had sympathized with the revolutionary movement in Hungary and left after that revolution had failed in the fall of 1919. Moving first to Vienna and becoming involved with the Ma circle of activists, and then to Berlin, Moholy-Nagy became associated with the Dada artists of the Communist Malik-Verlag group. Married on 18 January 1921, both were attracted to innovative ideas about art and society that could bring about a better future. Their disdain for the conventional allowed them to be open to the new and the experimental. Neither appears, however, to have joined the Communist Party as did many of their colleagues. Their activism and openness were reserved for their belief in the power of art to affect the people.[44]

They separated in 1929, but many years later, Lucia Moholy explained that their "working arrangements . . . were unusually close." She pointed out that she was "responsible for the wording and editing of the texts that appeared in books, essays, articles, reviews and manifestos," but at the time they did not acknowledge this collaboration.[45] Moholy-Nagy's German was not solid, and he was not interested in developing his photographs. Moreover, women at the Bauhaus, particularly those married to faculty members, often subordinated their own interest to their husband's work and were not encouraged to study painting but rather were directed to focus on crafts.[46] Moholy-Nagy did acknowledge his wife's assistance in the preface to his 1929 book, *From Material to Architecture,* included her photographs in the famous Film and Foto exhibition of 1929 in Stuttgart, and used her portrait photo of Feininger's wife, Julia, in the second edition of his well-known treatise (Figure 3.4).[47] Nonetheless, she did not receive credit for her photographs of Gropius's new Dessau building (Figure 3.5) for the school and of student and faculty designs.[48]

The only other female photographer who appeared in *Painting, Photography, Film* was the Berlin Dada photomontagist, Hannah Höch, who was represented by two works, perhaps as a tribute to her impact on Moholy-Nagy's own experiments with that technique. Moholy-Nagy is thought to have begun to experiment with photomontage in 1923.[49] Although few of the original montages exist, photographs of the montages allow us to see how he absorbed the lessons not only of German montagists such as Höch but also of the Soviet constructivists. In most of the photomontages that he produced, he used figures cut out from photographs and from commercial magazines, arranged in strong diagonal lines against a white or light background so that the images appear weightless as they move within the irrational and disorienting space. In *Circus and Variety Poster* (Figure 3.6), which he included in both editions of his major treatise, he contrasted the montaged performers straddling thin, high wires placed against

a light background with two suited men standing on a dark and solid-looking platform. Parallel diagonal and curved lines in addition to transparent and solid vertical planes and a transparent circle recall Malevich's suprematism and Lissitzky's Prouns.

Gropius assigned Moholy-Nagy to lead the metal workshop, and when Itten finally left the Bauhaus in the fall of 1923, Moholy-Nagy was put in charge of the preliminary course, which Itten had taught. He continued Itten's practice of introducing the students to a variety of mediums and materials. But students, especially in the metal workshop, were encouraged to move away from using precious material such as silver and use instead glass and base metal, materials with industrial associations. Gropius's request that the students design prototypes for industrial production so they could be "in a position . . . to exert a decisive influence on existing craft (enterprises) and industrial works,"[50] began to be taken seriously, and samples of lamps and other electric light fixtures, many by Marianne Brandt, were among the metal workshop's achievements after Moholy-Nagy took over. By 1926, when the school had moved to Dessau, Gropius would write: "The Bauhaus workshops are essentially laboratories in which prototypes of products suitable for mass production and typical of our time are carefully developed and constantly improved. In these laboratories the Bauhaus wants to train a new kind of collaborator for industry and the crafts, who has an equal command of both technology and form. . . .The prototypes that have been completed in the Bauhaus workshops are being reproduced by outside firms with whom the workshops are closely related."[51]

Moholy-Nagy did not teach photography in the metal workshops, but by 1925, with the production of the Bauhaus book series, including the publication of his own book on photography, he became recognized for his ability to handle type and layout for books and posters. *Painting, Photography, Film* became a primer for the new photographic medium. In this treatise, Moholy-Nagy explained that technology helped to level class and economic differences by making more products available and obtainable due to their lower costs.[52] Because photography allowed the possibility of multiple works, it also helped solve the problem of an artwork as a statement of a personal, idiosyncratic vision, made by one individual for another individual, an approach he felt

Figure 3.5. Lucia Moholy, photograph of southwest corner of the workshop wing, 1927. Bauhaus-Archiv, Berlin. Copyright 2005 Artists Rights Society (ARS), New York / VG Bild-Kunst, Bonn.

Figure 3.6. László Moholy-Nagy, *Circus and Variety Poster,* before 1925. Photomontage. From Moholy-Nagy, *Malerei, Fotographie, Film,* 106. Copyright 2005 Artists Rights Society (ARS), New York / VG Bild-Kunst, Bonn.

dominated painting. Not only was photography less costly than painting, it more dynamically transformed the familiar to allow the viewer to experience a new way of looking at the world.[53]

The treatise was illustrated in part with examples of vernacular photography that were to serve as models for the new vision he was prophesying. Including photos that were conceived of not as "high art" but as reports or documents of the ordinary, material culture of the modern world, Moholy-Nagy suggested possibilities for camera photography that he and many others in the mid- to late twenties would employ.[54] Reproducing photos that used unusual angles and close-ups, he described the sharp, upward tilt of a newspaper illustration depicting repair work on an outdoor clock as conveying the "experience of the oblique view and displaced proportions." A detail of a record was called the "heightened reality of an every-day object."[55] By 1925, Moholy-Nagy had begun experimenting with the technical apparatus of the camera itself to formulate what he called "productive creation." The following year, he and Lucia Moholy established a darkroom for developing film in their new Dessau quarters. Utilizing overhead and other disorienting viewpoints in addition to the principles of asymmetry that he had employed in his oils and photograms and that Gropius had used in designing the new buildings for the Dessau Bauhaus, Moholy-Nagy transformed the subjects he photographed through the principles of "dynamic construction." In *Balconies* (Figure 3.7) for example, published in the second edition of *Painting, Photography, Film,* he utilized a dizzying, sharp, upward focus of the cantilevered overhangs of Gropius's new building to convey by shock and disorientation its radical structure. In this edition, Moholy-Nagy also included photos that reflected his experiments with printing both the negative and positive versions of the same image. His explanation—"organized effects of light and shade bring a new enrichment of our vision"—for one of his earlier photograms could be applied to his figurative photographs as well.[56] But unlike his explorations in oil and sculpture, his photomontages and his photographs were not limited to abstract

Figure 3.7. László Moholy-Nagy, *Balconies,* circa 1927. From Moholy-Nagy, *Malerie, Fotographie, Film,* 58. Copyright 2005 Artists Rights Society (ARS), New York / VG Bild-Kunst, Bonn.

shapes. He included in his treatise a number of portrait photographs, including one (Figure 3.4) by Lucia, which he described as moving beyond the traditional, subjective approach to one of greater concreteness. Lucia had made a number of documentary photographs of Bauhaus goods and buildings, as well as portraits of Bauhaus faculty and students, and he viewed her work as another example of the transformation of the familiar.

The treatise itself was an example of how text and photographs could be arranged to emphasize communication. Alternating bold and regular type and using circles, rectangles, and lines to set off one section from another, Moholy-Nagy worked to produce pages that were not static. By the 1927 edition, he included a section of his manuscript for a film, *Dynamic of the Metropolis,* in which he arranged both text and photographs, highlighted by a vibrant pattern of vertical and horizontal black lines as well as words and letters on the same page (Figure 3.8) to display his concept of "typophoto." Earlier in the book, he explained that typophoto could be "the visually most exact rendering of communication," but the vernacular illustrated newspapers and posters that had begun this process used typography in too linear a manner to endow their productions with an appeal to both the emotion and the intellect. He stressed that "contrasts of typographic material (letters, signs, positive and negative values of the plane)," along with an "all-embracing use of the techniques of photography, zincography, the electrotype, etc.," were necessary to produce "a correspondence with modern life."[57] Photography, he further emphasized, could be utilized as "typographical material" by creating a "'phototext' in place of words, as a precise form of representation."[58] Drawing upon his own efforts, those of other faculty such as Herbert Bayer, and those of Lissitzky in producing books, book covers, posters, and advertisements, Moholy-Nagy stressed that the future of public communication lay in this direction.

Moholy-Nagy understood that even criticism of the new medium of photography generated interest in it. Explaining that discussions about painting and photography were especially topical, as photo editor of the Dutch periodical *i 10,* he helped place a querulous article by Ernst Kállai, another Hungarian émigré who would soon become the editor of the Bauhaus journal.[59] Kállai, with the terminology of Russian constructivism, critiqued photography for its lack of *Factur*—its lack of texture and variety in its physical material surface. For this Hungarian, photography had neither tension nor motion and thus could not represent struggle.[60] Moholy-Nagy then had the opportunity to organize a number of responses that lamented Kállai's polarization of the question. In his own response, Moholy-Nagy explained that *Factur* in photography had more to do with the gradations of light and dark than with the qualities of surface or tactility. Once again, he repeated that painting, especially of the abstract variety, and light formations, in addition to photography and film, offered much to future artists.[61] In his search for the unity of all things, and echoing Gropius's plea for harmony, Moholy-Nagy was even able to get Kandinsky to write a response denigrating the either/or position of Kállai.

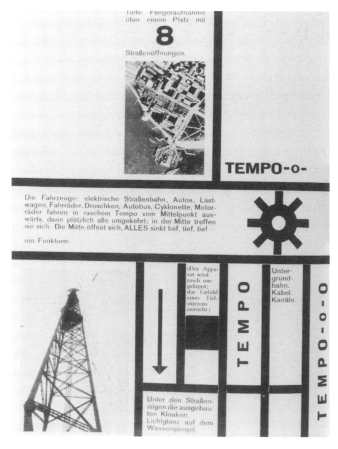

Figure 3.8. László Moholy-Nagy, typophoto from *Dynamic of the Metropolis,* 1927. From Moholy-Nagy, *Malerie, Fotographie, Film,* 126. Copyright 2005 Artists Rights Society (ARS), New York / VG Bild-Kunst, Bonn.

PHOTOGRAPHY UNDER MEYER AND MIES

Early in 1928, Gropius stepped down as director of the Bauhaus. With the appointment as his replacement of Hannes Meyer, whom Gropius had brought in to establish an architecture program, many of the faculty resigned. By this time, Moholy-Nagy was no longer seen as the enemy of the painters. When he and Lucia left for Berlin, Feininger lamented: "Now there will really be a gap that cannot be filled. . . . Moholy's friendly and strong voice. . . . He provided for the exchange and circulation of Bauhaus ideas and was the most amiable and helpful, most vital person."[62] Meyer maintained that the Bauhaus needed to become more practical, and he synthesized the curriculum. Although he hired Schlemmer as a full professor, allowed Kandinsky and Klee to teach free painting classes in addition to their basic design courses, and continued to support Gunta Stolzl (whom Gropius had elevated to a "junior master" in 1927)[63] and her direction of the weaving workshop, Meyer saw political implications in all artistic matters. Architecture was the main arena, with advertising and industrial design also important. Viewing photography as an integral part of productive work such as advertising, Meyer brought Walter Peterhans from Berlin to teach photography, and as a result instruction in photography became part of the curriculum. Students were continually urged to design model samples for industry, and to study political theory, sociology, and anthropology. Kandinsky and Klee were increasingly viewed as remnants of an older, more individualistically oriented school. Gropius's wife, Ise, had prophetically commented a year earlier: "The days of the painters at the Bauhaus appear to be truly over. They are estranged from the actual core of present activities and their influence is more restricting than inspiring."[64] By the spring of 1929, however, Schlemmer was describing Meyer as "a disappointment," and by fall, just after he left, he wrote: "The painters at the Bauhaus are not waging open battle against the opposition, which consists of architecture, advertising, 'relevant' pedagogy. . . . The students are supposed to do something on their own, fulfill a commission . . . ; even if the results are unsatisfactory, the sociological factor is considered an asset, something *new*."[65] Although the number of students increased and the income of the school rose from the product designs sold to industry, Meyer's and the students' increased political activity, particularly support for the Communists, led to his forced resignation two and a half years after he assumed the role of director.

When Mies van der Rohe took over as the next director in August 1930, the study of the theoretical aspects of architecture became even more dominant. Politics and sociology subsided, and workshops such as mural painting, metal, and furniture were combined into one called interior design, headed in 1932 by Mies's Berlin partner, Lily Reich. Of the original painters on the faculty, only Klee and Kandinsky were left, and Klee soon received a teaching position in Dusseldorf. Peterhans continued his photography instruction even when the school was forced to leave Dessau and move to Berlin in 1932. By that point, students were allowed after their first semester to specialize in photography. During their second and third semesters, photography could be signed up for under commercial art or under photography. The curriculum brochure described this course as offering "practical and theoretical fundamentals." The purpose of their fourth to seventh semesters was to move students "from purely technical experiment into independent work with reference to the requirements of advertising and reporting."[66] In his teaching, Peterhans continued to stress the technical aspects of photography, using rationalistic and scientific-sounding exercises as a means of professionalizing his field.[67] The emphasis was less on creative work and more on the productive usage of the photographic medium, an emphasis that continued to echo Gropius's concept of producing design for industry.

Many of the women, who continued to apply to the Bauhaus because of its reputation for experimentation and enthusiastic embrace of "modernity," gravitated to photography since it provided the possibility of creative work and a way to make a living through commercial portraiture and advertising. Although women did not make great inroads on the faculty and the leadership of the school, an increasing number of women such as Irene Bayer and Gertrud Arndt, both wives of faculty members, in addition to Ise Gropius, the wife of the first director, experimented with photography.[68] In its last years, the photography program itself attracted a number of women, among them the Hungarian Irena Blühová and the Berliner Grete Stern, who had studied privately with Peterhans. While taking photographic courses, Stern opened a studio in Berlin with the assistance of her longtime friend Ellen Auerbach. They used their childhood names of "ringl" and "pit" to indicate their joint efforts. Their use of photomontage in advertisements, particularly one that won a competition for the hair dye Komal, reveals an assimilation of Peterhans's love of fabrics and textures, as well as Moholy-Nagy's concept of "productive creation."[69]

Even after Moholy-Nagy left the Bauhaus, his promotion of the faculty and students helped to bring recognition to the school and to photography. Not only did he include Lucia Moholy's work in the famous Film and Foto exhibition of 1929 (which did more to publicize the medium of photography as a significant art form than any other exhibition of the period),[70] he also chose photographic examples from both the young men (Andreas and Lux Feininger, Otto Umbehr, known as Umbo) and women (Irene Bayer, Marianne Brandt, Florence Henri) who studied at the school. In addition, he included work by Peterhans and former faculty such as Herbert Bayer, and he devoted an entire section to documentary photos of student work in various mediums. Bauhauslers such as Marianne Brandt and Florence Henri who experimented with photography are more likely to have international recognition today than those, such as Kandinsky's students Eugene Batz and Fritz Tschaschnig, who focused on painting. Walter Benjamin's praise of photography as taking "the baton from painting" and for Moholy-Nagy's "new way of seeing" that he described in 1931 as unmasking the present in contrast to aesthetizing it,[71] also provided a wider arena of esteem for Moholy-Nagy and his direction.

By the time the Bauhaus was closed in 1933, painting no longer had the same influence on the school as it had enjoyed in its formative years. Photography had been utilized in a growing number of areas, for commercial and public use as well as for private experimentation, and had grown more influential in its own right. However, this is not to say that photography had not absorbed a number of concepts and ideas from certain painters. For example, the focus of Kandinsky and others on the communicative power of the visual arts, particularly when abstraction was involved, and on the concept of synthesis yielded results they might not have imagined at the time. Moholy-Nagy's experiments in different mediums, as well as his photographic variations, were a tribute to his acceptance of the concept of synthesis as a means of increasing the power of art to affect others. His concentration at first on the photogram with its abstract possibilities helped pave the way for the acceptance of photography as a creative rather than an imitative medium. By absorbing the compositional and spatial lessons of Russian painters such as Malevich and Kandinsky in his photomontages and photographs, in addition to assimilating vernacular approaches, he endowed the mechanical process of camera work with the potential for originality associated with painting. Following the constructivist concept of using personal work to guide practical output enabled Moholy-Nagy to move his work into the more public realm of typographic design, books covers, posters, and advertising, a direction encouraged by all the directors from Gropius to Mies. The publication of the eighth Bauhaus book, *Painting, Photography, Film,* with its proselytizing synthesis of the technological and the creative and its subsequent circulation throughout Europe and the United States, contributed to elevating the photographic image into a signifier of the material present as well as of a better future, thereby ensuring its continuation as one of the dominant mediums of the past century and, perhaps even, of the twenty-first.

ARCHITECTURE, BUILDING, AND THE BAUHAUS

4

Wallis Miller

Ever since Walter Gropius announced that the goal of the Bauhaus was to construct "the new building of the future," the school has loomed large in any discussion of modern architecture.[1] Not only did Gropius, along with his successors Hannes Meyer and Ludwig Mies van der Rohe, manage to gather together well-known architects along with those who showed great promise, but Gropius in particular also generated a huge amount of publicity to assure the Bauhaus a place in the history of architecture. The International Architecture Exhibition of 1923, the various Bauhaus books on architecture that followed it, Gropius's Bauhaus building, and the exhibitions, lectures, and publications he and others produced long after the school had closed continue to convince a majority of the public that if a work of architecture is modern it is "Bauhaus Architecture."

Various ideological statements made at the Bauhaus about architecture continue to serve as guides to understanding modern architecture more generally. The ambition to construct "the new building of the future," definitive for the school, crystallized the contemporary view that architecture was the catalyst for making art relevant to modern life. Meyer's essay "Building," published in the *Bauhaus Journal* during his first year as director of the school, portrays an even more radical version of the relationship between art and life. In it an emphasis on responding to physical demands eradicates the need for artistic principles in the design of a building. Mies did not publish a seminal text while he was director of the Bauhaus. Nonetheless, his designs for a series of courtyard houses, developed alone and with his students, are clear examples of his investigation of the relationships between structure and enclosure, interior and exterior, and the rational and the irrational definitive of modern architecture.

Gropius established the Bauhaus just as the principles of a modern architecture were being spelled out. Frustrated with the emphasis on perfecting form and the focus on drawing that came with the professionalization of architects, which began in the Renaissance but reached its height in the nineteenth century, architects had begun by the end of that century to look for ways to make their work more responsive to life around them. Along with artists of the time, those architects who wanted to create a modern architecture tested ways to escape rigid attention to a prescribed set

63

of standards and forms. They rewrote their own standards, relying initially on areas outside of architecture—functional preferences and construction technologies—to direct the development of their designs. Their attention shifted from the drawing, central up until then, to the building. Architects certainly continued to make drawings to represent their ideas, but architecture now manifested itself fully in the building, not in a geometrically perfect plan.

Despite its strong connection to the modern movement, the role of architecture at the Bauhaus was surprisingly ill defined. Architecture struggled for a position within a school whose reputation was based on its workshop program, especially while Gropius was the director. It had to find a place among the other fields of design, which were to be its collaborators in creating a building. Because of the scope of an architectural project and its consequent reliance on representation as a tool for developing a design, the various architecture curricula resisted the emphasis on realization that guided workshop training in the other areas of design. Instead, architecture at the Bauhaus emerged out of a combination of theory and practice that changed with each new director.

WEIMAR: WORKSHOPS OR LABORATORIES?

PEDAGOGY

Architecture made its most prominent appearance early in the history of the school. Gropius's well-known call to craftsmen and artists in his first manifesto of 1919 to conceive of their work in anticipation of its placement in a building—"Together let us conceive and create the new building of the future, which will embrace architecture and sculpture and painting in one unity"—was supported by a curriculum based in the workshop.[2] It is important to note that it was not only sculpture and painting but also architecture that found its realization in building. In his short statement, then, Gropius made an essential distinction: for architecture to be sublimated in building, he first had to regard the two as different practices.

The distinction implicit in Gropius's early statement may shed some light on the development of the architecture curriculum during his tenure as director and even afterward, when the Bauhaus became a more conventional school of architecture and design under the direction of first Meyer and then Mies van der Rohe. It is a well-known fact that there was no official architecture program during most of Gropius's tenure. Only during his last year, 1927, did Gropius establish an "architecture department" and appointed the Swiss architect Hannes Meyer as its director. More telling, however, is that there was never a workshop for architecture, as there was for all the other advanced courses in design. In the pedagogical context defined by Gropius, which linked a student's independent work to the workshop, this meant that there was no opportunity for students to develop their own designs in architecture because there was no workshop in which to realize them.

One might have expected Gropius to identify the building projects associated with the Bauhaus as the "architecture workshop." But while the projects satisfied the requirement of realizing an architectural design, they did not address an essential aspect of the workshop pedagogy because they failed to nurture students' independent work. Collaboration produced "buildings," according to Gropius, which precluded any focus on the creative contributions of individuals. (Furthermore, in these cases, students were not the architects.) Gropius's views also prevented him from accepting architecture as an exceptional case in the curriculum, in which representation, not realization, was the medium for design development. As a result, Gropius found himself with little room to maneuver as he tried to integrate architecture into the program of study. At first, he tried to maintain the distinction between architecture and building by treating architecture as a theoretical pursuit separate from realization or practice, which was the domain of building. But in this scheme, he still could not provide students with the opportunity to work on their own designs. In his later amendments to the curriculum, he proposed a segment on architectural research. Had it been possible to implement it, this curriculum would have allowed students to pursue theoretical work in architecture—their own design work—as a kind of practice and thus maintained the separation of architecture and building. Recognized as two forms of realizing a design, both architecture and building would then have fit neatly into the Bauhaus course of study. As the curriculum evolved under the direction of Meyer and Mies, so did the relationship between architecture and building, transcending the confrontation that characterized it in the early years of the school.

Gropius's ambivalent attitude toward architecture manifested itself from the moment he established the school, when, from among his colleagues at the Arbeitsrat für Kunst, he invited only the painters Lyonel Feininger and Gerhard Marcks, clearly excluding such architects as Bruno and Max Taut and Erich Mendelsohn.[3] Instead, he turned to Dr.-Ing. Paul Klopfer, the director of the neighboring Institute for the Building Trades (Baugewerkschule), and asked him to let the gifted Bauhaus students attend courses in construction and engineering there. Klopfer, in turn, accepted Gropius's invitation to deliver a series of lectures at the Bauhaus called "Principles of Architecture." The lectures, in which Klopfer intended "to show what was culturally, aesthetically, and technically valuable using illustrations of old and new buildings," must have been well received. His first series lasted almost a year (at least from May 1919 to March 1920), and he was invited back to deliver the lectures a second time during 1921–22.[4]

It was only at this point that Gropius began to lecture at the Bauhaus; his first series was titled "Space and Practical Drawing." As Klaus-Jürgen Winkler points out in *Architecture at the Weimar Bauhaus,* the lectures had "a philosophical and architecture-theoretical character and reflected the general principles of the Bauhaus program of 1919": that "buildings symbolized a spiritual perspective on the world."[5] The lectures eventually became seminars, for which Gropius's partner Adolf Meyer was the assistant. Here, students learned about "the laws of mathematical proportion," which, according to Gropius's announcement, were "an organic means of expressing our spiritual perspective and, in the future, would become a counterpoint in the fine arts."[6]

A report from the years 1921–22 by the Institute for the Building Trades openly acknowledged both the shared pedagogical spirit and the difference in formal approaches of the two schools. At the Bauhaus, "the new was sought out with great ambition while the Institute for the Building Trades emphasized the firmly entrenched."[7] Klopfer's own attitude toward architecture was equally complex: while "[h]e was open to attempts to renew architecture and art and sought the creation of an aesthetically complex environment," thus supporting the Bauhaus's goals and structure, he did not hesitate to criticize in matters of content because his theory of architecture was directly opposed to Gropius's. In contrast to Gropius's promotion of *Zeitgeist*-inspired form, especially in his lectures, Klopfer's theory was based on classical aesthetics and a universal concept of culture.[8]

Although there is no published evidence of the work of the institute students at the Bauhaus, who were sent there "to develop their artistic abilities," it certainly reflected the distinction between the two schools. In the course in building construction, taught by architect Ernst Schumann, students had to design every detail of a small single-family house. In a parallel class in shop drawings, they had to do the same for a piece of furniture. While the traditional appearance of the work they produced bore no trace of the forms produced in the Bauhaus workshops, Gropius was pleased with Schumann because he had a broad knowledge of building and apparently introduced the students to new construction methods and materials. Gropius probably supported the basis of the course as well, which presented architecture as a "constructive whole worked out in detail."[9] Clearly, Gropius was not ideologically threatened by Schumann's course, since he could appreciate the value of the information it communicated and totally ignore the formal consequences.

In general, then, the architecture courses served as sources for theories, information, and skills but neither provided students with opportunities to develop their own designs nor prepared them to use the information gained in class to develop their designs elsewhere. This approach to architecture was consistent with other theoretical courses taught at the Bauhaus. For most students, architecture as well as painting and sculpture were sources for essential principles that were meant to guide the design of objects in the workshops. The proposal for an official Bauhaus architecture program made at the same time also took this theoretical approach, and, as a result, the state certification board accepted it only as an introduction to the field. The first proposal—drafted by Klopfer and, in turn, presented to Gropius in the summer of 1919—included lectures in construction, drawing, building typologies, building codes, and structures. While this was never implemented, the state government approved a second proposal, which consisted of classes in construction, mathematics, and physics and existed for a year.[10] If the architecture course had followed through on the pedagogical model for other fields of design at the Bauhaus, there would have been an advanced component of architectural training in the workshop or on the project site itself. Students would have developed their own design ideas onsite, in the context of realizable projects.

Instead of offering students an architecture workshop, Gropius offered them building: experience on an experimental building site and apprenticeships in his office. In 1922, Gropius and the masters supported the creation of an experimental building site so that the Bauhaus would be the first school to realize the collaboration of art, industry, and trade through education promoted by the Werkbund ten years earlier.[11] There was no mention of it, however, as a place for architecture students to learn how to realize their designs. In the end, the site was never established, mostly because its director, Emil Lange, had too many responsibilities. (He was also working for Gropius's office and for the Bauhaus housing society on a project associated with the school, as well as acting as the school's union representative.)[12]

Despite the failure of the official plans for such a site, the Sommerfeld House, a project Gropius's office completed in 1922 (the same year the masters approved the creation of the experimental site) could be considered as such. The house itself was designed by Gropius and Adolf Meyer and the interior by Gropius's associate Carl Fieger. Students and masters collaborated on other aspects of the environment. Marcel Breuer designed several pieces of furniture, and Joost Schmidt designed the fine woodwork on the stairs, doors, and the exterior. The metal workshop produced the radiator grilles and the light fixtures, the weaving workshop made several carpets, and apprentices from the wall-painting workshop accompanied their master, Hinnerk Scheper, in painting the interior of the house.[13] Like the experimental building site and the Haus am Horn, built a year later for the Bauhaus's first major exhibition, the Sommerfeld House was a showcase for the ultimate goal of the school—a collaboration issuing in a building—rather than a training ground for beginning architects.[14]

Apprenticeships in Gropius's office introduced students to the work of the architect but, again, did not give them the chance to exercise creativity. Almost immediately after the Bauhaus had started admitting students, Gropius began making space for them in his office. The list of students he invited was small, reflecting Gropius's concern for maintaining high quality and his belief that only the best students should become architects.[15] It was clear that the apprenticeship was not simply an opportunity for Gropius to acquire employees—he hired students at all levels of experience—but another occasion for skill development. The students learned how to respond to the externally defined demands of construction, program, and the designs of other objects that, according to Gropius's manifesto, transformed architecture into building.

Despite the Bauhaus's progressive goal—to relocate the creative process from the isolated art studio to the context in which a practical object ultimately would be placed—the structure of architectural education at the school under Gropius's direction followed a traditional model. Students would learn theory in the academy and practice realizing a design in an apprenticeship; development of their creativity would occur when they had a commission of their own. At the same time, between 1918 and 1925, leading members of the architectural profession in Germany were discussing how to improve this traditional model; they identified the integration of theory and practice as the core of their programs for educational reform. They were not only concerned with complementing theoretical education with opportunities to build, however, but also required the implementation of an architecture program centered on studio-based learning. The studio, which would foster the development of an individual student's ability to convene formal principles, programmatic demands, and the limits and possibilities of construction, would be a crucial link between theory and practice.

Up until this point, there had been no studio education in architecture schools in Germany. Their pedagogical structure, like that of the Bauhaus, was based on lectures and apprenticeships. Architects such as Otto Bartning, Hans Poelzig, Walter Curt Behrendt, and Hermann Muthesius recognized that architecture could not remain confined to the lecture halls. They sought a stronger connection to practice in the academy itself, as did Gropius at the Bauhaus. As Behrendt suggested in 1923 in his article "The Education of Architects," students were trapped in lecture halls and drawing rooms, far away from the building site and the workshop. "The science of building was taught," he wrote, "rather than building itself." As a solution, they introduced a design studio and the use of representation, not a workshop, into the academy, breaking with Gropius and his strict commitment to the final object.[16]

Early on in this phase of reform, a proposal by Bartning breached the gap between theory and practice in other ways that were definitive for the academy. Bartning was an active member of the Arbeitsrat für Kunst and the radical faction of the Werkbund. In 1918, he outlined a new social structure for architecture schools that guaranteed equality among all members of the educational community. Included here was the substitution of the names *apprentice, journeyman,* and *master* for *student* and *professor* to suggest that education was a continuous process and not a confrontation between those who already knew the material and those who needed to learn it.[17] These new roles removed the academy from its isolation by recasting it as the source of practice. Bartning emphasized that art could not be taught but had to be "released and directed . . . through contact with a creative personality. . . . [O]nly 'knowledge,' techniques, and handicraft skills are really transmittable."[18] Bartning's vision of social equality and his support for a student's abilities (and, thus, freedom to develop an architectural language) made the independence of the students essential to his new pedagogy.

Gropius shared these particular goals and clearly promoted them during the first years of study at the Bauhaus: individual creative development defined the introductory course and the workshops, and the social structure of the entire school had the equality—or near equality—suggested by Bartning's scheme.[19] The study of architecture, however, remained an occasion for students to imitate the work of others rather than emulate the process of design and realization on their own.

The students often complained that Gropius refused to teach architecture; obviously his lecture course was not sufficient for students used to working on their own design projects in the preliminary courses and the workshops. According to George Adams, a student at the Bauhaus from 1921 to 1923,

> [Gropius] never taught at the Bauhaus and that was one of the complaints we leveled at him directly saying "Well, here you are, Director of the Bauhaus, architect, and you want integration of all the arts towards a new architecture and you don't teach architecture." To this he replied, I think very fairly, that first of all we students have got to learn a craft properly. "I think that a man has to have first four years of training before he is able to go into conceiving architecture."[20]

In retrospect, Gropius blamed the delay in establishing an architecture program on external circumstances. "[B]ecause of inflation," he said, "there was simply no money to build up a decent architectural department." When he arrived at Dessau, Gropius said that there was a bit more money, "and I got Hannes Meyer from Switzerland, who had done some very good design work for the United Nations and others which I liked, and so he started to build up this architectural department."[21] The fact that Gropius was willing to engage the students on the topic suggests that he too felt that his lectures and his offer of an office apprenticeship fell short of an adequate architecture program, one in which students could, as he put it, "go into conceiving architecture."

OUTSIDE THE CURRICULUM

Students did not abandon the issue easily. They found their own professors and started to design architectural projects as early as 1922. As a group, the wall-painting students seemed to understand the connection between their workshop lessons—wall painting as painting in an environment—and architecture the best. Several students in the wall-painting workshop produced architectural designs either at the Bauhaus or later in their careers. As students, Peter Keler concentrated on housing, including a mobile house, and Herbert Bayer designed several advertising kiosks and exhibition pavilions.[22] Both Bayer and Alfred Arndt, who worked on murals for Gropius's Auerbach House in Jena and for the 1923 exhibition, and on wall colors for the Haus am Horn, had apprenticed as architects before they studied at the Bauhaus and worked as architects after they had left. Arndt returned to the Bauhaus under Meyer and Mies to become director of the Interior Design Department, which had become a collection of the wall-painting, metal, and furniture workshops. In their architectural pursuits, students apparently followed the example of other painters at the Bauhaus: Oskar Schlemmer, one of their masters in Weimar, and Georg Muche, master of the weaving workshop until 1927. Schlemmer, highly praised for his transformation of the hall and staircase of the Bauhaus building for the 1923 exhibition, was also master of the Theater Workshop, which he presented as an investigation of bodies in space. Muche was the designer not only of the 1923 exhibition house but of several housing types, including a series of steel house types, in which the color of the material determined their configuration.

Although students pursued their architectural interests outside of the official curriculum, they did not completely turn away from Gropius. Their designs—at least the ones that have been published by Gropius and by Bauhaus scholars—were for housing projects, produced in the same spirit as some of Gropius's own work at the time. While Gropius had a variety of commissions when his office was in Weimar—for villas, a monument, an academy, a theater, office buildings, and housing—his development of an unbuilt flexible housing type exerted the most influence on student work. From 1920 to 1921, Gropius had developed a design for a Bauhaus *Siedlung,* a campus for the school that would include classrooms, housing, and buildings for other communal functions. He had invited students and masters to submit designs for the project but eventually put himself in charge of the design and made Fred Forbat, a young Hungarian architect who had been in the office for about a year, chief planner. While the project failed in the face of strong local opposition, and the site plan subsequently vanished, the building types developed by Forbat survived and immediately motivated the architecture work of both students and masters. Forbat had developed a series of houses—single-family, apartments, and studio-apartment combinations—that reflected Gropius's preoccupation with standardized parts and variable building forms, what he termed *Wabenbau,* or honeycomb construction.[23] Here, the notion of type in building, which linked a cultural interpretation of function to a specific form, shifted from the building in its entirety to the volumetric elements out of which it was composed. Along with Forbat, Gropius developed this strategy throughout 1922 and 1923 in a scheme he called *Baukasten im Grossen* (Large-Scale Building Blocks): a series of volumetric elements he combined into housing for varying numbers of occupants and various social situations (Figure 4.1). These were based on an earlier proposal for standardized housing for the AEG.[24]

While Gropius's explanation focused on the combinatorial source of the houses' form, the drawings and models (eventually shown in the Bauhaus exhibition of 1923) demonstrate clearly his affinity for the massing and articulation of surfaces and architectural elements identified with modern architecture. Despite their origin as agglomerations of various parts, the overall form of the houses was evidently based on the cube, a pure geometrical form that was a favorite of modernists. The smooth surfaces and corresponding lack of detail in the articulation of windows, doors, and roofs likewise bore witness to Gropius's attempt to make the buildings look modern.

Relying on Gropius's office for advice, the few students who had begun to design

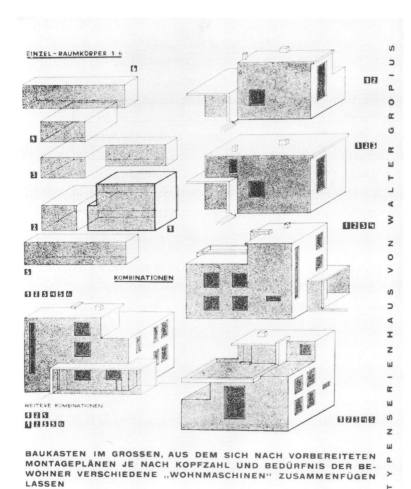

EINZEL-RAUMKÖRPER 1 h

KOMBINATIONEN

WEITERE KOMBINATIONEN

BAUKASTEN IM GROSSEN, AUS DEM SICH NACH VORBEREITETEN MONTAGEPLÄNEN JE NACH KOPFZAHL UND BEDÜRFNIS DER BEWOHNER VERSCHIEDENE „WOHNMASCHINEN" ZUSAMMENFÜGEN LASSEN

TYPENSERIENHAUS VON WALTER GROPIUS

Figure 4.1. Walter Gropius and Fred Forbat, *Large-Scale Building Blocks,* 1921–23. From Alfred Meyer, ed., *Ein Versuchshaus des Bauhauses* (Munich: Albert Langen, 1924), 8.

on their own worked with Adolf Meyer, Gropius's partner, and Ernst Neufert, an architect in the office, to design housing similar to Gropius's "building blocks." The best-known example is Farkas Molnár's single-family house, which he called *The Red Cube,* designed in 1922–23.[25] The student projects were never presented as an investigation of additive schemes. Nonetheless, they shared one important characteristic with Gropius's and Forbat's work: all were identified as "typical" and, due to the articulation of their massing or the systematic disposition of their structure, looked as if they could easily be mass-produced.

These early designs were a part of the 1923 International Architecture exhibit held in conjunction with the major exhibition celebrating the Bauhaus's fourth anniversary. The exhibition displayed examples of modern architecture by thirty architects from Germany, the United States, France, Holland, Denmark, Czechoslovakia, and Hungary, including Frank Lloyd Wright, Le Corbusier, Ludwig Mies van der Rohe, Erich Mendelsohn, Bruno Taut, Mart Stam, Willem Marinus Dudok, Gerrit Rietveld, J. J. P. Oud, and Theo van Doesburg. To collect the work, Gropius told well-known architects that he wanted to create an exhibition "with the sharpest international architecture that reflected a certain specific perspective." He wanted to show "the dynamically functional side of the development of modern architecture."[26] The exhibition, which Gropius presented under the slogan Art and Technology: A New Unity, was the first occasion for the Bauhaus to connect itself to the international movement in architecture and was one of the earliest exhibitions of modernism in Europe. One critic called the International Architecture exhibit "the actual heart" of the entire exhibition, which included displays of work by students and masters from every department as well as the experimental Haus am Horn.[27]

The Bauhaus was well represented by the work of architects affiliated with the school. Fifteen projects came from Gropius and Adolf Meyer; there was also work from Master Georg Muche, from Gropius office employees Fred Forbat and Carl Fieger, who also taught at the school, and from students Farkas Molnár, Marcel Breuer, Erich

Figure 4.2. Exhibition of International Architecture, Bauhaus, Weimar, 1923. Farkas Molnár's *The Red Cube* (1922–23) is on the left. From Bauhaus–Universität, Weimar, Bauhaus–Album "Ausstellung 1923" XXX/10.

Dieckmann, and Herbert Bayer. The alcove dedicated to the Bauhaus was filled with designs for housing types rather than for specific buildings (Figure 4.2). Visitors directly confronted models of Gropius's modern-looking *Large-Scale Building Blocks,* but also saw a perspective of the Bauhaus *Siedlung* with the early house types designed by Forbat (and drawn by Molnár). The rest of the student work flanked the sides of the alcove and included drawings as well as models of Molnár's *Red Cube* and Forbat's standardized single-family house. The commissioned work that Gropius had produced in his office was exhibited separately, and thus marked as distinct from the housing research. The configuration, which he presumably approved if not designed, allowed him to link his housing research to the independently produced student designs, suggesting the kind of intellectual exchange that he had envisioned but was never able to implement.

Many of these housing projects also appeared in the third Bauhaus book, *The Bauhaus's Experimental House* (1924), which documented the other example of architecture in the exhibition: the Haus am Horn (Figure 4.3).[28] Like Gropius's *Large-Scale Building Blocks,* and most of the other housing projects on display, the Haus am Horn had smooth white surfaces and a simple articulation of architectural elements, and relied on pure geometries (cubes, rectangles, and squares). But the symmetry of three of the four facades and the centrality of the largely symmetrical plan distinguished its composition from Gropius's housing types that were always asymmetrical. Some architects and critics viewed asymmetry as dynamic and clearly responsive to the functional requirements of the occupants. Symmetry, by contrast, was seen as the result of following formal conventions. Members of the Bauhaus community, however, did not seem to worry about the symmetry of their exhibition house, having faith in it as a modern response to function and methods of construction.

When the Council of Masters started planning the exhibition, they proposed that the building of a model house using the *Wabenbau* system should be the focus of the event.[29] Certainly a building that could demonstrate the collaboration of all the artists working at the Bauhaus had to be the centerpiece of the exhibition. But the decision to base its design on the housing strategy common to the work of Gropius, the architects at his office, and the students also marked a turning point for architecture at the Bauhaus: it showed that the masters recognized that architecture existed at the school. Furthermore, it consolidated the Bauhaus's unofficial architectural work—Gropius's research and students' designs—by effectively presenting it in one culminating effort. Ultimately, the house was designed not by Gropius but by Muche; nonetheless, Gropius accepted it as an example of the application of Bauhaus research to practice. According to him, the Haus am Horn, named after its location, was "to make a useful contribution to the general problem of housing and . . . act as a measure for most evaluations."[30]

Some critics regarded the Haus am Horn as the best part of the exhibition because of the way in which it fulfilled its role as a building; for them, it provided strong evidence of successful collaboration.[31] In his review for *Das Kunstblatt,* Walter Passarge criticized the exhibition for being overambitious in its claims to present "a radical break from the past," because, at that time, a new period had only just begun. "On the other hand," he wrote, "no one will be able to avoid seeing with what earnestness and determination the basic problem of the integration of craft, art, and technology has been tackled."[32] This integration was represented largely by student work. But while students provided the fixtures and finishes for the house, in the context of the workshops in wall painting, cabinetry, metal, weaving, and ceramics, they only participated in the design of its architecture indirectly: by overseeing the construction phase and creating its precedents and successors in their own projects.[33]

Although critics praised the Haus am Horn as a building, they criticized it as a work of architecture, complaining about its form. While many of the critics were simply pressed to recognize and accept something new, there were some who disagreed with the house's formal interpretation of mass production.[34] Others complained that the house was not even built using the mass-production methods that its form allegedly expressed. Adolf Meyer, project manager for the house, tried to ameliorate the situation by describing the house as an attempt to "[transcend] the present economic restrictions." This did not dissuade Passarge from pointing out that the Haus am Horn "does not yet represent a final solution, and as an experimental house using some quite expensive materials, it is not a model for a simple settlement house."[35] The other housing types that Gropius gathered together as examples of Bauhaus design work and that were clear influences on Muche's Haus am Horn also showed signs of having the same problem. They were either physically or financially impossible to build en masse, although their forms were inspired by the repetition that should have kept costs low.

Gropius's preoccupation with the influence of mass-production methods on form led members of the Bauhaus community to reject his scheme for the Haus am Horn and build the one by Muche. They believed that Muche's house represented a new lifestyle, whereas Gropius's design demonstrated a rationality that had little relationship to the way people lived.[36] In the Bauhaus book on the Haus am Horn, Muche and Gropius confirmed their polarization. On the one hand, Muche's essay explained the connection between individual living spaces and the activity that should go on in them but did not discuss the construction of the house at all.[37] On the other hand, Gropius's "Dwelling Industry," the first essay in the book, was dedicated to justifying standardization of form—specifically, of "spatial cells"—and to quelling the common fear that a standardized house would create standardized people.[38] For Gropius, standardization allowed the opposite: more flexibility in the planning of the house. Mass production provided Gropius with the material basis for a formal approach based on standardization. Under the photograph of his "large-scale buildings blocks" in the book *International Architecture,* Gropius wrote: "Models of Mass-Produced Houses. Variability of the same plan-type through the addition of repetitive spatial units in different ways. Basic principles: integration of the greatest degree of repetition with the greatest possible variability."[39]

As Winkler points out, however, no one at this time advocated the use of prefabricated parts or their assembly off-site. Gropius's real goal, he says, was to demonstrate that architects were confronting mass production by finding an appropriate expression for it rather than engaging it in practical terms.[40] Mass production seemed to be a cultural phenomenon for Gropius and not a construction process.

Aside from revealing his formalist motives, Gropius's integration of mass production and architectural design may have been his attempt to reconcile the conflict between his workshop-based curriculum and the study of architecture. Mass production and, specifically, the prefabrication process offered him and the others an alternate view of construction as something that could be determined before anyone approached the site. In this sense, architecture could be constructed before it was actually built (in Gropius's terms), and drawings were no longer provisional representations but the first view of a realized design. With this approach, Gropius could integrate architecture into the Bauhaus curriculum—to which realization was essential—and yet distinguish it as an individual endeavor from the collaborative effort of "building," which would necessarily transform the architecture once it was placed on a site.

If architecture were conceived of as prefabrication, however, students would produce drawings and models rather than concrete objects. This definition of architecture is at odds with a workshop setting. Instead, the laboratory would be the appropriate model. The laboratory accommodated the approach to architecture as a series of types, an approach already taken by various Bauhaus students and faculty. Types could only be articulated as drawings or models before they were transformed into buildings by the vicissitudes of external demands—represented by the other collaborators—that imposed themselves once the designs took their place on a specific building site. In this laboratory for housing types, design became research into a standardized world, and drawings and models became themselves sites of experimentation.

In fact, such a lab was central to Gropius's architecture curriculum, published on the occasion of the 1923 Bauhaus exhibition. Gropius used the curriculum along with the International Architecture exhibition to consolidate the unofficial architectural work done by members of the Bauhaus community. He presented it as "Theory and Organization of the Bauhaus" and illustrated it with the famous circular diagram that has "building" at its center.[41] In the diagram, however, "building" had two functions: it characterized the culmination of the preliminary and workshop courses, and it was a subject heading that subsumed "building site," "experimental site," "design," and "construction and structural knowledge." The diagram expressed Gropius's tenet that building had become an independent field of study that included design and was not just the result of the collaborative efforts of all artists. In the text, by contrast, he promised the best students "Instruction in Architecture"—not even "building." The course description bore some relationship to the diagram in that it did require "practical participation in buildings under construction," presumably by working in Gropius's office, but it also included "independent architectural training" in the "Bauhaus Research Department."[42] This, Gropius hoped, would be "a center for experimentation where it will try to assemble the achievements of economic, technical and formal research and to apply them to problems of domestic architecture in an effort to combine the greatest possible standardization with the greatest possible variation of form."[43] The architecture workshop was to become a housing lab, where students could realize their designs in a parallel world in which design was research, and construction—prefabrication—could occur on paper.

This proposal, which was Gropius's official acknowledgment of the existence of architecture at the Bauhaus and its integration into the pedagogical structure of the school, came just as the first group of Bauhaus students had finished their workshop training and were ready to apply to such a program.[44] But Gropius never implemented the curriculum that would have allowed him to reconcile of the study of architecture with his emphasis on building. In a footnote to the English translation of the curriculum that appeared in the catalog for the 1937 exhibition of "his Bauhaus" at the Museum of Modern Art, he explained that "The Research Department for experimental work was only partially realized, due to lack of space and funds."[45] The part that eventually came to exist emerged only in 1927, when Hannes Meyer arrived at the school; the Bauhaus building commissions, which would have examined the transformation of this research, never materialized.

The creation of the laboratory, however, did not depend only on Gropius. After 1923, it came to life in principle, if not in fact, in the continuing production of designs for housing types by students and faculty alike. These types emphasized the distinction between the architecture lab and the building site by working outside of the constraints of practice. Molnár's 1923 *Row House with High Living Space* was a three-story row house type that had the same dimensions as the Haus am Horn.[46] The entire building was essentially an extrusion of the form of a single unit and was to be built out of a new type of concrete block. Later that year, Molnár reworked his idea using reinforced concrete. As in the first scheme, the units were cantilevered, which would have posed enormous problems had the project been constructed. One could have viewed the project as impractical, but Gropius's placement of the project in his 1925 Bauhaus Book documenting the 1923 International Architecture exhibit offered another interpretation. He placed Molnár's project on the page following his *Large-Scale Building Blocks* and opposite Le Corbusier's *City for Three Million Residents*.[47] By this association, Gropius pronounced Molnár's design as visionary, legitimizing it by removing it from existing conditions of production and from expectations that it could not have fulfilled, at least at that time.

If Molnár's project suggested that the laboratory was a parallel world (or a fantasy), Breuer's 1924 design for an apartment house established a firmer connection between it and reality by showing that it had become a site of invention (Figure 4.4). At least in hindsight, the project, which was similar to one Muche produced in the same year, challenged rather than avoided reality.[48] Its regular structural form—presumably out of concrete—determined its image, and the design was often published as an example of recent Bauhaus work.[49] In an article titled "About the Practical Output of the Bauhaus," Siegfried Giedion refers to Breuer's design as *the* example of Bauhaus architecture:

> In the field of architecture only one example shall be mentioned. A new type of apartment house grew completely out of the atmosphere of the Bauhaus: the skyscraper made of glass panels, the skyscraper of eight to twelve stories, which is found everywhere today. This type

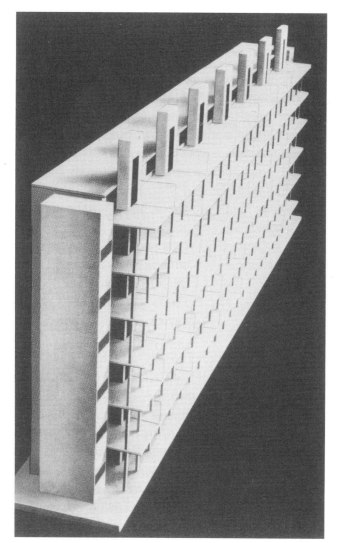

Figure 4.4. Marcel Breuer, model of a project for an apartment house, 1924. From Walter Gropius, ed., *Internationale Architektur* (Munich: Albert Langen Verlag, 1925), 90.

of skyscraper was designed by Marcel Breuer for the first time in a contest for inexpensive apartments held by the *Bauwelt* in 1924, disproving the idea of concentrated mass due to its plate-like shape. Walter Gropius fought in vain an intensive but hopeless battle for the realization of this type of dwelling up to 1933. The first glass-panel house in Rotterdam was built by van Tijen in 1934.[50]

For Giedion, Breuer's design did not simply ignore existing technology and conditions of practice, as did the Haus am Horn on the one hand, and Molnár's project on the other, but anticipated what might—or should—emerge in the future. Architecture was still separate from building, but the gap had narrowed.

While the students continued to produce architecture on their own, they persisted in their demands for a program in architectural design. Early in 1924, influenced by the 1923 exhibition and the prominence it had given to architecture, Breuer demanded, along with Molnár and Muche, that Gropius create an architecture department that would concentrate on the design of housing, specifically the development of norms, types, and standards. They also wanted to build a second model house, this time in an urban context, to integrate their research with practical experience in construction.[51] Like the other proposed programs in architecture, this one only admitted students who had completed the rest of the course and had "special artistic abilities."[52] The plan was similar to Gropius's insofar as its emphasis on norms, types, and standards cast architecture as research, giving architecture students the opportunity to realize their designs on paper. But the students characterized the architecture department as an office and planned to publish their designs in an effort to get commissions. Their program, which acknowledged the continuity between their designs and real buildings, no longer preserved Gropius's distinction between architecture and building, which implied that architecture could only exist on paper, and buildings, something very different, could only stand on a site. It was, instead, a harbinger of the curriculum Hannes Meyer would implement three years later.

Gropius agreed to their demands but never secured the funding to implement the proposal. The students did not abandon their demand for an official program in architecture, though, and one year later approached Gropius with another curriculum in hand, threatening to leave the school if he did not carry out their plan. Their new curriculum abandoned the emphasis on research as a form of practice. Instead, it favored developing the students' formal talents. It incorporated the existing courses on construction and structure and added, significantly, a course on the history of architecture and one in formal design, described as a studio to be taught by Gropius. Gropius later "corrected" the program by eliminating the history course and enlisting Adolf Meyer to teach design with him.[53] But it was already December 1924, and by the end of March the following year the masters would close the Weimar school and be on their way to Dessau. The Weimar Bauhaus never got its architecture program.[54]

AFTER WEIMAR: LABORATORIES AND STUDIOS

The remaining history of the Bauhaus could be read as an epilogue. After Gropius had moved the school to Dessau, he turned away from the quandary concerning the relationship between architecture and building definitive for the Weimar years. The implementation of an architecture program in Dessau demonstrates, on the one hand, that he and his successors instead accepted the new but eventually conventional approach to architecture defined in the programs for educational reform and abandoned the Bauhaus's singular celebration of building as collaboration. On the other hand, the incarnations of the Bauhaus in Dessau and Berlin might be read as a transformation of the quandary rather than as an escape from it. From this perspective, the curricula and designs proposed by Gropius as well as Meyer and Mies can be seen as transformations of the relationship between architecture and building from one of incompatibility to different forms of integration.

The Bauhaus building and the masters' houses—Gropius's first two Bauhaus commissions to be completed—together formed a compendium of the possible relationships between architecture and building. The Bauhaus building was not only a vision of the future but the embodiment of the school's complicated existence. Its architecture was an expression of transition. It opened on 4 December 1926 to a crowd of 1,500 guests, many of whom were important cultural, political, and industrial figures. The popularity of the building can be gauged by the number of visitors (20,000 in the first three years) and the continual praise it received. Writing after the opening ceremonies, the critic Max Deri called it "one of the most extraordinary modern buildings to be seen in Germany."[55] The great glass curtain wall that surrounded the workshops was the object of most of the attention. And while some critics recognized the innovative technology and structural design that made possible the curtain wall as well as the rest of the building, many of the comments made it clear that the importance of the building lay in its form.[56] Many years later, former Bauhaus student Howard Dearstyne even pointed out that Gropius had painted the columns black on the canteen/auditorium facade in order to make the windows look continuous.[57]

Dearstyne's observation certainly reveals the formalism for which Gropius's earlier work has often been criticized. Specifically, this aspect of the Bauhaus building embodied the final incarnation of the architecture curriculum in Weimar and the institution of the course titled "Formal Design." The canteen windows indicated that it was possible for the architect to force the built object into the form of the architecture, irrespective of its actual construction. Oddly enough, although the window arrangement came primarily from Gropius's preoccupation with appearance, it betrayed the same belief in the continuity between the architectural design and the built object that would later define Meyer's approach to architecture at the school. Here, Gropius's early distinction between architecture and building had collapsed.

Like the Bauhaus building, the masters' houses reflected the formal approach solidified in the last architecture curriculum from Weimar. While their architecture looked as if it were a product of a prefabricated construction process and, thus, an example of architecture that could be realized on paper, prefabrication was never implemented in this project. As in the case of the early housing types, the design of the repetitive units, which were rotated about an axis and reflected about a plane in order to provide a variety of accommodations, captured the repetition and variation of prefabrication in form alone. One can only explain them, to paraphrase Winkler, as the expression of mass production rather than as the result of it.

Gropius and Muche made some later attempts to use prefabrication methods in other projects. From 1926 to 1928, Gropius tried to move beyond his formalism in the Törten housing, where he designed a set of housing types in concrete and then tried to build them. Specifically, he sought to use a rationalized construction process in which the various architectural elements would be prefabricated and then assembled on the site. His intention was to construct architecture on paper, in keeping with his earlier approach to architecture and his later plans for an architecture research department. But when he tried to transfer his architecture to the site, the prefabrication process proved fraught with technical problems that prompted renovations to the buildings soon after their completion. The project failed because Gropius attempted to maintain total control over it while its architecture was transformed into a building. His failure underscored the necessity of the collaboration that was central to the Bauhaus manifesto but contradicted by his ambitions for control over the construction phase. Collaboration rather than an idea about construction distinguished architecture from building. One way to explain why Gropius could not successfully build Törten, then, is to say that he was caught between his early distinction between architecture and building and his later ambition to build architecture without allowing for collaboration. It is perhaps no accident that immediately after this project, Gropius decided to leave the Bauhaus to return to private practice.

Prefabricated building in steel proved to be as problematic as it was in concrete. Since 1924, while Gropius had been working on Törten, Muche had been developing housing types in steel in order to best accommodate the changing spatial requirements of the family. In 1927, a steel house he had designed with Richard Paulick was built on a site near the housing. Despite steel's promise for the realization of a flexible design, Muche had to acknowledge that its use in residential construction was not yet realistic. In an article about the house, he wrote: "At present all types of steel constructions for houses are still primitive. The amount of material needed is too large. Only specially developed constructions . . . will make the steel house into a modern industrial product with respect to purpose, form, and price."[58] Muche's reflections on building confirmed the earlier comments on Molnár's and Breuer's housing types, which said that existing technology could not yet support prefabrication and assembly and, in practice, remove the construction process from the building site. They were the only interpretations that would have saved construction for the architect. Otherwise, the practical impossibility of these examples would have debunked the dream of solitary architectural control over construction.

Despite the lack of collaboration between architects and builders in the construction of Gropius's Bauhaus building, the masters' houses, and the Törten housing, architecture was not completely alienated from building in the sense of his 1919 manifesto. Collaboration of the architects with various masters and the members of their workshops on the interior design of the projects contributed to the projects' transformation from architecture to building. The central location of Gropius's office in the

Bauhaus building expressed all the complexity of the architect's role in this transformation. On the one hand, the office reinforced the role of architecture as a catalyst for collaboration in the context of the design curriculum. On the other, it was an office where architects alone produced instructions for building. Most important, it displaced the studio space for architecture students during Gropius's tenure and effectively denied architecture, as originally defined, a place in the Bauhaus curriculum.

The curriculum continued to change during Gropius's last years and even displaced building from its central role. In October 1926, new statutes for the school took effect that remained valid until 1930. Building was no longer the ultimate goal, but realization still characterized the curriculum. The school provided training and preparation (no teaching) in the form of "practical experiments." Furthermore, it "[prepared talented people] for creative design work, particularly for architecture." Architecture was addressed directly, but now as one of many options; if students were not admitted into the architecture course at the end of their training, they could enter the "practical research department" and experiment with other design ideas.[59] The new curriculum elevated research from a transitional phase to an end as Gropius had tried to do in his Törten project. Rather than producing Gropius's types, students now produced prototypes. While the Bauhaus building was not literally the product of this research, the interpretation of some critics suggests that it certainly embodied the research. Many of them referred to the building as a factory (or something even better than a factory): the site of the mass-production methods that standardized the material world and transformed design into research as in Gropius's earlier model. Quite fittingly, they also described the workshops as laboratories.[60] There is little trace of Gropius's early emphasis on collaboration, construction, and building, but his later approach to architecture as research appears to have been fulfilled.

Gropius had managed to integrate this newer take on architecture successfully into the curriculum by the time Hannes Meyer arrived at the Bauhaus in April 1927 to teach in the newly formed architecture department. Meyer quickly became the head of the department and, one year later, the director of the entire school. His partner, Hans Wittwer, taught design with him until 1929 and lectured on acoustics, lighting, and heating.[61] Almost immediately after he had become director, Meyer hired Ludwig Hilberseimer, who already had a strong reputation as an art, architecture, and planning critic, to set up a department of city planning.[62] Anton Brenner, an Austrian who had learned architecture in a Russian POW camp during World War I, came to the Bauhaus in 1929, from designing housing with Ernst May in Frankfurt am Main.[63] He took over the architecture studio.[64] Alcar Rudelt, a construction engineer from Dresden, taught mathematics, statics, strength of materials, and steel and reinforced concrete construction from 1928 to 1933.[65] Edvard Heiberg from Oslo taught housing; Carl Fieger, an associate in Gropius's office in Weimar, returned to the Bauhaus to teach architectural draftsmanship part time; and Wilhelm Müller gave lectures on building materials.[66] Among the guests were Mart Stam, who lectured on elementary instruction in architecture and city planning; Rudolf Carnap, Otto Neurath, and Herbert Feigl, the philosophers; Hermann Finsterlin, the architect; Ernst Toller, the playwright; Dziga Vertov, the film director; and Karel Teige, the critic.[67] Former student Marcel Breuer continued to direct the furniture workshop until he left later in 1928. When an interiors department was established in 1929, which included the furniture workshop, another former student, Alfred Arndt, became its chairman.

The architecture department became a permanent fixture of the school until its closure in 1933. In the case of both Meyer and Mies, its head was also the director of the Bauhaus, a fact that seemed to express architecture's—or building's—dominance in the school. But a curriculum published in 1928 shows that architecture was only one of four courses of study—advertising, theater, and a seminar in free sculpture and painting—that defined a student's education. Building was now subsumed under the study of architecture and regarded as the exterior counterpart to interior design, which comprised the metal, wall-painting, and furniture workshops. Although participation in building was no longer the explicit goal of every program in the school, the interior design course partially recovered Gropius's original principles. The students in its various workshop components still designed with a consciousness of the environment in which their work would be placed. The great difference from Gropius's scheme was that the environment was not a tangible entity anymore. Under Meyer, every student, including the interior designers and the architects, would have to study "design for living" to be able to consider "the judicious incorporation of his work into the context of today's society" rather than into a physical environment.[68]

Meyer told an audience of prospective students something similar: "Those who pursue architecture will learn in this course a scientific way of architectural thinking according to the principle: Building signifies 'the design of all the activities of life.'"[69] Architecture did not involve the creation of form. This echoes Meyer's emphasis on building and rejection of architecture in his famous essay, "Building" which was published in the Bauhaus Journal around the same time.[70] Meyer did not reject architecture wholesale, only its alliance with art and formal conventions; "architecture [sic] as 'an emotional act of the artist' has no justification," he declared.[71] Despite the fact, according to several students and masters, Meyer did have an interest in painting and, more generally, composition after all, he implemented his ideology by isolating the art departments—painting and sculpture—from architecture and building. Mies maintained this split.[72]

"Instruction in Architecture" under Meyer was thus transformed from a creative into an analytic and largely quantitative project; as in the laboratory, the results of the "experiment"—the design—emerged from the definition of the parameters, here "the activities of life." In Meyer's architecture course, literally called "Analytic Building," one student presented his project for apartment units as the result of a detailed examination of movement and circulation, sun exposure, and air circulation relative to function in individual and multiple units. On the sheet of drawings, pie charts, flow charts, and shadow diagrams dominate the plans and sections that document the building.[73] Meyer introduced the students to this approach through a process he called *Projektierung,* which integrated the analysis of various factors that would affect the shape of a building with their documentation. Documentation and presentation thus became an integral part of the design process. Or, as a former student, Philipp Tolziner, described it, Meyer presented the projects and the students had to draw the diagrams (Figure 4.5).[74] In their design for an apartment house, Tolziner and his partner, Tibor Weiner, annotated their drawing of the apartment floor plans and sections with the initial remark "the plan is calculated from the following factors." Two-thirds of the sheet contained diagrams of sunlight, use patterns in the apartment, and notes on ventilation requirements. On the plans and sections on the remaining third of the drawing were indicated sight lines and sunlight penetration as well as the furniture. According to Arieh Sharon, another former student, Meyer was very specific about drawings since he viewed them as "a site for reprogramming ideologies and causalities."[75]

If Meyer's analytic drawings were the result of the students' "special training emphasizing theory," they were also the product of "a design studio that included the practice of building."[76] The drawings had a close relationship to Meyer's buildings, often characterized as "diagrammatic," and could be considered as a real site of building and collaboration. In contrast, Gropius's housing types, which represented his notion of architecture in drawing and model, could never be transformed into buildings; their identity as types confined them to paper. One has only to compare Gropius's with Meyer's designs for the Törten housing. Gropius's project had to be significantly altered after its completion, due to shortcomings in its construction and function. Meyer's project remained virtually untouched. Gropius approached the building of Törten as an architect for whom collaboration was not a part of the design method; he tried to invent a construction method for the project himself (and also probably tried to anticipate how the method might be applied).[77] Consequently, the project remained a work of architecture until it was altered by others to accommodate its existence on a real site. Meyer approached the project as a head of a building team. For him, collaboration shifted from the building site to the architectural drawing, where he considered the contributions of nonarchitects while working out his solution on paper. Meyer's curriculum aptly reflected the relationship between his designs and his buildings: it made architecture—his vision of a design on paper—the goal of collaboration or, in Bauhaus terms, building. Moreover, Meyer's curriculum rescued architecture for Gropius by linking the architect's design with realization and with collaboration. In the process, however, it devalued Gropius's definition of building as an object in its own right, distinct from architecture.

When Mies became the director of the Bauhaus in 1930, he consolidated it into a school of architecture and interior design (which had become an independent

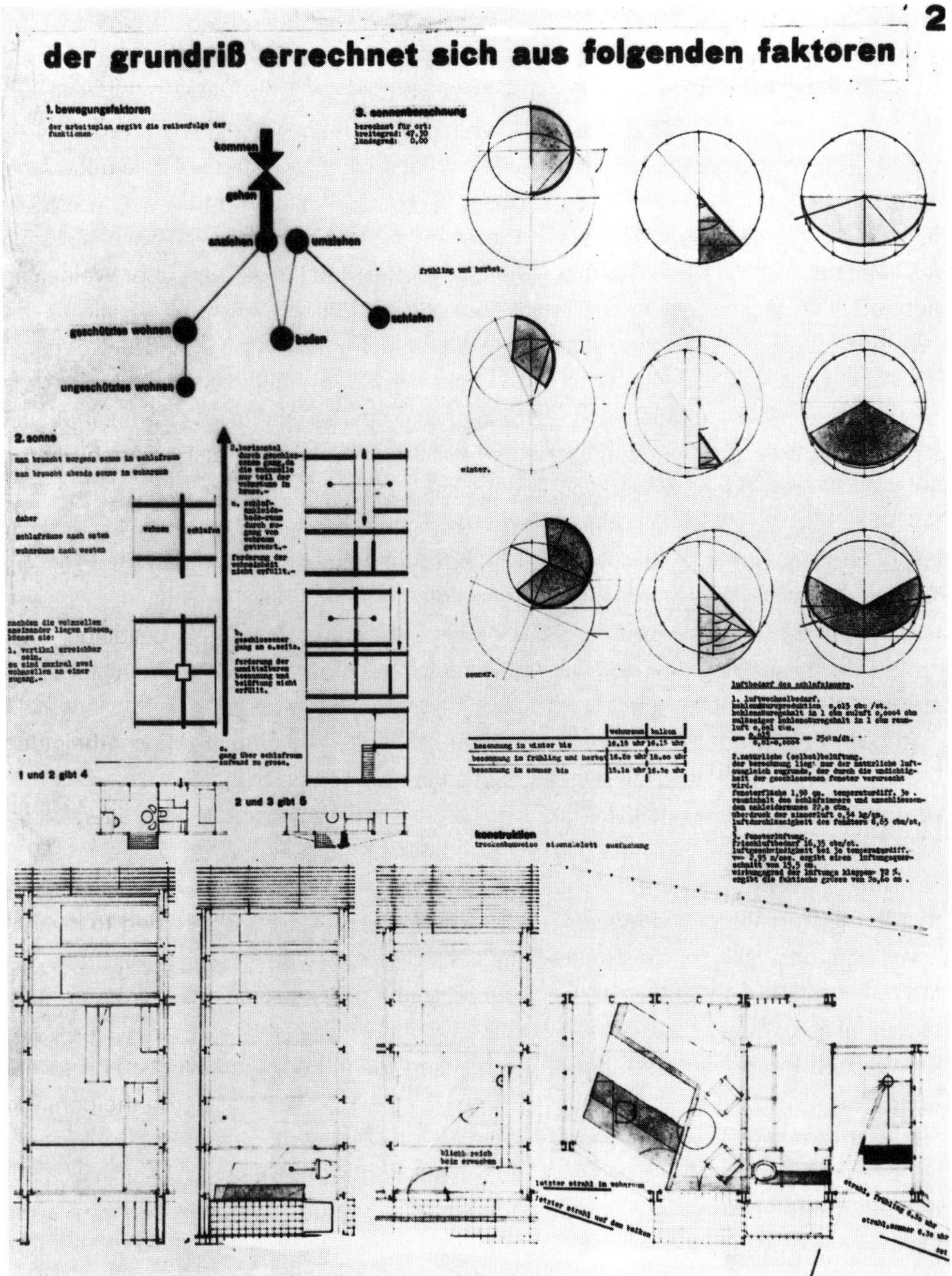

Figure 4.5. Student work from Hannes Meyer's course: Philipp Tolziner and Tibor Weiner, "The Plan Is Calculated from the Following Factors: Design for Units in an Apartment House," 1930. Bauhaus-Archiv, Berlin.

department in 1929, still including the metal, wall-painting, and furniture workshops) that also offered courses of study in commercial art, photography, weaving, and fine art. Hilberseimer and Mies taught architecture and planning; Arndt and then Lilly Reich directed the Department of Interior Design. The predominance of architecture coupled with a reduced curriculum illustrates Mies's interest in specialization and professionalization.[78] He apparently ignored building altogether, both as a collaborative project for the entire school and as an artifact of the construction process in the studio. Students learned about construction but concentrated on the study of architecture, which Mies openly portrayed as a spatial and aesthetic proposal rather than as the social or material proposal advocated by Gropius and later by Meyer. Furthermore, he transformed the preliminary course, long an anchor of the Bauhaus curriculum, into one called "Introduction to Artistic Creation," which was seen as a replacement for a student's lack of previous experience in construction or handcrafts.[79] (Students with this experience did not have to take the course.) Along with this course, students took other fundamental courses in theory (science courses in chemistry and physics; mathematics, materials) and skill development (lettering, shop, projective geometry, and representational drawing). Of these, Mies particularly insisted on the course in representational drawing because of its importance for the study of architecture.[80]

Mies emphasized professionalization in architecture and interior design (as well as in photography, commercial art, weaving, and fine art) but not in the context of practice. In Mies's Bauhaus, Gropius's workshop and factory were superseded by the school. He wanted to dissolve the "unfortunate" conflation of educational activities and production, certainly because it resulted in objects of poor quality, borne out by the number of complaints the Bauhaus received about its products. But Mies also believed that there were certain principles of architecture that students could only learn in school, where they were free of the constraints of practice.[81] Along with the general dissolution of Gropius's workshops, Meyer's architecture course, understood as "Bauen," became Mies's "Baukunst": architecture was no longer conceived as building but as art. In his architecture seminar, the third and final stage of the architecture curriculum, Mies presented the students with abstract problems and discussed them in terms of their composition of objects and space.

While students pursued their own projects in Mies's architecture studio, these looked very much like the designs for court houses that he was working on at the time. Students progressed through a series of assignments—Houses A, B, C—of increasing complexity. Student Pius Pahl's perspective of his design for House C (Figure 4.6) not only shares the architecture of Mies's court houses—the transparency; the relationship between the columnar structure and the windows and walls that form the enclosure; the overhanging roof; and the articulation of the living room as an exposed interior space—it also uses similar representational devices (the plants, vines, and furniture of Mies and Lilly Reich's design). While the work of Meyer's students also bore some

HAUS 'C'

Figure 4.6. Student work from Mies van der Rohe's course: Pius Pahl, House C, 1931–32. Bauhaus-Archiv, Berlin.

resemblance to his own work, the similarity in Mies's studio was the consequence of his pedagogy. Students learned architecture by imitating Mies's own designs; sometimes he even sat down at a student's desk and designed parts of his project.[82] Conversely, student work (at the Bauhaus and, later, in Chicago) had a strong influence on Mies's own designs, to the point where student work was sometimes identified as Mies's. Although Mies's teaching turned away from practice, his relationship to his students did not completely reject the roles and the closeness of master and apprentice. Mies's pedagogy was probably a transformation of the way in which he had learned how to design as an apprentice for Bruno Paul and Peter Behrens, an artifact of practice now used in the freer and more focused context of an academic institution.[83]

Mies was not the only one teaching architecture during his directorship. Late in 1930, Richard Neutra visited the Bauhaus to teach a seminar in modern architecture, in which he asked students to do the competition design for the state theater in Kharkov. More prominent in the curriculum was Ludwig Hilberseimer, who taught the other Bauhaus course in architectural design, the so-called second stage of a student's education. His class, first called "Instruction in Building" (which he also taught under Meyer) and later "Seminar for Apartment and Town Planning," complemented Mies's seminar in architecture in several ways.[84] Hilberseimer's seminar focused on the relationship of the housing unit to its context, while Mies's focused on the design of a unit. It also approached design as the implementation of theory, retaining the sense of design as an analytic project, central to the architecture program during Meyer's tenure. In Hilberseimer's class, students discussed theoretical questions of planning, building orientation, and the placement of infrastructure and thought about design as variable solutions to particular economic and functional problems rather than an open-ended compositional possibility, as they did with Mies. But they also took away some lessons on form. Along with Mies's court houses, Hilberseimer's L-shaped house as well as his design and graphic approach to planning turned up in many student projects.

If Mies's Bauhaus separated architecture from building, can one say that Mies had fully abandoned the Bauhaus's mission and transformed the school into, as it would later be viewed, a conventional school of architecture? In his essay on Mies and the Bauhaus, accompanying an exhibition on the same subject, Christian Wolsdorff notes that, as a consequence of this view, Mies's Bauhaus has the worst reputation of all the incarnations of the school; authors have only included it in the Bauhaus story, Wolsdorff argues, because they feel obligated to provide a complete chronicle of the school.[85] But this assessment is unjust. Certainly Mies presented students with a different relationship between architecture and building than that posed by Gropius and Meyer. Mies's view of architecture—like Meyer's—opposed Gropius's high regard for the built object by privileging the drawing (and the model) in the development of architecture. But Mies also turned away from Meyer's program when he rejected the identity of architecture and building in the curricula he implemented in Dessau and Berlin.[86] After having been forced to leave Dessau earlier in 1932, Mies managed to revive the Bauhaus in Berlin for the winter semester of 1932/33. In the brochure describing the new curriculum, he characterized the school as "an independent teaching and research institute," emphasizing the separation of architecture from building and practice.

Even after the Bauhaus closed in March 1933, Mies continued to teach architecture, first in private lessons in his Berlin studio and in Switzerland, and, from 1938 onward, as the director of the School of Architecture at the Armour Institute of Technology in Chicago (later the Illinois Institute of Technology). In Berlin, Mies insisted that he was only offering private instruction in the aesthetic questions of building and was not training prospective architects. In Chicago, he claimed that he had finally been liberated from the Bauhaus and could develop a curriculum appropriate for a school of architecture.[87] Only here, he (together with Hilberseimer) reunited architecture with building in the studio, following the "conventional" pattern.

Seen in the context of his architecture program for the Armour Institute, Mies's approach to architecture at the Bauhaus—as a formal project—was not at all that of a "conventional school of architecture." Instead, it was consistent with the Bauhaus's original program: that the goal of architecture, as well of the arts, was the *Gesamt-*

kunstwerk (Total Work of Art). Collaboration was central to creating the Total Work of Art, as it was to Mies's case that "nothing had changed in terms of the goals of the Bauhaus since the establishment of the school," despite Mies's differences with his predecessors.[88] The importance of collaboration made it virtually impossible for Gropius to reconcile the teaching of architecture with his emphasis on realization or building. Hannes Meyer solved the problem by relocating building and its realization from the construction site to the drawing board, preserving collaboration as a part of the Bauhaus experience but dispensing, at least rhetorically, with architecture. Mies, in turn, saw collaboration as a goal but assigned it, along with building, to practice. In doing so, he made room for architecture in the studio. He saw his role as preparing Bauhaus students to "create the building of the future," but only after they left the school.

The Bauhaus was always a school of building but never a school of architecture, despite its influence over our notion of modern architecture. Building was always the motivating force behind a curriculum in which architecture could never find a resting place. However contradictory this appears to be, and however frustrated the search for architecture was at the Bauhaus, it is this very situation that may tell us more about the possibilities for architecture than any "conventional school of architecture" ever did.

BAUHAUS THEATER OF HUMAN DOLLS

5

Juliet Koss

> But when I attempt to survey my task, it is clear to me
> that I should speak to you not of people, but of things.
> —**RAINER MARIA RILKE,** *Auguste Rodin* (1907)

In 1961, Walter Gropius grandly declared that "the Bauhaus embraced the whole range of visual arts: architecture, planning, painting, sculpture, industrial design, and stage work."[1] While the statement is not inaccurate, the straightforward inclusion of theater as one of six fundamental components of the visual arts belies the field's more complicated status at the Bauhaus. Gropius had not mentioned theater in the initial manifesto and program of the State Bauhaus in Weimar, the four-page pamphlet published in April 1919 that proclaimed, "Architects, painters, sculptors, we must all return to the crafts!"[2] But stage work soon became central, and theater proved to be a form of art that unified all the others; already in 1922, a drawing by Paul Klee of the idea and structure of the Bauhaus shows Bau und Bühne, or building and stage, firmly united at its core. The Bauhaus held performances frequently and sponsored many in other venues, causing delight and, intermittently, disturbing the neighbors. The theater workshop, created in the summer of 1921 and overseen initially by Lothar Schreyer, is associated most closely with Oskar Schlemmer (who ran it from early 1923 until his departure in 1929) and particularly with his *Triadic Ballet,* first performed in full in 1922.[3] Theater was also the subject of the fourth of the fourteen Bauhaus books, *Die Bühne im Bauhaus* (The Stage at the Bauhaus), which appeared in 1925.[4] When the Dessau Bauhaus was built that year, the auditorium was located near the center of the building's triadic pinwheel, between the entrance hall and the canteen, as if to indicate theater's pivotal status within the school's social and professional life.

The study of theater is often impeded by the nature of the medium: notoriously difficult to document and theoretically unruly, it falls easily between disciplines while claiming to incorporate them all. This amorphous quality gained particular significance at the Bauhaus, where experiments in stage and theater design occurred both on and off the premises, frequently in the context of costume parties and other festivities. In all of its incarnations, Bauhaus performances re-created the human body—literally and

90

symbolically, on stage and off—in the shape of the doll, its childlike simplicity combining a comforting and seemingly animate charm with an unnerving absence of human personality. Bauhaus dolls of various kinds maintained a playful ambivalence in the face of shifting models of subjectivity, toying with gender ambiguity and engaging with the notion of abstraction both at the level of the individual subject and as a unified group of creatures, delightfully difficult to differentiate. Vessels of empathy and estrangement, they expressed and encouraged a reciprocal relationship between performers and spectators, increasingly exemplifying the bond between gender and mass culture, to provide models of mass spectatorship for the Weimar Republic.

"The history of the theater is the history of the transfiguration of human form," Schlemmer asserted in 1925, with "the human being as the actor of physical and spiritual events, alternating between naïveté and reflection, naturalness and artificiality."[5] Such contradictory attributes often appeared simultaneously on the Bauhaus stage, where performances combined human subjectivity and its deadpan absence, as seen in a black-and-white photograph taken by Erich Consemüller of Schlemmer's *Space Dance* in 1926 (Figure 5.1). Three figures pose on an otherwise bare stage in padded monochrome unitards indistinguishable in everything but (presumably) color; their feet, in standard-issue dance slippers, appear dainty and petite below their stuffed bodies; and identical masks encase their heads in shiny metallic ovoids painted with wide-eyed expressions of mock surprise. Three hands near the center of the image seem to mark the only areas of visible human flesh, but even these look so rigid as to evoke those of shop window mannequins; the calculated angles of the dancers' arms and legs likewise suggest synthetic limbs. Facing frontally or in profile, the perfectly poised figures lack all trace of individuality, any sense of flesh and blood, or any hint of human skeletons at their core; they seem devoid even of a generic human personality. Their padded bodies, particularly at the hips and crotch, appear female. Underneath the costumes, however, lurk Schlemmer himself (in front on the left) and the dancers Werner Siedhoff and Walter Kaminsky. Conflating "naïveté and reflection, naturalness and artificiality"—to invoke Schlemmer's terms—they playfully embody a model of human subjectivity that reflects the instability of their era.

The unitards and masks resemble the protective gear of fencers; the poses call to mind the fencing ring or dance studio.[6] But despite the initial impression of active athleticism, the figures also seem like passive objects. They hold static, almost timeless postures, like modern parodies of the statues of ancient Greece that Johann Joachim Winckelmann had famously characterized by a "noble simplicity and a calm greatness, as much in the pose as in the expression."[7] The figure on the right especially, with its simplified forms and its arms tucked invisibly behind its back, evokes a ruin with missing limbs and weathered features. "The artificial figure permits any movement, any position for any desired duration," Schlemmer explained. "It permits—an artistic device from the periods of the greatest art—the variable scale of the figures: significant large,

Figure 5.1. Oskar Schlemmer, *Space Dance*, performed by Schlemmer, Werner Siedhoff, and Walter Kaminsky, Dessau Bauhaus, 1926. Photograph by Erich Consemüller. Nachlass Erich Consemüller, Cologne, private collection. From Wulf Herzogenrath and Stefan Kraus, *Erich Consemüller: Fotographien Bauhaus-Dessau: Katalog der Fotographien aus dem Nachlass von Erich Consemüller, dem Bauhaus-Archiv, Berlin, and dem Busch-Reisinger-Museum der Harvard University, Cambridge, Mass.* (Munich: Schirmer/Mosel, 1989), Plate 123.

insignificant small."[8] Without human faces or individualized bodies, the figures in *Space Dance* are easily read as miniature humans, although the padding enlarges their forms. Comforting and disturbing in equal measure, they simultaneously resemble children's toys expanded to adult size and oddly overstuffed little people, in keeping with Schlemmer's declaration in 1930 that representations of the human figure belonged "in the realm of the doll-like."[9] The photograph's uncertainty of scale is meanwhile intensified by the absence of anything else on stage with which to compare the figures, effectively rendering each one an unreliable standard for judging the other two. Receding upstage from left to right, they become smaller, but their heads remain at the same height.

Within the image, the choreography leaves no doubt that the intended spectator is in fact the camera lens; Schlemmer's careful arrangement of the figures on stage coincides precisely with Consemüller's photographic composition. Symmetrically arranged within the frame, shining out from the center of the surrounding darkness, the three heads divide the photograph vertically into four equal areas and horizontally into three, with the dark space behind them—the blank backdrop behind the stage—comprising the top two-thirds of the picture. The bodies are arranged in space, but the image reads as flat; only the straight, deep shadows linking Schlemmer's feet to the center of the horizon line (and the shorter, parallel shadows behind the other figures' feet) suggest recession into depth. The three vertical bodies—and the limbs attached to them—likewise divide the image like the lines of a geometry diagram, despite the figures' apparent difference in size and arbitrary poses. A painted line down the center of the stage floor also bisects the photograph vertically; interrupted by the feet of the central figure (Siedhoff), it continues along his body and through Schlemmer's outstretched hand to end at Siedhoff's artificial head. But Siedhoff's head is also Schlemmer's; identical to that worn by the director, it is made according to his design.

These representations of the human figure in the late 1920s—both the stage image and the photograph—test the limits of recent art historical scholarship in the United States on Weimar subjectivity. Scholarship in this field has concentrated on Dada imagery, robots, and other technological creatures, frequently emphasizing disjuncture of various kinds—from the aesthetics of montage to the prevalence of dismembered bodies in the wake of World War I.[10] Following the arguments of the artists themselves, formal disjuncture is often aligned with the politics of resistance, with the visible montage fragment treated as a marker of the "real" that questions the logic of representation and thus acts as a destabilizing force in the political, cultural, and social realms.[11] Such an equation of aesthetic and political radicalism is often convincing—as, for example, in Hannah Höch's photomontage *Dompteuse* (Tamer), of about 1930, a willfully uncertain depiction of the Weimar New Woman. A collation of partial, mismatched, roughly torn images from contemporary magazines, *Dompteuse* shows various accoutrements of control from the circus arena and public life, challenging prevailing notions of idealized feminine beauty and troubling the relationship between tamer and tamed.[12] The equation's inverse—that an aesthetic "return to order" signifies political conservatism—is often equally powerful, with positive images of physical wholeness and the healthy body produced as National Socialist propaganda, as in Leni Riefenstahl's two-part film *Olympia* of 1938.[13]

Particularly in contrast to the gritty photomontages of John Heartfield and Höch or the political theater of Bertolt Brecht and Erwin Piscator, it may be tempting to read Schlemmer's creatures, Consemüller's photograph, and Bauhaus dolls generally as ominous harbingers of the National Socialist obsession with physical culture and rationalized subjectivity. Whether openly celebratory of such tendencies or simply blind to political reality, the dolls (by this line of thinking) are, at best, liable to co-optation by right-wing forces; at worst, their physical amplitude and seemingly apolitical posturing prove their guilt. Insistently whole—more than whole—they seem optimistically to embrace the mounting mechanization of Weimar Germany; their robotic poses softened, literally, by their costumes, they stave off the threat of dismemberment with a denial both charming and disquieting. Three more figures, standing proudly with linked arms in Consemüller's photograph of Schlemmer's *Gesture Dance III* in 1927, might be cited as further evidence. Like a trio of padded fops, Schlemmer, Siedhoff, and Kaminsky here are buried in costumes resembling tuxedos, ostensibly useless spectacles appended to their identical masked heads. They seem blind, deaf, and dumb to the escalating troubles of the Weimar Republic; Siedhoff even faces upstage, turning his back to spectators and camera lens alike—without suffering an ensuing reduction in personality.

In fact, no amount of padding could protect the inhabitants of the Bauhaus from continuous charges of communist leanings, with their festivities cited as evidence of political radicalism. The Ministry of Culture in Weimar responded to allegations in 1920, for example, that the school was "spartacistic and bolshevistic," noting that "a complaint has been made that the neighborhood of the Bauhaus . . . is often disturbed by noise during the night hours."[14] While right-wing harassment is no proof of leftist tendencies, Bauhaus activities certainly undermined authority and threatened conservative local governments.[15] Funding in Weimar was canceled in the autumn of 1924, prompting the school's dissolution the following spring; its Dessau incarnation was closed by a bill put forward by the National Socialists in September 1932; and in Berlin the school was shut down by the Nazis after only six months, in April 1933. But despite such ongoing victimization, ample connections exist between the Bauhaus and National Socialism, as recent scholarship attests.[16] Schlemmer's approving citation of Josef Goebbels in a letter of June 1933 reveals both his own political bent and his sense of the convergence of his life and work. "I consider myself pure, and my art strong," he declared, "in keeping with nat. soc. principles—namely 'heroic, steely-romantic, unsentimental, hard, sharp, clear, creative of new types,' etc."[17] And one need look no further than Schlemmer's design, the following year, for a mural for the congress hall in the Deutsches Museum in Munich to witness the chilling offspring of his earlier dolls. Roughly sketched in blue and purple chalk, an orderly litter of identical, dark blond women stand in profile, their right arms raised in a Nazi salute. Hailing a greater power that lies beyond our sight, they are unified in a grid of support—although the feminine silhouette of their flowing, floor-length skirts suggests a return to Jugendstil ideals following the androgynous padding of their 1920s forebears.

But while such textual and visual evidence reveals much about Schlemmer in 1933 and 1934, it proves little about the figures he designed in the 1920s. Creative work never merely illustrates a political position that has been fully worked through years in advance, and the dolls at the Bauhaus were neither Nazi sympathizers nor leftist troublemakers, neither wholly celebratory nor entirely critical of their environment.[18] The figures in *Space Dance* and *Gesture Dance III* demonstrate the danger of applying preconceived equations to works of art in retroactive assessment of protofascist potential. Insistently refusing to postulate a firm stance of any kind, the dolls seem instead to adopt the position of profound patience described by Siegfried Kracauer in 1922:

> Perhaps the only remaining attitude is one of *waiting*. By committing oneself to waiting, one neither blocks one's path toward faith (like those who defiantly affirm the void) nor besieges this faith. . . . One waits, and one's waiting is a *hesitant openness,* albeit of a sort that is difficult to explain.[19]

In light of these words, one might view the extraordinary static poses of Schlemmer's theater dolls—their noble simplicity and calm greatness—as uncertain, expectant, and hopeful. Seriously playful creatures, construction sites of modern subjectivity, they might even be seen to embody the synthesis of "the most extreme fantasy with the most extreme sobriety" with which the art critic Franz Roh characterized the technique of photomontage itself in 1925.[20]

AUTOMATA, MARIONETTES, AND DOLLS

Waxworks, dolls, marionettes, and puppets had long substituted for humans in the German literary imagination, famously appearing in the work of E. T. A. Hoffmann and Heinrich von Kleist in the early nineteenth century. "Grace," Kleist decreed in 1810, "appears purest simultaneously in the human body that has either none at all or else infinite consciousness—that is, in the puppet or god."[21] Such artificial creatures gravitated easily to the stage. In late-nineteenth-century France, for example, Léo Delibes's ballet *Coppélia* (1870) and Jacques Offenbach's opera *The Tales of Hoffmann* (1881) took up these literary precursors, their leading characters melding mechanization and the performance of femininity as if testing a new model of female subjectivity. Replica humans—and female dolls in particular—pervaded the visual arts of early-twentieth-century Germany, from the paintings of the Blaue Reiter to Hans Bellmer's creations and photographs. Such treatments of the relation between subjectivity and objectification occurred with particular fervor after the birth of visual abstraction, as they permitted the continued investigation of human subjectivity despite the demise of figurative painting. "At a certain point in time," as Walter Benjamin declared in the allusive, telegraphic prose characteristic of his Arcades Project, "the motif of the doll acquires a sociocritical significance."[22]

At the Bauhaus, dolls of a traditional size were created as well, such as the marionettes designed by Kurt Schmidt for *The Adventures of the Little Hunchback* and pictured in *Die Bühne im Bauhaus* in 1925.[23] They performed in private and in public, acting as scale models for theater costumes and as miniature people, manipulated by human hands and enjoyed by human spectators. Between 1916 and 1925, Paul Klee created for his son, Felix, a puppet theater with fifty marionettes, including a self-portrait, a crowned poet, and a matchbox genie. As Felix later reminisced with regard to these creatures, "Some hilarious performances were held at the Weimar Bauhaus, during which various confidential matters were aired in an unsparing and sarcastic way, vexing to those concerned and highly amusing to the others."[24] Blending child's play with serious adult activity, performances could serve both as entertainment and as psychological ventilation along the model of Sigmund Freud's "talking cure." The playfulness of the dolls made by Klee and others in this period suggests a determination to re-enchant the world, in keeping with Schlemmer's lament that, outside the Bauhaus, "the materialistic-practical age has certainly lost the genuine feeling for play and wonder. The utilitarian frame of mind is well on the way to killing it."[25] Proudly bearing the marks of their makers' hands, dolls embodied the drive to unify art and craft that governed the Bauhaus in its early years.

After 1923, however, with the arrival at the school of László Moholy-Nagy—and increasingly after the move to Dessau—technology became the guiding force of Bauhaus creativity, and theater provided an ideal showcase for contending with the body's increasing reification, mechanization, and androgyny.[26] "The integration of humans into stage production must not be burdened by the tendency to moralize, nor by any . . . INDIVIDUAL PROBLEMATIC," Moholy-Nagy argued.[27] As if in response, the small playful objects at the Bauhaus—toys, essentially—grew to human size; their transformation accompanied a change in status, transforming Bauhauslers into their counterparts on stage. Despite borrowing conceptual authority from their Romantic antecedents, Bauhaus dolls—after the school's initial years—were not marionettes controlled by someone who, as Kleist had written, ideally "imagines himself at the puppet's center of gravity" to create "*the path of the dancer's soul*" in the movement of its limbs.[28] The Bauhaus director was now more likely to perform as a doll than to hold its strings behind the scenes. Creator and performer became theoretically interchangeable, dissolving the fundamental distinction between them that the traditional theater maintained both physically and conceptually. And, as performers took on the guise of passive objects, spectators—implicitly—were increasingly rendered their equals.

Unlike the puppet and marionette, the automaton—a machine figure operating as if human, without need of human assistance—more closely approximates the model of the Bauhaus doll. From the Renaissance to the late nineteenth century, automata had enchanted audiences throughout Europe with mechanical ingenuity and magical performances, demonstrating the wondrous qualities of the modern machine while confirming the mechanistic nature of the human body.[29] An automaton capable of reproducing a short sentence on a sheet of paper, made by Pierre-Jacquet Droze and Jean-Frédéric Leschot in 1773 and now in the collection of the Musée d'Art et d'Histoire in Neuchâtel, Switzerland, may be taken as representative. An astounding replica of human capabilities, it embodies a humanist conception of individuality: civilized, educated, and unique. In his book *Machine Man* of 1747, Julien Offray de La Mettrie described the activity of spectatorship as a physical reflex: "We take everything—gestures, accents, etc.—from those we live with in the same way as the eyelid blinks under the threat of a blow that is foreseen, or as the body of the spectator imitates mechanically, and despite himself, all the movements of a good mime."[30] Immersed in the performance, a spectator cannot resist imitating a performer's movements, even those of an inanimate automaton. Figuratively speaking, the relationship is reciprocal. Just as a spectator mimics the actions of the performer, the latter imitates its spectators, reflecting contemporaneous conceptions of what it means to be human.

"Automata represent the dream, the ideal form, the utopia of the machine," Jean-Claude Beaune has argued; "the gauge of their absolute perfection is their independence, which endows them from the first with an anthropomorphic or living quality."[31] Like the human model on which it was based, the automaton was essentially individualistic. A suggestion of technical replication combined with the magic of irreproduceability; both as a mechanical invention and as a human substitute, the measure of its success was its uniqueness. "It is often possible to discern some temptation toward group activity" within an automaton, Beaune allows, "but not yet to such an extent as to affect its insularity."[32] Individual performers in *Space Dance* and *Gesture Dance III*, stiff and machinelike, almost pass for overgrown, padded automata. But despite the morphological resemblance, the model of subjectivity they embody is very different: they belong implicitly within a group of identical creatures. Individual automata would seem to have continued to captivate the Weimar cultural imagination, exemplified, perhaps, by the character Maria in Fritz Lang's film *Metropolis*, released in early 1927; even she, as a prototype for later replicas ("we will put one in every factory!"), represents the wondrous potentials of serial production. So, too, does the *Steel R.U.R. Automaton* photographed in *Variétés* in 1928. The letters emblazoned across his chest stand for "Rossum's Universal Robots," in reference to the 1921 play of that title by Karel Čapek, who introduced the term *robot* in its pages.

By the 1920s, German stages were well prepared for such creatures. The weakened authority of narrative, the disappearance of bourgeois characters on view in the privacy of their own drawing rooms, and the dismantling of the invisible "fourth wall" dividing the stage and auditorium—all provided evidence of the demise of naturalism in the theater, as in literature and the visual arts.[33] In Germany and Russia, in particular, performances increasingly emphasized nonrepresentational movement; Schlemmer's *Gesture Dance III* may thus be seen to stand at the intersection of modern dance and theater as both art forms sought to abandon naturalism, and its attendant psychologist impulses, in favor of abstraction.[34] "The theater, the world of appearances, is digging its own grave when it tries for verisimilitude," Schlemmer asserted in 1922, citing Hoffmann and Kleist with approbation.[35] Moholy-Nagy also embraced theatrical abstraction. While commending the futurists, expressionists, and Dadaists for helping theater to overturn naturalism's "predominance of values based exclusively on logic and ideas," he criticized their reliance on figures based on subjective emotional effects and literary models, demanding instead that a new abstract human be developed for the stage.[36] Rather than resting at the top of the theatrical hierarchy, central to the activities on stage, this new model would remain, as he put it, "OF EQUAL VALUE TO THE OTHER CREATIVE MEANS."[37] Performers at the Bauhaus were to be rendered abstract both at the level of the individual figure and in groups; such traditional versions of the mechanized body as the automaton would be replaced with a new model, infinitely replicable and potentially universal.

Bauhaus dolls echoed the radical transfiguration of the human subject in early-twentieth-century Germany, when an emphasis on *Sachlichkeit,* or objectivity, joined the potentially universal "urge to abstraction" described by the young art historian Wilhelm Worringer in 1908.[38] Following World War I, *neue Sachlichkeit,* or new objectivity, delivered a new creature, one that has been termed posthumanist; drained of psychological autonomy, this Weimar subject—visible in such works as Raoul Hausmann's *The Engineers* of 1920—retained only a lingering pretense of humanist individuality.[39] With standardized clothing, bodies, and faces, the engineers present an image of studied efficiency and anonymous uniformity, an effect reinforced by the presence of a ruler and urban plan, as well as by the surrounding urban environment. Simultaneously spontaneous and mechanized, playful and unsettling, their forms increasingly abstract, Bauhaus dolls of this period likewise pass for posthumanist. "The sign of our times is *abstraction,*" Schlemmer himself declared in 1925, "which, on the one hand, functions to disconnect components from an existing whole, leading them individually *ad absurdum* or elevating them to their greatest potential, and, on the other, results in generalization and summation to create a new whole in bold outline."[40] Abstraction, in other words, helped dismantle a given object—such as the human body—into its constituent elements, rendering each one essentially useless or making it more purely and forcefully itself. At the same time, it provided a new standard in keeping with the new age.

Schlemmer's *Highly Simplified Head (Profile)* from the late 1920s indicates the extent of his fervor for pictorial abstraction. Reducing the head to two abstract components—a flat circle and a rectangle expanded to three dimensions—the drawing would seem to calculate their structural relation. It also posits a "new whole in bold outline," a radically new model of human subjectivity: devoid of psychology and emotion, absent of all signs of individual identity, it can be measured with the instruments of geometry and, in theory, infinitely reproduced by machine. For Schlemmer, this achievement was only to be admired. "Because the *abstraction* of the human form . . . creates an image in a higher sense," he maintained in 1930, "it does *not* create a *natural human being,* but an *artificial* one; it creates a *metaphor,* a *symbol* of human form."[41] This symbolic figure surpassed the limits of naturalism, providing an abstract, artificial model prepared for the challenges and delights of the posthumanist era. One suspects that some human dolls designed at the Bauhaus were inspired by the wooden figures

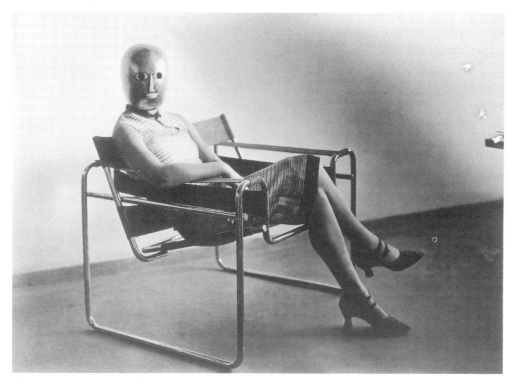

Figure 5.2. Erich Consemüller, photograph of a woman wearing a Schlemmer mask at the Dessau Bauhaus, 1925–26. Nachlass Erich Consemüller, Cologne, private collection. From Herzogenrath and Kraus, *Erich Consemüller,* Plate 1. Photograph copyright Bauhaus-Archiv, Berlin.

that were used in drawing classes in place of traditional nude models, as seen in a photograph taken around 1932 by Alfred Eisenstaedt of a Bauhaus drawing class. Looming over the five students gathered attentively below, the artificial figure appears, as it were, larger than life. Cause and effect are inextricable; given this image, it is little wonder the human doll would set the standard for human subjectivity.

A photograph by Consemüller from 1925–26 presents this new figure, the human doll, and exemplifies the impossibility of distinguishing Bauhaus life from performance, identity from anonymity (Figure 5.2). Stylishly dressed in the fashion of the day, a woman reclines in a tubular steel armchair designed by Marcel Breuer. The surrounding room is empty, with the floor beneath her and the wall behind her cleared of other objects as if she were placed on a bare stage in preparation for the photographic performance. Her dress, designed without curves, was made by Lis Beyer in the Bauhaus weaving workshop; her shoes epitomize elegance. Her head a Schlemmer mask, she gazes benignly, blankly, and directly at the camera. Her upper torso and head face the camera, but with her right elbow casually resting on the arm of the chair and her right leg crossed over the left—a strikingly modern pose—visual access to her body is impeded. Her Bauhaus environment has encased and absorbed her: chair, dress, head. She is clearly female, but her slim body, ovoid head, and the pared-down fashions of the Weimar New Woman all suggest androgyny, reproducing the effect of Schlemmer's padded dolls from the other side of the gender divide. She is in fact anonymous, now documented only as either Beyer herself or Ise Gropius, who was known to possess the dress.[42] That the figure cannot be identified, rather than detracting from the documentary value of the photograph, certifies a central feature of Bauhaus life: the defining presence of the doll, seemingly female, but androgynous and certainly anonymous.

Three photographs taken in the late 1920s illustrate the pronounced interest in androgyny at the Bauhaus. In one, two students—one male, one female—sport matching haircuts and spectacles; photographed from above, they are lying down with their heads angled toward each other, the tips of their cigarettes meeting in an ashy kiss (Figure 5.3). Boy and girl are almost identical; the modern habit of smoking links them physically and symbolically, marking the sexual spark between them like the "equal" sign in a mathematical equation. Another photograph, titled *Posierende Mädchen* (Girls Posing) and taken by Umbo (Otto Umbehr) in 1927, shows a row of four seated women, equally stylish from their haircuts to their shoes, sitting almost identically. Their heads slightly tilted and their hands almost on their hearts, they parody a cliché of maidenly sentimentality. Three of them cross their legs, but one does not—and the disparity, intentional or not, threatens to break down the machine of modern femininity.

Figure 5.3. Photograph of Gerhard Kadow and Else Franke, 1929. The J. Paul Getty Museum, Los Angeles.

The third photograph is a self-conscious self-portrait of pensive solitude from 1927 by Ise Gropius. Her hair also in a fashionable, mannish bob, she has used the reflections of a mirror to repeat her own image infinitely, as if internalizing the seriality of the posing women. At the Bauhaus as elsewhere in the Weimar Republic, the New Woman embraced *neue Sachlichkeit*.[43] Drained of psychological autonomy and individualism, she allowed the trappings of androgyny to transfer her from the realm of sexual reproduction to that of serial production.

The advent of *neue Sachlichkeit* and the birth of the posthumanist subject intensified the attention to doll figures while shifting the focus from individual replicas to figural groups. With the rise of the mass audience, and in conjunction with the emerging machine aesthetic, the individual body lost its value as the privileged site of human identity. It was replaced in the Weimar cultural imagination by the corporate body, a group entity comprising a set of identical forms operating mechanistically, in unison. The mechanical woman of the late nineteenth century had transmogrified into a larger performing machine, an elaborate configuration made up of mechanized female bodies. The urge to abstraction thus inspired the mass ornamental designs—chorus lines of identical creatures, almost always female—that Kracauer described as "indissoluble girl clusters whose movements are demonstrations of mathematics."[44] The new human dolls acquired their significance in groups, gaining identity by association; those who "consider themselves to be unique personalities with their own individual souls," Kracauer added, "fail when it comes to forming these new patterns."[45] Chorus lines sometimes provided a literal model for Bauhaus high jinks, as in a photograph taken by Irene Bayer in the mid-1920s (Figure 5.4). Fourteen male figures—all slender and boyish, all wearing bathing costumes, some with hats, the first (Xanti Schawinsky) holding aloft a woman's sun parasol—kick back their heels in an impressive, messy row. "One need only glance" at a chorus line, Kracauer believed, "to learn that the ornaments are composed of thousands of bodies, sexless bodies in bathing suits. The regularity of their patterns is cheered by the masses, themselves arranged by the stands in tier upon ordered tier."[46] Here, the spirited conflation of participation and performance faces the camera lens, that singular mechanical spectator standing in for the expanded photographic audience.

If the camera's presence could gather a group of people into a chorus line, photography as a medium likewise structured Bauhaus activities, inspiring a wide variety of experimental activity. Dolls cavorted on the exterior architecture of the Dessau Bauhaus as often as they appeared in its indoor theater. They perched on several levels of the building in *The Building as Stage,* for example, a photograph taken by Lux Feininger in 1927. Generally reproduced with the lowermost figure cropped from the image, the original photograph contains five human dolls, each one standing on its own architectural platform, while a sculpted head gazes blindly from the building's penultimate story.[47] Each figure, enclosed in its costume and holding aloft at least one large

Figure 5.4. Irene Bayer, *On the Beach at Mulde,* **1926–27. Bauhaus-Archiv, Berlin.**

and unwieldy prop, seems simultaneously expressive and speechless, communicative and dumb. Both on and off the stage, Bauhaus dolls proved remarkably photogenic, as seen in an image commemorating a performance of Schlemmer's *Triadic Ballet* at the Metropol Theater in Berlin in 1926. A visual cacophony of bulbous forms and geometric shapes encases the bodies of eight performers, suppressing their individual identities and personalities. Their limbs and torsos are held at awkward angles; their gestures seem to have been inspired by the movements of modern machinery. But the sense of functionalism is undermined both by their whimsical costumes and their careful arrangement before the camera, rather than in relation to one another. Compositionally attractive as a group, they are unconvincing as robots, or as a potential machine. Overall, the effect is one of uncontrollable exuberance, not rationalized efficiency.

The existential groundwork for these new figures had already been laid a decade earlier, in 1914, when Rainer Maria Rilke had articulated the viewer's ambivalent relation to the figure of the doll. "At a time when everyone still tried hard to answer us quickly and soothingly," he wrote,

> it, the doll, was the first to inflict on us that larger-than-life silence that later wafted over us again and again from space when somewhere we approached the frontiers of our existence. Across from it, while it stared at us, we first experienced (or am I mistaken?) that hollowness

of feeling, that heart pause, in which one would perish if the whole of gently persistent nature did not lift one, like a lifeless thing, over abysses.[48]

Owing to its extraordinary capacity to absorb empathy, Rilke writes, the doll is the first figure to impose on a child the experience of estrangement. Staring blankly, it offers a comforting presence while cruelly inflicting a silence both uncomprehending and incomprehensible. A pivotal figure in human development, the doll prefigures relationships with others and, subsequently and figuratively, with the spaces of architecture and the world. Its Bauhaus incarnations were similarly passive, but capable of provoking intense emotional responses. Their padded bodies and masked heads simultaneously endearing and alienating, they provided a sentimental education for their audience, encouraging both emotional engagement and the absence of feeling.

SPECTATORS

Rather than describing opposing models of subjectivity among spectators and the objects of their attention, empathy and estrangement exist on a theoretical continuum, each one implying the other's presence. Afforded their historical specificity, they connote more than generic attraction and repulsion; rather, they are embedded within several decades of discussion concerning the nature and function of the work of art and the aesthetic response it elicited. In 1873, the young German philosopher Robert Vischer explained that the viewer's body "unconsciously projects its own bodily form—and with this also the soul—into the form of the object," a process from which, he wrote, "I derived the notion that I call 'empathy,'" or *Einfühlung* (literally, the viewer's "feeling into" an object).[49] Over the following decades, empathy theory appeared within a range of disciplines, including aesthetic philosophy, perceptual psychology, and visual and architectural theory. Variously describing the perception of space and form, it presented aesthetic experience as an embodied vision that helped create the work of art. In 1961, Gropius evoked the concept, claiming that Schlemmer "experienced space not only through mere vision but with the whole body, with the sense of touch, of the dancer and the actor," before making the reference explicit: "With empathy, he would sense the directions and dynamics of a given space and make them integral parts of his mural compositions—as, for instance, in the Bauhaus buildings in Weimar."[50]

However, the process of aesthetic empathy undergone by Weimar audiences differed from that of the nineteenth-century spectator, whom theorists had treated as a solitary male viewer, his cultivated soul transported by a unique work of art within a tranquil environment. With the emergence of the modern mass audience and the newly developed media to which it attended—in particular, the cinema, which absorbed the attention of women as well as men—ideas about spectatorship and the construction of modern subjectivity underwent continual reconfiguration. By the early twentieth century, empathy had fallen from favor among psychologists and aesthetic theorists alike, owing partly to experimental research that found perceptual differences among its subjects. The concept was soon recoded as passive, describing an uncreative process of identification to which weak-willed audiences easily and happily succumbed. If the fully empathetic individual spectator of the nineteenth century had proved his profundity by "losing himself," as it were, in the privacy of his own home, the mass audience was now sometimes accused of empathizing too much. Benjamin would claim in 1936: "He who concentrates before the work of art becomes absorbed within it; he enters into this work. By contrast, the distracted mass absorbs the work of art into itself."[51] The absorption of the isolated individual, requiring time and erudition, was thought to lift the viewer to the nobler plane of art appreciation, while the masses—an undifferentiated group whose proletarian tastes inspired an aesthetic of reproducible objects—lowered the work of art to their own cultural level.

Concurrent with the advent of *neue Sachlichkeit* in the 1920s, the aesthetic experience of the mass audience came to be described more positively—to be valued, that is, as much for its capacity to induce critical thinking as for its radical political potential. Brecht's concept of *Verfremdung* (alienation or estrangement), for example, developed both theoretically and theatrically, interrupted sustained absorption to render the familiar strange and, in the process, to construct a spectator who was actively engaged intellectually.[52] Directly opposing the concept of estrangement in Brecht's schema, empathy represented a traditional, passive model of bourgeois spectatorship.[53] Where empathy encouraged emotional transport, estrangement prevented such passive spectatorship, maintaining the audience's critical awareness of its distance from the work of art. The intermittent use of estrangement, Brecht argued, was "necessary to avoid the intoxicating effects of illusion," to prevent the audience from becoming too absorbed by the aesthetic experience.[54] As he acknowledged in his journals, however, both techniques were necessary to achieve theatrical success.[55] Estrangement was impossible without the intermittent presence of empathy—as the dolls at the Bauhaus, of course, were well aware.

Moholy-Nagy's discussion of the mechanical stage figures of futurism, expressionism, and Dada reveals the extent to which the intertwined models of empathy and estrangement—identification and shock—were expressed and encouraged by the performing bodies of the 1920s. "The effect of this bodily mechanics," he wrote, "essentially lies in the spectator being astonished or startled by the possibilities of his own organism as demonstrated to him by others."[56] Reproducing the machine in human form, such robots replaced the bourgeois characters of the naturalist stage with mechanical creatures. But as literal representations of modern mechanization, he believed, they still relied on the traditional technique of empathy. Spectators would identify their own bodies with those on stage, recognizing their differences with a pleasant frisson of shock. By contrast, the figures he demanded (and that Schlemmer and others would design) represented posthumanism at a symbolic level. Rather than simply reflecting modern machines literally, through their forms, Bauhaus dolls absorbed them into their structures. They did so both individually, through gesture, and—more crucially—at the level of the group. Individual dolls could be invested with personality by empathetic viewers; gathered together in photographs or on the stage, they formed the quintessential objects of estrangement. Trained by dolls to understand their own posthuman potential, spectators learned to discard their individuality and join the mass audience.

Surrogates of human *Sachlichkeit* on stage faced the *sachlich* humans in the audience: mirror images so interchangeable as to render the orchestra pit almost obsolete. Benjamin, expert equally in allegorical drama and children's toys, went so far as to claim that, in the auditoriums of the Weimar Republic, "the abyss that separates the players from the audience like the dead from the living . . . has become functionless."[57] Kracauer, too, noted the trend, writing in 1926 that "the surface glamour of the stars, films, revues, and spectacular shows" in Berlin mirrored its viewers' shallow collective consciousness. "Here, in pure externality," he explained, "the audience encounters itself; its own reality is revealed in the fragmented sequence of splendid sense impressions."[58] Like Benjamin—but with an ambivalence that stemmed from his own appreciation of the movies—Kracauer opposed such effortless viewing habits to the intense absorption of the traditional spectator. He ascribed the change in spectatorship to a change in spectators themselves, citing especially the increased number of salaried workers, the growing presence of women in the workforce, and the exacerbation of capitalism's rationalizing impulses.[59] In Kracauer's view, women visiting the cinema on their evenings off work were particularly prone to the shallow pleasures and perils of distraction. "Furtively," he wrote with a combination of sympathy, snobbery, and sexism, "the little shopgirls wipe their eyes and quickly powder their noses before the lights go up" at the end of each film.[60] His opinions were prompted not only by actual changes in the composition of audiences but also by the widespread tendency, in the Weimar Republic as elsewhere, to treat mass culture as female—in its models of spectatorship no less than the objects of its attention.[61]

THE TRIADIC BALLET

Bauhaus performances occurred in a remarkable variety of venues, from the experimental stage of the Dessau building to its balconies and roofs, where students and masters cavorted before the camera both in and out of costume—or from the German National Theater in Weimar, where the *Triadic Ballet* appeared as the culminating event of the celebrations of Bauhaus week in August 1923, to the unbuilt designs for theaters for mass audiences. The *Triadic Ballet* nevertheless remains the production most often associated with the school; begun by Schlemmer in 1912 and first presented in full at the Landestheater in Stuttgart ten years later, the project was reincarnated several times

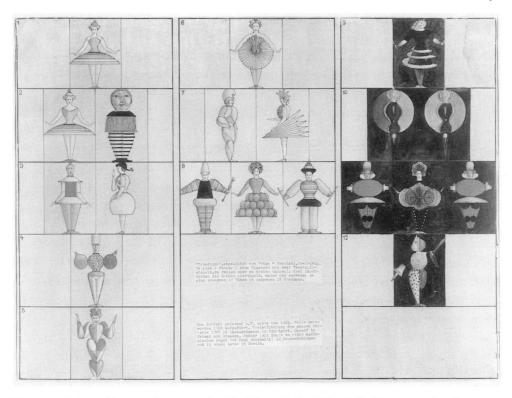

Figure 5.5. Oskar Schlemmer, figure plan for *The Triadic Ballet,* 1926. India ink, watercolor, zinc white, and bronze on paper. Harvard University Art Museums, Cambridge, Massachusetts. Copyright 2004 Bühnen Archiv Oskar Schlemmer / The Oskar Schlemmer Theatre Estate, IT – 28824 Oggebbio [VB], Italy.

over the course of the following decade to critical and popular acclaim. In addition to the Stuttgart and Weimar productions, others took place in Dresden, Donauschingen, Berlin, Frankfurt, and Paris, either as full-length performances or within larger revues.[62] Delighted by the favorable response, Schlemmer transcribed some reviews into his diary for further analysis.[63] "The Triadic Ballet," he explained in an essay of 1926, "which avoids being actually mechanical or actually grotesque and which avoids actual pathos and heroism by keeping to a certain harmonious mean, is part of a larger entity—a 'metaphysical revue'—to which the theoretical investigations and the actual work of the Bauhaus stage at Dessau are also related."[64] The absence at the Bauhaus of any strict demarcation between traditional theater performances and more general theatrical experimentation helps explain the presence of the work's costumes in a range of photographs unconnected to particular productions, with *The Building as Stage* offering only one of many examples.

Schlemmer laid out one version of the play's structure in a drawing of 1926, arranging the acts into columns, each divided horizontally into numbered scenes (Figure 5.5). The tripartite structure of the *Triadic Ballet*—performed by three dancers, two men and a woman—contained three acts with five, three, and four scenes, respectively. (This structure was variable; the three acts of the Weimar production in 1923, for example, contained six, three, and three scenes, respectively.) The three features of the ballet, according to Schlemmer, were "the costumes which are of a colored, three-dimensional design, the human figure which is an environment of basic mathematical shapes, and the corresponding movements of that figure in space."[65] He also considered the "fusion of the dance, the costumes, and the music" to operate triadically, an association perhaps more wisely ascribed to his own tendency to think in threes. In his plan, the characters appear either frontally or in profile, equal in height to the rectangles that contain them, which are painted yellow, white, and black according to the dominant color of each act. The fanciful, brightly colored costumes are composed of circles, spheres, triangles, and spirals; the padded forms with masks and hats appear inflatable. The symmetrical bodies seem no less abstract; stilted postures render limbs unlimber. Whimsical and awkward, the figures evoke marionettes, circus clowns, and the ultimate machine creatures of the 1920s.

Overall, the performance described the trajectory of dance history, leading from a relatively traditional dance in the first scene of the first act to a dance of pure movement in the last scene of the third act. It traveled, in other words, from naturalism to abstraction, its sequence of costumes proceeding from almost human to thoroughly artificial. The first scene was performed by a female dancer wearing a modified ballerina's tutu; the third-act finale, by a solitary creature who possessed a spiral for a chest, a face composed of three nonrepresentational forms (all sharing one eye), and outstretched arms that brandished the tip of a spear and a rounded stick. This last figure—whom Schlemmer labeled "the abstract"—exceeds the boundaries of its rectangle, as if breaking through the realm of representation at the end of the performance, into the world beyond.[66] An entire production of the *Triadic Ballet* thus appears within a grid; each row depicts, at a glance, the characters, costumes, and background color of each scene, with intermissions occurring, as it were, between the columns.

Beyond its utilitarian function, the design of the drawing is doubly significant at the level of its structure. First, rather than providing traditional diagrams of stage blocking—aerial views of the characters on stage—the rectangular images present frontal views in a vertical sequence; individual scenes are legible from top to bottom. Using traditional artistic mediums (ink and watercolor on paper), in other words, the depiction operates like three reels of film, evoking what was at the time the most technically advanced form of visual representation. The affinity of Bauhaus dolls for photography is here set in motion; if these abstracted figures were to feel at home in any context, it might well be that of the cinema, the exalted medium of the age of mechanical reproducibility. Shadow puppets of the machine age, they embody the existential shallowness of celluloid modernity. At the same time, they appear fundamentally incapable of feeling "at home" anywhere, exuding instead a sense of the uncanny articulated by Freud in 1919. "The uncanny [*Unheimlich*] is that class of the frightening which leads back to what is known of old and long familiar," Freud argued, describing the doubled sensation of familiarity and strangeness.[67] Adorably animistic and uncomfortably inhuman, eerily charming, the dancing Weimar bodies of Schlemmer's drawing offer, simultaneously, the familiar playfulness of dolls and the sinister hollowness of mechanical creatures.

The logic of the film strip operates in tandem with a second structural feature of Schlemmer's drawing, which not only re-creates human bodies as dolls in the individual depictions, but also reproduces this new creature at another scale. The first and third acts form larger figures, their bodies outlined by the colored backgrounds of the individual scenes. A yellow figure at the left, the height of the page itself, stands to attention with its arms at its sides: its head consists of the dancer in the first scene, its torso a perfect rectangle of four figures, and its legs the two soloists of the act's final scenes. The black figure at the right, meanwhile, four rectangles high, possesses a head and feet of equal size and a triangular body in between, with two identical dancers surmounting three more standing symmetrically below. Read in this way, the ballet's first and third acts form the bodies of, respectively, a man and a woman. He stands like a rectangular robot. She has breasts formed by the halos behind the upper bodies of the two dancers in scene 2; the metal winding in spirals around the female dancer at the center of scene 3—the "wire figure"—suggests pubic hair above the dotted lines that delineate, simultaneously, her legs and the crotch of the larger figure. Viewed in this context, the little dolls in each scene may be considered ideal participants in the mass ornamental forms that, as Kracauer wrote, "are never performed by the fully preserved bodies, whose contortions are the smallest component parts of the composition."[68] Between the yellow man and the black woman, meanwhile, the scenes of the second act (with one, two, and three dancers, respectively) together form an equilateral triangle, a visual triad symbolizing the ballet's overall schema. Below this platonic shape are glued two paragraphs of typed text: notes on the ballet's formal components and performance history.[69]

In Stuttgart in 1922, Schlemmer played one of the parts of the *Triadic Ballet*; Albert Burger and Elsa Hötzel, partners in dance as in marriage who had appeared together in the ballet before, filled the two main roles. A photograph shows the two performing the third dance in the first act, a duet accompanied by the music of Marco Enrico Bossi. Their feet turned out in classic ballet position, their expressions stark like those of pantomime figures, and their arms gesticulating woodenly, Burger and Hötzel are formally linked, but do not seem to interact. In their polka-dotted, bulbous, or cylindrical costumes, they are uncanny but appealing, human yet mechanical; they are simultaneously dolls reconceived in human size and humans re-created as dolls. A confusion over gender parallels that of scale: if it is initially unclear in Schlemmer's diagram that the cylindrical figure is male and the spherical one female (their genders are reversed from the previous scene), the photograph is easily legible, but the male dancer nevertheless wears something akin to a tutu both around his waist and around his neck. The gender ambiguity is significant; in his diary that year Schlemmer registered his approval for the use of masks and his nostalgia for the use of men to represent women on stage. "Dates that historians consider high points," he wrote, "should rather be called declines: 1681, the first appearance of female dancers—until then female roles had been performed by men. 1772, the abolition of face masks."[70]

COSTUME PARTIES AND THE TOTAL WORK OF ART

"Today the arts exist in isolation," Gropius proclaimed in 1919 in the initial Bauhaus program; he found this a regrettable condition, "from which they can be rescued only through the conscious, cooperative effort of all craftsmen."[71] To idealize the unification of all the arts in early-twentieth-century Germany was almost a cultural cliché, heavily indebted to Richard Wagner's formulation of the *Gesamtkunstwerk,* the exalted total work of art. "The highest shared artwork is the *Drama,*" the composer had declared seven decades earlier; "true Drama is only conceivable as emerging from the *shared urge on the part of all the arts* toward the most direct communication to a shared *public.*"[72] One might draw a parallel between this unification of the arts and the way in which the umbrella structure of the general introductory course at the Bauhaus sheltered the specialized training of students within particular workshops.[73] "Together, let us desire, conceive, and create the new structure of the future," Gropius entreated, echoing the composer's formulation of "the artwork of the future" from his essay of that title.[74]

Wagnerian echoes overlapped with those of the composer's erstwhile disciple, Friedrich Nietzsche, whose importance for artistic thinking in Germany in the early twentieth century (and particularly in Weimar, where his archives were located) was unrivaled. As Count Harry Graf Kessler, one of the city's leading cultural figures, stated categorically, "The way in which Nietzsche influenced, or more precisely possessed, us cannot be compared with the effect of any other contemporary figure or poet."[75] By 1919, the creative, internationalist idol of prewar Germany had become a cult figure of right-wing nationalism, but pan-Nietzschean sentiments continued to captivate Germans across the political spectrum. A romantic Nietzscheanism lurked at the Weimar Bauhaus, inhabiting the souls of its artistically inclined idealists.[76] Gropius, no exception to this tendency, advocated the "mutual planning of extensive, Utopian structural designs—public buildings and buildings for worship—aimed at the future," but he posited churches, not theaters, as the communally constructed buildings that would incorporate all forms of art. Omitting both theater architecture and such subsidiary arts as costume and set design, stage decor painting, and the making of props, the program mentioned performance only in the context of extracurricular entertainment.

"Encouragement of friendly relations between masters and students outside of work," it noted; "therefore plays, lectures, poetry, music, costume parties."

Exactly as Gropius decreed, theatrical events ranging from plays to costume parties, from organized fetes to spontaneous festivities, operated as essential binding agents for social life at the Bauhaus. "We worked on them as if obsessed," Felix Klee later recalled; "Oskar Schlemmer presented his stage plays especially for them. On May 18 we celebrated Walter Gropius's birthday. Every year was the traditional lantern party."[77] Wassily Kandinsky's acquisition of German citizenship in early 1928 provided another occasion for a celebration, which he attended wearing traditional German lederhosen. Parties dissolved the boundaries between spectators and performers, with all in attendance taking part in the larger spectacle. At a professional level, they provided innumerable opportunities for the design of invitations, posters, costumes, and room interiors, as well as for performances by various Bauhaus groups.[78] One of the most famous of these was the Beard, Nose, and Heart Party, organized by the Bauhaus band and held in Berlin on 31 March 1928—coincidentally, Gropius's last day as director—with invitations designed by Herbert Bayer. As a fund-raiser for the Bauhaus with an entrance fee of ten marks (half-price for art students), the event featured performances by the Bauhaus Theater group.

A photograph by Umbo is thought to depict two revelers at this Bauhaus party: two identical clowns wearing jackets and ties and sporting dark painted mustaches and metallic beards, eyebrows, noses, and thick, curly hair (Figure 5.6). While one stares intently at the viewer, the other, identical save for the addition of a pair of spectacles, appears in profile, gazing with equal seriousness to the left; together they seem to present the front and side views of the same party specimen.[79] The funnels perched upside down on their heads seem to bear a functional relation to the long tubes, held in their mouths like straws, that cross each other before disappearing over what appears to be the figures' shared shoulder—possibly to reappear at the tops of their funnels. Their heads held close, their bodies appear to merge, while the tubes and funnels share a delightful mechanical uselessness. Despite an absence of background detail, one senses the event's overlapping sounds, swirling movements, and multitude of other guests; emerging from the darkness with the blurred clarity of an alcoholic gaze, the two revelers embody a deadpan glee. Bodily interference—the clown tripping over his feet, the prankster falling from his chair—infused Bauhaus parties, accompanied by musical bands, dancing, recitations, and general merriment.[80] Under their funnels, the two revelers seem prime candidates for the happy irritation produced by their own bodies; nothing would appear to please them more than the prospect of tripping over their own feet.

Except, perhaps, for the possibility of tripping over each other's feet—and, the photograph suggests, these two revelers might not even register the difference. Identically dressed and decorated, they are mimetically twinned like mirror images in a carnival

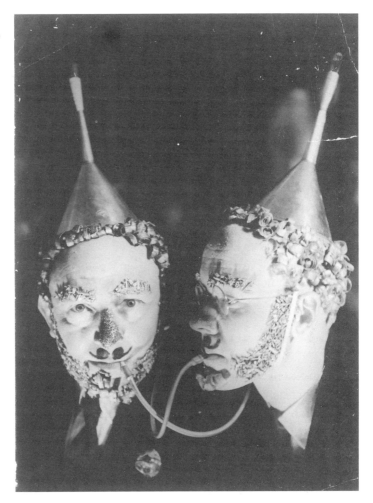

funhouse, their doubled presence destroying any sense of individuality. Encrustations of face paint render their faces as masks, devoid of the outward manifestations of human personality. With identical poise, they reflect each other on either side of the photograph; the crossed tubes emanating from their mouths mark a hinge between them. While the figure on the left stares directly at the camera, and at the viewer, his twin presents a more ambiguous gaze. If he is staring into the distance, then the two look past each other, peering at cross-purposes: a face and profile exemplifying serious silliness. If, however, he stares at his partner, then the viewer is incorporated into a triangular *mise-en-abîme* of clown vision, a construction of gazes interrupted only by the viewer's doubling back to return the gaze of the figure on the left. The viewer—perhaps on the verge of sensing an inverted funnel atop his or her own head—might well suppose that the crowd of partygoers outside the frame contains more copies from the same mold: an assembly line of identical clowns in formal attire, purposefully sipping from useless straws. Here, as elsewhere, theatrical exuberance at the Bauhaus is undermined by uncanny repetition.

Although probably taken in 1928, the photograph could also depict the infamous Metallic Party held in Dessau early the following year. Originally titled the Church Bells, Doorbells, and Other Bells Party, this event was renamed, it is said, in an effort to keep the noise level down. Guests came attired in metallic objects of all kinds, from tin foil to frying pans. They entered the party by sliding down a large chute that deposited them in the first of several rooms decorated for the occasion. An anonymous report printed in a local newspaper several days later described the event's delightful confusion:

> And then there was music in the air everywhere, and everything was glitter wherever one turned. The rooms and studios of two floors, which normally are used for serious work, had been decorated with the greatest variety of forms placed together all over the walls, shinily metallic and fairy-like, the ceilings hung with bizarre paper configurations. . . . In addition music, bells, tinkling cymbals everywhere, in every room, in the stairways, wherever one went.[81]

With breathless syntax, the text reproduces the sense of exhilaration fostered by the party's carnival atmosphere, as musical bands played in competition with one another while other sounds, less easily categorized, wafted through the Bauhaus air. The Metallic Party also featured more traditional performances in the building's auditorium, where, the newspaper reported, "a gay farrago of film pictures alternated with various stage presentations."[82]

Such theatricality manifested itself both in formal performances and in the guise of general exuberance. "One does not want simply to see the play on the stage, but to perform the play oneself," Karl Friedrich Schinkel—perhaps Germany's most famous theater architect—had declared in 1810.[83] Reciprocity between spectator and performance, a trope of theater discourse increasingly prevalent after 1900, was explored explicitly at the Bauhaus. Bemoaning the structural and symbolic "isolation of the stage," for example, Moholy-Nagy stated:

> In today's theater, STAGE AND SPECTATOR are separated too much from each other, divided too much into active and passive, for creative relationships and tensions to be produced between them. An activity must be developed that does not let the masses watch silently, that does not simply excite them inwardly, but that instead lets them take hold of, participate in, and—at the highest level of a redemptive ecstasy—merge with the action on stage.[84]

The aesthetic response was not meant to occur too far beyond the limits of spectators' bodies; rather, performances would inspire a seated audience to a cathartic communal surge of emotion, an active but relatively contained experience. These efforts would

Figure 5.7. Erich Consemüller, photograph of Werner Siedhoff, Oskar Schlemmer, and Andreas Weininger on the Dessau Bauhaus stage, 1927. Nachlass Erich Consemüller, Cologne, private collection. From Herzogenrath and Kraus, *Erich Consemüller,* Plate 118.

be especially encouraged by the designs for three Bauhaus theaters: Farkas Molnár's U-Theater, seating 1,590; the Spherical Theater of Andreas Weininger; and Gropius's Total Theater of 1926, a 2,000-seat amphitheater intended for the productions of Erwin Piscator.[85] This last structure was to contain neither private boxes nor other architectural subdivisions, such as aisles, to divide the audience hierarchically.

Within the Dessau auditorium, 164 steel-frame tubular chairs designed by Breuer, with folding canvas seats, formed a unified block of spectators: eight identical rows of 19 chairs preceded a back row comprising 12 chairs that flanked the room's wide entryway. Designed to present both lectures and more elaborate stage performances, and raked very gently to improve sight lines, the room expressed the *sachlich* ideals of practicality and functionalism with a block of seats awaiting a block of identical spectators.[86] As in Gropius's Total Theater, designed the same year, the unity of the audience is emphasized. No spatial or architectural elements subdivide the spectators, whose identity as a group—and reciprocal relationship with the posthumanist performers—is thereby encouraged.[87] A photograph by Consemüller, taken one year earlier from the back of this auditorium, appears to show a rehearsal in progress (Figure 5.7). At the center, Schlemmer perches in profile on a set of three steps. With his right hand, he gestures at the dancer Siedhoff, who stands on a wooden platform at left in a Schlemmer doll outfit, mask in hand, and leans against another structure. The relationship of the audience to the stage is thus reproduced within the photograph, as Schlemmer observes

BAUHAUS THEATER OF HUMAN DOLLS **113**

Siedhoff's performance and the two Breuer stools between them evoke the more comfortable seats in the auditorium. Revealed in the wings on the right, Andreas Weininger, clothed in worker's coveralls, directs a movie camera out the window, toward the building's terrace. An unidentified man plays the grand piano in the auditorium at right, while another stands at the center, watching the scene from the canteen behind the stage, its floor level with the stage. Another figure lurks at the left: its body a padded Schlemmer costume hung from a giant ladder, its head resting on the steps below. Hardly a spontaneous rehearsal image, the photograph presents the Bauhaus theater as *Gesamtkunstwerk:* music, dance, film, stage direction, spectatorship, and a decapitated Bauhaus doll gather together on the stage, poised equally for the camera.

Creatures simultaneously without affect and fully invested with personality performed on a range of Bauhaus stages, occupied its auditoriums, celebrated at its costume parties, and clambered over its architecture to be captured by its cameras. Seven decades earlier, Wagner had imagined the following ideal scene at the theater:

> The spectator completely transports himself on to the stage by looking and hearing; the performer becomes an artist only by complete absorption into the audience; the audience, that representative of public life, disappears from the auditorium . . . . It lives and breathes now only in the work of art, which seems to it life itself, and on the stage, which seems to be the whole world.[88]

In the 1920s, the Bauhaus theater aimed at something similar. Complete identification would transpire between performers and spectators; the auditorium walls would fall away to reveal the entire world as the ultimate Bauhaus stage. But such developments ultimately depended on the receptivity of its audience, in Schlemmer's eyes. "It begins with building the new house of the stage out of glass, metal, and tomorrow's inventions," he maintained in 1925. "But it also begins with the spectator's inner transformation."[89] Recognizing themselves in the Bauhaus dolls, Weimar spectators experienced a communal heart pause worthy of Rilke as all of nature lifted them, like lifeless things, across the abyss of modernity itself.

UTOPIA FOR SALE

THE BAUHAUS AND WEIMAR GERMANY'S CONSUMER CULTURE

6

Frederic J. Schwartz

The utopias of the Bauhaus were numerous and varied. From the dream of a new community centered on building "cathedrals of socialism"[1] to the search for an expressionist "new man"; from the goal of uniting "art and technics"[2] by producing well-designed goods for the modern mass to the attempt to "put life in order":[3] many of these projects have come to be emblematic of the interwar avant-garde.

And yet these utopias found no lasting home in Weimar Germany. This fact is due, say some, to political opposition to the school's aims, bureaucratic sabotage, or public hostility to its aesthetics or ideologies. Others point to the contradiction of trying to reform a culture without transforming its social base, the absurdity of a social vision that is at its core aesthetic, the fraught and slippery relation of art and politics. In this essay, however, I would like to ask more modest but more specific questions about the difficulties faced by this most famous "crucible of modernity,"[4] leaving to one side the question of whether its project was hopelessly utopian, simply technocratic, or a cynical acceptance of capitalist industry. What happened to the Bauhaus when its products went beyond the world of "theory" and discursive debate and confronted the real, non-utopian capitalist economy that actually existed in Weimar Germany? How did these objects, with their geometric clarity and rigor, fare as commodities on the open market? Indeed, did they ever get there? To answer these questions, so long unposed, we must look at some forgotten but fateful episodes in the history of the Bauhaus that show its confrontation with the capitalist consumer culture of Weimar Germany. These events amount to the misadventure of utopia on the market.

BAUHAUS STYLE

Was there a "Bauhaus style"? During the "classic" period of the Bauhaus—from the turn to constructivism and industry around 1922–23 to the departure of Walter Gropius and László Moholy-Nagy in 1928—the existence of such a style was routinely denied. In a text published in the 1926 Bauhaus book *New Products of the Bauhaus Workshops* and separately as a prospectus, Gropius describes what he calls "Principles of Bauhaus Production." The design criteria are decisively technical, and not artistic:

[T]he Bauhaus is seeking—by systematic practical and theoretical research into formal, technical, and economic fields—to derive the design of an object from its natural functions and relationships. . . .

An object is defined by its nature. In order, then, to design it to function correctly—a container, a chair, or a house—one must first of all study its nature; for it must serve its purpose perfectly, that is, it must fulfill its function usefully, be durable, economical, and "beautiful."[5]

Specifically, he calls for:

A resolute affirmation of the living environment of machines and vehicles
The organic design of things based on their own present-day laws . . .
The limitation to characteristic, primary forms and colors . . .
[E]conomical utilization of space, material, time, and money.[6]

With his quotation marks around the word *beautiful,* Gropius distances himself from aesthetic concerns; and with his invocation of objects' "laws" and the goal of designing "correctly," he removes the task of design from the realm of taste. Marcel Breuer, whose tubular steel furniture remains to this day perhaps the very symbol of this phase of the institution, was even more direct in his denial of stylistic concerns: "metal furniture is a part of modern [interior] space. it is "styleless," for it should exhibit only its function and the necessary construction, and otherwise no intentional composition."[7]

Few today would concur with the Bauhaus's own claims for the design process followed and its transparency to functional and constructional concerns. In the famous lamp designed by Karl Jucker and Wilhelm Wagenfeld (Figure 6.1), it is easy enough to see the inspiration of Moholy-Nagy's paintings: lamp and canvas share the concern with transparency and translucency, with the intersection and interpenetration of circles and ruled lines, with the sharp edge and the renunciation of the artist's hand. In the way it suspends the sitter in a three-dimensional rectilinear grid, Breuer's "Wassily" armchair is clearly a cognate of Gerrit Rietveld's De Stijl chairs; similarly, its bewildering array of delicate parallels and right angles recalls the Prouns of El Lissitzky, while its carefully delineated intersection of two cubes in space is hardly unrelated to the experiments of the suprematists. However, my point is not the undeniable existence of an a priori formal idiom or the extent to which it is justified. I want to look instead at how the very popularity and easy recognition of this idiom came to play a role in the history of its namesake.

In the popular parlance of the Weimar period, the word *Bauhaus* did not necessarily refer only to the institution itself but to the tendency of which it became emblematic. In the popular press—whose illustrated pages came to be the surfaces across which images circulated with an unprecedented speed and in unprecedented numbers—the first contact most readers had with the developments of the avant-garde was almost certainly in the highly publicized reports about the political battles over the Bauhaus—

gesch.
Höhe ca. 35 cm
AUSFÜHRUNG
Messing vernickelt, Glasschirm, Zugfassung

ME 2

TISCHLAMPE AUS METALL

VORTEILE
1 beste Lichtzerstreuung (genau erprobt) mit Jenaer Schottglas
2 sehr stabil
3 einfachste, gefällige Form
4 praktisch für Schreibtisch, Nachttisch usw.
5 Glocke festgeschraubt, bleibt in jeder Lage unbeweglich

Metallwerkstatt

its exhibition of 1923, its expulsion from Weimar, the move to its stunning new building in Dessau, and so on. Gropius had, without a doubt, an eye and ear for publicity; and his position as head of the first government-sanctioned bastion of artistic modernism in Germany made him both the most obvious target for the many opponents of the avant-garde and a cause célèbre for its supporters. The Bauhaus was, in any case, a major focus of attention when it came to progressive ideals and modern artistic developments. In its highly visible and controversial period during the so-called stabilization phase of the Weimar Republic, the term Bauhaus came to be synonymous with tendencies we now recognize as larger than the single school, tendencies usually called New Objectivity (*neue Sachlichkeit*) in design and New Building (*neues Bauen*) in architecture. This is the balance drawn by Ernst Kállai, editor of the school's in-house newspaper, in an article of 1930: "Houses and even whole housing settlements are being built everywhere—all with smooth white walls, horizontal rows of windows, spacious terraces, and flat roofs. The public accepts them, if not always with great enthusiasm, at least without opposition, as the products of an already familiar 'Bauhaus style.'"[8]

The notion of the "Bauhaus," however, was stretched, distended, and distorted beyond the scope of the avant-garde, further clouding the issue of whether we can talk of a Bauhaus style The problem was the presence of imitations, objects that were labeled by their manufacturers or retailers "Bauhaus" but that represent counterfeits, cheaper versions, surrogates, perhaps even sincere attempts to emulate the products of the school. All of them traded on the tendency to be identified with the school of that name. Kállai, again:

> Today everyone's clued in. Houses with glass and gleaming metal: Bauhaus style. The same goes for hygienic homes without home atmosphere: Bauhaus style. Tubular steel armchair frames: Bauhaus style. Lamp with nickel-plated base and a matte glass shade: Bauhaus style. Wallpaper with cubes: Bauhaus style. No picture on the wall: Bauhaus style. Picture on the wall, but what does it mean? Bauhaus style. Printing with bold rules and sans serif letters: Bauhaus style. everything in lowercase: bauhaus style. EVERYTHING IN CAPITAL LETTERS: BAUHAUS STYLE.
>
> Bauhaus style: one word for everything.[9]

A particular source of concern was a marketing ploy used by Wertheim, a fashionable Berlin department store that set up a furniture department and used the word Bauhaus as a draw (whether they sold the properly produced or licensed products remains unclear).[10] Other businesses that trafficked illicitly with the name were instead cause for amusement. A clipping from the Viennese journal *Woman's World* circulated through the school in 1928: "'Bauhaus style' is what one calls the geometric decoration on modern bed linen, a contrast to the somewhat fluffy flower, tendril, and garland motifs that the modern woman quite properly considers old-fashioned."[11] "Bauhaus is a fashion," despaired Hannes Meyer in a lecture of 1929. "All the ladies at the cocktail parties chatter about Bauhaus constructivism. Their calling cards are in lowercase letters."[12]

Imitation is, of course, the sincerest form of flattery, and the matter had its comic side. But the presence of surrogates, imitations, and counterfeits was much more, and much more pernicious, than a mere confusion of categories or a crudeness of classification. It was dangerous to the school in two ways. First, the administration of the school could not prevent the production of imitations that traded on and diluted the hard work and daring innovations of its students and masters (more on this later). Second, because of their fame, they ended up bearing responsibility for the "high-fashion kitsch"[13] associated with them. In the area of popular opinion, in a sector of culture not self-policed by the connoisseurs of the higher market niches, the presence of what many referred to—incorrectly—as a "Bauhaus style" represented a force beyond control of the institution that bore the name.

There is, in other words, no denying the existence of a Bauhaus style, even if it had only a very tenuous connection with the school of that name. The reader of the popular press thought there was one, the department stores capitalized on its attractions, women bought their cheap underwear and bed linen thinking they were modern because of the name. "Let us keep the slogan 'Bauhaus style,' since it has already become a household word, even where it is no more than a cover for a corruption of originally more sincere intentions," wrote Kállai in resignation; but he adds, "With all due respect to the difference between these intentions and the commercialization of the Berlin Broadway."[14]

"Berlin Broadway": the reference is to the United States, a society seemingly without the roots of old cultural forms, where the representations appearing on the mass market, in what Max Horkheimer and Theodor W. Adorno called the "culture industry," represented for many the only native culture available.[15] By the first decade of the twentieth century the market and the popular press that manifested the rapidly accelerating commodification of word and image in this stage of modernity, the drafting of an increasing proportion of signs into the service of sales, had reached Germany. The market may have been wrong: what was regularly referred to as Bauhaus was most likely to be derivative, imitative, lower in quality, and designed without a real understanding of avant-garde developments. But authentic or not, the motley and unruly set of images, objects, and environments so thoughtlessly labeled Bauhaus style was a functioning reference point, a very real fact in the popular imagination of Weimar Germany; and this imagination was one formed in the chaotic and expanding market for consumer goods, commodified information, and commercialized entertainment.

ADVERTISING AND COMMERCE

At some level, then, the design principles of the avant-garde—white walls and flat roofs; glass and chrome steel; geometry, impersonality, and precision—caught on. In the face of developments controversial yet esoteric, the dynamic of commercial publicity and public opinion produced some widespread and crude oversimplifications; a better way of putting it is that it generated a sort of shorthand that identified many of the more bewildering and exciting tendencies of artistic innovation with the two simple syllables—the compelling neologism Bauhaus—most often associated with them. This need not have been so disturbing a state of affairs. We need to ask why the victory in the battle for the public eye and favor was a pyrrhic one, precisely why the Bauhaus's relation with the mass market through which industrial goods were distributed and exchanged was so strained.

For the Bauhaus could hardly be said to be in any way opposed or hostile to the mass market for consumer goods. In the tradition of the reform movements from art nouveau to the German Werkbund, those affiliated with the school rejected much of what they found there, but their goal was, arguably even more than that of their predecessors', to reform the look of the products offered consumers and not so much the system itself (the consumer sector of a highly developed capitalist economy) through which these goods were offered. Generalizations are risky here. The Bauhaus was a complex institution, and the shifting, manifold political positions represented there cannot be summarized or elided. Certainly the school started in a mood and mode that would have to be termed expressionist anticapitalism. Its second director, Hannes Meyer, was a committed socialist, one more interested in providing good products to those with little disposable income than in producing luxury items with a high profit margin. And many of the projects associated with the school and its avant-garde circuit were placed in the service of local Social Democratic authorities in order to provide public housing that would circumvent capitalist real estate speculation. But regardless of this radical or left-wing cachet, it is abundantly clear that in the years following the turn to "art and technics," the Bauhaus was as much implicated in consumer capitalism as it was its victim. It sought an alliance with industry; it was willing to work within the system, not outside or against it; it sought to use the everyday object and the market through which it moved as a site of cultural intervention, the consumer commodity as a vehicle for a utopia that was usually aesthetically and not politically or economically defined. However high flown the rhetoric or uncompromising the pose, the Bauhaus was in no way an ivory tower.

The story of the attempt to cooperate with industry in the development of prototypes for mass production is often told. It is worth noting, however, that those at the school were, in various ways, thinking hard about the role of visual form in a modern economy beyond the realm of industry, production, or "technics." They knew that everyday objects in an industrial economy were not only *produced* and *consumed* but also had to move through a system of *distribution* and *exchange*—the unruly realm of commerce. The history of the Bauhaus shows not only an awareness of this fact but often excitement about it, and occasionally even sophistication in dealing with it. Bauhauslers learned from the sphere of commercialized mass culture, and they saw it as an area in which they could make their mark.

This becomes clearest when one considers the steady and intense involvement of various Bauhaus figures and studios with the task of advertising. Herbert Bayer's 1924 photomontage designs for kiosks and exhibition stands are certainly an instance of the impact of De Stijl, with their primary colors, shifting planes, and strict rectilinearity, but it is clear that they respond as much to Dada's delight in the chaotic storms of commercialized text and image in the modern metropolis as to the architectonic rigors of international constructivism (Figures 6.2 and 6.3). One shows the sales window's array of newspaper titles as a photomontage, each title cut out from the front page and standing literally for itself; the right side wall is a full-blown, if carefully ordered, Dadaist work combining kitsch images of beauty, a cubist violin ironically whole, the hyperbolic claims of unspecified products, and intimate testimonials for various patent medicines. There are even flashing lightbulbs in the light box above the giant arrow pointing to the sales window. A cigarette pavilion from the same series flirts with the absurd: it shows a towering "P," fifty feet in height, illuminated with lightbulbs—undoubtedly a reference to a brand name—with an equally monumental cigarette beside, its smoke revealing its literal three-dimensionality. The absurd, however, was a trick not only of the avant-

Figure 6.2. Herbert Bayer, design for a newsstand, 1924. Tempera and collage. Bauhaus-Archiv, Berlin. Photograph by Hermann Kiessling.

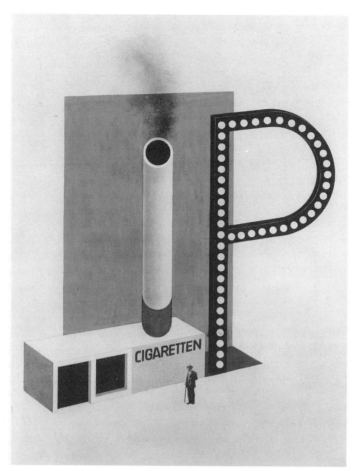

Figure 6.3. Herbert Bayer, design for a sales and advertising kiosk for a cigarette brand, 1924. Watercolor, tempera, and collage. Bauhaus-Archiv, Berlin. Photograph by Hermann Kiessling. Copyright 2005 Artists Rights Society (ARS), New York / VG Bild-Kunst, Bonn.

garde but also of the attention-grabbing techniques of advertisers, and the giant smoking cigarette was not just a flight of fancy. In fact, it resembles closely the sort of advertising pavilions erected in the trade fairs of the time.[16] It also uncannily echoes a passage from Erich Kästner's novel *Fabian,* a satirical account of an intellectual's fall from grace—from university to advertising copy writing (and then to unemployment). Here is an episode from his work at the advertising agency:

> "I still have to work on the text for the photomontage posters," said Fabian. . . .
> Fabian unrolled a poster and pinned it to the wall. He stood in the far corner of the room and stared at it—a photograph of Cologne Cathedral and, put next to it by the maker of the poster, a cigarette just as large.[17]

As an example of advertising practice, Bayer's pavilion might well have been Kästner's inspiration: the design was reproduced in the advertising journal *Gebrauchsgraphik*

(Applied Graphics), where professionals of the field (like the fictional Fabian) would have seen it.[18]

Affinities and involvement with the advertising trade were neither coincidental nor accidental, for advertising was, in many ways, central to the activities of the Bauhaus. The way printing was taught at the school shows this clearly. In Weimar, the craft aspect gave this part of the curriculum its name: it was called the "print workshop." Its activities were various, including the printing necessary for use within the school, but also, especially in the early years, art printing (woodcuts, etching, original lithographs). With the move to Dessau, the studio was renamed the "print and advertising workshop" and began to concentrate more on assignments of the type usually carried out by commercial printers.[19] Their products and assignments show books, leaflets, posters, and other kinds of job printing. In 1927, the "advertising department" became, along with architecture, theater, and free painting/sculpture, one of the four major areas in which instruction was offered.[20] In the Hannes Meyer era, this instruction included lectures on economics and advertising psychology. Of the leaders of the print and advertising studio (Moholy-Nagy, 1923–25; Bayer, 1925–28; Joost Schmidt, 1928–32), only Schmidt did not go on to have an important career in advertising.[21] The Bauhaus's profile in the professional world of advertising was high, and in 1927 the school hosted a major conference under the auspices of the Association of German Professional Advertisers.[22] If the Bauhaus started out offering instruction in the craft of the artistic print, it ended giving professional education in the field of advertising.

The products of the advertising studio are significant in many ways. The brochures and posters of the studio were widely distributed, and the series of Bauhaus books came to represent a small but prestigious library of the contemporary avant-garde, including works by not only Gropius, Moholy-Nagy, Paul Klee, and Wassily Kandinsky but also Piet Mondrian, Theo van Doesburg, Kazimir Malevich, J. J. P. Oud, and Albert Gleizes. More important, perhaps, the *style* in which books, brochures, posters, and handbills were printed was distinctive, influential, and widely imitated—another example of the "Bauhaus style." Along with the work of Jan Tschichold, Johannes Molzahn, and El Lissitzky, the work of the Bauhaus advertising workshop under Moholy-Nagy, Bayer, and Schmidt was a center of innovation in the realm of typography. The Bauhaus and the other so-called New Typographers pioneered the exclusive use of sans serif letters; and following the contemporary reforms suggested by Wilhelm Porstmann, they often printed in lowercase only, the rationale being that the need to use two separate alphabets—upper- and lowercase—represented needless and uneconomical duplication and extra labor.[23]

The very appearance of the "Bauhaus" typographic style was novel and unforgettable. Writing in a special Bauhaus issue of the printers' journal *Offset* in 1926, Josef Albers summed up the principles of the New Typography. He stressed the need to read *quickly*—on the move, in a train, tram, or automobile. Instead of the "running type of uniformly placed elements, corresponding to running speech," and which he equated with old-fashioned, "epic" language, Albers invoked the current demand for the speed and economy of the "stenogram and telegram and code." Textual communication must become more *pictorial,* with relevant sections accented, underscored, abbreviated. "We must read fast, as we must speak sparely. Only the schools still forbid us to speak in incomplete sentences, and this is wrong. . . . So we must distance ourselves from the book. Most printed matter no longer consists of books."[24]

What did this look like in practice? We can look at the Bauhaus's own *Catalog of Designs,* a set of loose-leaf pages in the new A4 normal size. The page showing the famous nickel-and-glass lamp displays many of the characteristics (Figure 6.1). Text is not laid out as a centered gray block; instead, words, photographs, and nontypographical elements such as circles and heavy rules are incorporated into a composition that looks nothing like the "running type" of the traditional book. Type is freed from the usual left-to-right, top-to-bottom movement dictated by printed pages for centuries; instead, the eye can follow the graphic elements, garnering information freely from image, letter, and symbol. Type is set not only horizontally but also vertically, allowing one to rotate the book ninety degrees and leaf quickly through the long side to check for different sections, just as it allows the printing information (format, date) at the lower left to melt into the gutter (the adjoining inside margins). Not only the photographic image but also color and shape communicate: the sections of the catalog are divided by workshop, the names of which appear in black sans serif letters against a red ground, while every model designation—the code—appears in red in a circle near the textual description. There are no complete sentences but rather a syntax of word, image, and symbol that is free, flexible, and immediate.

One might consider this a "functionalist" form of typography, and many of the written statements emerging from the printing and advertising workshop encourage this line of thought. But this is only half the story. Listen to Moholy-Nagy, writing in 1925: "The majority of our books [today] are by no means superior to Gutenberg's productions in their typographical-visual-synoptical form. . . . As far as newspapers, posters and job printing are concerned, the situation is much better, since whatever typographical development has taken place has only been in these areas."[25] The typographers of the Bauhaus, in other words, sought to break down the fundamental and long-standing distinction between books and commercial "job printing." They sought to make "newspapers and posters" their model for all use of type, for all visual communication. One day, wrote Moholy-Nagy, "all literary works, including probably philosophical ones, will be printed using the same means for illustration . . . as current American magazines."[26] The visual experience of the modern city—the assault of advertising, the warnings of traffic signs and on underground doors and platforms, the speed with which information was absorbed, the photographs of the front pages, the new experience of the cinema—these came to be the conditions assumed as relevant for all types of visual communication. Since the principles of commercial communication from advertisements, catalogs, illustrated magazines, billboards, and neon advertisements came to determine the nature of visuality in modernity, they would thus determine the way any printed page would be viewed. In their attempt to adapt to this development, the contemporary commodity culture of Weimar Germany came to be central, built in, the very precondition of Bauhaus typography. The post-1923 Bauhaus did not conceive of itself as above the fray: its affirmation of modernity extended to the new conditions of visuality, textuality, and commercial exchange.

BAUHAUS LTD.

The Bauhaus was successful in promoting itself, in turning its name into a household word. "What did I find at the time of my appointment?" asked Meyer rhetorically on his departure. "A Bauhaus whose potential exceeded its achievements by orders of magnitude and which was the object of an unprecedented amount of advertising."[27] And the Bauhaus was at the forefront of certain developments in the advertising business. But how did the school fare in what must be considered its true goal, the production of "mass consumer goods" that could be "offered at a reasonable price . . . by utilization of all the modern, economical methods of standardization (mass production by industry) and by large-scale sales"?[28]

From a business point of view, not very well. For all the popularity of the "Bauhaus style," the school received little direct benefit. To see how and why this happened, we can look at examples from three stages in the development of the Bauhaus's relationship with the larger world of industry.

Early attempts to capitalize on the Bauhaus's design work and facilities were ad hoc and uncoordinated. In Weimar, only shortly before the large exhibitions of the 1923 "Bauhaus Week," Gropius appointed Emil Lange as the school's first business manager.[29] Not a businessman by training or experience, Lange was an architect who came to the Bauhaus to instruct in his field but was prevented from taking up these duties due to the institution's lack of funds. His job was to find manufacturers for products designed at the school and to find commissions for the workshops. But, as Anna Rowland writes, his real task was "to struggle for the financial viability of the school."[30] Though Lange and subsequent business managers performed their duties conscientiously, their role seems to have been limited to that of financial caretaker, seeking to ensure the survival of the school by capitalizing on what happened in the course of instruction. Their brief was clearly narrowly circumscribed, and they were unable to reorganize the activities of the school more fundamentally, to make it a business from the ground up. The result was improvised and unsatisfactory. When the managers succeeded in gaining workshop commissions, the workshops often lacked the required production capacity to cope with orders in a timely fashion. When classics such as the Wagenfeld-Jucker lamp were presented at trade fairs, they drew interest, but of the wrong kind: at the renowned Leipzig Trade Exhibition, Wagenfeld reported, "[r]etailers and manufacturers laughed at our efforts. These designs which looked as though they could be made inexpensively by machine techniques were, in fact, extremely costly craft designs."[31] The greatest successes seemed to be in the area of toys—hardly objects that would justify the stern, forward-looking rhetoric of "art and technics."[32] The problems of the Bauhaus at this stage can be summarized as follows. First, as a school, the Bauhaus did not have the facilities to operate as an industrial producer: it remained, as Anna Rowland writes, a "cottage industry," and the objects that could be supplied were for a higher "craft" market niche.[33] Second, since the Bauhaus was not organized as a business, it could not orient production according to criteria that were fundamentally neither pedagogic nor artistic but instead commercial. In general, Lange complained that the workshops were simply not interested in producing suitable objects that would capture the interest of manufacturers at the trade fairs.[34]

The second stage emerged in Dessau; it is marked by a more consistent strategy that sought to focus the work of the Bauhaus on *design* and not production per se. On 7 October 1925, the corporation "Bauhaus GmbH" or "Bauhaus Ltd." was founded; its purpose was to serve as sole agent for Bauhaus designs and products.[35] In other words, the school no longer needed to be a factory; other firms would be licensed to manufacture Bauhaus designs in exchange for the payment of fees. The Bauhaus could be the laboratory for design and development, while other businesses with more experience would be responsible for production and distribution.

It was a far better way of handling involvement with the market, but Bauhaus Ltd. was not always so successful. This can be studied through the classic example of Bauhaus innovation: the tubular steel furniture from the early Dessau years.[36] From the Weimar days, Marcel Breuer had been experimenting with bending steel; he also collaborated in his experiments with a metalsmith and the Dessau airplane manufacturer Junkers. Others in the avant-garde were working on similar designs; and it seems to have been his Dutch colleague Mart Stam (very briefly, under Meyer, a lecturer at the school) who produced the first cantilevered chair, shown at the Weissenhof exhibition in 1927. In any case, with the help of the Bauhaus, Breuer patented many of his innovations in tubular steel design.[37]

The registration of patents was professional and proper: it protected the economic value of discoveries by preventing the copying of innovations by others, allowing the inventor the rights to economic exploitation. But the Bauhaus and its members proved to be naive in their attempt to adapt to business practices and ultimately unable to exploit their innovations for their own gain. The first problem of many was that the patents emerging from the work at the school were in Breuer's own name, and not that of Bauhaus Ltd. They were thus his to sell or exploit, which is exactly what he did: in 1926 or 1927, Breuer, owner of the patents, and a partner founded a firm called Standard-Möbel to produce his designs, and it did so in direct competition with the Bauhaus

Arch. Marcel Breuer

B 33
Thonet

Figure 6.4. Marcel Breuer, B33 chair, 1927/28. From the Thonet Stahlrohrmöbel loose-card catalog of 1930–31.

directorate, which had already been negotiating for the serial production of the innovative furniture in its own right. The result was the so-called Breuer crisis of 1927, which prompted the designer to tender his resignation. As it turned out, Breuer stayed, and his firm (which was later bought by the bentwood furniture manufacturer Thonet) began production without paying royalties to the school.

The problems, however, did not end there. Breuer continued to make designs, among others for a cantilever chair. Breuer's design for Standard/Thonet was hollow and sprung (Figure 6.4); this represented the significant improvement over Mart Stam's visually similar but stiff and internally reinforced model from Weissenhof. But a canny and informed businessman who had bought the rights to Stam's design sued Thonet for infringement of copyright. He claimed that Breuer's design represented a *technical* modification of Stam's *artistic* design. The crux of the issue was whether the chair would be considered, legally, a work of art.[38] "Artistic" developments were considered, under the law, the domain of copyright—the traditionally "fine" artist's exclusive right to reproduce or have reproduced, to distribute, and to sign original work for the duration of his life (heirs inherited this privilege for a specified period after the artist's death). Although they could be licensed or sold, these rights, which were extended to architects and applied artists in 1907, were the intellectual property of the "artist." "Technical" innovations, however, were the property of whoever registered them for patent, provided the proper documentation, and paid the relevant fees. They covered not so much form or appearance as the principles narrowly considered technical "function."

In the extensive litigation that unfolded over several years, the courts ruled that the tubular steel cantilever chair was a work of art—and thus the intellectual property of Stam. Its essence was considered the *form* given it by the Dutch architect and not Breuer's technical innovation in the use of hollow steel. As a result, many of Breuer's designs had to be marketed under Stam's name, with the payment of fees to the purchaser of this copyright. This is a brief summary of a complex and not always transparent set of episodes, but one thing is clear: the union of art and industry was nothing new. Artistic form was property that regularly changed hands for purposes of economic exploitation; it could be registered, and anyone working in areas considered by the courts to be "applied arts" or "architecture" enjoyed the privilege of copyright. Meanwhile the system of patents similarly regulated the relation between imagination and economy from another angle, that of technical innovation. The union of "art and technics" was an old one, with long-established but ambiguous and occasionally conflicting rules, rules to which the innovations of the Bauhaus were subject. The avant-garde in design and architecture considered their work in terms of its radical newness, but this work was assimilated into and absorbed by the prevailing economy, which had long since developed structures governing the convergence of art and industry. Precisely here the Bauhaus showed little business sense. Thus the occasional laughter of those with less vision but more experience; and thus the failure of the school to make any earnings from innovations such as the tubular steel chairs. As so often, others with more practice were able to borrow, steal, or exploit—however one wishes to describe what happens to intellectual property left to the market's unbridled energies—the work of the school.

The third example comes from the Meyer era. Interestingly, for all of Meyer's socialist credentials the school showed far more business savvy under him than under Gropius. This example is an exception, a story of success; but the terms of this success are revealing about the difficult and ultimately unsatisfactory way the Bauhaus worked in the market. The product in question is the "Bauhaus wallpaper" produced by Rasch Brothers & Company, near Hannover, using designs developed at the Bauhaus.[39] On

1 March 1929, a contract was signed between the two limited corporations whereby Emil Rasch paid the Bauhaus a generous fee plus expenses for a set number of wallpaper designs. The first collection of fourteen papers, meant as an alternative to bare paint in large-scale settlements, was prepared by the wall-painting workshop under Hinnerk Scheper and was ready in September 1929. The papers were essentially monochrome, structured, and delicately tinted, and showed gently waving lines and varied grids that gave a mild textured effect. With ambitious, indeed aggressive, marketing by their firm, they were a considerable success, despite the fact that they were not so very different in kind from patterns offered by other firms (and later, other patterns offered by Rasch under different names). Still, the contract provided the first opportunity for the Bauhaus Ltd. to make a profit.[40]

A brief look at the contract casts considerable light on the way the Bauhaus interacted with the market for everyday goods. Here I would like to single out two points from the document, quaintly typed in lowercase letters. Point number eight involves the Bauhaus in the business beyond the simple preparation of the designs: Rasch agreed to use the services of the advertising workshop for the bulk of the posters, notices, and catalogs used to promote the papers; he would, however, receive a 20 percent discount for designs and 10 percent for production from the studio's normal rates. Rasch, in other words, bought a Bauhaus package—not only design for the objects for sale but for the publicity as well. And in point number five, we read that "the Bauhaus agrees not to distribute any other wallpaper designs *under its name*."[41] Rasch did not seek an exclusive license for all wallpaper products designed at the school, but secured himself the only line of "Bauhaus wallpaper" on the market.

Rasch, of course, bought the school's design talent—yet the *product* did not look so different from other similar products on the market, and was certainly not obviously avant-garde in origin. He bought, one could say, the "Bauhaus style"—but in the *advertising* more than in the product designs themselves. Most important, he bought not the style but the *name*. Rasch was the only firm that could legally and properly sell this product under the Bauhaus label. They did so effectively, even after the school had closed under pressure from the National Socialist authorities; it was apparently still profitable far into the 1930s. In the end it was the name, the cachet, one could say the aura of the Bauhaus that was its chief asset. Business success for the Bauhaus thus depended, paradoxically, on the same principles behind the imitations and frauds— the separation of name from product. The name had a greater and longer-lasting value than particular designs—a sad state of affairs for an institution that sought to privilege the technical criteria of functionality over representative style, that sought to propose a more straightforward or logical approach to the objects of everyday life. The consumer market continued working according to its own, much older criteria, and success for the Bauhaus could be achieved only on these terms.

This exceptional success of the Bauhaus's project of providing prototypes for a popular, industrially mass-produced product also provides a foil, an episode that casts into sharper relief the more frequent failures of the Bauhaus as a business. We can say that the innovative but unclear position of the institution—art or industry, school or business—prevented its members from taking adequate steps to capitalize on their products and their popularity, and also to prevent this popularity from being diluted by its use designating derivative work. It becomes clear that the members of the school underestimated the energies of the market, its ability to copy, adapt, spread into different niches, and to combine elements in the rhythm of the cycles of changing fashion. The design research of the school ended up profiting others—those with the business sense to know what to do with a good idea. These are the businesses that did—whether legally or well is not the issue—what the Bauhaus simply could not. In short, the Bauhaus failed

- to achieve its own goal of designing cheap, mass-producible objects, to make objects that were both better and more affordable than the mass-market alternatives;
- to work effectively with businesses to design objects those businesses would want to produce and the public would want to buy (at the Bauhaus there was often surprise that "industry" did not come knocking at its door);
- to identify promising markets and adapt its production to them; and
- to set up structures by which it could protect its most valuable assets: its specific designs and its *name,* those two syllables that it had successfully convinced a broad public represented new principles of design, a new start, the look of the twentieth century, the appearance of the modern world.

The profits went instead to those who knew how to achieve these basic business goals by means that were effective, if often crude. They capitalized on the inaccurate but insistent popular equation of the name with a set of formal idioms and in the process robbed the avant-garde of the financial capital generated by their cultural work.[42] As part of this process, the Bauhaus in its derivative forms came to represent merely one style among many, a consumer option and not a design imperative. The Bauhaus thus lost its authority, its purity, its claim to provide a *correct* set of design principles for the modern world. It was no longer the *modern* but merely the *latest,* and the latest loses its status quickly.

WHOSE BAUHAUS?
I have thus far tried to reconstruct what happened to the Bauhaus when its products, its formal idiom, and its name came to be factors in the consumer-oriented sector of the German economy of the time. But that is not the whole story. We need to look at what happened to the products, the idiom, and the name in the hands of the

consumers. We need to see what role the Bauhaus played in a market that was stratified in complex ways in terms of class. What, specifically, could or did the Bauhaus mean to those for whom its objects and environments were designed? To whom did the Bauhaus belong?

The currency of the Bauhaus was not its particular approach to design or specific design solutions but rather its perceived *newness*. And the new—the radically original that challenges, confounds, and disrupts the practiced gaze on the world—is classless. For a moment, however brief, it resists the social codes, the social semiotics, that allow one to manipulate and interpret objects as signs so as to make statements and assumptions about identity. Once the new is identified as such, even in its status as the "latest," it can be recognized and read; yet nonetheless this is perhaps the most interesting moment for a historian of visual culture. For the object or sign has now entered into a territory in which meanings can be attached to objects and also, more crucially, signs can be tried out, fought over, contested, negotiated. There were many competing views about what modern Germany should be (few thought that the first German republic was a final or stable form), and each could claim certain forms to represent its cause. At issue was a complex process of negotiation about the future of modernity—politically, socially, ideologically—and how it should look.

Objects signify, they are signs; and in the twentieth century an increasing proportion of objects enters into the system of social semiotics in the form of commodities—produced to be sold, accompanied on the market by the representations of advertising and display that seek to channel the meanings in specific (though not always unambiguous) directions.[43] The consumer marketplace is one of the preeminent signifying realms in modernity. It may not displace all other organizations of signs such as church and state; instead, it has become another field across which those more traditionally defined meanings could be made. The marketplace becomes political as the objects that circulate across it make competing claims about the purchaser and his or her view of the world (a woman wearing a tie and trousers expresses, in some contexts, a constellation of views about gender politics; a man in a suit and tie asserts, even if only ironically, bourgeois identity). And political battles are fought over a terrain that is occasionally indistinguishable from the consumer marketplace (National Socialism turned itself into a political brand by methods well known to advertisers of automobiles and soap).[44] It is in this less definable field of the market that we must now seek to locate the Bauhaus.

For many, the Bauhaus meant the socialist left; and though there was, as we shall see, nothing *inherently* progressive about the *neue Sachlichkeit* in a political sense, this identification of objects and buildings with a political stance had a certain logic. The hallmark of the New Architecture and the New Objectivity was, of course, the rejection of applied ornament; and this was discussed by architects and critics as a rejection of the traditional visual language of bourgeois education and prestige.[45] In the eyes of some, the New Objectivity seemed to speak for a society no longer traditional in power and organization; it might be a meritocracy, a technocracy, an American-type land of opportunity.[46] The rhetoric of socialism was prevalent in the first or expressionist phase of the Bauhaus; and many of the chief practitioners of this mode of design in Germany identified themselves in various ways with the left (Gropius, Bruno Taut, Meyer, Stam).[47] In terms of sheer numbers, the new principles of design were most often put into practice by forces considered socialist: in Berlin, the housing societies associated with the trade unions commissioned the vast settlements designed by Taut and Martin Wagner; in Frankfurt, the Social Democratic government underwrote the gleaming white satellite communities designed in May's office; and the Bauhaus was institutionally secure only in Social Democratic municipalities.[48] The range of furniture and accessories in the style of radical "objectivity" offered to the residents of the Ernst May settlements represents probably the most extensive range of products in this tendency. And finally many ideologues of the right confirmed this identification by their very rejection, naming the style "bolshevist."[49]

So the new design style was in many ways "claimed" by social democracy and taken as a sign of it.[50] But though it may have been identified with the left, the working class did not always want it. Research has shown that the residents of the "New Frankfurt" at times resisted the furniture style they felt was imposed upon them.[51] Furthermore, in identifying the principles behind the New Architecture with means-end rationality and the prevailing logic of production, the sympathetic socialist critic Alexander Schwab felt forced to equate it with the rationalizing tendency of bourgeois capitalism. "The New Architecture," he wrote, "has a double face: it is fact both haut-bourgeois and proletarian, high-capitalist and socialist. One could even say both autocratic and democratic."[52] Indeed, many of the finest examples of the new principles of architecture were expensive one-offs, luxurious villas by Gropius, Ludwig Mies van der Rohe, Erich Mendelsohn, and others; and there is no doubt that the tubular steel furniture by Breuer and others appealed to the upper end of the market.[53] Just another form of prestige, wrote Kállai: "His Majesty the snob wants something new. . . . The historical costume is replaced with a technoid edge. But it's just as bad. A bourgeois is always a bourgeois. His home remains a luxury object, all 'objectivity' aside. . . . The 'objectivity' of the new kind of living in Bauhaus style has its two sides: one for the many, the other for the few who can afford it."[54]

Indeed there is good anecdotal evidence that the Bauhaus style was seen, in the late 1920s, as haute bourgeois or fashionable, or at least that people could recognize the difference between the New Frankfurt and the radical chic, and that they did so by means of images provided by the illustrated press. Consider the case of the radical theater director Erwin Piscator, who took up his friend Gropius's offer to renovate his apartment, complete with Breuer's latest Bauhaus designs. Here is his own account:

Instead of doors with panels and applied ornamentation, flush doors were fitted; the rooms were painted white and equipped with steel furniture. But even while the apartment was in its original condition, people in the know were whispering that Piscator was building a castle. . . . Old proletarian friends would swear blind they had just seen me drive past in a Rolls-Royce. . . . And so when Stone, our theater photographer, took pictures of the apartment and published them against my will in *Die Dame,* a women's magazine, my condemnation was complete.

How can a man like that claim to be a Communist?[55]

Thus the "newness" represented by the Bauhaus was tied to hopes for a new and egalitarian society; yet a similar sort of novelty entered the stratified market of changing fashions at the upper market level (as fashions so often do). It would necessarily have a middle ground, one shown in a drawing by the Karlsruhe artist Karl Hubbuch called *With Hair Dryer and Bicycle* (Figure 6.5). Here Hubbuch shows us his wife, Hilde, as a "New Woman." She is relaxed, with bobbed hair, and independent (the mobility provided by the bicycle)—and sitting in an early Wassily chair by Breuer. This is the world not of the wealthy and established consumers of luxury, nor of the industrial proletariat. This is the world of the young, the fashionable-on-a-shoestring, the office workers, salespeople, clerks, and secretaries who were seen to represent a "new middle class" at the time—new because it was one that could represent the upwardly mobile from a working-class background or the downwardly mobile from the bourgeoisie, and new because it was a class that had bourgeois claims to status and prestige but wages as low and employment as precarious as the traditional proletariat. In the end, it was this market niche—the urban office workers—that came to be most closely identified with the New Objectivity and the Bauhaus. The market idiom came to be identified with the small, fashionable, and nontraditional objects such a young urban class aspired to (a Wassily chair in a crowded flat), and to the sites of commercialized entertainment that they frequented. Feuilletonist Joseph Roth took the steam out of the rhetoric of the avant-garde by depicting these objects in the cheap but trend-conscious milieu of the white-collar workers:

> That these white, hygienic operating theaters are in fact cafés is something I know already. But I still confuse the long glass rods on the walls with thermometers. But now they are lamps. . . . A tabletop out of glass is not meant to allow guests conveniently to inspect their shoes while eating, but rather to generate bone-shattering scratching noises when the metal ashtray is drawn across the transparent material.[56]

One cannot fail to recognize the avant-garde in the description of furnishings that "have no feet, resemble crates and are hollow. One sits on these objects."[57] In his extraordinary study *The Salaried Masses* of 1930, the cultural critic Siegfried Kracauer similarly pokes gentle fun at the way the Bauhaus style came to characterize the bars

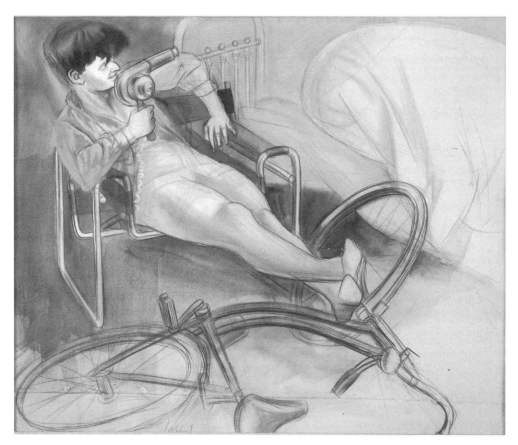

Figure 6.5. Karl Hubbuch, *With Hair Dryer and Bicycle,* **1927/28. Lithographic crayon and watercolor. Photograph courtesy Volker Huber.**

and nightclubs of Weimar Berlin, havens of glamour for the office workers who paid to spend their evenings there, the sites of industrialized leisure he termed "pleasure barracks."[58] His example is the massive "Haus Vaterland," which featured a gleaming entryway in the new style: "Since only the most modern is good enough for our masses, this exaggerates the New Objectivity style."[59] The interior was divided into theme rooms with panoramas for walls, each offering a different experience: "In other rooms adjoining the New Objectivity the Rhine flows past, the Golden Horn glows, lovely Spain extends far away in the south."[60] This is the consumer market's Bauhaus, merely one style among many, valued for the superficial pleasures it might fleetingly offer.

Even the classic account of the white-collar Berlin milieu, Hans Fallada's *Little Man, What Now?,* provides perspective on the phenomenon we might call commercial constructivism. There Pinneberg, a junior salesman in a department store, strives to make good in Berlin with his wife, Lämmchen (the diminutive nickname has been translated as "Bunny"). A central scene is Fallada's fable of consumer desire in which, soon af-ter their arrival in Berlin, Pinneberg and Lämmchen are mesmerized by the apparition of a dressing table in a shop window display showing a bedroom suite. "God," says Lämmchen, "if only we could buy it. I think I'd cry for joy. . . . It would be beautiful . . . wonderful."[61] When Pinneberg gets his first paycheck, this spell turns into a frenzy: he rushes to the store and foolishly, impulsively, rudely, and insistently spends nearly all of it on the useless object (which the frightened salesman had not wanted to separate from the suite). The description of Pinneberg's psychology, his rage before everything standing between him and the object, is the real subject of this scene. But is not the brief portrayal of the object itself relevant here—is it not New Objective, something that might have been considered "Bauhaus style"? "So there's the shop window with the bedroom, and here on the side is the dressing table. The mirror in its brown frame is strictly rectilinear; so are the drawers beneath with their runners to the left and the right."[62] Fallada does not tell the reader in so many words—perhaps he did not have to—but the dressing table sounds uncannily familiar, like many others made by small manufacturers at the time in a diluted or derivative but nonetheless fashionable Bau-haus style. A grainy photograph of one such example reveals the utter banality of the object of Pinneberg's disproportionate desire (Figure 6.6).

Like other styles, the New Objectivity of the Bauhaus came to be diffused through-out a market with its class-specific niches, niches filled with objects that could be rec-ognized by members of many different constituencies and used to fashion their identi-ties and speak to their desires. But that social and formal diffusion is not the only thing that happens to the social semiotics of the Bauhaus as it filtered through the market. Let us consider one final example that shows the effect of the consumer market on this set of forms, materials, and practices, this avant-garde mode of design, and the effect on its ability to make an artistic or ideological intervention across the consumer field. That example is one of the most noteworthy moments when forms of artistic prac-tice confronted each other with all the ideological force and tensions with which they could be laden in the explosive atmosphere of Weimar Germany, where the avant-garde faced the forces of more conservative reform, where left faced center-right in a confrontation of two fundamentally and dramatically opposing views of what the mod-ern world should look like. This is the famous "battle of the roofs" in the Berlin suburb of Zehlendorf.

Starting in 1926 and in the half-decade following, Taut, with Hugo Häring and Otto Rudolf Salvisberg, built the settlement Waldsiedlung Zehlendorf, in popular parlance "Uncle Tom's Cabins."[63] The settlement was for the left-leaning, trade-union-affiliated building society GEHAG, and it remains a classic example of the New Architecture with flat roofs, bright colors, standardized housing units, and clear geometry. A few years into the project, the more conservative white-collar building society GAGFAH applied for permission to build its own settlement at the edge of the GEHAG project;

Figure 6.6. Dressing table from a bedroom suite by Paul Giesser. From Paul Giesser, *Die neue Wohnung und ihre Möbel* (Stuttgart: Julius Hoffmann, 1930).

GAGFAH's purpose was to work toward a "perfected form for the middle-class home."[64] The term used for "middle class" was the old-fashioned designation *Mittelstand,* referring to the traditional, and traditionally conservative, segment of small tradesmen representing modest professions. Sixteen architects, members of the aesthetically and politically conservative group "The Block"—the more radical group, which included Taut, called itself "The Ring"—united in the building of the settlement called Am Fischtal, consisting of various clearly individualized houses and apartment blocks, built in a self-consciously traditional and crafted mode and unified by a prerequisite forty-five-degree angle of the roofs. "Like a barrier wall from an entirely different era,"[65] they stood, writes

136 FREDERIC J. SCHWARTZ

Figure 6.7. Walter Gropius and László Moholy-Nagy, pavilions for the exhibition Bauen und Wohnen at the GAGFAH settlement Am Fischtal, 1928. Photograph by Lucia Moholy. Bauhaus-Archiv, Berlin. Copyright 2005 Artists Rights Society (ARS), New York / VG Bild-Kunst, Bonn.

Annemarie Jaeggi, "in stark and intentional contrast to the serially constructed GE-HAG buildings."[66]

So far, the situation is clear. As homes, the building styles were controversial and politically coded. But where did the Bauhaus fit in? Marginally, to be sure; but its former director Gropius was represented there, along with Moholy-Nagy. The two had designed the café and pavilions for a temporary exhibition called "Bauen und Wohnen" (Building and Dwelling) (Figure 6.7) mounted by the GAGFAH to mark the opening of the conservative "countersettlement."[67] They did so in an uncompromisingly radical style: flat roofs, building frames visible and used for the support of large, sans serif lettering, strip windows, with the Bauhaus advertising studio responsible for the glass and steel furniture on which the conservative GAGFAH displays were mounted. It might seem odd that the GAGFAH agreed to be exhibited in a style to which their buildings stood so crassly opposed. A critic writing in the German Werkbund journal *Die Form* noted the disparity from a point of view sympathetic to the claims of the progressive architects: "It is a strange feeling when one steps out of these [GAGFAH] houses and into the café of the exhibition, where Gropius, Breuer and Moholy-Nagy have mounted an excellent exhibition. . . . Here dominates a modern spirit . . . that one hardly finds in the [GAGFAH] settlement."[68]

Why, then, would the Bauhaus style have been acceptable to represent the conservative exhibition? It has to do, I think, with the specific context and function of this work, and the context and function are very revealing indeed. Gropius and Moholy-Nagy were building a café and temporary exhibition, areas considered commercial and representing an architecture of entertainment. Buildings in this realm of leisure did not represent polemical statements, like the embattled dwellings that were the real issue in Zehlendorf. It seems, strangely enough, that ideological foes could meet happily here, could sit in metal chairs and drink coffee or sip lemonade under flat roofs. Leisure was not always, in Weimar Germany, an ideological safe haven, a politically neutral zone; but the obvious acceptability and unspoken appropriateness of this occasionally polemical and powerfully politicized mode of design show that the world of urban and commercialized entertainment had the tendency to neutralize, to reframe artistic interventions as mere glamour, to refigure the complex work of the avant-garde into mere surface style.

Perhaps the interaction of the avant-garde with the world of commerce and industry, with consumer culture, need not have taken this turn; but the remarkable adventures of the artistic tendency whose center was the Bauhaus are a case study of the functioning of the consumer market and the forces to which the work of an artistic avant-garde was subject when it dared to enter this field. Within the short space of five or six years the Bauhaus had achieved one of its central goals: the set of innovations that it had developed moved into mass production and was available to all—whether the objects themselves, or their short-term use in the spaces of leisure and entertainment. But the artists had lost control—of the set of forms, of their own names, and of the aesthetic, economic, and social conditions under which their design utopia would be experienced.

The market had its own way of uniting art and industry, and in its brief history the Bauhaus never mastered it. These practices were articulated by laws, manipulated by experts, and tested by profits. And the market itself was chaotic and unruly. Forms could be circulated there and products distributed, but this would happen on the terms of capitalist commerce's own dynamic, the energies of which those working at the famous school understood very poorly. The consumer market was a cultural field as dangerous as it was unavoidable to ambitious designers in the twentieth century, and it made the Bauhaus the victim of its own otherwise considerable success.

BAUHAUS ARCHITECTURE IN THE THIRD REICH

Winfried Nerdinger

Translated by Kathleen James-Chakraborty

> No one can doubt, however, that the new building
> methods as such question absolutely nothing about
> men or about human goals. Sing Sing [prison] will be
> built in as modern a way as a new market hall, a depart-
> ment store as fashionably as a new housing colony,
> and when a somewhat larger new prison becomes im-
> portant for a new military—or maybe even a giant new
> factory for gas bombs, so they too will be truly modern.
> —**ADOLF BEHNE**, *Wohnungswirtschaft* (1930)

In 1935, in order to obtain material for a publication about the Bauhaus, Walter Gropius, then living in England, wrote numerous Bauhaus colleagues in Germany and
asked them to send him their recent work. Of the few answers that he received, Ernst
Göhl's is certainly the most striking:

> I want to be honest.—When I received your letter, I thought instinctively about a fairy-tale
> prince and a silent fairy-tale garden out of the old times.—We live in the year 1935. It has
> changed some. We (I speak of the Bauhauslers I know) stand in the middle of a struggle for
> existence and have at the best been able to salvage a small remnant of the old ideal in en-
> tirely personal areas . . . but you will never experience what the Bauhaus people in Prague,
> Paris, or Berlin really do, which would be interesting but maybe not so nice to hear about.[1]

Göhl spoke about the large group of Bauhaus renegades whose revisionist work is today justifiably forgotten. Whether, how, and at what price individual Bauhauslers tried
to salvage the remnants of the ideal is the theme of this chapter. It was not just former
students who were relatively well informed about the political conduct in National Socialist times of their former colleagues. In 1940, for example, Alfred Arndt wrote W. J.
Hess, ". . . have spoken by telephone with Scheper, who is still painting the Karin Hall
for Hermann Göring. A fine job, isn't it? We have not had such good fortune."[2] Those
abroad also knew about it. A shocked Ivo Pannagi wrote Gropius in 1934 about Ludwig Mies van der Rohe's signature on a "Summons to the Creators of Culture."[3] Martin Wagner told him that he and Hugo Häring had declined an invitation from Mies to

follow suit,[4] and Kósa Zoltan reported to Gropius in 1939 about "traitors"[5] equal to Farkas Molnár.

Waldemar Alder gave his old teacher Hannes Meyer a detailed report in a letter of 16 July 1947. He named the "public and camouflaged Nazis"[6] at the Berlin Bauhaus in 1933—the group "Heide, Chors, Rohbra, Lindner, etc."—and was infuriated that the last had been named a professor at the newly opened architecture school in Weimar.[7] Alder enumerated further examples of party members and of Hubert Hoffmann's "activity with the SS," which would result in his dismissal in Dessau. In response to Meyer's question about the fate of those who returned home from Russia, Alder wrote: "As far as I know nothing happened in 1936. On the contrary a great percentage of them . . . were enlisted in the factories of Hermann Göring." Alder was certainly right. The returning members of the Meyer and May brigades and others who had also helped in Russia, such as Gustav Hassenpflug, Konrad Püschel, Werner Hebebrand, Walter Kratz, and Rudolf Wolters, received commissions and positions in Nazi Germany. In particular, Herbert Rimpl's enormous office, which looked after the architectural aspects of Göring's factories, featured the largest collection of Bauhaus-associated and modern architects. His survey occasioned in Adler a resigned conclusion: "Here a cult will develop, that the Bauhauslers were a special sort of people. . . . It is not so. In twelve years I certainly was able to establish that our worthy colleagues felt the Third Reich to be correct, and when there was a spark of opposition, it was prompted only because this formal direction was dismissed as cultural Bolshevism. If Mussolini had been at the tiller instead of Hitler, everything would have been in order."

In contrast to the subjective opinion of Adler, who certainly spoke for many, it must be admitted that some Bauhaus architects avoided all entanglements with the National Socialist system. They withdrew to unproblematic positions—as much as these existed within such a system—in such fields as construction, film architecture, or underground engineering (Peter Keler, Selman Selmanagic, etc.).[8] A historically correct appraisal of the life and careers of the Bauhauslers during the Nazi period must certainly investigate each case individually. Still more biographies must be scrupulously researched to fill in the gaps and to illuminate especially the self-serving Bauhaus cult of the postwar period.[9] The following overview cannot account for every personal fate, but it will point out the variety of directions individual lives took and the possibility of a modern architecture within the Nazi system.

Even the deportment of Gropius, the Bauhaus's founder, displays a characteristic ambivalence. On the one hand, Gropius, together with Martin Wagner and Wilhelm Wagenfeld, voiced opposition to the collapse of the German Werkbund.[10] He also defended modern buildings in letters to the president of the National Board of Visual Arts, Eugen Hönig, and to the president of the Werkbund and of the Association of German Architects, Carl Christoph Lörcher.[11] On the other hand, these letters certainly document Gropius's hope for the establishment of the modern as "German" art according

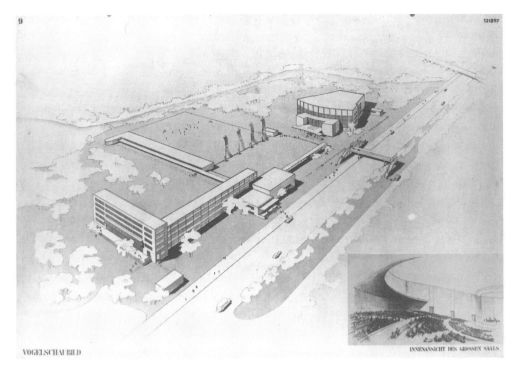

Figure 7.1. Walter Gropius with Rudolf Hillebrecht, competition for Haus der Arbeit, 1934. Bauhaus-Archiv, Berlin.

to the Italian model, a hope that he shared with Häring, Martin Mächler, Mies, and Martin Elsässer.[12] Architectural expression of this conception can be found in a competition entry for a "Building for Work" on which he collaborated with Rudolf Hillebrecht in 1934 and in which swastikas appear in the perspective drawing (Figure 7.1).[13] Along with numerous other exponents of modern architecture, Bauhausler Gustav Hassenpflug and Ernst Hegel also took part in this competition.[14] Like Gropius, their contributions based upon the Italian model were unsuccessful.

Gropius's engagement went still further. Together with the Bauhaus alumni Joost Schmidt and Walter Funkat he designed the Nonferous Metal Section of the 1934 exhibit German People—German Work.[15] About a dozen Bauhauslers or their employees worked on this Nazi propaganda show for the "German race" and "German work," installing in total six sections of the great Hall of Honor as well as additional showrooms. Moreover, Gropius on 2 February 1934 sent an exposé he had written with Martin Wagner about the industrialization of East Prussia to Hans Weidemann, Goebbel's official in the Propaganda Ministry. In a detailed analysis, they made recommendations about how the "idle workers in the area of city planning"[16] could be employed; that is, they tried to obtain an official planning commission.

Gropius shared a lack of commissions and poor finances with nearly all architects in those years. He was, however, a registered member of the Reichskulturkammer (National Cultural Council) and was given no special restrictions like Carl Fieger,[17] nor was he entirely denied permission to work, as Ferdinand Kramer was.[18] On the contrary, when Gropius demanded help from Hönig to defend himself against slander, the answer came that Hönig valued him as "German-feeling."[19] Gropius should calmly defend himself, "since your admission in the National Cultural Council of Visual Arts can be given" to people "as proof of your worth." Gropius's emigration to England in the fall of 1934 was for financial reasons, and he traveled back to Germany repeatedly in 1935–36, so the terms *flight* and *asylum seeking* cannot be used to describe his departure. Until 1939 Gropius obviously hoped to return to Germany and exerted himself intensively to avoid any political complication. His friend Alexander Dorner wrote him in 1941, "Thus you wanted first to fight the Nazis with their own weapons, and then you tried to rescue what could be saved."[20]

Gropius sent his (doctored) statement annually to the German Finance Office; he signed important letters "with German greetings." He even asked Hönig in 1936 for a confirmation that his activity in London was "in the German interest";[21] and many times he stressed, in opposition to the way he was described in the English press, that he remained a "German citizen."[22] In order to be permitted to bring his household belongings from Berlin to the United States, he organized through Theodor Heuss and Ernst Jäckh an agreement with Goebbels's ministry: the German press could report that for the first time "this cultural teaching position was occupied by a German."[23] To Hönig he wrote in addition that "as before I will conduct myself in the future loyally and see my mission in Harvard as serving German culture."[24] When, in 1938, after he became a professor at Harvard, the German government tried to tax him for leaving the country, he wrote furiously to State Secretary Frank that he "found it shameful, to be treated without cause as a deserter," and that he remained a "loyal German citizen."[25] Finally, until the outbreak of the war he ostentatiously kept his distance from all German immigrants and their efforts. With the exception of a signature for the Congress "Of the Free Word"[26] in February 1933, he declined each opportunity to make a political statement and refused even as late as 1938 to add his name to the "American Guild for German Cultural Freedom."[27]

By the same token, Gropius met with Hönig in London, and the Sturmabteilung (storm trooper, or Brownshirt) member Lörcher came to eat at his house. According to the testimony of his wife, he got along with both "very well."[28] He also met in 1936 in London with his former collaborator Ernst Neufert, and subsequently declared himself to be enthusiastic about the further development of Neufert's ideas concerning the teaching of architectural design, even reviewing his book favorably.[29] Only after 1945 did Gropius see in Neufert the "Nazi-Spirit"[30] that would hinder the renewal of Germany if the reconstruction proceeded according to Neufert's teachings. To be sure,

Gropius himself compiled a file, "Own Struggle with the Nazis,"[31] but this collection of letters is incomplete and conceals his ambivalent posture. The brilliant postwar reputation of "Mister Bauhaus" eventually completely transformed this phase of his life.

It is astonishing, furthermore, how many important members of Gropius's office deserted to the Nazis. Beside Neufert, Speer's commissioner for issues of standardization, these included Hans Dustmann,[32] who would become the architect for the Hitler Youth, Otto Meyer-Ottens,[33] the chief construction supervisor for Rimpl, and Walter Tralau,[34] who managed urban planning in the Salzgitter area and was in charge of residential architecture for Göring's factories. Coming directly from the office of the founder of the Bauhaus obviously occasioned no occupational problems in the Nazi period.

The staff members of the last director of the Bauhaus, Mies van der Rohe, also obtained Nazi commissions and in some cases were elevated above party members. For instance, Sergius Ruegenberg and Ernst Walther designed the Hall of Honor and other showrooms for the Nazi propaganda exhibit German People—German Work; Eduard Ludwig,[35] the display for the timber industry; and Siegfried Giesenschlag,[36] the one for the metalwares industry. Giesenschlag eventually worked as an architect and construction supervisor at the Air Ministry, and Karl Otto[37] became an air raid defense expert at Göring's ministry. Ernst Walther received through Mies's personal intercession with Dr. Maiwald, the commissioner of the Association of German Industry, the job of designing the Industrial Exhibit of 1933 in Berlin.[38] The advancement of his career was not hindered by his membership in the SS; after 1945 Walter became a professor at the College of the Arts in Berlin. Eventually Mies wrote a generous whitewash for his old associate.[39]

The deportment of Mies in regard to National Socialism is rather more complicated than that of Gropius. Already, at the time of the Bauhaus's closing, he had complained to Martin Mächler that "some sordid scoundrel spreads the rumor that I am a Dutch Jew."[40] He became without any problem a member of the National Cultural Council. In 1934 he joined two additional Nazi organizations[41] and signed his name to the notorious "Summons to the Culturally Creative." In the same year he designed the mining section of German People—German Work. In June 1934 he was one of six architects officially invited by the National Cultural Council to compete for the design of the German Pavilion for the 1935 World's Fair in Brussels.[42] Here the worldview of the Nazis was supposed to be expressed. In a cover letter, Mies compared his swastika-decorated design to the "character of German work."[43] It is true that it was not he but Ludwig Ruff who was awarded the commission, but as compensation Mies and his companion, Lilly Reich, immediately were promised the design of the chemical and textile industry displays.[44] Nothing came of the design, as Germany withdrew at the end of 1934 from the exhibition. Still in 1937 he and Lilly Reich designed the German textile industry installation that was exhibited in Speer's pavilion at the Paris World's Fair.[45]

Within a few years Mies had designed a memorial for the Communists, a pavilion for the Weimar Republic in Barcelona, and a propaganda building for the Nazis. Richard Pommer dubbed him "the Talleyrand of architects,"[46] but this is not true insofar as Mies did not, on the one hand, really care much about party politics and, on the other, remained true in all his designs to his artistic principles. What is problematic rather is that for Mies, modern forms were transferable to any context, that for him they were only a formal canon. One could perhaps pointedly say that he served each politically without, however—in contrast to Hans Scharoun, Sep Ruf, or Egon Eiermann—making any formal compromise.

Financial reasons would scarcely have accounted for this behavior. For his first place entry in the competition for the Reichsbank, which Sibyl Moholy-Nagy foolishly characterized as a "deadly fascist design,"[47] Mies had received 5,000 reichsmarks, for the Brussels plan yet another 5,500 reichsmarks. In addition, he was paid for the exhibit installations mentioned above, for gas stations, and for the factory building for the Verseidag in Krefeld, as well as private planning and royalties.[48] He was able in 1936 to declare 3,600 reichsmarks as taxable income.[49] He reported, moreover, that he still had at this point two employees. His move to the United States in 1938 was hardly for political and only partially for financial reasons. It was inspired above all by the hope of the recognition that the Nazis had refused him.

In contrast to the rather apolitically conservative Mies, one might have expected his friend Ludwig Hilberseimer, for many years a writer for the *Sozialistische Monatshefte,* to make a political statement about Nazi Germany or to have his work impaired. The Nazis included the removal of Kandinsky and Hilberseimer in their requirements for the reopening of the Bauhaus.[50] But they did not put Hilberseimer under any restrictions. In 1935 he was able to erect two houses in Berlin with all the characteristics of the "New Building,"[51] and in 1937 he planned cubic high-rise blocks inspired by Le Corbusier for a competition for the new University of Berlin (Figure 7.2). Until his emigration to the United States in July 1938 he designed large modern projects for housing developments, a hotel complex, and a garden city.[52]

Among the Bauhaus architects who stayed in Germany, a large proportion adjusted to the official taste, and a few even made careers in the Nazi system. Because many at the closing of the Bauhaus had not received a final degree, they had to transfer to other architecture schools. It is nevertheless astonishing that Mies personally recommended to the young Rudolf Ortner that he go not to Heinrich Tessenow in Berlin but to Paul Schulze-Naumburg in Weimar, as he could receive good technical training there.[53] The handwriting of Schulze-Naumburg and Fritz Norkauer thus appears in the buildings that Ortner, as "Chief Architect of the Magdeburg Fire Society," planned and executed until the beginning of the war. Modern forms à la Mies first reappeared in his case, as in many others, only after 1945.

Like the party member Ortner in Magdeburg, Siegfried Ebeling in Hamburg and party member Helmuth Weber in Jena[54] worked conventionally and adjusted without

Figure 7.2. Ludwig Hilberseimer, competition design for Berlin University, 1937. Photograph copyright The Art Institute of Chicago.

being conspicuous. Modern formal language also vanished from the work of Hermann Bunzel, who had supervised the construction of Hannes Meyer's ADGB-Bundeschule in Bernau and until 1934 led Otto Haesler's design atelier in Celle.[55]

Those who went to city building administrations or entered the architectural office of an official Nazi architect also made their peace with Nazi-specific building tasks and often polished their careers through party membership. Thus Hans Vogler,[56] the city architect of Krefeld, designed a new monumental administration forum for Oldenburg, while Hans Cieluszek worked in the office of Hermann Alker on the redevelopment of Munich as the "capital of the movement." Fritz Koch was an associate of Roderich Fick on the construction of the head house of the bridge in Linz. Party and SS member Waldemar Hüsing planned the national train management center for Augsburg and, beginning in 1942, worked on the reconstruction of Lübeck.[57] Rudolf Sander, as leader of the Bremen office of Friedrich Tam, designed a general construction plan for Schwerin before beginning in 1940 to construct, under Speer, countless military buildings such as the Munitions Ministry in Berlin and the Air Research Office in Lübben.[58] Ernst Kanow planned many housing developments for a residential building society as a part of Speer's redesign of Berlin.[59] Finally, Gerhard Weber was the leader of Rimpl's large private office and designed the central administration building of the Reichswerk Hermann Göring as well as the south train station on Speer's great North-South Axis for Berlin.[60]

Still more Bauhauslers ascended through the Nazi system to more or less high offices and honors. Lothar Lang[61] became construction manager and local administrator of the Nazi public relief tax; Hubert Hoffmann,[62] state planner for Lithuania; and Erich Brendel,[63] leader of the building department of the agricultural settlement Westmark-Saarbrücken as well as building adviser for all agricultural construction in occupied Lorraine. Carl Bauer[64] obtained the important position of confidential architect of the DAF for the district of South Hanover-Braunschweig. In this role, Bauer had much to do. He erected countless housing developments, model houses, and social buildings, such as the social hall for the Senking factory (together with his Bauhaus colleague Fritz Schreiber), which was published as a model building by the "Office of Beauty in Work." In the war, Bauer, like many others, turned to industrial architecture. His work included the Hanover copper forge, today the HAKU factory.

Those who wanted to survive as private architects in the years between 1933 and 1939 also had to make compromises. Practically no residential buildings without saddle or hipped roofs were given construction permits. What took place under the "German" roof, however, was considered much less sternly. So countless "Einfa"[65] housing developments in Berlin maintained, for example, the model of the residential buildings of the Weimar Republic. In private single-family houses the opportunities to experiment with the garden facade were greater, and each architect arranged the interior as he wanted and could. Thus one finds in the work of Gustav Hassenpflug[66] a series of interiors in the best Bauhaus style, not only for living rooms as in the Matthes House of 1938 (Figure 7.3), but also for offices or exhibitions such as the Junkers exhibit stall of 1937 and the Junkers training show of 1938. Although conventional on the outside, the Tornow House in Luckenwalde by the Bauhausler Ernst Hegel,[67] for which he even won in 1938 the Berlin Academy of the Visual Arts' Great State Prize for Architecture, displays on the interior the clear influence of Mies's Tugendhat House. Such examples of the divide between rather conventional street and modernistic garden facades are often found in the residential buildings of "New Building" architects such as Scharoun, Eiermann, Schwarz, or Ruf.[68] Rudolf Lodders described this behavior with the formula: "Show a cold shoulder to the brown environment, to the garden build a Tusculum."[69]

Finally, architects made a virtue out of the required slanted roof. Whereas Eiermann brilliantly operated with slanted and hipped roofs, others recalled not only the modern flat roofs of Gropius and Le Corbusier, but also the hipped roofs of Frank Lloyd Wright's Prairie houses. One finds this in many buildings by Emanuel Lindner, Gustav Hassenpflug, Rudolf Lodders, and Fritz Schleifer,[70] whose hipped roofs were especially accented by being both raised higher and projected outward. The facade underneath receded in comparison somewhat and, in conjunction with the bundling

Figure 7.3. Gustav Hassenpflug, study of Walter Matthes House, Grossglienicke bei Berlin, 1938. Photograph by Hannah Leiser. Bauhaus-Archiv, Berlin.

together of the windows, can, as in the case of Wright, counteract the impression of a massive building.

Such a consideration of "modern" details must nevertheless immediately address two misunderstandings: on the one hand, almost all the architects mentioned simultaneously built entirely conventionally when the clients wished or required it. Thus Hassenpflug erected, at the same time as the Matthes House, the conservatively vernacular Kranz House. On the other hand, the microscopic search for modern details distorts and disguises the reality of everyday Nazi building. There must be a clear distinction between the trace elements, which the historian collects and then bundles together, and the overwhelming bulk of conservative reactionary buildings, except for factories.

In contrast to the concealed remnants of modernism in residential architecture, modern architectural forms could be employed in the area of private and state industrial buildings with relatively little restriction. Connecting technology with industrial production, speed, and progress on armaments promoted the use of technical materials such as glass, steel, and concrete, as well as the architectural representation of technical values such as rationalization and functionality, even encouraging a Nazi-specific concept of the "beauty of technology."[71] Goebbels explained in November 1939 that "National Socialism has performed the miracle in regards to the technology of this century of making people excited about the new and of filling them with the spirit not only of its purposefulness but also of its aesthetic beauty."[72] This cult of technology was combined, however, with a view of architectural types that remained stuck in the nineteenth century. Thus Hitler in 1937 insulted Adolf Abel's design for the new art exhibition building in Munich as a "bathing establishment,"[73] "markethall," "train station," or "Saxon thread factory," because it did not correspond to his conception of "suitable" representative architectural forms for art. During his visit to the Hermann Göring factory in Linz, Hitler explained to Speer: "Look at this facade from a distance of 300 meters. How beautiful these proportions are! Here exists another assumption than in a forum for the party. There our Doric style is the expression of a new order; here, on the other hand, the technical solution is suitable."[74]

Modern form was thereby assigned in Nazi ideology the task of expressing technical values. In the field of private and state industrial buildings, modern architects thus found a wide field of activity. Just as Eiermann (who worked for Herbert Hirche from 1939 to 1945) designed for the Total factory,[75] Lodders[76] for Borgward, Vaeth for Mannesmann, and Kremmer and Schupp for mines in the Rhineland, so also some Bauhauslers designed private industrial facilities with all the hallmarks of the "New Building." By way of example one could cite Mies and Erich Holthoff's Verseidag factory in Krefeld,[77] Emanuel Lindner's wire factory Lang in Brandenburg, Heinrich S. Bormann's plant in Braunschweig, or the buildings produced by Fritz Pfeil as chief architect of the Junkers factories in Breslau.[78] Ernst Neufert, the house architect of the Lausitzer glass factories, carried the title "industrial architect" on his letterhead and had in his Berlin office ten employees, among them the Bauhauslers Kurt Debus and Gustav Hassenpflug, as well as five construction supervisors for out-of-town sites.[79] The Bauhausler Heinrich Kölling[80] specialized from 1940 in the building of animal remains management installations that produced nitroglycerine that was important for the war. The sixty building projects, which he planned with the assistance of seven employees and partly implemented, occupied a "rank of national importance" with highest priority.

With the beginning of the war, individual Bauhauslers such as Egon Hüttmann, Fritz Schleifer, or the party member Hans Georg Knoblauch became construction supervisors and architects for "industrial buildings," that is, armament installations for the air force and the army. Their activity is today hardly possible to reconstruct, because they later only made at best vague statements about it. So, for instance, Gropius's former colleague Wils Ebert noted only "planning for hydrogen and aluminum factories, industrial buildings, specifically general development plans,"[81] about what was probably an active occupation.

The largest collection of the modern architects who remained in Germany was found, however, in Rimpl's construction office for the "National factories of Hermann Göring," founded in July 1937.[82] With the growth of this enterprise, which in 1940 numbered more than 600,000 employees and represented the world's "largest

Figure 7.4. Heinrich S.
Bormann, steel fabrication
hall, Salzgitter, about
1940. From *Baukunst und
Werkform* 1 (1947): 15.

concentration of industrial power," Rimpl's office, which was responsible for its architecture, also grew. It opened branch offices throughout the Reich and had around
seven hundred employees, among them the Bauhauslers Gerd Balzer,[83] Heinrich S.
Bormann, Wilhelm J. Hess, Hubert Hoffmann, Max Enderlein, Fritz Koch, Pius Pahl,
Walter Tralau, and Gerhard Weber. Here, too, the Bauhauslers were in no way "hid-
den" in subordinate positions. Instead, Tralau led the entire residential construction
division, Bormann built three hundred apartments in Salzgitter as experimental construction with gas concrete,[84] and Weber was division leader of the coal, iron, and
steel construction staff. The catalog of these architects' work reveals that several of
them planned and built a number of the largest industrial installations between Narvik
and the Ukraine.[85]

Because all the buildings resuscitated the appearance of modern architecture and because Rimpl did not value party membership and during the war arranged many army exemptions for his collaborators, the legend arose immediately afterward that there had been room in industrial architecture for the concealment of the modern. As early as 17 January 1946, Rudolf Lodders explained in a lecture that industrial buildings had been "escape hatches"[86] for his generation, and in the first issue of *Baukunst und Werkform* noted, "That a small number of architects found a fundamentally loyal path in industry as a way out and refuge, made possible that some German buildings can still be acknowledged by the rest of the world."[87] The first illustration is a steel factory by Heinrich S. Bormann from Rimpl's office (Figure 7.4). Industrial installations from Eiermann and Gerhard Weber follow. The idea, which would be constantly repeated, ran simply: Whoever employed modern forms during the time of the Nazis could not have been a Nazi. Modern forms rehabilitated the architects and legitimized them immediately as democratic in spirit or even as members of the resistance. This biographical lie on the part of an architectural generation is the counterpart of another exoneration formulated by Gottfried Benn and cited by Bruno E. Werner in *Die Galeere,* the key novel of the "internal emigration": namely, that "the army was the aristocratic form of emigration."[88]

The call to industrial architecture can be unmasked as false in two respects. On the one hand, it deals in many instances with what are in no way functionally planned buildings in the sense of the "New Building." The installations are symmetrical throughout and excessively monumentalized (Figure 7.5), and their ground plans are forcibly laid upon their sites as upon a parade ground. So, for example, the courtyard of the often cited Heinkel factory in Orianienburg[89] was only created because the long arm of the toilet installations formed the right wing at the main entrance (Figure 7.6). On the other hand, this argument completely represses the fact that the modern industrial installations almost without exception served as military production locations, which, as the original sources of the technical means of mass murder, handled everything from

Figure 7.5. Fritz Kremmer and Martin Schupp, Zeche Zollverein Schacht XII, Essen, 1932. From Gerdy Troost, ed., *Das Bauen im Neuen Reich* (Bayreuth: Gauverlag Bayerische Ostmark, 1938), 108.

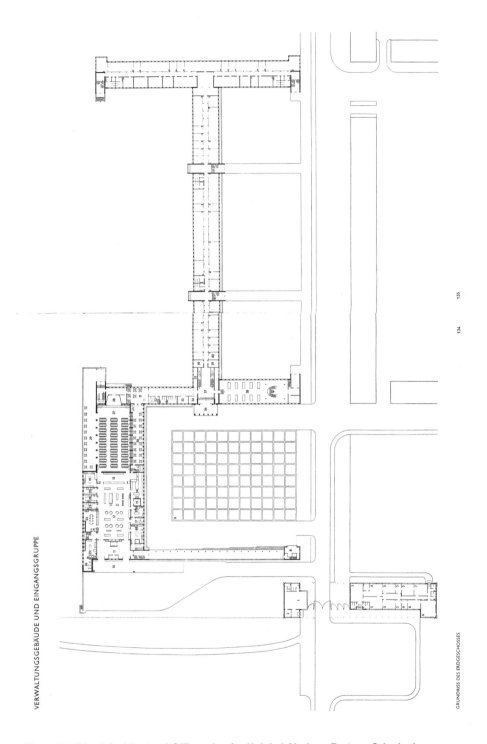

VERWALTUNGSGEBÄUDE UND EINGANGSGRUPPE

GRUNDRISS DES ERDGESCHOSSES

134

135

Figure 7.6. Rimpl Architectural Office, plan for Heinkel Airplane Factory, Orianienburg, about 1938. From Hermann Mäcker, *Herbert Rimpl* (Berlin: Wiking Verlag, after 1935).

tanks and shells to Zyklon B. Modern architectural form is not human or democratic per se; such qualities depend upon its function and the community purpose for which it is used.[90] The meaning of a form is determined foremost by the communal and architectural entirety of each case. In this sense the most modern industrial buildings and their architects were an integral component of the Nazi system. Modern architecture did not shield collaboration.

FROM ISOLATIONISM TO INTERNATIONALISM

AMERICAN ACCEPTANCE OF THE BAUHAUS

Kathleen James-Chakraborty

8

The Museum of Modern Art's 1932 exhibition of modern European architecture and the immigration to the United States of the two Bauhaus architects highlighted in it, Walter Gropius and Ludwig Mies van der Rohe, have been widely credited with transforming American architecture and design.[1] This is a myth. The Great Depression and World War II, not the presence of the émigrés, were responsible for far more substantial changes in both fields. These shifts led to the adoption of forms that in most cases bore little resemblance to their supposed European antecedents.[2] Bauhaus-associated architects, designers, and artists succeeded in the United States in exact proportion to the degree to which they or their supporters could inscribe their work into specifically American conditions. Many tried to assimilate into the culture of their adopted homeland. Their efforts met with greatest success, however, only when a relatively small coterie of Americans adopted European modernism as a badge of their own sophistication and, by extension, their country's new cold war status as a global superpower.

Mapping the causes for new approaches to architecture and design replaces hagiography with a more nuanced assessment. Although it challenges the sometimes self-aggrandizing accounts of participants, it also buffers them from those critics who hold a small circle of conspirators responsible for having foisted an alien vocabulary upon a docile public.[3] This account also exposes the limits of the most widespread accusation leveled at the émigrés today: that their new engagement with American capitalism betrayed an originally socialist project. The Bauhaus never existed at a pristine remove from the marketplace, as Frederic Schwartz's essay in this volume demonstrates. In the postwar United States, however, the assumption that there had been a great distance between the two often aided those who had been associated with the school. Paradoxically, the Bauhaus's apparently objective designs would become emblematic of an American corporate capitalism whose wealth it represented only opaquely.

If the Museum of Modern Art exhibit and the immigration of significant figures from the Bauhaus were not the most important catalysts for the reorientation of American architecture and design that occurred during the course of the 1930s and 1940s, what were? Economic factors were crucial. During the Depression, few clients could afford to build magnificently. Architects, who competed with builders for even modest commissions, trimmed costs by emphasizing functional plans and inexpensive construction in buildings that were generally smaller and more simply finished than would have been the case during the Roaring Twenties. World War II exacerbated this process, bringing a profession whose practitioners had until recently thought of themselves as artists into closer contact with industry. Architects became more involved in designing factories and in making efficient use of their products to further lower construction costs.[4] Finally, postwar inflation, which dramatically raised the cost of labor as well as materials, made a return to earlier standards impossible.[5]

The same events, the Depression and World War II, also provoked changes in government policies that had profound implications for architecture and planning. The New Deal engaged the federal government in comprehensive regional planning and housing construction. State management of the national economy increased to unprecedented levels during the war. Even before Pearl Harbor, the government began to provide housing for defense workers. After the war, federally guaranteed mortgages encouraged veterans to move their families into the suburbs, which would eventually be linked to downtowns by federally financed highway construction. Fears of nuclear war helped provoke this and other government-sponsored shifts of resources away from central cities.[6]

Meanwhile, by the late 1940s the cold war demanded that American economic and military prowess be buttressed by cultural achievement. This imperative shaped the perception of changes that had already touched the lives of the vast majority of Americans, affecting the appearance of the places where they lived, worked, shopped, and were educated. It dignified cost cutting and the adoption of new construction technologies by placing them within a modernist cultural tradition with a sophisticated European provenance.

Gropius's talent for effective propaganda blossomed in this setting. After being hired by Harvard University in 1936, he began, as Paul Betts first demonstrated, to orchestrate the fable that the goals of the Bauhaus had reached fulfillment only in the democratic conditions offered by the United States.[7] Conversely, only by assimilating European culture could America itself come of age, replacing an exhausted Europe as the keeper of the modernist flame. This account, which benefited all those émigrés who had been affiliated with the Bauhaus, required Gropius to purge the history of the school he had founded of those elements least likely to be accepted by Americans. Expressionism and socialism, and with them the important contributions made by Johannes Itten and Hannes Meyer, were eliminated in favor of focusing upon an aesthetic that was justified as the logical artistic response to mass production.[8] According with cold war politics, this narrative eventually proved to have enormous appeal, not least because it validated key American institutions, from Harvard University to the State Department.

For years, however, the position of the Bauhaus émigrés remained tenuous even as their numbers grew. Gropius and Mies each brought former faculty with them when they accepted prestigious teaching positions in the United States (Mies became head of the Department of Architecture at the Armour Institute of Technology, later renamed the Illinois Institute of Technology, in 1938). Gropius hired Marcel Breuer, while Ludwig Hilberseimer and Walter Peterhans were key to Mies's reconfiguration of the IIT curriculum. Other former Bauhaus faculty continued their educational mission at innovative new institutions. Josef Albers, who arrived as early as 1933, taught at Black Mountain College in North Carolina until 1949; László Moholy-Nagy, who came to Chicago in 1937, founded the New Bauhaus (later the School of Design) there. Herbert Bayer arrived in 1937. Lyonel Feininger, the one American-born member of the Bauhaus faculty, returned to his native land in the same year. Former Bauhaus students, a few of them Americans to begin with, also came to the United States. These included a number of alumnae of the weaving workshop, among them Anni Albers.[9]

Success came slowly. What appeared later as an unqualified triumph took at least fifteen years to achieve, years in which the outcome was almost always uncertain. The émigrés initially found themselves in a country where both their international orientation and the abstract, often almost mechanical art they espoused were viewed with considerable suspicion.[10] When the climate finally became more hospitable, it was less due to their individual efforts than to the cultural politics of the cold war.

REGIONALISM AND ASSIMILATION

Henry-Russell Hitchcock and Philip Johnson, the two young curators of the exhibit devoted to the "International Style" sought to convert Americans to a new architectural style, one that gained much of its cachet from being both modern and European. There was little more place in Depression-era America, however, for this agenda than for Johnson's almost simultaneous attempt to start a fascist movement.[11] Instead, the inroads that modernist architecture and design did make in the United States during the thirties were largely the product of economic austerity and the political activism it helped spawn.[12] Neither the industrial aesthetic nor the international outlook espoused by the architects singled out in the New York exhibition initially had much resonance across the Atlantic. During the thirties, Americans, like many of their European counterparts, instead looked inward, focusing their attention on issues of regional and national identity. Bauhaus émigrés reacted differently to this situation. Working as partners, Gropius and Breuer initially strove for a measure of assimilation, whereas Mies made little attempt to ingratiate himself.

In the twenties many American architects had turned their attention toward Europe, but they had been more often been captivated by the Continent's historical monuments or by art deco than by the International Style. Already in the latter part of the decade a vague awareness of many of the architects whose work was displayed in the Modern's galleries had infiltrated the American architectural community.[13] The austerity espoused by these Europeans was initially totally out of step, however, with the prosperity that encouraged American architects to embellish even relatively modest commissions with a rich veneer of ornament. At times, history lent an air of stability to the cherished institutions of a society and an economy that were, in fact, in flux; at other points, exotic imagery, some of it entirely of the moment, celebrated the dynamic quality of contemporary life.[14]

The Depression restrained but did not entirely erase this dual impetus for decoration. The Georgian and Gothic Revival dormitories under construction at Harvard and Yale Universities and the jazzy new cinemas in which the ordinary American found a temporary escape from the country's dire economic situation were seldom featured in the professional press, however. Many younger members of the profession began to focus their attention upon housing, mostly for the middle and working classes.

The flirtation of a handful of American architects with the white stucco boxes exhibited by Hitchcock and Johnson at the Museum of Modern Art soon gave way to designs that addressed more specifically American conditions. American advocates of modern architecture became proud of the degree to which their country's architects had moved away from European precedent.[15] In their place, Frank Lloyd Wright and William Wurster, in particular, emphasized the use of natural materials in their design of relatively modest single-family houses that were models of sensitive integration into their sites.[16] Although much of this work was understood as regional, it was widely dispersed throughout the country and shared affinities, as well, with the recent work of the two leading modernists who had remained in Europe, Le Corbusier and Alvar Aalto. Meanwhile, less adventurous architects were drawing upon a range of local vernaculars, from the colonial cottages of Cape Cod to the ranch houses of the Great Basin, to develop the modest evocations of traditional domesticity that would serve as models for postwar developers. Even politically engaged architects dedicated to the improvement of housing for the working class adhered more closely to Garden City than International Style models.[17]

Housing was not the only kind of architecture being constructed in the United States, of course, but it was the building type that most clearly reflected the changes in American architectural culture. With the exception of the influence upon streamlining of Erich Mendelsohn, singled out in the introduction to the catalog of the International Style exhibit for being less "modern" than his Bauhaus-affiliated colleagues, European modernism had even less impact upon the design of American industrial and commercial buildings.[18] Civic architecture, meanwhile, remained dominated by the planning precedents of the French academic tradition in which most American architects had been trained. These could be dressed up in a variety of styles, from Georgian to art deco. Even the engineering marvels of the day—Boulder, Grand Coulee, and Norris dams—reveal relatively little debt to the European architects who so admired American technology.

156 KATHLEEN JAMES-CHAKRABORTY

A snapshot of American architecture sponsored by the same institution that had launched the International Style in the United States revealed the ways in which even the most modernist architecture of the period differed from its supposed parent. In the exhibit Built in the USA 1932–1944, curated by Elizabeth Mock, the Museum of Modern Art showcased what it deemed the most noteworthy new American buildings (Figure 8.1).[19] Almost nothing in this show remotely resembled the buildings selected by Hitchcock and Johnson a dozen years earlier, although they are remembered today in almost direct proportion to the degree to which they were later assumed to be products of European influence. From wall surfaces to floor plans, most of the buildings on display owed more to Wright than to Le Corbusier or Mies. Except for steel sash windows, there was little trace of the industrial imagery so crucial to buildings like the Bauhaus.

The catalog, too, emphasized the distance that Americans had come on their own. In the introduction Philip Godwin denied that the museum had ever sought "to impose a foreign style."[20] Mock herself noted that "some process of humanization was necessary before the new architecture could be whole-heartedly accepted by the average man, European or American. She credited Wright's reemergence and "a revaluation of that very dark horse—traditional vernacular building" with accomplishing this.[21]

Gropius and Breuer arrived at Harvard ready to integrate themselves into this way of working. Gropius wrote Breuer, who was still in England:

> It's wonderful here. . . . All around an unspoiled, untamed landscape, most of which has not been degraded into parks and in which one doesn't always feel like a trespasser. In addition, fine wooden houses in the Colonial style, painted white, which will delight you as much as they do me. In their simplicity, functionality, and uniformity, they are completely in our line. The inviting appearance of these houses mirrors the incredible hospitality of this country, which probably stems from old pioneer times.[22]

Gropius was certainly well aware of the respect that Breuer repeatedly voiced in the mid-1930s for vernacular architecture's "tendency toward the typical, the unfashionable, that which is developed by set rules."[23]

Two of the partnership's most ambitious designs illustrate the balance they sought to maintain between respect for local traditions and the modernist ideals of convenience and efficiency. Although Gropius's own house of 1938 in the Boston suburb of Lincoln reprised aspects of the house he had built himself in Dessau, it also reveals the two men's respect for vernacular traditions, including stone walls and screened porches, as well as clapboard farmhouses (Figure 8.2). Neighbors, however, could be forgiven for focusing their attention instead upon the flat roof, exterior spiral stair, and flush siding, features that many considered a radical intrusion.[24] Local opposition to Aluminum City in New Kensington, Pennsylvania, just four years later, was predicated as much on class as design when in 1941 the federal government placed subsidized

Figure 8.1. Gardner A. Dailey, architect, and Marie Harbeck, landscape architect, L. D. Owens House, Sausalito, California, 1939. From Elizabeth Mock, ed., *Built in USA since 1932* (New York: Museum of Modern Art, 1945), 33.

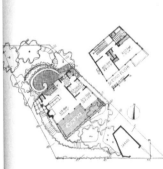

Gardner A. Dailey, architect; Marie Harbeck, landscape architect: House for L. D. Owens, 39 Atwood Avenue, Sausalito, California. 1939

Ingratiatingly modest evidence of the advantages of a flexible architecture. The architect met the problems of a wedge-shaped lot, narrow, windy and inordinately steep, with admirable directness, forsaking the characteristic horizontality of the California vernacular.

Since too much sun was impossible in that climate, the house could be designed like a wide-angle camera. Splayed side walls open up the horizontal view, and floor-to-roof glass on two sides gives full vision **down** to San Francisco Bay and **up** to the almost vertical garden which rises behind the house like a curving tapestry.

33

workers' housing into a middle-class suburb of Pittsburgh. Ignoring what was typically American—materials (wood and brick), density (low), and relationship to the landscape (it was laid out along the contours of its hillside site)—critics labeled the results "chicken coops." The original tenants were more enthusiastic. They cherished the provision of such amenities as the open land surrounding their units and the well-equipped kitchens and bathrooms.[25] After the war these features proved easily detachable, however, from modernist styling.[26]

Gropius and Breuer realized that their success in America would depend upon their ability to integrate themselves into their new surroundings. Only in an unbuilt project for Black Mountain College, itself an outpost of Bauhaus pedagogy, did they return without reservation to the International Style. Mies, on the other hand, quietly enjoyed the opportunities his position at IIT offered him to continue his own highly disciplined investigation into the relationship between form, material, and function. Despite Johnson's aggressive lobbying, it was almost a decade before he got any work other than the design of inexpensive two- and three-story buildings for the new IIT campus. Although these would eventually become icons of American architecture, they initially had little impact at home or abroad. All this would change, however, with the onset of the cold war.[27]

COLD WAR INTERNATIONALISM

The coalition represented by Mock's catalog did not last. Based on an appreciation of regional production, if not of truly individual regional styles, it depicted a nation where even the most innovative architects balanced an appreciation of deeply rooted cultural traditions, especially sensitivity to the landscape, and American preferences regarding building materials with their growing appreciation for European abstraction. She also painted a portrait of limited ambition. The buildings she illustrated were for the most part modest in scale and inexpensive to construct. They captured the spirit of contemporary American society at a time when almost everyone was learning to live

Figure 8.2. Walter Gropius and Marcel Breuer, Gropius House, Lincoln, Massachusetts, 1938. Courtesy of Society for the Preservation of New England Antiquities.

more simply, but did not give adequate scope to the country's postwar position as a global superpower.

The end of World War II brought middle- and working-class whites at least much of the social consensus and economic prosperity Americans had been promised. At the same time the expression of privilege became more difficult. Amid increasing homogeneity, modern architecture usefully conveyed status based on taste more than on wealth.[28] At the same time, although many middle-class Americans continued to suspect modernism of being communist, the image of the United States promoted in elite circles at home as well as abroad was of a tolerant and progressive sponsor of advanced, even experimental art.[29]

Once again the Museum of Modern Art led the way. In 1947, Johnson, who had reassumed the leadership of the museum's Department of Architecture and Design, organized an exhibit devoted to Mies. Johnson's catalog was the first monograph on Mies to be published in any language.[30] This fact demonstrates the extent to which the former director of the Bauhaus had been neglected in the years since his victory in the Reichsbank competition had briefly inspired the hope that his architecture would serve as the template for that of the Third Reich.[31] The reception of two projects completed in the years immediately following the exhibit delineate the limits of the extraordinary success Mies was to have in the years to come.

In a pair of apartment towers on Chicago's Lake Shore Drive, Mies realized buildings on the scale of the breakthrough designs for high-rise offices he had made for Berlin just after World War I (Figure 8.3). Faced finally with the opportunity to detail the glass skins of which he had long dreamed, he chose a system of ornamentation so representative of their skeletal steel construction that untutored observers would often assume it was structural. Steel I-beams longitudinally framed the carefully proportioned windows, marching across the facade in a rhythm that remained constant across both towers.[32]

Although these were not the first curtain-walled towers built in the United States following the war, they did garner the most attention.[33] This was in part because they seemed to make earlier American architecture a crucial predecessor for the International Style. Mies became simultaneously the heir to the Chicago school of the late nineteenth century and the badge of his adopted country's new architectural maturity. This triumph was confirmed by the facts that his towers were less expensive to construct than traditional masonry-clad buildings and that their condominium units quickly established themselves, despite minor problems with heating and cooling, as extremely good investments.[34] The stage was set for a generation of Miesian towers that, despite their German origins, would come to be seen whenever they were erected outside the United States as evidence of encroaching Americanization.

Mies's determination to design buildings whose ideal forms, conceived in detachment from all but the most abstract considerations of function or context, bestowed an

Figure 8.3. Ludwig
Mies van der Rohe,
860–880 Lake Shore
Drive Apartments,
Chicago, Illinois,
1951. Photograph
by Ezra Stoller.
Copyright Esto.

almost spiritual dignity upon the mundane activities they housed. They also coincided conveniently with the relatively egalitarian anonymity of midcentury American corporate capitalism. Abstraction ostensibly untainted by crass commercialism imparted artistry and thus dignity to what was in fact a highly efficient deployment of people as well as materials. Mies himself appeared largely oblivious to the issues of representation that might have distinguished his commercial from his civic and other institutional commissions. His focus on proportion and construction as sites of resistance to architecture as fashion or fad discouraged inquiries into the way in which he was actually blurring the boundary between the two.[35] His example encouraged the American architectural profession to focus on issues of style to the exclusion of any critique of the social and economic forces embedded in the windfall of corporate patronage they were enjoying.[36]

Americans accepted the International Style, however, only when it did not conflict with more cherished values. In his weekend house for Dr. Edith Farnsworth, Mies paid no attention to the conventions of American domesticity or construction. Instead, he pursued his apparently objective—but actually quite personal—investigation into ideal geometry and the elegant detailing of a minimalist structure into what had remained in Europe uncharted territory. Farnsworth found the resulting glass box expensive and almost uninhabitable. Although she lost her lawsuit against the architect, her position won support from Elizabeth Gordon, the editor of *House Beautiful,* who took the occasion to condemn the International Style in language that echoed the general distrust of foreigners common in cold war America.[37] Even Mies's most ardent supporters found it impossible to defend this design as a possible prototype for American domestic architecture.[38]

The furor over the Farnsworth house reprised many of the themes that had provoked the Modern's second major postwar contribution to the institutionalization of the International Style. In 1947 Lewis Mumford published an article in his *New Yorker* column, "Skylines," in which he challenged the importance of the machine to modern architecture. "The modern accent," Mumford stated, "is on living, not on the machine." He added parenthetically, "This change must hit hardest those academic American modernists who imitated Le Corbusier and Mies van der Rohe and Gropius, as their fathers imitated the reigning lights of the Ecole des Beaux-Arts."[39] Like Mock, who was Wurster's sister-in-law, Mumford offered in its place a half century of architecture from the San Francisco area.

One reason for the alarm bells this piece sounded for the émigrés and their supporters may have been the point of view epitomized in two pieces published in 1948 by Jean Murray Bangs. Bangs was the wife of the prominent California architect Harwell Hamilton Harris, whose Berkeley house for Wesley Havens was perhaps the Bay Area's most celebrated new building. Her articles on Bernhard Maybeck and the Greene brothers published in two of the nation's leading architectural journals, *Architectural Record* and *Architectural Forum,* were instrumental in drawing attention to the local roots of the Bay Area school, which she pointedly contrasted with the suspect European origins of other architectural modernisms.[40]

In response ostensibly to Mumford, the museum organized a symposium entitled "What Is Happening to Modern Architecture?" Although the initial results were ambivalent, the event marked the eclipse of Wurster and his circle by those affiliated with the Bauhaus and its American successors.[41] Hitchcock, Johnson, Gropius, and Breuer were among the speakers. Breuer, whose own work was perhaps the closest to that of the Bay Area school, voiced the most pointed of the many barbs slung at Wright, Wurster, and their many admirers: "'Human' seems to me more than just a pleasant forgiving of imperfection and an easy-goingness as to precision of thinking, as to the quality of planning, as to consequences of materials, details and construction."[42]

Others focused on the larger issues at stake. Hitchcock denied the usefulness of Wright, the figurehead for what he and Alfred Barr, the museum's founding director, caricatured as the Cottage Style, even while expressing great respect for his work. He drew attention instead to Sigfried Giedion's recent call for a monumentality appropriate to the International Style's impending triumph over its rivals.[43] Ignoring Johnson's flirtation with fascism, Barr sought to establish the political context of this triumph, which he ascribed in particular to the influence the International Style had had in the United States since 1932 as antifascist and anticommunist:

> Of course the Style has developed and changed and mellowed. It has even generated reactions and created new opponents here and abroad. We may mention in passing the bitter hostility of Hitler and his National Socialist architects to the International Style. Fortunately, this is now a matter of history. But parallel to the German reaction has been the Soviet revival of the stylistic chaos and pomposities of the nineteenth century in the name of proletarian taste and socialist realism. In this country, I would say that our best architects take the style for granted so far as large buildings are concerned.[44]

To buttress its position the museum commissioned Breuer to design a house that it displayed in its sculpture garden the following summer (Figure 8.4). The construction of his butterfly-roofed model house encouraged Americans, especially on the East Coast, to forget that such dwellings were not a fashionable new import from Europe. Nonetheless, in its own publicity, the museum stressed that "the plan of the house is closely fitted to the requirements of a typical American family" and that "the type of construction used . . . is familiar to builders in all parts of the country."[45]

In 1952, the museum once again surveyed contemporary American architecture. Hitchcock, who made the choices, used the occasion to consolidate an interpretation that replaced Mock's position with one that simultaneously emphasized the greatness of the American present and its dependence upon European precedent.[46] "In architecture, as in many other things," he declared, "we are the heirs of Western civilization." As evidence he offered not only Wright but also the fact that "we have . . . provided important commissions hardly attainable today abroad for several distinguished Europeans who have settled in our midst or who have been invited to design or to advise on the design of major structures."[47] In the exhibit Mies stood alongside Wright as the major American architect of the day, while the younger generation was represented for the most part by those who had studied under Gropius and Breuer at Harvard.[48]

This account was further institutionalized in the decade's two most important comprehensive accounts of recent architectural history. These were Giedion's third edition of *Space Time and Architecture: The Growth of a New Tradition,* published in 1953, and Hitchcock's volume for the influential Pelican History of Art series, *Architecture: Nineteenth and Twentieth Centuries,* which appeared five years later. Both authors further stressed the seamless continuity between the European modernism of the 1920s

Figure 8.4. Marcel Breuer, House in the Museum Garden, Museum of Modern Art, New York, 1948–49. Photograph by Ezra Stoller. Copyright Esto.

and contemporary American work. Giedion declared: "There are moments in the lives of nations when, like certain plants, they require extraneous fertilization in order to achieve a further phase of their cultural evolution. . . . America . . . needed a new spiritual orientation. The laws of chance made this need coincide with the exodus of many of the best European minds. [They] provided the rather devious means by which Americans were at last enabled to recognize their own pioneers."[49] Hitchcock brought the story up to date. Citing "the universality of the new architecture," he emphasized the role of a new generation of Americans who were building upon European precedent not only at home, but in buildings around the world.[50]

Indeed, support for the International Style came from precisely those who best understood the impact its imagery could have abroad. The museum's promotional efforts were buttressed, for example, by the architectural patronage meted out by the State Department. Although Congress was not always willing to fund its vision of enlightened democracy, the State Department was a crucial promoter of modern American architecture.During the 1950s and early 1960s, many American embassies and consular offices were designed by Gropius, Breuer, and their students, as well as in a Miesian manner by the firm of Skidmore, Owings, and Merrill.[51] Because the Soviets espoused socialist realism, which even many of Europe and Latin America's most committed Marxist intellectuals found difficult to take seriously, America's apparent commitment to all forms of artistic modernism was widely understood to be an effective cold war weapon. The patronage of private American companies, such as the Hilton hotel chain and IBM, in buildings erected in Europe and the Middle East further reinforced this image.[52]

The importance of the Museum of Modern Art in disseminating Bauhaus architecture in the United States, and of the State Department in confirming its impact, hints at the limited ways in which that influence actually functioned. Sleek steel and glass cages remained relative rarities throughout the United States during the 1950s, while on the East Coast even Breuer's more palatable wood-sheathed angular boxes found an enthusiastic reception only in "advanced" circles.[53] Furthermore, even though new federal legislation gave city planners increased control over the layout of many urban neighborhoods, most construction remained stubbornly out of the hands of design professionals. Real estate developers both shaped and responded to consumer demands when they created vast new suburbs with little input from the International Style.[54] Only the poor, who had little say over such matters, would be warehoused in buildings whose failure to fulfill their needs was more a consequence of social than of architectural factors.[55]

MULTIPLE MODERNISMS

That Gropius, Mies, and their students did not dominate the design of the environments in which most Americans lived, worked, studied, and played does not mean that Americans remained averse to modernism. A substantial audience existed for blatantly commercial variants of the style. Sandy Isenstadt recounts that "cubic forms, flat roofs, spare geometries, reduced ornament, and glass walls only added another aisle to the postwar supermarket of style."[56] Even within the canon supported by the Museum of Modern Art and the State Department, there was ample evidence of a modernist tradition far broader than the Bauhaus and its progeny. During the postwar period this broader tradition was responsible for the innovative design of a wide range of popular consumer-oriented commodities. Modernism's range remained largely unacknowledged, however, because it did not neatly dovetail with the narratives that validated postwar architectural practices. Comparing the lives and work of two European-born textile designers, Anni Albers and Marianne Strengell, who immigrated to the United States within four years of one another, illustrates the way in which this interpretation generated substantial gaps between artistic and commercial recognition.

Anni Albers, née Fleischmann, was born in Berlin in 1899, Strengell three years later in Helsinki. Albers enrolled at the Bauhaus in 1922. Like most female students at the otherwise progressive school, she was encouraged to join the weaving work-shop. Here, Gropius believed, they could focus on a gender-appropriate activity without threatening the seriousness with which the school's core enterprises were taken. Although it remained something of a ghetto, the weaving workshop thrived, as did the enthusiastic young Albers. Under the influence of her instructors, the form master Paul Klee and the head of the workshop, Gunta Stölzl, she began to experiment with the design and production of woven fabrics whose abstract patterns accentuated the structure of warp and weft. She also met and married Josef Albers, a fellow student who was quickly promoted to a teaching position in the important preliminary course.[57] Meanwhile Strengell, who received more conventional training, was gaining exposure to modernist design through her work on international exhibitions in Stockholm and Milan.[58]

In the United States, both women became influential teachers at new institutions increasingly dedicated to modernist art and design. Anni and Josef Albers were perhaps the first native German Bauhauslers to move to America, arriving in 1933. After being recommended by Johnson, they both obtained teaching positions at Black Mountain College. With an innovative curriculum that encouraged experimentation across the fine arts and an energetic young faculty, Black Mountain quickly became the closest thing there was to an American successor to the Bauhaus, in spirit if not in name. During the Alberses' sixteen years at Black Mountain, their colleagues and students included Ruth Asawa, John Cage, Merce Cunningham, Kenneth Noland, and Robert Rauschenberg.[59]

Strengell arrived in the United States in 1937 to teach at the Cranbrook Academy, where from 1942 until 1961 she was the head of the Department of Weaving and Textile Design. Cranbrook, founded a decade earlier by the Finnish architect Eliel Saarinen, accounted for much of the vitality of postwar American architecture and design. It eventually proved relatively easy to fold the work of many former Cranbrook students into a history of modern architecture and design in which only the Bauhaus and its American successors were accorded iconic status.[60]

Cranbrook was initially far more securely rooted in the Arts and Crafts movement than the Bauhaus, despite Gropius's earliest intentions, had ever been. This was reflected in the architecture of the campus, located in the Detroit suburb of Bloomfield Hills. The almost monastic character of Cranbrook's courtyard-oriented campus entirely avoided the Bauhaus's frank acceptance of industrialization.It also reflected the ten-year difference in age between Saarinen, who in Finland had moved from the recollection of rustic charm to an increasing engagement with civic monumentality, and Gropius. Like many of his fellow National Romantics, Saarinen anticipated the reassuring integration of permanence and individuality into designs of increasingly forthright simplicity that would distinguish Scandanavian design in the middle decades of the twentieth century.[61]

In some cases the influence of Cranbrook and the Bauhaus clearly overlapped. Between 1939 and 1941, Florence Schust Knoll studied at Cranbrook, in London, and at IIT. She also worked briefly during this period for Gropius and Breuer. Under her leadership, Knoll International would make the American office interior a showcase for contemporary furniture and textiles.[62]

Other Cranbrook alumni enjoyed equally stunning success despite their lack of Bauhaus credentials. Charles and Ray Eames's designs for everything from molded plywood furniture to exhibit installations featured a lively integration of function and abstraction that appealed simultaneously to their corporate and governmental clients and to the publics they were hired to reach.[63] A similar flair for creating architectural identities whose purpose was often commercial distinguished the architectural career of Eliel's son Eero, who during the 1950s rivaled Mies as America's most respected and influential architect.[64]

Cranbrook's influence enlivened, and thus made palatable, the structural changes in the American economy that had prompted much of the acceptance modernist design did indeed enjoy. New materials, especially plastics and synthetic fibers, made inexpensive manufactured goods more durable and comfortable. For the most part Bauhaus products were too austere for either the general public or those who candidly sought to influence their choices as consumers. The Bauhaus remained crucial, however, because it dignified the simplification and standardization of objects of daily life with the principles of a high art apparently divorced from the crudity of the marketplace.

From the beginning textiles were central to the understanding at Cranbrook of the relation between the fine and decorative arts. Eliel Saarinen's wife Louise (Loja) Gesellius Saarinen was a widely exhibited weaver and textile designer, as was their daughter Eva Lisa (Pipsan) Saarinen Swanson. Studio Loja Saarinen, established in 1928, initially concentrated on producing fabrics for the Cranbrook campus. By the forties, however, Strengell and Swanson shifted much of their attention to providing printed and woven prototypes for industry.[65]

Meanwhile, Albers began to achieve fame as a new kind of weaver, one who combined considerable distinction as an artist—she was awarded a solo exhibit at New York's Museum of Modern Art in 1949—with an admiration for machines, their products, and the standardization they encouraged. Her handwoven tapestries and mass-produced upholstery fabrics, the latter manufactured by Knoll, offered architects, including Johnson, Gropius, and Breuer, as well as interior decorators durable and abstract patterns and textures that complimented modernist architecture, while serving as an alternative to conventional ornament (Figure 8.5).

Like Albers, Strengell gave students a solid grounding in the technical aspects of weaving, but she also encouraged them to consider economic as well as technical and aesthetic issues. Her sensitivity to the questions of marketing ignored by Albers

enabled Strengell to achieve the integration between art and industry prophesied by Gropius. Less active as a fine artist than Albers, she instead worked closely with a wide array of manufacturers, designers, and architects. Her corporate clients included Ford, Chrysler, and General Motors. She collaborated as well with the industrial designer Raymond Loewy on the interior design of United Airlines jet planes and with Eero Saarinen on the General Motors Technical Center, for which she designed carpeting as well as upholstery fabrics.[66]

The move into printed fabric liberated Strengell from the woven grid that kept Albers loyal to Bauhaus rectilinearity (Figure 8.6). Her emphasis on surface rather than structure ensured that Strengell's work was more decorative than that of her Bauhaus counterparts. This distinction accounted for much of her commercial success at the same time that it hindered her recognition as an artist. Strengell remains overshadowed by her Bauhaus-trained counterpart, who has been accorded most of the credit for changes in textile design for which Strengell and her students were at least equally responsible.

As this example demonstrates, the presence of Bauhaus figures such as Gropius, Mies, Breuer, and Albers on American shores was less important in effecting the very real changes that took place in architecture and design during the 1930s and 1940s than it was in explaining them after the fact. Accounts of the Bauhaus that situated the replacement of a romantic celebration of craft with the uncritical acceptance of the machine within a European school renowned for its fine artists and its principled liberal politics enabled postwar American modernists to see themselves as courageous pioneers.[67] Conveniently forgotten was the degree to which these "pioneers" were allied with many of their new homeland's most powerful people and institutions in ways that reinforced rather than challenged American cultural stereotypes and corporate capitalism, if not aesthetic conventions. The efficient production, using inexpensive new materials, of highly functional buildings and objects instead appeared as freedom of artistic

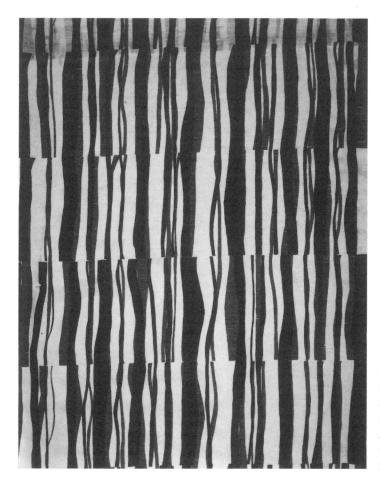

Figure 8.6. Marianne Strengell, drapery fabric, circa 1955–60. Printed silk. Collection of Cranbrook Art Museum, Bloomfield Hills, Michigan (museum purchase CAM 1981.7).

expression. Modernism never won universal acceptance in the United States, not least because ornament could be as cheaply mass-produced as its own clean lines. By converting consumerism into abstract art, however, it dignified the increased standardization that was the cost of the general rise in the postwar American standard of living. Such elevated rhetoric, although useful at home, was equally important abroad. As the next essay underscores, the American afterlife of the Bauhaus offered the United States one of its most appealing weapons against the Soviet bloc.

THE BAUHAUS IN COLD WAR GERMANY

Greg Castillo

The history of the Bauhaus was not only written during the cold war, it was also a cold war artifact. The immigration of Bauhauslers to the United States during the 1930s was the launching point for narratives about the Americanization of European avant-garde design. Triumphalists interpreted the new world successes of Mies, Gropius, and other Bauhaus figures as evidence of the global preeminence of American post-war culture.[1] Bauhaus histories largely ignored the ongoing development of Bauhaus pedagogy in its German homeland. Three disparate efforts to revive Bauhaus peda-gogy in early postwar Germany—two in the Soviet-affiliated eastern sector, and one in the U.S.-allied west—provide case studies of how Bauhaus revivals promoted oppos-ing cold war ideologies: an aspect of the school's legacy studiously ignored or strate-gically dissimulated in postwar histories.

As the anthropologist Katherine Verdery has observed, the cold war was not only a military standoff but also "a form of knowledge and a cognitive organization of the world."[2] As the cold war split the world into opposing geopolitical camps, it also divided structures of cultural knowledge. At the broadest scale, the cold war's processes of bi-nary partition yielded the twentieth century's two largest, deliberately designed experi-ments in globalization: one pursued by the Soviet Union in the name of international so-cialism, the other led by the United States in defense of what it called "the free world." By 1950, each of these global orders had adopted a signature aesthetic. The Soviet bloc's was socialist realism, a hybrid neoclassicism said to be "national in form and socialist in content." This straightforward equation of style with geopolitical content was short-lived. By the late 1950s, reforms championed by Stalin's successor, Nikita Khrushchev, increased tolerance of modernist design on the part of Communist Party authorities across the Soviet bloc.

Prior to the imposition of cold war politics on the Bauhaus legacy, it had been ideologically indeterminate. Arguments for the application of Bauhaus pedagogy to promote socialism or capitalist democracy both could be found within the school's eclectic political past. Gropius's progressive outlook, forged in Germany's revolution of 1918 and tempered by the Weimar Republic's social democracy, characterized the school's early years. Hannes Meyer, Gropius's successor, put modernism at the service of a socialist cultural agenda. The school's last director, Mies van der Rohe, cultivated political disengagement as a survival strategy in his unsuccessful attempt to prevent right-wing extremists from closing the school. Postwar Bauhaus revivals typically enthroned one of these institutional personas and its politics as "authentic" and dismissed all others as deviations.

Attempts to resuscitate the Bauhaus in postwar Germany, while differing in ideological goals, shared certain values and tactics. The school's philosophy of harnessing art to industrial production was a common strategy for the speedy recovery of a war-ravaged economy and the efficient manufacture of scarce consumer goods. Bauhaus advocates often embraced a more sweeping concept of reform as well. The proposition that design could reshape postwar citizens was a leitmotif in Germany's attempted Bauhaus revivals, both in the east and west. Credence in environmental determinism—the power of objects and surroundings to determine human behavior—led many modernists to argue that Bauhaus culture would yield a new German citizen, usually described as "democratic."[3] This yearning for the empowerment of form (and form givers) was ironic when invoked in the name of democracy, since granting designers absolutist authority for a totalizing reconstruction of human environments constituted the opposite of democratic process. Schemes for social reform through Bauhaus pedagogy also invoked shared beliefs about the school's political heritage. The Nazi closure of the Bauhaus in 1933 provided the school with sterling "antifascist" credentials that were maintained through ignorance, willful or otherwise, of the collaboration of Bauhaus-trained architects in the construction of the Third Reich's military-industrial complex. This historical fact, had it not been dissimulated and repressed from memory, might well have compromised postwar use of the Bauhaus legacy as a symbol of social progress.[4]

HUBERT HOFFMANN AND THE NEW DESSAU BAUHAUS: 1945–47

Like its German homeland, Walter Gropius's Bauhaus building in Dessau entered the postwar era in ruin. In 1933, a year after Dessau's newly Nazified city government had sent Gropius's art academy packing, the research division of the Junker works, one of the largest producers of warplanes for the Luftwaffe, had moved into the modernist masterpiece. During an American bombing raid in March 1945, a single incendiary device pierced the building's roof, falling into a drafting studio. Incandescent magnesium ignited mechanical drawings of weaponry, and then everything around them. Plate glass shattered in the searing heat. Metal window frames became ductile, bulging outward under their own weight. At the epicenter of the blaze, concrete roof planks buckled, and crumbling plaster rained down from ceilings and walls.[5]

On 23 April 1945, after two days of fierce ground fighting, the U.S. Army Seventh Corps occupied Dessau. Assigned to the armored division that rumbled through the ravaged city was Henry Cohen, an officer who in a distant civilian past had studied architecture at MIT. He found the Bauhaus building gutted and abandoned. Cohen waded through hallways strewn with blueprints of German aircraft, exploring the concrete hulk "room for room and floor for floor." Although the top floor of the workshop wing was "a rubble pile of plaster surrounded by badly damaged bare walls," the building apparently was structurally sound.[6]

Cohen left Dessau to push east with his unit toward a historic convergence with the Red Army. Between naps stolen en route, he penned a note to William Wurster, his former MIT professor. Cohen's letter contained the first news to reach America concerning the fate of the Dessau Bauhaus, as well as a confession. He admitted that the spectacle of terrified locals in flight to avoid Soviet troops left his platoon unmoved: "we . . . do not care one iota over what happens to the Germans." But the fate of Gropius's institute still could elicit a scrap of compassion for the design school's homeland:

> It is safe to say that the Bauhaus has outlived the fiendish uses to which it was put. Though allied bombing damaged it, and harassed the aircraft planning within its walls, Germany will again have an opportunity to use the Bauhaus for progressive purposes. Gropius had to come to America to display his architectural ideas, to help out in forward looking housing and construction, and in educating students toward those purposes. Hitler could not use that kind of stuff. . . . With a slight effort, Germany can again have the Bauhaus and the things it stood for.[7]

In the course of the next few years, however, the nature of the Bauhaus legacy and "the things it stood for" would prove far more ambiguous than Cohen seemed to think.

The U.S. Army, ironically enough, made possible the first postwar attempt to revive the Bauhaus as an institute for the design of objects and environments calculated to hasten the triumph of socialism. Although Dessau had fallen within the Soviet occupation zone mapped out by Roosevelt, Churchill, and Stalin, American forces reached the city first. U.S. Army officers purged the city government of Nazi administrators and appointed Fritz Hesse as mayor. He was well qualified for the post, having held it two decades earlier. Hesse had been responsible for bringing Gropius's design academy to Dessau in the 1920s. He resolved to resuscitate the Bauhaus and assigned the project to Hubert Hoffmann, one of its few alumni to have experienced the school under all three of its directors: Gropius, Meyer, and Mies van der Rohe.

Although Hoffmann had made his leftist sympathies explicit as early as 1931 through work on the Proletarian Building Exhibition, held in Berlin on the eve of the Nazi ascent to power, his subsequent career was a tangle of political paradoxes. He had led a double life during the war. While retaining allegiances to left-leaning Bauhaus comrades, he worked as a planner engaged to redevelop Nazi-occupied Lithuania as a Third Reich colony. During the final days of the war, hoping to avoid capture by vindictive Soviet troops, Hoffmann deserted his post at Berlin's Imperial Academy of Urban Planning. He and his colleagues jolted their way westward in the back of a truck heading toward the advancing American front. In the snowy silence of a forest outside the village of Bismark, Hoffmann buried his Third Reich uniform and papers—and with them, he hoped, his wartime employment history.[8] In July 1945, Hesse tracked Hoffmann down and lured him to Dessau with the shared dream of a postwar Bauhaus resurrection.[9]

Hoffmann's attitude toward his alma mater was an amalgam of veneration for its unfulfilled promise and contempt for its commercial achievements. Postwar Bauhaus design was to live up to an aphorism coined in the 1920s by Bauhaus director Meyer: "People's necessities instead of luxury goods." The school could thus avoid what Hoffmann decried as "the fate of the old Bauhaus, which (with exceptions) created a few pieces of furniture, houses, and appliances for snobs."[10] Hoffmann's indictment, while ignoring numerous interwar experiments in proletarian housing overseen by Gropius, Meyer, and a host of Bauhaus students, demonstrated another Weimar-era revival: the penchant for charging onto politically volatile territory bearing the Bauhaus banner. In pronouncements regarding the Dessau Bauhaus and its planned postwar successor, Hoffmann consistently associated the school's legacy with leftist cultural politics.

Hoffmann's scheme for the battered modernist monument foresaw the installation of new workshops for carpentry, painting, textiles, metalwork, printing, and architecture—a plan that far exceeded available resources. He began assembling the new Bauhaus by securing facilities and faculty that had survived the war. He recruited former alumni as prospective teachers: Carl Fieger, Carl Marx, Georg Neidenberger, Rolf Radack, Hinnerk Scheper, and Max Ursin were among the first wave to return to Dessau. Hoffmann also oversaw makeshift repairs to Gropius's building. The roof was patched, and fire-damaged walls were replastered, but a nationwide glass shortage made restoration of the famous curtain-wall facade impossible. Where floor-to-ceiling glazing had proclaimed a revolution in architecture, window openings were sealed with walls of scavenged brick (Figure 9.1).

Interwar Bauhaus pedagogy provided a springboard for the school's postwar successor. Preparatory training in its broadest sense would be the agenda of a preliminary course, just as it had been at Gropius's Bauhaus. Similarly, an ensuing phase of instruction would familiarize students with design's diverse subdisciplines. Specialized proficiency would accrue through apprenticeships. For their final stage of training, students would participate in team research in partnerships with the nonacademic world.[11] However, a philosophical divide separated this postwar Bauhaus from its Weimar predecessor, as revealed by Hoffmann's curriculum chart (Figure 9.2). Prewar Bauhaus pedagogy had positioned architecture at the center of all design endeavors, as depicted graphically in Gropius's bull's-eye diagram of his academy's curricular goals. At the postwar Bauhaus, the core competency informing design training was to be an

Figure 9.1. Bauhaus building, Dessau, photographed in the early 1950s. Stadtarchiv Dessau.

innovative, interdisciplinary concept of "horticulture." This academic abandonment of the machine metaphors favored by Weimar modernism was a posttraumatic response to the technological nightmare of "total war." The new curricular emphasis would instill reverence for nature, establishing its patterns and processes as the paradigm for all creative enterprises: a revisionist outlook underscored by Hoffmann's nomination of landscape architect Hermann Mattern as the school's future director.[12]

To ensure the school's postwar revival, Hoffmann set out to establish a dominant position for himself in Dessau's administrative hierarchy, taking control of the city's planning department through his ties to the mayor. Hoffmann also took a seat on the town parliament and appointed himself local chairman of the influential Cultural Union for the Democratic Renewal of Germany: "all in order to realize the Bauhaus idea 'to reunite art and life,' proceeding from a concrete position of power," as he explained decades later.[13] This arrogation of authority, invoked in the name of postwar democracy

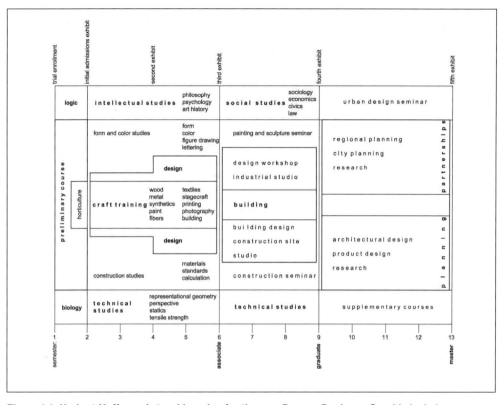

Figure 9.2. Herbert Hoffmann's teaching plan for the new Dessau Bauhaus. Graphic by Luis Bustamante, based on an original diagram in the Archiv Hubert Hoffmann, Archiv Hoffmann, St. Veit, Austria.

but manifestly incompatible with it, was bitterly resented by Hoffmann's political competitors, including representatives of the Soviet-backed SED (Sozialistische Einheitspartei Deutschlands), the German Socialist Unity Party.

As the SED assumed control of the Soviet sector in the fall of 1946, Hoffmann lost a crucial ally. The party removed Hesse from the mayor's office, replacing him with a Soviet-trained German.[14] "The new mayor heard the word 'Bauhaus' for the first time when I used it in conversation," Hoffmann ranted.[15] Worse yet, Dessau's new mayor soon discovered Hoffmann's former credentials as a Third Reich planner, an employment episode discreetly omitted from his résumé. Hoffmann was fired and his food ration card withdrawn amid threats of arrest and deportation to Russia.[16] "The methods that were used before 1933 [to vilify the Bauhaus] are harmless compared to the kind of denunciations, political defamations, etc., that have been set in motion against us," he reported to Gropius. "We have all but given up on Dessau."[17] With his options exhausted in the Soviet sector, Hoffmann emigrated to West Berlin.

MART STAM, DRESDEN'S "BAUSCHULE,"
AND THE BERLIN-WEISSENSEE ART ACADEMY: 1948–52

A subsequent attempt to retrieve Bauhaus pedagogy in the name of postwar German socialism achieved provisional success. Its sponsor was Mart Stam, a Dutch-born architect who had taught at the Dessau Bauhaus under Meyer. After spending the war years in Nazi-occupied Holland working with the resistance movement, Stam's commitment to communism inspired his postwar emigration to East Germany. In 1948, he approached Gerhard Strauss, a top official in the Ministry of Education, and announced: "The [party] central committee sent me. I want to help build socialism. What can I do? Where can you use me?"[18]

In fact, Stam had in mind a project of his own. He outlined a plan to replace art school instruction with a curriculum of architecture and applied design based on Bauhaus precedent. A preliminary course would instill basic design philosophy. Subsequent specialization in painting, graphics, textiles, product design, or architecture would link students with state industries and the party's centrally managed socialist reconstruction. The proposal was perfectly timed. In June 1948, the U.S. military government enacted a currency reform that coupled Germany's western occupation zones to the capitalist West. Before the month was out, the Soviet sector unveiled its alternate economic future in a two-year plan modeled on Soviet precedent. By October, Stam's bureaucratic patron, Strauss, was promoting the linkage of nationalized industry and art schools in order to cultivate a cadre of designers trained to create objects for mass production.[19] The Stalinization of East Germany, heralded by the replication of a Soviet-style economy and its supporting structures of party-managed education and culture, was to be aided and abetted by Stam's Bauhaus-inspired pedagogy.

Stam was named rector of both Dresden's Academy of Fine Art (Kunstakademie) and the city's College of Arts and Crafts (Hochschule für Werkkunst), and given the mandate to merge both institutions into a single entity, which he named "bauschule." Academic atelier culture would be abolished. Student recruitment would favor candidates from working-class backgrounds. Education would emphasize the design of "progressive household goods" for working class consumers.[20] Bauhaus pedagogy, in other words, would be exercised by and for the proletariat. Although these changes enchanted government officials like Strauss, the same could not be said for the school's faculty. Stam dismissed conservative instructors under the pretense that they were compromised by Nazi collaboration. In fact, the purge was based on aesthetic rather than political allegiences, as demonstrated by Stam's recruitment of Bauhaus alumna Marianne Brandt, a former member of the Third Reich's Kulturkammer.[21] His dictatorial manner, contempt for academic art, and privileging of architecture sparked a faculty mutiny. Within a year, the plan to forge a new socialist design school in Dresden had reached a stalemate. Convinced that Stam's talents might be better applied elsewhere,

Strauss and the party transferred him to the Berlin-Weißensee Art Academy, another institution in need of an overhaul.[22]

Upon arrival in Berlin, Stam began transforming Berlin-Weißensee into a laboratory for socialist industrial design. He was an engaging host of new instructors, including Bauhaus alumnus and fellow party comrade Selman Selmanagic. They found the school hobbled by limited resources and mediocre pupils. Stam cracked down on the poor work quality and lack of application among a cohort of students he diagnosed as suffering from "fear of creativity." He believed that "first and foremost, the size of this group should be reduced"—a disciplinary campaign that would come back to haunt him.[23] Stam also struggled to build a research collective applying the school's best talents to actual design commissions. In collaboration with the [East] German Bureau of Standardization and Product Testing, and the state Ministries of Heavy Industry and Popular Education, Berlin-Weißensee's Institute of Industrial Design, Ceramics [Division], was established in 1951. It received an initial state commission to design ceramic heaters. Additional research divisions for textiles, wood, and metal products also were planned. Stam seemed well on his way to linking design education with socialist state industries, and taking working-class consumers to "a higher plane of taste and culture." Design research at Berlin-Weißensee would transform East German material culture, he believed: "There are hundreds of superfluous and tasteless petit-bourgeois products to be scrutinized and discontinued."[24]

Although Stam championed the party's hegemony over the means of industrial and cultural production, he was oddly out of touch with the standards of taste it entailed. In 1951, East Germany was in the throes of a Stalinist cultural revolution; what made Stam's myopia remarkable was that he had witnessed the original in Russia during the 1930s. He had gone to the USSR in 1929, driven eastward, along with hundreds of German architects, by capitalism's global depression, the promise of a socialist alternative, and the professional opportunities inherent in Stalin's Five-Year Plan and its agenda of new construction and industrial modernization. But the Kremlin soon abandoned its patronage of modernism in favor of socialist realist neoclassicism. Stam left Russia in 1934, just as a wave of Soviet xenophobia was casting all foreigners, communist or otherwise, as potential saboteurs.[25] A brief relaxation of party oversight had occurred in the early 1940s as the Kremlin mobilized to wage war against Nazi aggression rather than internal aesthetic deviance. The party reasserted its authority over art in a postwar crackdown known as the *Zhdanovshchina* after its initiator, Andrei Zhdanov of the Party Central Committee. Zhdanov demanded that artists and intellectuals renounce aesthetic values associated with the contemporary West. Those who persisted in their enthusiasm for modernist modes of expression were accused of "toadying to the West," persecuted, and forbidden to distribute their work.[26] In the late 1940s, this cultural battlefront moved into the newly minted People's Republics of Eastern Europe.

Figure 9.3. Mart Stam, architect, model of competition design for Böhlen Palace of Culture (unbuilt), 1949. Sächsische Landesbibliothek, Deutsche Fotothek.

While the decorative flourishes defined as "progressive" under socialist realism defied Stam's conception of realism, Stalinist indoctrination had left its mark. Although the provenance of specific product prototypes remains too vague to be attributed with confidence to Stam, the paper trail left behind demonstrates a cross-fertilization of modernist and Stalinist rhetoric. He proclaimed the necessity of a "new style" expressing socialist society's "comradely and life-affirming" qualities: the stock tropes of Stalinist collective pathos.[27] An accommodation of socialist realist monumentality is evident in his little-known project of 1949 for a "Palace of Culture" at the Böhlen Chemical Works (Figure 9.3). Its attenuated columnar portico is perched atop a stepped stylobate; heroic bas-reliefs crown the entry. This resuscitation of classicism is so out of keeping with the rest of Stam's oeuvre that it seems like the work of a different architect. In a sense, it was.[28] Stam searched diligently for the unlikely (and, as it turned out, unwanted) Hegelian resolution of the clash between Bauhaus modernism and its self-appointed antithesis, socialist realism.

The *Zhdanovshchina* arrived at the art academy in Berlin-Weißensee in February 1950, just prior to Stam's directorship. The school's use of "hostile" avant-garde imagery in posters and invitations circulated for a school celebration was the catalyst for a purge in which six modernist instructors were forced out of their jobs for their "bourgeois" and "reactionary" views.[29] As a leader in the school's party organization, Stam was expected to ferret out other faculty suspected of aesthetic deviance. It was a responsibility that he evaded, as indeed he had to. By the party's newly Sovietized cultural criteria, Stam was himself guilty. On 26 January 1951, a six-member delegation from the SED and the Ministry of Education arrived at Berlin-Weißensee demanding a clarification of school policy regarding cultural degeneracy. A handful of faculty voiced their disappointment with the campaign's reductive logic and combative tone; Stam urged a measure of tolerance for aesthetic diversity and disagreement among comrades. A transcript of these comments went directly to the SED Central Committee.[30]

As the party shifted East Germany's cultural revolution into high gear, Stam and his modernist faculty became national role models for ideological deviance in the arts. Denunciations were obtained from disgruntled students, regarded as design mediocrities under Stam's disciplinarian regime, but now declared by party authorities to be "politically and ideologically further along than their professors."[31] Stam and Selmanagic were condemned as being "stuck back in the Bauhaus tradition."[32] At the Fifth Congress of the SED Central Committee in March 1951, the party elaborated on the politics of such backwardness. "Today, where are the architects who represented the Bauhaus, such as Gropius, Mies van der Rohe . . . and others? They are in America, they appear to like it there, and from this we can infer that they have decided in favor of American imperialism."[33] As made clear by SED party chairman Walter Ulbricht, resistance to socialist realist neoclassicism rendered a designer unfit to participate in the building of socialism. "In the wake of functionalism and the formalism of the so-called Bauhaus style, which—particularly in West Germany, as introduced by the Americans—have led architecture to a dead end, it is necessary to base the architecture of a new Germany on the classical legacy and . . . above all, Soviet architecture."[34] Given a cultural revolution that depicted the Bauhaus legacy as an American pathology and celebrated neoclassicism as progressive, Stam's attempt to create a "new style" for socialist Germany was a lost cause. A call for his resignation surfaced in the Party Central Committee as early as March 1951.[35] In September 1952, he was replaced as director of the Berlin-Weißensee Art Academy. A restraining order prohibited him from setting foot on the school's grounds. On New Year's Day 1953, Stam became an immigrant again. Discarded by the political system he had spent much of his life trying to serve, he left East Germany "sick in heart and soul," as his wife later testified.[36]

WALTER GROPIUS AND THE AMERICANIZATION
OF THE BAUHAUS LEGACY

Any hope of reviving Bauhaus pedagogy in the name of socialism was shattered by the infiltration of the cold war into the domain of culture, a geopolitical process in which the founder of the original Bauhaus played no small part. Even before SED leaders in East Berlin began equating the Bauhaus with U.S. expansionism, Gropius was forging that myth's cold war complement from his home base at Harvard, reinterpreting Bauhaus design as intrinsically democratic and incompatible with totalitarianism in any form. When Donald Drew Egbert, an art historian, asked him to comment on the history of the Bauhaus "in relation to socialism [. . . and] the forms (if not the content) of Russian Constructivist art," Gropius deemed the request an inquest. "When I read your letter I felt that picking out some of these points and putting them together gives altogether a distorted picture which reminds me of the activities of the Thomas Committee [on un-American activities]." Gropius's denial of socialist influence at the Bauhaus was categorical: "Many of the members of the Bauhaus were interested in social improvement, but the main tendency was very much anti-Marxist."[37] Given this claim, one can only imagine his reaction to letters sent to him from Dessau by his former student, Hubert Hoffmann, eulogizing the Weimar-era design community founded by Gropius as "a true socialist team," and proclaiming that in postwar Germany "the designation 'Cultural Bolshevik,' which Nazis used to stigmatize Bauhaus disciples, will become an honorary title."[38] "Discussing the collapse of Hoffmann's plan for a Soviet-zone Bauhaus, Gropius wrote to one of its participants: "I'm not surprised that the experiment failed. Circumstances today are completely different."[39]

Gropius's own situation was not least among the circumstances that had changed. His position as the chair of Harvard's Department of Architecture situated him within a pool of academic expertise that would eventually guide West Germany's political and economic reconstruction. In 1942, he offered his services to a Harvard think tank assembled to plan the future of a postwar Europe under U.S. occupation. The committee's director, Carl J. Friedrich, himself a German émigré, gave Gropius "the assignment of naming reliable figures in [Germany and Italy] in the field of architecture and art, in the event of a Nazi defeat."[40] By war's end, Friedrich had risen to a position of influence as the U.S. military government's chief adviser on the reestablishment of a constitutional democracy in Germany. In 1947, he used his position to push for Gropius's assignment as a reconstruction consultant to the U.S. high commander, General Lucius Clay.[41] In just five years, Gropius had been transformed from a German émigré classified by U.S. immigration authorities as an "enemy alien" to an American cultural ambassador and internationally recognized authority on democratic approaches to urban planning.

During a western German lecture tour sponsored by the the U.S. high commander in 1947, Gropius advanced a new world modernism that fused Bauhaus design with distinctly American developments: domestic consumer technology, universal automobile ownership, and the "neighborhood unit" planning propounded by Clarence Stein and Henry Wright.[42] Gropius portrayed this suburban paradigm as the ideal incubator for democratic subjectivities. After attending his lecture in Berlin, Hans Scharoun commented: "For Gropius, the Bauhaus was the path rather than the goal. In America, the path continued onward."[43] The concept of a Bauhaus tradition that had found refuge and new sustenance in America advanced U.S. State Department goals in several ways. It cast the United States as the conqueror that had preserved Germany's cultural heritage; a more flattering reputation than that of having bombed it to rubble. American patronage of cutting-edge modernism also countered communist propaganda depicting the United States as a superpower ruled by parvenus.[44] By the mid-1950s, the U.S. State Department was touting American avant-garde culture abroad as exemplary of democratic freedom of expression. In this dubious marriage of politics and aesthetics, art that was by definition "nonrepresentational" was used to represent core American values: a propaganda achievement so unlikely that it was nothing short of sublime.[45]

Gropius's visit to the U.S.-occupied zone provided good reason for Soviet authorities to view the Bauhaus legacy with suspicion. They learned that Gropius had arrived in Germany charged with a clandestine commission—to begin planning for the reconstruction of Frankfurt am Main as the future West German capital.[46] Gropius revealed the nature of this covert assignment to reporters in December 1947, just as negotiations on German unification were collapsing. His leak made international headlines and provoked outrage among Communists. The fact that his design commission had begun nine months before Germany's official split into two separate cold war states demonstrated that American diplomats had considered the partition a fait accompli, despite assurances to the contrary.[47] Gropius proved better at keeping a secret of his connection to Berlin's CIA headquarters. In the summer of 1946, he wrote a letter introducing Scharoun to a Harvard couple that had recently relocated to Berlin. Gropius casually noted: "Mr. Durand is politically active in the American military administration. The Durands have asked us to introduce them to our friends—those who still live in Berlin."[48] Scharoun evidently complied with the request. In a letter written to Gropius from the Soviet sector, Hoffmann mentioned meeting the Durands during a trip to Berlin.[49] Dana B. Durand had moved to the city to replace Richard Helms as the chief officer of the OSS Berlin Operations Base, and presided over its transformation into the CIA's most important cold war outpost.[50] In addition to pitching modernist reconstruction for the U.S. State Department, Gropius appears to have provided the CIA with contacts involved in Soviet zone reconstruction, including one inside East Berlin's Institut für Bauwesen, the organization headed by Scharoun until 1950 and entrusted with strategic East German rebuilding projects.[51]

MAX BILL AND THE FOUNDING OF THE ULM HOCHSCHULE FÜR GESTALTUNG: 1949–53

A less covert alliance between Gropius and U.S. military authorities involved the reintroduction of modernist design pedagogy into West Germany. During his 1947 visit, Gropius had been instrumental in suppressing traditionalist architectural instruction in Stuttgart. There, at the urging of militant local modernists, he and an entourage of U.S. Army administrators met with professors and students of the local architecture school to discuss the reinstatement into the faculty of Paul Schmitthenner, a longtime adversary of "the new architecture." By the meeting's end, the previous position of U.S. administrators was overturned, and, according to a student eyewitness, "it was decided that Prof. Schmitthenner should not return to his teaching position."[52] Gropius's direct role in suppressing academic traditionalism was limited to Stuttgart. More decisive for the broader landscape of postwar design education was his support for the Ulm Hochschule für Gestaltung (Academy of Design, or HfG), often considered the West German successor to the Bauhaus.

The HfG was the brainchild of Inge Scholl and Otl Aicher, former colleagues of the members of an anti-Nazi dissident group called the "White Rose," which had been brutally suppressed by the Gestapo. As a postwar memorial to her martyred siblings, Scholl dreamed of founding a progressive institute of higher learning. She approached Germany's capitulation as an opportunity to redirect the nation toward a socialist democracy. "The world of bourgeois imagination is no longer sufficient," Scholl wrote in 1946. "[Socialism] should no longer be merely the cry of the dispossessed, but must become the obligation of a new culture."[53] Faith that design could cure German social disorders secured a role for Bauhaus pedagogy within Scholl's agenda for educational reform. While teaching design at Ulm's city college (Volkshochschule), she and Aicher met Max Bill, a Bauhaus alumnus employed by the U.S. occupation government as a consultant on popular education.[54] Bill's position on the faculty of Zurich's Kunstgewerbeschule (Arts Trade School) provided credentials that could help realize the goal of founding a postwar institute, and he agreed to join this joint effort.

When Scholl presented her ideas late in 1949 to the new the U.S. high commissioner for Germany, John McCloy, his response was positive. A "quiet arrangement" emerged from their meeting. The United States would contribute half of the cost of establishing a school if Scholl could locate donors for the other half. She was given six months to assemble an international advisory board and produce a document specifying educational goals, curriculum, and construction plans.[55] American advisers began a series of visits to Ulm to discuss the school and check up on its founders, much to Aicher's annoyance. "We were being tested to see if we were good democrats," he complained to Bill.[56] John P. Steiner, a U.S. educational adviser, made a pointed inquiry to Scholl: "I put forth the question: how will your planned institute help in the reconstitution of a free and democratic nation?"[57] As military occupation authorities made clear, funding would be contingent on the new school's ideological program, not on its approach to design.

Scholl's proposal aimed to put such questions to rest. The curriculum would offer training in politics, the press, broadcasting, film, photography, advertising, industrial design, and urbanism: disciplines that supported liberal capitalist democracy across a spectrum of practices, ranging from the technologies of shaping public opinion to the design and promotion of objects of international mass consumption, a keystone of the

U.S. Marshall Plan and its blueprint for political stability through economic prosperity. Training in painting and sculpture, creative pursuits that Scholl associated with arts-and-crafts dilettantism, would have no place at Ulm. Her elimination of any mention of socialism was also consistent with the expectations of the school's principal patron. According to Scholl's notes, the new school would cultivate a "democratic elite" and contribute the design skills that would make German products competitive in the global marketplace.[58]

After being reviewed and amended by Bill, the curriculum plan for the new Ulm school was submitted to U.S. authorities in June 1950. Training would begin with a foundation course modeled after the Bauhaus *Vorkurs*. Specialization within one of several small ateliers under the guidance of a "master" would constitute the next phase of education. Seven disciplinary areas—methodology of politics, press/broadcasting, publicity, visual design, product design, architecture, and town planning—would be supported by "form-workshops" investigating specific materials.[59] The proposal satisfied the the U.S. high commissioner, who praised Scholl's "crusade to enlighten the German people" in a speech given in Boston in 1950, and asserted that her efforts coincided with America's plan to "help the German people take a democratic road" and "find a close association with the peoples of Western Europe."[60]

The commitment to politics that commended the proposal to McCloy set off alarms for another authority. Seeking support for the Ulm project, Bill sent Gropius a copy of the proposed curriculum in May 1950.[61] Gropius's response challenged the intended curricular focus on political education. He advised emphasizing design "clearly and unambiguously," with architecture and urban planning heading the inventory of coursework, followed by product design, and politics at the bottom of the list. "However," he wrote, "I believe it quite possible that the inculcation of democratic attitudes could be included as a peripheral pursuit of the institute." Despite these misgivings Gropius pledged his support, adding, "If you want me to help with the American officers who are in charge of cultural issues under McCloy, please let me know."[62]

A political crisis made the backing of a figure associated with democratic reconstruction invaluable. In 1951, one of Scholl's local detractors, a former Gestapo officer, denounced her as a communist sympathizer. It took nearly a year to convince the school's U.S. and German patrons that the charge was a fabrication.[63] Bill's effort at damage control painstakingly extricated the Ulm project from the historical legacy of Hannes Meyer's "red" Bauhaus and its contemporary East German offspring, informing McCloy that

> the object of the school in Ulm is not simply to educate new people, but to stiffen the spine of a larger cohort already active [in society] so that they do not fall into the communist camp. It is a known fact that the "Bauhaus" was politically neutral, yet in practice took on German leftist tendencies. At that time, the "light from the east" appeared to many as the only

possible solution to social problems . . . for the most part they have changed their minds. Others, however, are still working in East Germany, albeit under increasing difficulties, since the agenda of a progressive contemporary culture is incompatible with the conditions that they strive for there.[64]

McCloy's decision to continue U.S. support for the Ulm project also may have been influenced by a letter from Gropius asserting that modernist design pedagogy supported democratic subjectivities. "Every successful student leaving the school to enter as a designer into the field of industry or teaching will represent a broad method of approach based on a consistent democratic conception which then will make him a potential cultural factor in his environment." Design instruction at Ulm could have broad social repercussions, "as happened in the Bauhaus," Gropius pledged.[65]

On 23 June 1952, McCloy presented Scholl with a check for one million DM. He funded a school from which the major in politics had been replaced with a minor under the anodyne title of "cultural information." Aside from Gropius's claims about the democratic influence of modernist pedagogy, McCloy's rationale for funding an institute devoted to design paralleled the motives of West German industrialists who cofunded the school. McCloy's previous job had been as director of the financial institution later known as the World Bank. He was an ardent supporter of political stability through free trade and had contemplated "complete economic union" as the ultimate answer to Europe's economic problems.[66] In the context of the Marshall Plan, mass-produced consumer goods had strategic value. They undermined the appeal of communism by offering material rewards to workers who remained enfranchised within the capitalist system; and a transnational market in consumer goods could link former enemy nations in economic coexistence.[67] With Marshall Plan recovery in full swing, McCloy's support for Ulm's industrial design pedagogy was consistent with cold war economic and geopolitical diplomacy.

Bill's design academy fostered capitalist consumption while rejecting many of its social underpinnings. Inaugurated in 1953, the HfG reinvigorated functionalism as the hallmark of high-quality West German consumer goods. Hans Gugelot, a commanding presence in the school's Department of Product Design, led the way in his work for the Max Braun Company, beginning with elegant, minimalist home audio equipment (Figure 9.4). Gugelot and Aicher refined modernist graphic conventions for corporate branding and identity, with Braun and Lufthansa being notable early clients. Bill's interest in merging functionalist pedagogy and material culture also was expressed in the collaborative design of the Ulm Hocker, a multipurpose object used by students as a shelf, stool, side table, and, when turned upside down, cafeteria tray. The universal logic of the Ulm Hocker recalls one of the earliest tubular metal furnishings developed by Marcel Breuer at the Dessau Bauhaus: a small piece intended for use as either a stool or table. But unlike Breuer's hard-edged elegance of sinuous nickel-plated

Figure 9.4. Braun consumer goods display, German Radio and Television Exhibition, Frankfurt am Main, 1955. The "D 55" demountable exhibitions display system was developed for Max Braun AG by Otl Aicher and Hans G. Conrad; many of the home electronics products showcased were designed by Hans Gugelot. From Klaus Franck, *Exhibitions: A Survey of International Designs* (New York: Praeger, 1961). Photograph courtesy of Braun GmbH.

tubing, the raw wood surfaces of the Ulm Hocker repudiated luxury. Bill's design for the school's facilities, a collision of geometric solids tossed across a hillside overlooking Ulm, espoused the same ascetic stringency. Bare concrete and right angles reigned supreme within this "Cartesian cloister," as it was dubbed by a journalist, where austerity and modernism were a way of life.[68] Student novitiates shed their surname, adopted the simplified *du* form of address, and cropped their hair to the skull as a ritual induction into the collective.[69] The minimalism taught at the HfG was echoed in language, imprinted upon the body and embraced as identity. At Bill's "city on a hill," modernism's new objects generated their own postwar subjects, and design theory became a postwar ontology.

Conflicts over Bill's authoritarian methods culminated in his resignation in 1957. But his approach to design persisted as one of several undercurrents continually reshaping the HfG's institutional persona.[70] Bill was succeeded by a triumvirate consisting of

Scholl, Aicher, and Tomás Maldonado. By the close of the 1950s, West Germany's miracle economy used Ulm's neofunctionalism as just one of many viable strategies for consumer seduction. Key HfG faculty began to reappraise their relationship to industry.

Maldonado championed a new rationalist methodology he called "scientific operationalism." It was rooted in semiotic and information theory, and purged of the aestheticized idealism implicit in Gropius's Bauhaus. In 1960, Maldonado dissolved the HfG's first-year foundation course, asserting that Bauhaus-style pedagogy had become technologically out of date.[71] While he intended his new design methodology to depart decisively from the arts-and-crafts philosophy that he believed haunted Bauhaus-inspired pedagogy, one positivist underpinning of that tradition remained evident in his proposals. Maldonado insisted that the task of industrial design "should not consist of designing products according to an outlined demand, as is still the custom in our free economy. Rather, the product designer should be the one who contributes to the creation of demand, otherwise he will be able to play only a subordinate role."[72] Whether presented as hero-artist or engineer of material culture, designers were privileged with awesome power to shape human subjectivity under Ulm pedagogy, despite its rather different iterations by Maldonado and his predecessor, Bill.

A group of Ulm's junior instructors, embracing a design methodology based on systems theory and the questioning of aesthetic training, were attracted to the legacy of Hannes Meyer's Bauhaus, a chapter of the school's past dismissed as a leftist aberration in Western cold war discourse. Faculty member Claude Schnaidt published a biography of Meyer and his work in 1965.[73] It was the postwar era's first critical reassessment of the Bauhaus legacy to come from within that tradition, and the only major work of historical scholarship to emerge from the HfG under Maldonado's administration.[74] Maldonado ventured onto even more treacherous territory in his appreciation of socialist central planning and its potential to institute rational design practices.[75] His attitude was one of analytical detachment rather than overt partisanship, however. He criticized the Eastern bloc's acceptance of "frankly pathological manifestations of American and European industrial design . . . as models worthy of emulation and perfection."[76] But this attempt to establish an objective middle ground, independent of cold war categories, proved impossible to defend, especially as internecine quarreling fragmented HfG faculty into warring tribes of "methodolators" and "Maxists." In 1968, after the West German government canceled its contribution to the school's budget, the HfG dissolved itself rather than submit to a fiscal bailout contingent on loss of its independent status.

Just as Meyer's legacy was suppressed from the West's cold war celebration of the Weimar Bauhaus, Ulm's appreciation for Meyer's socialism marginalized the HfG as a historic successor to Gropius's hallowed insititute. Hans Wingler dedicated a single paragraph to the HfG in the second edition of his canonic history of the Bauhaus, but an entire chapter to the revival of Bauhaus pedagogy at Chicago's "New Bauhaus." This historiographic act of revenge was payback for the unflattering comment in Schnaidt's 1967 essay "Architecture and Political Committment," which claimed that Bauhaus design in the Weimar era had succumbed to "the commerical instincts of the bourgeoisie . . . for the purposes of money-making":

> Utility quickly became synonymous with profitability. Anti-academic forms became the new décor for the ruling classes. . . . The architects of the trade unions, co-operatives and socialist municipalities were enlisted in the service of the whisky distillers, detergent manufacturers, the bankers and the Vatican. Modern architecture, which wanted to play its part in the liberation of mankind by creating a new environment to live in, was transformed into a giant enterprise for the degradation of the human environment.[77]

From Wingler's influential perspective, the Ulm experiment had abdicated any historical claim as the legitimate heir to the Bauhaus legacy, given the school's reversion to what the author termed "Meyer's scientific-dogmatic tendencies."[78]

A LEGACY REVISITED AND REVISED

The inauguration of the Ulm HfG as a "new Bauhaus" in 1953 was just one of several events that year marking the maturation of the cold war's ideologically polarized, but politically symbiotic, Bauhaus myths. The Weimar-era school had become, according to a 1953 article by the director of England's Council for Industrial Design, "a symbol for all that is anti-totalitarian in design, as much in contrast with the socialist realism of the East as the [bygone 'blood and soil' aesthetic] of Nazism."[79] The West's appraisal of the Bauhaus as cultural legend was mirrored in reverse in the Soviet bloc. There, Bauhaus design was said to be a signifier of capitalist cultural imperialism. Mart Stam's forced flight from East Germany demonstrated a zero-tolerance policy toward designers unwilling to renounce Bauhaus pedagogy. Yet even in its role as pariah, Bauhaus modernism remained central to East German culture as a definitive counterexample to the aesthetic system imported from Moscow.

Pressure to conform to a standardized interpretation of Bauhaus modernism was by no means unique to Stalinist Eastern Europe, as revealed in the West German "Bauhaus Debate" of 1953. The controversy was triggered by the publication of a blistering critique of Gropius and the Bauhaus. Its author was Rudolf Schwarz, an architect and city planner whose work defied easy stylistic categorization. Like his modernist buildings using traditional materials and craftsmanship, Schwarz's rhetoric mixed positions associated with clashing ideologies: a recipe for trouble in politically polarized Germany. The torrent of outraged responses to his article staked new limits for acceptable design discourse and demonstrated the cult status of the Bauhaus in postwar West Germany.[80]

Schwarz's article, titled "Artists Should Create, Not Orate," railed against "the anti-intellectual terrorism of [two] dictatorial groups: namely, the Bauhaus literati and later, of course, the masters of the thousand-year Reich." This correlation might have been unremarkable in communist East Berlin, but was shocking coming from a West German. Schwarz's claim that the literature of Weimar modernism "wasn't German, but rather the jargon of the Communist International," again confounded cold war notions of the Bauhaus and its relationship to Marxism. Anyone expressing doubts about the school's theories, Schwarz insisted, had been "berated and mocked." His charge that Bauhaus proponents "wanted a dictatorship, not a discussion," reversed the familiar story line of the school's suppression by Nazis, casting modernists in the role of oppressors.[81]

Rejoinders to Schwarz's confusing polemic condemned the author, speculated on the ideological nature of his offense, and above all put Gropius and the Bauhaus back into their proper laudatory context. "You have overstepped all boundaries, [but] there is *one* that you *must* respect," intoned one rebuttal. "It lies before the name *Walter Gropius*."[82] Hoffmann, another scandalized respondent, lumped Schwarz with "Mr. Goebbels, Mr. Schulze-Naumberg [a notoriously racist spokesman for anti-Bauhaus sentiment], and the Nazi administrators of Thüringen and Sachsen-Anhalt."[83] Conversely, Schwarz was defamed as a closet Communist in a denunciatory letter from an association of Hamburg modernists: "We would not want to leave unmentioned that the condemnation of the Bauhaus in this dramatic way is also practiced by the other side."[84] The most creative appraisal of Schwarz's brand of apostasy depicted him as a conspirator in a "Catholic campaign against the modern," and urged Gropius to do "something extremely decisive against this clique of papists."[85] The consensus among mainstream West German modernists was that Schwarz was some sort of extremist, but just what sort remained unclear. The lesson, in any case, was apparent: Gropius and the Bauhaus had become sacrosanct elements of West Germany's emerging national myth. "In this period," the cultural historian Paul Betts has observed, "the Bauhaus assumed a privileged position within West German culture in part because it played a crucial role in the larger cold war project to draw the Weimar Republic and the Federal Republic into the same elective liberal lineage, while at the same time conjoining West German and American cultural modernism."[86] By 1953, to belittle either the Bauhaus or its founder was considered an act of heresy, as Schwarz had discovered.

The trajectory of cultural change that ultimately dismantled the cold war's symbiotic Bauhaus interpretations was set into motion by another event of 1953. Stalin's sudden death in March initiated a struggle for succession within the Kremlin. The ultimate victor, Nikita Khrushchev, galvanized support by initiating a program of populist reforms originally proposed by his rival, Georgi Malenkov. Crucial to this campaign was the improvement of the USSR's appalling housing conditions.[87] At the Soviet All-Union Conference of Builders and Architects held at the Kremlin in 1954, Khrushchev attacked the interlocking systems of architectural theory, pedagogy, and construction that had been cultivated for decades under Stalin. Architecture, specifically that of housing, began to be decoupled from socialist realism's decorative imperatives. Design theory went through the same cut-and-paste revisionism that had been used earlier to edit out modernism, but this time Stalinist neoclassicism was dumped from the cultural script.

Throughout the Soviet bloc, a new generation of apartment buildings arose, their elemental look more an artifact of industrial construction systems than a reflection of any particular aesthetic tradition. By 1959, a heated debate had erupted in East Germany over modernist functionalism and the relevance of the Bauhaus as a "signpost to socialist architecture."[88] A rehabilitation of the Bauhaus legacy as socialist design could not proceed until a positive signal from Moscow was perceived. It came in a 1962 issue of the Soviet journal *Decorative Arts*. Its feature article, "The Creative Legacy of the Bauhaus," was published in translation a year later in East Berlin.[89] A homegrown example of post-Stalinist architectural scholarship, Lothar Lang's study, *The Bauhaus 1919–1933: Idea and Reality*, was published two years later by East Germany's Central Design Institute. While aesthetic revisionism opened the floodgates to a new appreciation for Bauhaus design, the sensitive topic of the school's political and social history remained off limits until the mid-1970s, when the Bauhaus was certified by common consensus in the Eastern bloc as a "socially progressive" phenomenon.[90]

During the party's denigration of modernism as "cosmopolitan formalism," Gropius's Bauhaus building had remained intact but indifferently repaired. Although dirty and scabrous, the structure attracted an ever-greater number of visitors over the course of the 1960s. The SED was deeply embarrassed by what it termed "protest pictures" comparing the building's condition in the 1920s and 1950s. The images were circulated internationally with their publication in Leonardo Benevolo's *History of Modern Architecture*.[91] Internal documents record the SED's fear that the monument's wretched state nurtured "a deep alienation among circles of the intelligentsia, artists and architects in the East and West, that harms the image of our nation at home and abroad. . . . The restoration of the Bauhaus building would address this and eliminate a source of aversion and doubts regarding the East German republic and its cultural policies."[92]

On 6 December 1976, at a fiftieth anniversary party for the Dessau Bauhaus, the SED celebrated the school's full political rehabilitation and its new status as an ingredient in East Germany's socialist national culture (Figure 9.5).[93] Renovation had begun just nine months before. The facade and formal public areas of Gropius's building, including the auditorium, stage, exhibition gallery, and café, had been the primary targets of the reconstruction effort. Carl Marx, a Bauhaus alumnus and artist who had lived at the margins of East German society ever since his involvement with Hoffmann's ill-fated attempt to revive the school in the late 1940s, provided expert advice for the project. Ironies such as this one were multiplied at the grand opening. While the SED feted Gropius, the Bauhaus figure most actively involved in the cold war struggle to extend American cultural influence in postwar Germany, Hoffmann, remained uninvited

Figure 9.5. Bauhaus building, Dessau, view from the northeast after DDR renovation, 1978. Busch-Reisinger Museum, Harvard University Art Museums; gift of Ise Gropius.

as a persona non grata. Nor was Stam anywhere to be found. Decades after his denunciation by the SED, he lived in isolation in Switzerland, fully retired from the design profession and unresponsive to attempts at contact by old party comrades. His former bureaucratic patron, Strauss, reflected upon Stam's silence in a publication commemorating the Bauhaus anniversary and restoration. Echoing Stam's colleague Hans Schmidt, he wondered "how one could explain the sudden obscurity of such a gifted talent, the sudden silencing of the creative impulse with which Stam engaged modern architecture and the rise of a new era."[94] The answer should have been apparent to Strauss, since he had been a party to the process. With the reopening of Gropius's building and the final Eastern bloc revision of its design legacy, memories of the Stalinist suppression of the Bauhaus were themselves suppressed from public discourse, and would remain so until the collapse of East Germany in 1989. The Bauhaus was canonized within a new "invented tradition" of Soviet bloc design during that coalition's final decade. Avant-garde experiments of the 1920s were attributed to "the wave of socialist revolutions after 1917," a Russocentric reading that placed Lenin's October Revolution at the fulcrum of all architectural innovation. Modernist buildings scattered across Eastern Europe were revered as premonitions of social change that "achieved their complex realization in architectural practice only during the last few decades."[95] This updating of the socialist realist formula for national tradition cast its horizons beyond the confines of individual nations to imagine a unified architectural heritage shared by the entire Eastern bloc, and valorized the Bauhaus as a harbinger of post-Stalinist functionalism.[96] However, the conflation of East Germany's modernist inheritance with banal concrete-panel housing blocks was contested by professional and populist critics who, from the late 1970s onward, questioned the equation of functionalist monotony with socialism's professed goal of human liberation.[97]

In West Germany, the integration of the Bauhaus legacy into the cultural mainstream was confirmed in the creation of the school's permanent archive and museum, designed by Gropius's firm, The Architects' Collaborative, and dedicated by the city of West Berlin in 1978. However, new Bauhaus scholarship set the stage for a general reassessment of the Bauhaus legacy as it had been reconstructed for cold war use. A resurgence of interest in the school's more subversive tendencies was also sparked by the malaise many Western intellectuals felt toward a postwar culture they regarded as a hollow exercise in consumerist technocracy. Gert Selle's 1978 study of the emergence of modernist German design eulogized the radicalism of Meyer's Bauhaus and decried the postwar use of functionalism as bourgeois cultural capital.[98] Peter Blake's 1977 manifesto, *Form Follows Fiasco*, undermined the orthodox cold war idea that Bauhaus design was socially progressive. Blake claimed that Weimar Germany's modernist *Siedlungen* (residential complexes) were designed to assert control over residents "by trade unions and other forms of workers' collectives" just as surely as company towns attempted to exert management's control over labor: a critique formulated a decade earlier by Schnaidt at Ulm, and illustrated by Blake with a perspective drawing of a Bauhaus-designed housing project of 1928.[99] The modernist radicalism that Blake regarded as tragic became fodder for parody in Tom Wolfe's *From Bauhaus to Our House* of 1981. Wolfe mocked Gropius as "the Silver Prince" and caricatured Bauhaus social idealism as a comedy of manners in which architects competed with each other to produce the most "nonbourgeois" design.[100] While dismissed by architectural historians as superficial, Wolfe's satire was historically significant. The popular bestseller was a graveyard for the cycle of myths that heroized Bauhaus personalities and bonded the school's legacy to liberal democracy, freedom of expression, and postwar modernity: virtues extolled in America's cold war struggle against communism.

As cold war hostilities gave way to détente, the Bauhaus returned to its initial postwar status as a radically unstable signifier of political ideology. The Bauhaus legacy's use as an symbol of liberal Western democracy was a transient phenomenon. It was contingent on a suppression of the memory of Nazi patronage of Bauhaus talents; affiliation with the goals of U.S. occupation and Marshall Plan reconstruction; the more enduring need on the part of Germans to salvage a credible twentieth-century heritage; and—of critical importance—the repudiation of Bauhaus pedagogy by Soviet socialism. Had East German officials accepted Mart Stam's prescription for a modernist design academy fulfilling the mandates of a centrally managed Stalinist economy, the utility of the Bauhaus legacy as a cold war weapon might have been considerably altered. In understanding the Bauhaus's bequest to the postwar era, knowing what the school's advocates failed to achieve is as important as their more familiar roster of accomplishments.

NOTES

INTRODUCTION

1 For divergent perspectives see Karl-Heinz Hüter, *Das Bauhaus in Weimar* (Berlin: Akademie Verlag, 1976), and Elaine Hochman, *Bauhaus: Crucible of Modernism* (New York: Fromm International, 1997).

2 This is confirmed by the documentation offered by Hans M. Wingler, *Bauhaus: Weimar, Dessau, Berlin, Chicago,* trans. Wolfgang Jabs and Basil Gilbert (Cambridge, MA: MIT Press, 1978), and the analysis in Barbara Miller Lane, *Architecture and Politics in Germany, 1918–1945* (Cambridge, MA: Harvard University Press, 1968).

3 Herbert Bayer, Walter Gropius, and Ise Gropius, *Bauhaus 1919–1928* (New York: Museum of Modern Art, 1938), and Wingler, *Bauhaus,* offer the positive view; Tom Wolfe, *From Bauhaus to Our House* (New York: Farrar, Straus and Giroux, 1981), and Hochman, *Bauhaus: Crucible of Modernism,* the negative.

4 A significant exception is the degree to which issues of gender feature in recent accounts of the school. See Anja Baumhoff, *The Gendered World of the Bauhaus: The Politics of Power at the Weimar Republic's Premier Art Institute, 1919–1932* (Frankfurt am Main: Peter Lang, 2001); Magdalena Droste, *Bauhaus, 1919–1933* (Berlin: Bauhaus-Archiv, 1993); and Sigrid Wortmann Weltge, *Women's Work: Textile Art from the Bauhaus* (San Francisco: Chronicle Books, 1994).

5 Droste, *Bauhaus, 1919–1933.* See also Frank Whitford, *Bauhaus* (London: Thames and Hudson, 1984).

6 For more details about pedagogy, see in particular Rainer Wick, *Teaching at the Bauhaus* (Ostfildern-Ruit: Hatje Canz Verlag, 2000). Johannes Itten, *Design and Form: The Basic Course at the Bauhaus*

and Later (New York: Van Nostrand Reinhold, 1975), is a valuable source on the original preliminary course.

7 See, for instance, Eckhard Neumann, *Bauhaus and Bauhaus People: Personal Opinions and Recollections of Former Bauhaus Members and Their Contemporaries* (New York: Von Nostrand Reinhold, 1993), and Frank Whitford, *The Bauhaus: Masters and Students by Themselves* (Woodstock, NY: Overlook Press, 1993).

8 Important exceptions are the essays collected in Jeannine Fiedler and Peter Feierabend, *Bauhaus* (Cologne: Könnemann, 1999).

9 See, for instance, Andreas Huyssen, *After the Great Divide: Modernism, Mass Culture, Postmodernism* (Bloomington: University of Indiana Press, 1986). Examples of the application of this approach to architectural history include K. Michael Hays, *Modernism and the Posthumanist Subject: The Architecture of Hannes Meyer and Ludwig Hilberseimer* (Cambridge, MA: MIT Press, 1992); Kathleen James, *Erich Mendelsohn and the Architecture of German Modernism* (Cambridge: Cambridge University Press, 1997); Kathleen James-Chakraborty, *German Architecture for a Mass Audience* (London and New York: Routledge, 2000); and Janet Ward, *Weimar Surfaces: Urban Visual Culture in 1920s Germany* (Berkeley and Los Angeles: University of California Press, 2001).

10 Siegfried Kracauer, *The Mass Ornament,* ed. and trans. Thomas Y. Levin (Cambridge, MA: Harvard University Press, 1995). See also the slightly later Theodor Adorno and Max Horkheimer, *Dialectic of Enlightenment,* trans. John Cumming (1947; New York: Herder and Herder, 1972).

11 See in particular the pioneering work of Maud Lavin, especially *Cut with a Kitchen Knife: The Wei-*

mar *Photomontages of Hannah Hoch* (New Haven, CT: Yale University Press, 1993). Although my conclusions differ, I am also indebted to Hays, *Modernism and the Posthumanist Subject.*

12 For the most important exposition of the universality of abstraction see Wassily Kandinsky, *Concerning the Spiritual in Art* (1912; repr., New York: Dover, 1977), written by one of the Bauhaus's most influential masters.

13 James, *Erich Mendelsohn,* especially 140–200, and Ward, *Weimar Surfaces,* especially 92–141.

14 For the coupling of the Dessau Bauhaus with stores by Erich Mendelsohn, see Ludwig Hilberseimer, "Internationale neue Baukunst," *Moderne Bauformen* 9 (1927): 332. Hilberseimer began teaching at the Bauhaus two years after this article was published.

15 Elisabeth Förster-Nietzsche, letter of 16 April 1925 to Henry van de Velde, Henry van de Velde Papers, Bibliothèque Royale Albert Ier, Brussels, Belgium, for a right-wing denunciation of Gropius's talent for promotion.

16 The classic account of the road leading to the Bauhaus remains Nikolaus Pevsner, *Pioneers of the Modern Movement, from William Morris to Walter Gropius* (London: Faber and Faber, 1936). The most comprehensive assessments in English of the impact of the November Revolution upon the Bauhaus are Marcel Franciscono, *Walter Gropius and the Creation of the Bauhaus in Weimar: The Ideals and Artistic Theories of Its Founding Years* (Urbana: University of Illinois Press, 1971), and Joan Weinstein, *The End of Expressionism: Art and the November Revolution in Germany, 1918–19* (Chicago: University of Chicago Press, 1990).

17 See Frederic J. Schwartz, *The Werkbund: Design Theory and Mass Culture before the First World War* (New Haven, CT: Yale University Press, 1996), and Vittorio Magnago Lampugnani and Romana Schneider, eds., *Moderne Architektur in Deutschland 1900 bis 1950: Reform und Tradition* (Stuttgart: G. Hatje, 1992).

18 One such effort, the Centennial Hall in Breslau, is chronicled, however, in James-Chakraborty, *German Architecture for a Mass Audience.*

19 For an important revision of this view see Geoff Eley, ed., *Society, Culture, and the State in Germany,* *1870–1930* (Ann Arbor: University of Michigan Press, 1996).

20 This is the crucial difference between Schwartz, *The Werkbund,* and Joan Campbell, *The German Werkbund: the Politics of Reform in the Applied Arts* (Princeton, NJ: Princeton University Press, 1978), or even Stanford Anderson, *Peter Behrens and a New Architecture for the Twentieth Century* (Cambridge, MA: MIT Press, 2000).

21 Howard Dearstyne, *Inside the Bauhaus,* ed. David Spaeth (New York: Rizzoli, 1986), 221–22.

22 Paul Betts, *The Authority of Everyday Objects: A Cultural History of West German Industrial Design* (Berkeley and Los Angeles: University of California Press, 2004), 46.

23 Winfried Nerdinger, ed., in collaboration with the Bauhaus-Archiv, Berlin, *Bauhaus-Moderne im Nationalsozialismus: Zwischen Anbiederung und Verfolgung* (Munich: Prestel, 1993).

24 See also Lane, *Architecture and Politics in Germany,* and Richard Pommer, "Mies van der Rohe and the Political Ideology of the Modern Movement," in *Mies van der Rohe, Critical Essays,* ed. Franz Schulze (New York: Museum of Modern Art, 1989), 96–145.

25 Alfred Barr, "Preface," Bayer, Gropius, and Gropius, *Bauhaus,* 7–9. For a thoughtful examination of this exhibit in the context of exile, see Karen Koehler, "The Bauhaus, 1919–1928: Gropius in Exile and the Museum of Modern Art, N.Y., 1938," in *Art, Culture, and Media under the Third Reich,* ed. Richard Etlin (Chicago: University of Chicago Press, 2002), 287–315.

26 For the degree to which Le Corbusier was also willing to work for less than enlightened patrons, see Mary McLeod, "Le Corbusier and Algiers," *Oppositions* 16–17 (1980): 55–85, and Zeynip Celik, "Le Corbusier, Orientalism, Colonialism," *Assemblage* 17 (1993): 58–77.

27 The seminal example of this approach was Franciscono, *Walter Gropius and the Creation of the Bauhaus in Weimar.*

28 Éva Forgács, *The Bauhaus Idea and Bauhaus Politics* (Budapest: Central European University Press, 1995).

1. WILHELMINE PRECEDENTS FOR THE BAUHAUS

1 Accounts of the school and its origins include Hans M. Wingler, *Bauhaus: Weimar, Dessau, Berlin, Chicago,* trans. Wolfgang Jabs and Basil Gilbert (Cambridge, MA: MIT Press, 1978); Marcel Franciscono, *Walter Gropius and the Creation of the Bauhaus in Weimar: The Ideals and Artistic Theories of Its Founding Years* (Urbana: University of Illinois Press, 1971); and Gillian Naylor, *The Bauhaus Reassessed: Sources and Design Theory* (New York: Dutton, 1985).

2 For the German architectural profession's changing nineteenth-century identity in the face of rapid industrialization, see Mitchell Schwarzer, *German Architectural Theory and the Search for Modern Identity* (Cambridge: Cambridge University Press, 1995).

3 Gillian Naylor, *The Arts and Crafts Movement: A Study of Its Sources, Ideals, and Influence on Design Theory* (London: Studio Vista, 1971); Peter Stansky, *Redesigning the World: William Morris, the 1880s, and the Arts and Crafts* (Princeton, NJ: Princeton University Press, 1985); Wendy Kaplan, "The Lamp of British Precedent: An Introduction to the Arts and Crafts Movement," in *"The Art That Is Life": The Arts and Crafts Movement in America, 1875–1920,* ed. Wendy Kaplan (New York: Little, Brown, 1987), 52–60.

4 Paul Greenhalgh, ed., *Art Nouveau, 1890–1914* (London: V & A Publications, 2000); for a broader view of relationships between architecture and ideas of national renewal in the late nineteenth century, see Barbara Miller Lane, *National Romanticism and Modern Architecture in Germany and the Scandinavian Countries* (Cambridge: Cambridge University Press, 2000).

5 For a detailed account of pre–World War I government and private precedents to the Bauhaus, see John V. Maciuika, *Before the Bauhaus: Architecture, Politics, and the German State, 1890–1920* (Cambridge: Cambridge University Press, 2005).

6 Frederic J. Schwartz, *The Werkbund: Design Theory and Mass Culture before the First World War* (New Haven, CT: Yale University Press, 1996); Joan Campbell, *The German Werkbund: The Politics of Reform in the Applied Arts* (Princeton, NJ: Princeton University Press, 1978).

7 John Heskett, *German Design, 1870–1918* (New York: Taplinger, 1986); also Laurie A. Stein and Irmela Franzke, "German Design and National Identity, 1890–1914," in *Designing Modernity: The Arts of Reform and Persuasion, 1885–1945,* ed. Wendy Kaplan (New York: Thames and Hudson, 1995), 49–78.

8 In the extensive literature on Second Empire Germany, brief accounts of the structure of the empire can be found in Gerhard Loewenberg, *Parliament in the German Political System* (Ithaca, NY: Cornell University Press, 1967), 1–18; James Retallack, *Germany in the Age of Kaiser Wilhelm II* (New York: St. Martin's Press, 1996), 34–52; see also the contributions by Roger Chickering, Dan S. White, Michael John, and Andrew Lees in *Imperial Germany: A Historiographical Companion,* ed. Roger Chickering (Westport, CT: Greenwood Press, 1996).

9 Over time, the term *Heimat* took on new meanings that blurred the distinctions between the local "hometown," "homeland," and the nation. This made it possible for local *Heimat* traditions as well as new local initiatives to take on significance as contributions to national culture. See Peter Blickle, *Heimat: A Critical Theory of the German Idea of Homeland* (Rochester, NY: Camden House, 2002); Celia Applegate, *A Nation of Provincials: The German Idea of Heimat* (Berkeley and Los Angeles: University of California Press, 1990); Alon Confino, *The Nation as Local Metaphor: Württemberg, Imperial Germany, and National Memory, 1871–1918* (Chapel Hill: University of North Carolina Press, 1997); also classic is Mack Walker, *German Home Towns: Community, Estate, General Estate, 1648–1871* (Ithaca, NY: Cornell University Press, 1971).

10 See Michael John, "Constitution, Administration, and the Law," and Dan S. White, "Regionalism and Particularism," both in Chickering, *Imperial Germany,* 185–214, 131–55; also see Loewenberg, *Parliament in the German Political System,* 1–19.

11 Charles-Edouard Jeanneret, *Étude sur le mouvement d'art décoratif en Allemagne* (1912; repr., New York: De Capo Press, 1968), 15. On Jeanneret's extensive study tour of Germany in 1910–11, see H. Allen Brooks, *Le Corbusier's Formative Years: Charles-Edouard Jeanneret at La Chaux-de-Fonds* (Chicago: University of Chicago Press, 1997), especially 235–46.

12 Ian Latham, *Joseph Maria Olbrich* (New York: Rizzoli, 1980); Sabine Michaelis, ed., *Joseph Maria Olbrich, 1867–1908* (Darmstadt: Matildenhöhe Darmstadt, 1983); Maciuika, *Before the Bauhaus,* 35–45.

13 Klaus-Jürgen Sembach, *Henry van de Velde,* trans. Michael Robinson (New York: Rizzoli, 1989); Klaus-Jürgen Sembach and Birgit Schule, eds., *Henry van de Velde: Ein europäischer Künstler seiner Zeit* (Hagen: Osthaus Museum, 1992).

14 See Wingler, *The Bauhaus,* 21–26; Maciuika, *Before the Bauhaus,* 57–63.

15 Heinrich Waentig pointed out in *Wirtschaft und Kunst,* his study of 1909, that the percentage of manufactured goods in German exports rose from 40.1 in 1873 to 70.2 in 1907, and correctly believed this growth to be part of a long-term upward trend; quoted in Matthew Jeffries, *Politics and Culture in Wilhelmine Germany: The Case of Industrial Architecture* (Oxford: Berg, 1995), 168; see also Maciuika, *Before the Bauhaus,* 69–170.

16 John V. Maciuika, "Hermann Muthesius and the Reform of German Architecture, Arts, and Crafts, 1890–1914" (Ph.D. dissertation, University of California–Berkeley,1998), 148–49, and Maciuika, *Before the Bauhaus,* 106–12.

17 David Bindman and Gottfried Riemann, eds., *Karl Friedrich Schinkel "The English Journey": Journal of a Visit to France and England in 1826* (New Haven, CT: Yale University Press, 1993); also Barry Bergdoll, *Karl Friedrich Schinkel: An Architecture for Prussia* (New York: Rizzoli, 1994).

18 Hermann Muthesius, *The English House,* trans. Janet Seligman, intro. Dennis Sharp (New York: Rizzoli, 1979); this is an abridged translation of the original, three-volume work, Hermann Muthesius, *Das englische Haus: Entwicklung, Bedingungen, Anlage, Aufbau, Einrichtung und Innenraum* (Berlin: Ernst Wasmuth, 1904–5).

19 Biographical information is available in Hermann Muthesius, "Mein Lebens- und Bildungsgang" (25 September 1900), Muthesius Estate, Werkbund-Archiv Berlin; see also Eckhard Siepmann and Angelika Thiekötter, eds., *Hermann Muthesius im Werkbund-Archiv* (Berlin: Werkbund-Archiv, 1990), 105–28.

20 Maciuika, "Hermann Muthesius," 80–142.

21 Hermann Muthesius, *Style-Architecture and Building-Art: Transformations of Architecture in the Nineteenth Century and Its Present Condition,* intro. and trans. Stanford Anderson (Santa Monica, CA: Getty Center for the History of Art and the Humanities, 1995), 79.

22 Theodor Möller, quoted by Otto March in a letter from Otto March to Hermann Muthesius, 26 October 1904, Muthesius papers, Werkbund-Archiv, Berlin (Nachlass Muthesius im Werkbund-Archiv).

23 Gisela Moeller, *Peter Behrens in Düsseldorf: Die Jahre von 1903 bis 1907* (Weinheim: VCH Verlag, 1991); Stanford Anderson, *Peter Behrens and a New Architecture for the Twentieth Century* (Cambridge, MA: MIT Press, 2000), 69–94.

24 Hermann Muthesius, "Künstlerischer Unterricht für Handwerker in England," *Dekorative Kunst* 1 (1898): 15–20.

25 The English study tour is detailed in F. Dönhoff, J. von Czihak, and H. Muthesius, "Das Gewerbliche Unterrichtswesen in Grossbritannien, auf Grund einer Studienreise im Jahre 1903," in Preussischen Haus der Abgeordneten, 20. Legislatur-Periode, I. Session 1904–5, Drucksache Nr. 70, 1347–80; Muthesius's Prussian schools tour is detailed in "Ergebnisse der Besichtigung der Kunstgewerbe- und Handwerkerschulen in Duesseldorf, Crefeld, Elberfeld . . . im Juli und August 1903," 15 October 1903, in Prussian State Archives (Geheimes Staatsarchiv Preussischer Kulturbesitz, hereafter GSPK), I.HA Rep.120 EX Fach 1. Nr. 1 Bd. 13, File IIIb.8130, 42 pp. (hereafter cited as "Ergebnisse").

26 Instructional Workshops Decree ("Lehrwerkstätten Erlass"), 15 December 1904, GSPK, I.HA Rep. 120 EX Fach 1. Nr. 1 Bd. 14, File IIIb.8731.

27 Karl-Heinz Hüter, *Henry van de Velde: Sein Werk bis zum Ende seiner Tätigkeit in Deutschland* (Berlin: Akademie Verlag, 1967), 33–34.

28 Walter Gropius, "Proposed Budget for the Art Academy and School of Fine Arts in Weimar, 1919–1920," in Wingler, *Bauhaus,* 26.

29 Letter from Walter Gropius to Deutscher Werkbund, 30 January 1920, and Gropius to Rudolf Bosselt, 3 February 1920, Thuringen State Archives in Weimar (Thüringisches Hauptstaatsarchiv Weimar, hereafter ThHSAW), File 6, 56, 73.

30 Letter from Henry Cole to J. W. Henley, 10 March

1852, as quoted in Harry Francis Mallgrave, *Gottfried Semper: Architect of the Nineteenth Century* (New Haven, CT: Yale University Press, 1996), 209. See also John Physick, *The Victoria and Albert Museum: The History of Its Building* (Oxford: Phaidon, 1982), 13–32.

31 The establishment of nineteenth-century museums as centers of crafts education and revival is discussed in Barbara Mundt, *Die deutsche Kunstgewerbemuseen im 19. Jahrhundert* (Munich: Prestel, 1974), 152–64.

32 Muthesius, "Künstlerischer Unterricht für Handwerker in England," 19.

33 GSPK, I.HA Rep. 120 EX Fach 1. Nr. 1 Bd.14, File IIIb.8731. The full text of the published decree appears in the *Landesgewerbeamt*'s first administrative report, *Verwaltungs Bericht* 1 [1905], 159–61 (hereafter cited as *VB*). Subsequent quotations from the decree refer to page numbers from the *VB* [1905] edition.

34 "Ergebnisse," pp. 22–30; *VB* [1905], 159.

35 A London County Council report from 1895/96 on the founding of the Central School of Arts and Crafts is quoted in Julius Posener, *Anfänge des Funktionalismus: Vom Arts and Crafts zum Deutscher Werkbund,* Bauwelt Fundamente 11 (Frankfurt/Berlin: Ullstein, 1964), 27.

36 See Alan Crawford's excellent discussion of this point in *C. R. Ashbee: Architect, Designer, and Romantic Socialist* (New Haven, CT: Yale University Press, 1985), 410.

37 *VB* [1905], 159.

38 *VB* [1905], 159–60.

39 Muthesius, "Instructional Workshops Decree" draft, 5.

40 Maciuika, *Before the Bauhaus,* 121–25.

41 Walter Gropius, Memorandum to Bauhaus Workshop Heads, 10 April 1922, ThHSAW, File 2 (Werkstätten Satzungen), 52.

42 The memorandum discussing the need for and purpose of the State Trades Board is the "Denkschrift über die Begründung eines Landesgewerbeamts und eines ständigen Beirats," in *Anlagen zum Staatshaushalts-Etat für das Etatsjahr 1905,* II. Band (Nr. 16, Beilage G, Handels- u. Gewerbeverwaltung), 92–95.

43 Ibid., p. 92.

44 The Standing Committee's full title was "General Section of the Standing Committee for Trades' Educational Policy and the Support of Commerce." It is discussed fully in "Organisation des Landesgewerbeamtes und des Beirates," *VB* 2 (1906): 1–33.

45 Support for new commercial colleges, or *Handelshochschulen,* was part of the Commerce Ministry's expanding educational policy by the 1890s as well. See Friedrich Facius, *Wirtschaft und Staat: Die Entwicklung der staatlichen Wirtschaftsverwaltung in Deutschland vom 17. Jahrhundert bis 1945,* Schriften des Bundesarchivs 6 (Boppard am Rhein: Harald Boldt Verlag, 1959), 60.

46 Hermann Muthesius, "Die Bedeutung des Kunstgewerbes," *Dekorative Kunst* 15 (1907): 184, 190.

47 Letter from Minister Delbrück to the Association for the Economic Interests of the Crafts, 15 May 1907, reprinted in "Der Fall Muthesius: Ein Vortrag mit Akten und Briefen," *Hohe Warte* 3 (1907): 238.

48 *Verhandlungen des Preussischen Hauses der Abgeordneten,* 23. Sitzung am 3. Februar 1908, 1527, as cited in Hans-Joachim Hubrich, *Hermann Muthesius: Die Schriften zu Architektur, Kunstgewerbe, Industrie in der "Neuen Bewegung"* (Berlin: Gebr. Mann Verlag, 1981), 277.

49 Ordnung der Handelshochschule der Korporation der Kaufmannschaft von Berlin, in GSPK, I.HA 120 E XIII Fach 3. Nr. 5 Bd. 1, 41–42.

50 Maciuika, *Before the Bauhaus,* 248–82.

51 See the detailed analysis of Behrens's career in Anderson, *Peter Behrens.*

52 Peter Behrens, *Kunst und Künstler* 5 (February 1907): 207.

53 Tilmann Buddensieg, *Industriekultur: Peter Behrens and the AEG, 1907–1914,* trans. Iain Boyd Whyte (Cambridge, MA: MIT Press, 1984).

54 Anderson, *Peter Behrens,* 138.

55 Ibid., 138–45.

56 Schwartz, *The Werkbund.*

57 Reyner Banham, *A Concrete Atlantis: U.S. Industrial Building and European Modern Architecture 1900–1925* (Cambridge, MA: MIT Press, 1986), 188–94.

58 See "Werkbundaktivitäten zur Konsumentenerziehung," in Siepmann und Thiekötter, *Herman Muthesius im Werkbund-Archiv,* 61–66.

59 Auswärtiges Amt, "Die deutsche Werkbund Ausstellung in Köln 1914," Bundesarchiv Berlin, R901/file 18350, 51.

60 See Adelheid Rasche, "Peter Jessen, der Berliner Verein Moden-Museum und der Verband der deutschen Mode-Industrie, 1916 bis 1925," *Waffen- und Kostümkunde* 37 (1995): 79–82.

61 Undated letter from Hermann Muthesius to Ernst Jäckh (mid–1912), as reprinted in Ernst Jäckh, *Der goldene Pflug* (Stuttgart: Klett Verlag, 1957), and cited in Angelika Thiekötter, "Vorbereitung der Deutschen Werkbund-Ausstelung Köln 1914," in Siepmann and Thiekötter, *Hermann Muthesius im Werkbund-Archiv,* 67.

62 These figures are from Campbell, *The German Werkbund,* 296.

63 Letter from Walter Gropius to Karl Ernst Osthaus, 26 February 1914 (KEOA Kü 335/187), as quoted in Siepmann and Thiekötter, *Hermann Muthesius im Werkbund-Archiv,* 76.

64 Angelika Thiekötter, "Vorbereitung der Deutschen Werkbund-Ausstellung Köln 1914," in Siepmann and Thiekötter, *Hermann Muthesius im Werkbund-Archiv,* 68.

65 Ibid., 67.

66 Jäckh, *Der goldene Pflug,* 196.

67 Maciuika, "Hermann Muthesius," 364–80.

68 Hermann Muthesius, "Das Formproblem im Ingenieur-Bau," *Jahrbuch des Deutschen Werkbundes* (1913): 23–32; reprinted in Posener, *Anfänge des Funktionalismus,* 191–98, see especially 191, 197.

69 See "Muthesius/Van de Velde: Werkbund Theses and Antitheses," in *Programs and Manifestoes on 20th-Century Architecture,* ed. Ulrich Conrads, trans. Michael Bullock (Cambridge, MA: MIT Press, 1970), 28–31; see also Maciuika, *Before the Bauhaus,* Appendix B, 300–39.

70 See theses four through seven in ibid., 28.

71 Quoted in Siepmann and Thiekötter, *Hermann Muthesius in Werkbund Archiv,* 69, 74; see also the discussion in Maciuika, "Hermann Muthesius," 367–72; see also Maciuika, *Before the Bauhaus,* 270–77.

72 See Conrads, *Programs and Manifestoes,* 28–31.

73 Henry van de Velde, as quoted in Franciscono, *Walter Gropius and the Creation of the Bauhaus in Weimar,* 35.

74 See Wingler, *Bauhaus,* 20–21; also "Walter Gropius über Typisierung im Hausbau (1912)," in Siepmann and Thiekötter, *Hermann Muthesius im Werkbund-Archiv,* 94.

75 Hermann Muthesius, "Die Werkbundarbeit der Zukunft," in Hermann Muthesius, "Die Werkbundarbeit der Zukunft und Aussprache darüber," Sonderdruck zur 7. Jahresversammlung des Deutschen Werkbundes vom 2. bis 6. Juli 1914 in Köln (Jena: 1914), 33–49; reprinted in Posener, *Anfänge des Funktionalismus,* 199–204, quotation from 199.

76 Ibid., 200.

77 Ibid., 202–3.

78 Ibid., 203–4.

79 "Schlusswort von Hermann Muthesius auf der 7. Jahresversammlung des Deutschen Werkbundes, Köln 1914," in Siepmann and Thiekötter, *Hermann Muthesius im Werkbund-Archiv,* 95–98; excerpts from the debates are in Posener, *Anfänge des Funktionalismus,* 208–21.

80 "Schlusswort," in Siepmann and Thiekötter, *Hermann Muthesius im Werkbund-Archiv,* 95–98; also Julius Posener, *Berlin auf dem Wege zu einer neuen Architektur* (Munich: Prestel, 1979), 528.

81 "Muthesius' Rückzug aus dem Werkbund 1916–26," in Siepmann and Thiekötter, *Hermann Muthesius im Werkbund-Archiv,* 99.

82 Nikolaus Pevsner, *Pioneers of the Modern Movement from William Morris to Walter Gropius* (London: Faber and Faber, 1936).

2. HENRY VAN DE VELDE AND WALTER GROPIUS

1 Max Bill to Walter Gropius, letter of 15 December 1951, Reginald Isaacs Papers, Archives of American Art, Washington, DC.

2 Walter Gropius to Max Bill, letter of 31 December 1951, Isaacs Papers. See also Walter Gropius to Donald Drew Egbert, letter of 26 April 1951, Isaacs Papers.

3 Henry van de Velde, *Die Renaissance im modernen Kunstgewerbe* (Berlin: Bruno and Paul Cassirer, 1901), 30–35.

4 Birgit Schulte, "Henry van de Velde: Die Lebensreise," in *Henry van de Velde: Ein europäischer Künstler seiner Zeit,* ed. Klaus-Jürgen Sembach and Birgit Schulte (Cologne: Wienand Verlag, 1992), 19–53.

5 Compare Donald Drew Egbert's discussion of van de Velde's politics in *Social Radicalism and the Arts: Western Europe* (New York: Knopf, 1970), 609–19, with Walter Gropius to Donald Drew Egbert, letters of 14 October 1948 and 26 April 1951, Isaacs Papers.

6 Karl-Heinz Hüter, "Hoffnung, Illusion und Enttäuschung: Henry van de Veldes Kunstgewerbeschule und das frühe Bauhaus," in Sembach and Schulte, *Henry van de Velde,* 285–337.

7 Monographs on van de Velde proliferated during these years, as did more comprehensive studies of art nouveau. The most notable examples of the former are Abraham Marie Hammacher, *Le Monde de Henry van de Velde* (Anvers: Édition fonds Marcator, 1967); Karl Heinz-Hüter, *Henry van de Velde: Sein Werk bis zum Ende seiner Tätigkeit in Deutschland* (Berlin: Akademie Verlag, 1967); Léon Plaegaerts and Pierre Puttemans, *L'Oeuvre architecturale de Henry van de Velde* (Brussels: Atelier Vokuer, 1987); and Klaus-Jürgen Sembach, *Henry van de Velde* (New York: Rizzoli, 1989).

8 The following discussion depends on the account offered by Schulte, "Henry van de Velde: Die Lebensreise."

9 Susan M. Canning, "Soyons Nous: Les XX and the Cultural Discourse of the Belgian Avant-Garde," in *Les XX and the Belgian Avant-Garde: Prints, Drawings and Books, ca. 1890,* ed. Stephen H. Goddard (Lawrence, KS: Spencer Museum of Art, 1992), 28–54.

10 Alexander Murphy and Carl Strikwerdh, "Brussels and the Belgian Avant-Garde in Historical and Geographical Perspective," in Goddard, *Les XX,* 18–27.

11 John Ruskin, *Stones of Venice* (London: Smith, Elder, 1851–53), and William Morris, *News from Nowhere; or, An Epoch of Rest, Being Some Chapters from a Utopian Romance* (Boston: Roberts, 1890).

12 For van de Velde's theory, see the books he published while living in Germany: *Die Renaissance im modernen Kunstgewerbe, Kunstgewerbliche Laienpredigten* (Leipzig: Hermann Seeman Nachfolger, 1902), *Vom neuen Stil* (Leipzig: Insel Verlag, 1907), and *Essays* (Leipzig: Insel Verlag, 1910).

13 Van de Velde's critique of representation fore-

shadows that offered by one of the Bauhaus's most important masters. See Wassily Kandinsky, *On the Spiritual in Art* (1912; repr., New York: Dover, 1973).

14 Amy Fumiko Ogata, *Art Nouveau and the Social Vision of Modern Living: Belgian Artists in a European Context* (Cambridge: Cambridge University Press, 2001); Deborah Silverman, *Art Nouveau in Fin-de-Siècle France: Politics, Psychology, and Style* (Berkeley and Los Angeles: University of California Press, 1989), 272–82; and Gabriel Weisberg, *Art Nouveau Bing: Paris Style 1900* (New York: Harry N. Abrams, 1986), 57–88.

15 Ingeborg Becker, *Henry van de Velde in Berlin* (Berlin: Reimer, 1993), and Birgit Schulte, ed., *Henry van de Velde in Hagen* (Hagen: Neuer Folkwang Verlag, n.d.).

16 Murphy and Strikwerdh, "Brussels and the Belgian Avant-Garde," 23–24.

17 For evidence of this shift, see van de Velde, *Renaissance,* 131–48. Van de Velde's socialist sympathies have almost certainly been exaggerated, in particular by those historians who have sought to ally artistic experimentation with progressive politics. See, for example, Silverman, *Art Nouveau,* 158, 173, 210–11, 272–74.

18 For the rejection of Jugendstil as fashion, see Frederic J. Schwartz, *The Werkbund: Design Theory and Mass Culture before the First World War* (New Haven, CT: Yale University Press, 1996), 26–43.

19 Van de Velde, *Essays,* 41–74.

20 Van de Velde, *Geschichte,* 210–13.

21 Hüter, "Hoffnung, Illusion und Entwicklung," 320–24, and Sigrid Wortmann Weltge, *Women's Work: Textile Art from the Bauhaus* (San Francisco: Chronicle Books, 1993), 41–45.

22 Dieter Dolgner, *Henry van de Velde in Weimar, 1902–1917* (Weimar: Verlag und Datenbank für Geisteswissenschaft, 1996); Alexandre Kostka, "Der Dilettant und sein Künstler: Die Beziehung Harry Graf Kessler–Henry van de Velde," in Sembach and Schulte, *Henry van de Velde,* 260–73; Léon Ploegaerts, "Van de Velde and Nietzsche; or, The Search for a New Architectural Style for the Man of the Future," in *Nietzsche and "An Architecture of Our Minds,"* ed. Alexandre Kostka and Irving Wohlfarth (Santa Monica, CA: Getty Research Institute for the

History of Art and the Humanities, 1999), 233–55; and Günther Stamm, "Monumental Architecture and Ideology: Henry van de Velde's and Harry Graf Kessler's Project for a Nietzsche Monument at Weimar, 1910–1914," *Gentse Bijdragen tot de Kunstgeschiednis* 23 (1973–75): 303–42.

23 Steven E. Ashheim, *The Nietzsche Legacy in Germany, 1890–1990* (Berkeley and Los Angeles: University of California Press, 1992), 33–35, 48–50; and Kostka and Wohlfarth, *Nietzsche and "An Architecture of Our Minds."*

24 See the correspondence in file 534 of the van de Velde archives. The file contains a draft of a letter of 28 July 1914, written by van de Velde's Belgian friend Charles Lefèbure on his behalf to King Albert as well as a letter of 6 July 1914 in which Lefèbure warns van de Velde that such an effort is unlikely to be successful.

25 For van de Velde's letters to Gropius describing this effort, see Hans M. Wingler, *Bauhaus: Weimar, Dessau, Berlin, Chicago* (Cambridge, MA: MIT Press, 1978), 21.

26 Hermann Muthesius and Henry van de Velde, "Werkbund Theses and Antitheses," in *Programs and Manifestoes on 20th-Century Architecture,* ed. Ulrich Conrads (Cambridge, MA: MIT Press, 1971), 28–29.

27 For a survey of the literature on the debate, as well as an important revisionist interpretation, see Schwartz, *The Werkbund,* 147–212, 241. Another important recent discussion is Stanford Anderson, "Deutscher Werkbund—the 1914 Debate: Hermann Muthesius versus Henry van de Velde," in *Companion to Contemporary Architectural Thought,* ed. B. Farmer and H. Louw (London: Routledge, 1993), 462–67.

28 Ulrich Schulze, "Formen für Reformen: Henry van de Veldes Theaterarchitektur," in Sembach and Schultz, *Henry van de Velde,* 341–57. See also Dennis Sharp, *Henry van de Velde: Theater Designs, 1904–1914* (London: Maurice Culot, 1974).

29 Van de Velde, *Von neuen Stil,* 15.

30 Hermann Muthesius, *Style-Architecture and Building-Art: Transformations of Architecture in the Nineteenth Century and Its Present Condition,* intro. and trans. Stanford Anderson (Santa Monica, CA: Getty Center for the History of Art and the Humanities, 1994).

31 He thus followed the example set by the Austrian architect Otto Wagner. See his *Modern Architecture: A Guidebook for His Students to the Field of Art,* intro. and trans. by Harry Mallgrave (Santa Monica, CA: Getty Center for the History of Art and the Humanities, 1988).

32 Van de Velde, *Vom neuen Stil,* 65–69.

33 Gropius's inability to draft his own designs is a central point of the most comprehensive study of his work, Winfried Nerdinger, *Walter Gropius* (Berlin: Gebr. Mann Verlag, 1985). A second important biography is Reginald Isaacs, *Gropius: An Illustrated Biography of the Creator of the Bauhaus* (Boston: Little, Brown, 1991).

34 Joan Weinstein, *The End of Expressionism: Art and the November Revolution in Germany* (Chicago: University of Chicago Press, 1989).

35 Walter Gropius, "Bauhaus Dessau—Principles of Bauhaus Production," reprinted in Wingler, *Bauhaus,* 110.

36 Marcel Franciscono, *Walter Gropius and the Creation of the Bauhaus in Weimar: The Ideals and Theories of Its Founding Years* (Urbana: University of Illinois Press, 1971), and Éva Forgács, *The Bauhaus Idea and Bauhaus Politics* (Budapest: Central European University Press, 1995).

37 Nikolaus Pevsner, *Pioneers of Modern Design from William Morris to Walter Gropius* (Hammondsworth, UK: Penguin Books, 1964).

38 Pierre and Françoise Loze, *Belgique Art Nouveau de Victor Horta à Antoine Pompe* (Brussels: Eiffel Editions, 1991), 19–41.

39 As quoted in Peter Reed, "Alvar Aalto and the New Humanism of the Postwar Era," in *Alvar Aalto: Between Humanism and Materialism,* ed. Peter Reed (New York: Abrams, 1998), 97.

40 Walter Gropius, *Apollo in der Demokratie* (Mainz: Florian Kupferberg Verlag, 1967), 26.

41 Van de Velde, *Renaissance,* 64–68.

42 Barbara Miller Lane, *Architecture and Politics in Germany, 1918–1945* (Cambridge, MA: Harvard University Press, 1968), 69–86, describes this process, as, in a far more hostile fashion, does Elaine Hochman in *Bauhaus: Crucible of Modernism* (New York: Fromm International, 1997).

43 Walter Gropius to Günther Stamm, letter of 18 December 1967, Isaacs Papers.

3. FROM METAPHYSICS TO MATERIAL CULTURE

1 Oskar Schlemmer, letter to Meyer, mid-December 1925, in *The Letters and Diaries of Oskar Schlemmer,* ed. Tut Schlemmer, trans. Krishna Winston (Middletown, CT: Wesleyan University Press, 1972), 184.

2 Schlemmer, letter to Meyer, 13 February 1924, in *The Letters and Diaries of Oskar Schlemmer,* 151.

3 Walter Gropius, Bauhaus Program (1919), reprinted in *German Expressionism: Documents from the End of the Wilhelmine Empire to the Rise of National Socialism,* ed. Rose-Carol Washton Long (Berkeley and Los Angeles: University of California Press, 1995), 247–48.

4 For further discussion of the status of women, see Magdalena Droste, *Bauhaus, 1919–1913* (Berlin: Bauhaus-Archiv Museum für Gestaltung, 1990), 38–39, 72–74, 150–51, 184; and Anja Baumhoff, *The Gendered World of the Bauhaus: The Politics of Power at the Weimar Republic's Premier Art Institute, 1919–1932* (Frankfurt am Main: Peter Lang, 2001), especially 53–71 and 76–115. Baumhoff also discusses distinctions that were made between *Handwerk* (craftsmanship, such as carpentry) and *Kunstgewerbe* (arts and crafts, such as weaving); see 19, 71, and passim.

5 Walter Gropius, "Architecture in a Free Republic" (1919), reprinted in Long, *German Expressionism,* 193–97.

6 Bruno Taut, "A Necessity" (*Der Sturm,* 1914), reprinted in Long, *German Expressionism,* 123–25.

7 Gropius, letter to Edwin Redslob, 13 December 1920, Bauhaus-Archiv, Berlin.

8 Gropius, speech to Bauhaus students, July 1919, reprinted in Long, *German Expressionism,* 246–51.

9 Ibid.

10 Schlemmer, letter to Meyer, 7 December 1921, in Schlemmer, *The Letters and Diaries of Oskar Schlemmer,* 113–15.

11 Schlemmer, letter to Meyer, June 1922, ibid., 123.

12 As a Russian national, Kandinsky was obliged to leave Germany. He arrived in Moscow on 22 December 1914, and with the exception of a trip to Sweden in 1916, he remained in Russia until the end of 1921.

13 Taut, "A Necessity," reprinted in Long, *German Expressionism,* 123–25.

14 In 1914, the critic Paul Fechter described expressionism as having two strains: "intensive," which he used to refer to the work of Kandinsky, and "extensive," by which he described the less abstract and more detailed work of Max Pechstein; see Paul Fechter, from *Der Expressionismus* (1914), reprinted in Long, *German Expressionism,* 81–83. By 1919, the critic Oswald Herzog was using the term "abstrakte Expressionismus" to describe works that did not depict objects; see Oswald Herzog, "Abstract Expressionism" (1919), reprinted in Long, *German Expressionism,* 117–19.

15 Wassily Kandinsky, "Steps Taken by the Department of Fine Arts in the Realm of International Art Politics" (1920), reprinted in *Kandinsky: Complete Writings on Art,* ed. Kenneth C. Lindsay and Peter Vergo (Boston: G. K. Hall, 1982), 1:451.

16 Theo van Doesburg, "Ausstellung von Arbeiten der Lehrlingen im Staatlichen Bauhaus" (1922), cited in Claudine Humblet, *Le Bauhaus* (Lausanne: L'Âge d'Homme, 1980), 189.

17 Gropius, "The Viability of the Bauhaus Idea," 3 February 1922 circular to the Bauhaus Masters, reprinted in Hans M. Wingler, *Bauhaus,* 3rd rev. ed. (Cambridge, MA: MIT Press, 1978), 52.

18 Patricia Railing, *About 2 Squares and More about 2 Squares,* 2 vols. (Cambridge, MA: MIT Press, 1991). For essays on the impact of Lissitzky in Berlin, see those by Nancy Perloff, Christiana Lodder, and Éva Forgács in *Situating El Lissitzky: Vitebsk, Berlin, Moscow,* ed. Nancy Perloff and Brian Reed (Los Angeles: Getty Research Institute, 2003).

19 For a discussion of Kandinsky's interest in space and spatial effects, see Rose-Carol Washton Long, *Kandinsky: The Development of an Abstract Style* (Oxford: The Clarendon Press, 1980), 134–36.

20 For an illustration and discussion, see Droste, *Bauhaus,* 86–88, and also the discussion in Clark V. Poling, *Kandinsky: Russian and Bauhaus Years* (New York: Solomon R. Guggenheim Museum, 1983), 43–46.

21 For an illustration of the cradle, see *Bauhaus,* ed.

Jeannine Fiedler and Peter Feierabend, English ed. (Cologne: Könemann, 2000), 404, and Frank Whitford, *Bauhaus* (London: Thames and Hudson, 1984), Figure 173.

22 Wassily Kandinsky, *Point and Line to Plane* (Munich, 1926), reprinted in *Complete Writings*, 2:645.

23 Wassily Kandinsky, "The Value of the Teaching of Theory in Painting" (1926), reprinted in Wingler, *Bauhaus*, 13.

24 Linda Dalrymple Henderson, *The Fourth Dimension and Non-Euclidean Geometry in Modern Art* (Princeton, NJ: Princeton University Press, 1983), 238–94.

25 Wassily Kandinsky, letter to Will Grohmann, 12 October 1930, reprinted in *Künstler schreiben an Will Grohmann,* ed. Karl Gutbrod (Cologne: DuMont Schauberg, 1968), 56.

26 Kandinsky, *Point and Line to Plane,* reprinted in *Complete Writings,* 2:671.

27 For an illustration of *Several Circles,* see Hans K. Roethel and Jean K. Benjamin, *Kandinsky: Catalogue Raisonné of the Oil Paintings,* vol. 2 (Ithaca, NY: Cornell University Press, 1984), Figure 767.

28 Kandinsky, "Art Education" (1928), reprinted in Wingler, *Bauhaus,* 147.

29 El Lisickij (Lissitzky), "Exhibitions in Berlin" (May 1922), reprinted in *Vešč' Objet Gegenstand,* reprint ed. (Baden, Switzerland: Verlag Lars Müller, 1994), 122.

30 Ludwig Kassak and Ladislaus Moholy-Nagy, *Buch neuer Künstler* (1922), reprint ed. (Baden: Verlag Lars Müller, 1991).

31 For a discussion of reactions to Moholy-Nagy's work in Germany, see Magdalena Droste, "László Moholy-Nagy–Zur Rezeption seiner Kunst in der Weimarer Republik," in *Über Moholy-Nagy: Ergebnisse aus dem Internationalen László Moholy-Nagy Symposium, Bielefeld 1991, zum 100. Geburtstag des Künstlers und Bauhauslehrers,* ed. Gottfried Jäger and Gudrun Wessing (Bielefeld: Kerber Verlag, 1997), 23–36.

32 László Moholy-Nagy et al., "Manifesto" (*Egység,* 1923), reprinted in Krisztina Passuth, *Moholy-Nagy* (New York: Thames and Hudson, 1985), 289.

33 Moholy-Nagy, "On the Problem of New Content and New Form" (*Akasztott Ember,* 1922), reprinted in Passuth, *Moholy-Nagy,* 287.

34 Lyonel Feininger, letter to Julia Feininger, 9 March 1925, reprinted in Wingler, *Bauhaus,* 97.

35 To de-emphasize their individualism and to stress his orderly approach, Moholy-Nagy often titled his works, the oils in particular, with letters and numbers and/or with references to their color and form.

36 Moholy-Nagy and Alfred Kemeny, "Dynamic–Constructive System of Forces" (*Der Sturm,* 1922), reprinted in Passuth, *Moholy-Nagy,* 290; emphasis in the original.

37 Eleanor M. Hight, *Picturing Modernism: Moholy-Nagy and Photography in Weimar Germany* (Cambridge, MA: MIT Press, 1995), Chapter 4, especially 57, 72–76.

38 Oliver A. I. Botar, "Prolegomena to the Study of Biomorphic Modernism: Biocentrism, László Moholy-Nagy's 'New Vision' and Erno Kállai's Bioromantik" (Ph.D. diss., University of Toronto, 1997), especially Chapters 3 and 4. Botar believes that Raoul France's theories of *Biotechnik* had considerable impact on Moholy-Nagy.

39 Moholy-Nagy [and Lucia Moholy], "Production–Reproduction" (*De Stijl,* 1922), reprinted in Passuth, *Moholy-Nagy,* 289.

40 Lucia Moholy, *Marginalien zu Moholy-Nagy: Moholy-Nagy, Marginal Notes* (Krefeld: Scherpe Verlag, 1972), 59.

41 Moholy-Nagy, *Painting, Photography, Film,* trans. Janet Seligman (1925; repr. from the 1927 ed., Cambridge, MA: MIT Press, 1987), 27 (page citations are to the reprint edition).

42 Moholy-Nagy, *Painting, Photography, Film,* 8.

43 See Rolf Sachsse, "Die Frau an seiner Seite," *Fotografieren hiess teilnehmen: Fotografinnen der Weimarer Republik,* ed. Ute Eskildsen (Essen/Düsseldorf: Museum Folkwang/Richter Verlag, 1994), 67–75; and Sachsse, *Lucia Moholy* (Düsseldorf: Edition Marzona, 1985).

44 For discussion of their connection to anarchist and pacifist groups, see Oliver A. I. Botar, "From Avant-Garde to 'Proletkult' in Hungarian Émigré Politico-Cultural Journals, 1922–1924," *Art and Journals on the Political Front, 1910–1940,* ed. Virginia Hagelstein Marquardt (Gainesville: University Press of

Florida, 1997), 100–147; and Botar, "An Activist-Expressionist in Exile: László Moholy-Nagy 1919–1920," in *László Moholy-Nagy: From Budapest to Berlin, 1914–1923* (Newark: University Gallery, University of Delaware, 1997), 70–86. Also see Magdalena Droste, "László Moholy-Nagy," 36.

45 Moholy, *Marginalien,* 55.

46 Baumhoff, *Gendered World,* 53–75.

47 Moholy-Nagy, "Vorwort," *Von Material zu Architektur* (1929; repr., Mainz and Berlin: Florian Kupferberg, 1968), 7; by the English edition of 1930, this statement of gratitude had been removed. See also *Internationale Ausstellung des Deutschen Werkbundes Film und Foto Stuttgart 1929,* reprint ed. Karl Steinorth (Stuttgart: Deutsche Verlags-Anstalt, 1979), 69.

48 See, for example, Will Grohmann, "Das Neue Bauhaus in Dessau," *Das Kunstblatt* (January 1927), 18–30; and Gropius, *Die Bauhasbauten in Dessau* (Munich: Bauhausbuch 12, 1930).

49 Hight, *Picturing Modernism,* 147. Moholy-Nagy called his photomontages "Fotoplastiken." See also Irene-Charlotte Lusk, *Montagen ins Blaue: László Moholy-Nagy, Fotomontagen und –collagen, 1922–1943* (Giessen: Anabas-Verlag, Werkbund-Archiv 5, 1980).

50 Gropius, "The Viability of the Bauhaus Idea," 3 February 1922 circular to the Bauhaus Masters, reprinted in Wingler, *Bauhaus,* 52.

51 Gropius, "Bauhaus Dessau–Principles of Bauhaus Production," March 1926, reprinted in Wingler, *Bauhaus,* 110.

52 Moholy-Nagy, *Painting, Photography, Film,* 25.

53 Ibid., 29.

54 See Peter Galassi, "Rodchenko and Photography's Revolution," in *Aleksandr Rodchenko,* ed. Magdalena Dabrowski, Leah Dickerman, and Peter Galassi (New York: Museum of Modern Art, 1999), 113–25.

55 For illustrations of these two photos, see the English reprint *Painting, Photography, Film,* 57 and 62.

56 Ibid., 74

57 Ibid., 39.

58 Ibid., 40.

59 Under Hannes Meyer, Kállai edited the periodical from 1928 to 1930. For discussion of Kállai's career

and attitudes, see two articles by Éva Forgács: "Erno Kállai: The Art Critic of a Changing Age," *NHQ: The New Hungarian Quarterly* 17, no. 64 (1976): 174–81, and "Enter Malevich: The Conflict between Kállai and Moholy-Nagy," *Budapest Review of Books* 5 (Fall 1995): 139–42.

60 Ernst Kallai, "Malerei und Photographie," *i 10,* no. 4 (1927): reprinted in *Een Keuze vit de Internationale revue i 10* (The Hague: B. Bakker, 1963), 148–57; English translation in Edigio Marzona and Roswitha Fricke, eds., *Bauhaus Photography* (Cambridge, MA: MIT Press, 1985), 132–34; excerpt in English translation in *Photography in the Modern Era: European Documents and Critical Writings, 1913–1940,* ed. Christopher Phillips (New York: Metropolitan Museum of Art/Aperture, 1989), 94–99.

61 Moholy-Nagy, from "Diskussion über Ernst Kállai's Artikel 'Malerei und Fotografie'" (no. 6, 1927), reprinted in *Een Keuze vit de Internationale revue,* 233–34; English translation in Marzona and Fricke, *Bauhaus Photography,* 136–37; excerpt in English translation in *Photography in the Modern Era,* 101–3.

62 Lyonel Feininger, letter to Julia Feininger, 29 June 1928, reprinted in Wingler, *Bauhaus,* 141.

63 Stolzl was forced to retire in 1931; see Baumhoff, *Gendered World,* 95–99.

64 Ise Gropius, diary, 2 March 1927, cited in Droste, *Bauhaus,* 161.

65 Schlemmer, letters to Willi Baumeister, 8 April 1929, and to Otto Meyer, 8 September 1929, in Schlemmer, *Letters and Diaries,* 241 and 248.

66 Baubaus Berlin, Syllabus and Curriculum, October 1932, reprinted in Wingler, *Bauhaus,* 182.

67 See Katherine C. Ware, "Photography at the Bauhaus," in Fiedler and Feierabend, *Bauhaus,* 519–29; see also Jeannine Fiedler, "Walter Peterhans: A 'Tabularian' Approach," in *Photography at the Bauhaus,* ed. Jeannine Fiedler (Cambridge, MA: MIT Press, 1990), 84–107.

68 For reproductions of the many photographs produced by women at the Bauhaus, see Fiedler, *Photography at the Bauhaus.*

69 For a reproduction of the advertisement for Komol, see Ute Eskildsen and Susanne Baumann, *ringl+pit: Grete Stern, Ellen Auerbach* (Essen: Fotografisches Kabinett, Museum Folkwang, 1993), 26.

70 For a discussion of two other major exhibits in which Moholy-Nagy's photographs were displayed in addition to the Film und Foto exhibition of 1929, see Vanessa Rocco, "Before *Film und Foto:* Pictorialism to the New Vision in German Photography Exhibitions from 1909–29" (Ph.D. diss., City University of New York Graduate Center, 2004), Chapters 3 and 4.

71 Walter Benjamin, "Little History of Photography" (1931), in *Walter Benjamin: Selected Writings,* vol. 2, ed. M. Jennings, H. Eilaud, and G. Smith (Cambridge, MA: Belknap Press of Harvard University Press, 1999), 523. In "Little History of Photography," Benjamin castigates Albert Renger-Patzsch for aesthetization and commercialism. Also see Frederic J. Schwartz, "The Eye of the Expert: Walter Benjamin and the Avant Garde," *Art History* 2, no. 3 (June 2001): 401–44; and Michael Jennings, "Agriculture, Industry, and the Birth of the Photo-Essay in the Weimar Republic," *October* 93 (Summer 2000): 23–56.

4. ARCHITECTURE, BUILDING, AND THE BAUHAUS

1 Walter Gropius, "Programme of the Staatliches Bauhaus in Weimar" (1919), translation in part from *Programs and Manifestoes on 20th-Century Architecture,* ed. Ulrich Conrads (Cambridge, MA: MIT Press, 1980), 49. Conrads translates "den neuen Bau der Zukunft" as "structure" rather than "building," as I have here.

2 Ibid.

3 George Baird, "Bauhaus Conflicts Seen Now" (BBC radio broadcast, transcript: October 18, 1968; transmission: October 25, 1968, 21:25–22:25), 4. Mies van der Rohe Papers, Library of Congress.

4 Letter from Paul Klopfer to Gropius, 3 May 1919 in Klaus-Jürgen Winkler, *Die Architektur am Bauhaus in Weimar* (Berlin and Munich: Verlag für Bauwesen, 1993), 23 and 162 nn. 40, 41.

5 Winkler, *Die Architektur am Bauhaus in Weimar,* 29.

6 Ibid., 28.

7 Ibid., 25.

8 Ibid., 23–24.

9 Ibid., 25.

10 Despite the fact that the local government rejected the first proposal as a weak replacement for a "real" study of architecture, sixteen students signed up for the course. The second proposal made in 1923 was equally popular; fourteen students were enrolled from 1924 to 1925, when the school moved to Dessau. Ibid., 24, 28.

11 As Georg Muche pointed out, "The decisive origins of the Bauhaus lay in the decade preceding its founding. In March 1912, the Werkbund had already published something like a Bauhaus program in one of its yearbooks. 'The aim of the Werkbund is the penetration of work by the collaboration of art, industry, and trade through education.' In the foreword the co-operation of industry and artists in the field of mass production is already mentioned. Gropius, however, restricted the Bauhaus originally when he emphasized a romantic return to handicrafts." Georg Muche, "Bauhaus Epitaph," in *Bauhaus and Bauhaus People,* ed. Eckhard Neumann (New York: Van Nostrand Reinhold, 1970), 202.

12 Winkler, *Die Architektur am Bauhaus in Weimar,* 127.

13 Ibid., 37, and Gillian Naylor, *The Bauhaus Reassessed: Sources and Design Theory* (New York: Dutton, 1985), 104–5.

14 Gropius's design for a theater in Jena was also the product of a collaboration with Oskar Schlemmer and apprentices in the wall-painting workshop. Magdalena Droste, *Bauhaus, 1919–1933* (Berlin: Bauhaus-Archiv Museum für Gestaltung, 1990), 110, and Winkler, *Die Architektur am Bauhaus in Weimar,* 114.

15 Marcel Breuer, Fred Forbat, and Joost Schmidt were among the Bauhaus students who worked in the office between 1920 and 1925. Winkler, *Die Architektur am Bauhaus in Weimar,* 35.

16 Bernhard Gaber, *Die Entwicklung des Berufsstandes der freischaffenden Architekten* (Essen: Verlag Richard Bacht, 1966), 127.

17 Marcel Franciscono, *Walter Gropius and the Creation of the Bauhaus in Weimar: The Ideals and Artistic Theories of Its Founding Years* (Urbana: University of Illinois Press, 1971), 129.

18 Ibid.

19 The reference to masters, journeymen, and apprentices became official when it was included in the Bauhaus statutes, first published in 1921. See Berndt Vogelsang, "Chronology," in *Bauhaus Weimar–*

Designs for the Future, ed. Michael Siebenbrodt (Ostfildern-Ruit: Hatje-Cantz, 2000), 284.

Gropius maintained his support for the equality (or near equality) of students and faculty at Harvard. In a 1968 interview with the BBC, he complained that even at Harvard, students did not get to participate in the deliberations of the faculty. "In the Bauhaus, right in the beginning, we took two student representatives into all our council meetings and there were wild arguments all the time, but we never had any riots, because they took part in the responsibility." Baird, "Bauhaus Conflicts Seen Now," 21.

20 Ibid., 12.

21 Ibid.

22 Winkler, *Die Architektur am Bauhaus in Weimar,* 133–34.

23 Ibid., 84.

24 Naylor, *Bauhaus Reassessed,* 95. AEG is the Allgemeine Elektricitäts-Gesellschaft or, roughly translated, General Electric Company. Peter Behrens was its artistic director from 1907 to 1914.

25 Ibid., 129. Other students, such as Friedl Dicker and Franz Singer, also produced designs for single-family houses. Winkler, *Die Architektur am Bauhaus in Weimar,* 93.

26 Winkler, *Die Architektur am Bauhaus in Weimar,* 139 and 168, n. 365 (letter from Gropius to Mies, 4 June 1923). Mies also sought to present modern architecture as a unified movement in the Weissenhof Siedlung exhibition in 1927.

27 Walter Passarge, "The Bauhaus Exhibition in Weimar," *Das Kunstblatt* 7 (1923): 309ff., in Hans M. Wingler, *Bauhaus* (1962; repr., Cambridge, MA: MIT Press, 1984), 67.

28 Adolf Meyer, ed., *Ein Versuchshaus des Bauhauses,* Bauhausbücher no. 3, (Munich: Albert Langen, 1924). The book did not appear until after the move to Dessau in 1925.

29 Winkler, *Die Architektur am Bauhaus in Weimar,* 95.

30 Ibid., 109.

31 Ibid., 106.

32 Passarge, "The Bauhaus Exhibition in Weimar," 67.

33 Workshop students participating in the Haus am Horn were Cabinetry: Marcel Breuer (living room and woman's room), Alma Buscher and Erich Brendel (children's room), Erich Dieckmann (dining room and man's room), Benita Otte and Ernst Gebhardt (kitchen); Metal: Alma Buscher (lighting in children's room), C. J. Jucker (desk lamps), Julius Pap (standing lamp in the living room); Wall-Painting: Alfred Arndt and Josef Maltan (painting of the interior rooms); Weaving: Lis Deinhardt (carpet in man's room), Martha Erps (carpet in living room), Benita Otte (carpet in children's room), Agnes Roghé (carpet in woman's room), Gunta Stölzl (carpet in living room niche); Ceramics: Theo Bogler and Otto Lindig (ceramic vessels). In addition, Josef Hartwig, the master of the sculpture workshop, made the model of the house. Meyer, *Ein Versuchshaus des Bauhauses,* 65.

34 Adolf Behne quoted in Naylor, *Bauhaus Reassessed,* 117.

35 See Wingler, *Bauhaus;* Passarge, "The Bauhaus Exhibition in Weimar," 67; and Adolf Meyer, "The Construction of the Experimental House," 66.

36 Winkler, *Die Architektur am Bauhaus in Weimar,* 96.

37 Georg Muche, "Das Versuchshaus des Bauhauses," in Meyer, *Ein Versuchshaus des Bauhauses,* 15–23.

38 Walter Gropius, "Wohnhaus-Industrie," in Meyer, *Ein Versuchshaus des Bauhauses,* 5–14.

39 Walter Gropius, *Internationale Architektur,* Bauhausbücher no. 1 (Munich: Albert Langen, 1925), 99.

40 Winkler, *Die Architektur am Bauhaus in Weimar,* 86.

41 Gropius, "Idee und Aufbau des Staatlichen Bauhauses Weimar," in *Staatliches Bauhaus Weimar, 1919–1923,* ed. Walter Gropius (Weimar and Munich: Bauhausverlag, 1923), 7–18. The essay was also published as a pamphlet: Walter Gropius, *Idee und Aufbau des Staatlichen Bauhauses Weimar* (Weimar and Munich: Bauhausverlag, 1923); and it was translated and abridged as "The Theory and Organization of the Bauhaus," in *Bauhaus 1919–1928,* ed. Herbert Bayer, Walter Gropius, and Ise Gropius (New York: Museum of Modern Art, 1938), 20–29. The diagram first appeared in *The Statutes of the Staatliches Bauhaus Weimar* of 1922. See Karin Wilhelm, "The Three Bauhaus Directors," *Bauhaus,* ed. Jeannine Fiedler and Peter Feierabend (Cologne:

Könemann, 2000), 183, and Rainer K. Wick, *Teaching at the Bauhaus* (Ostfildern-Ruit: Hatje-Cantz, 2000), 68–69.

42 Gropius, "The Theory and Organization of the Bauhaus," 24.

43 Ibid., 28.

44 Gropius acknowledged that the introduction of a course in design was new to the Bauhaus, but not original, and cited the reform proposals by Bartning and others in order to legitimize his own project. Franciscono, *Walter Gropius,* 130.

45 "The Theory and Organization of the Bauhaus," 24.

46 Muche, "Das Versuchshaus des Bauhauses," in Meyer, *Ein Versuchshaus des Bauhauses,* 23.

47 Winkler, *Die Architektur am Bauhaus in Weimar,* 130, and Gropius, *Internationale Architektur,* 100.

48 Winkler, *Die Architektur am Bauhaus in Weimar,* 131.

49 Ibid., 132.

50 Siegfried Giedion, "About the Practical Output of the Bauhaus," in Neumann, *Bauhaus and Bauhaus People,* 200–201.

51 Winkler, *Die Architektur am Bauhaus in Weimar,* 27.

52 Ibid., 31–32. Only men were included in this group; Gropius and the other masters did their best to confine women to the weaving workshop because they believed that the women's alleged "arty-crafty" tendencies would have detracted from the rest of the school's activities. See Droste, *Bauhaus,* 38, 40.

53 Winkler, *Die Architektur am Bauhaus in Weimar,* 32.

54 It was the Berlin architect Otto Bartning who finally brought an architecture department to Weimar when he took over the directorship of the school that succeeded the Bauhaus after its move to Dessau in 1925. At the new Staatliche Hochschule für Handwerk und Baukunst, he succeeded in keeping the workshops and adding a building department with a studio and a model and experimental workshop. Ibid., 45. The design studio was one of the first of its kind in Germany, following a model established in the United States and in Great Britain.

55 Max Deri, "Das Bauhaus," *B.Z. am Mittag* (7 December 1926), in Walter Scheiffele, "'You Must Go There'—Contemporary Reactions," *The Dessau Bauhaus Building 1926–1999,* ed. Bauhaus Dessau Foundation and Margret Kentgens-Craig (Basel: Birkhäuser, 1998), 116.

56 See Wolfgang Thöner, "A Symbol of Hope, or of Failure? The Bauhaus Building in Publications," in *The Dessau Bauhaus Building 1926–1999,* 123–25, in which he cites Giedion and the constructivists among other critics on this subject. By placing the building in the 1932 International Style show, Hitchcock and Johnson ensured that this reputation would endure.

57 Howard Dearstyne, *Inside the Bauhaus* (New York: Rizzoli, 1986), 203.

58 Winkler, *Die Architektur am Bauhaus in Weimar,* 417, and *Bauhaus Journal,* no. 2 (1927).

59 Bauhaus Dessau, "Statute," in *Bauhaus Dessau, Satzung–Lehrordnung* (Dessau, 1927), in Wingler, *Bauhaus,* 122.

60 For example, see Scheiffele, "You Must Go There," 116.

61 Wittwer and Meyer became partners in 1926, as documented in Naylor, *Bauhaus Reassessed,* 142. In 1929, Wittwer ended the partnership and left the Bauhaus. Together, they had won the competition for the German Trade Union School building. Meyer took over the project as its sole author; the Bauhaus students worked on its development in Meyer's Berlin office. See Philipp Tolziner, "Mit Hannes Meyer am Bauhaus und in der Sowjetunion (1927–1936)," *Hannes Meyer 1889–1954: Architekt Urbanist Lehrer,* ed. Magdalena Droste and Werner Kleinerüschkamp (Berlin and Frankfurt am Main: Ernst und Sohn, Bauhaus-Archiv, Deutsches Architekturmuseum, 1989), 241.

62 Dearstyne, *Inside the Bauhaus,* 212.

63 Wingler, *Bauhaus,* 502.

64 Martin Kieren, "From the Bauhaus to Housebuilding—Architecture and the Teaching of Architecture at the Bauhaus," in Fiedler and Feierabend, *Bauhaus,* 563.

65 Wingler, *Bauhaus,* 503.

66 Ibid., 151 and 503.

67 Ibid., 151 and 429, and Naylor, *Bauhaus Reassessed,* 168.

68 "The Course of Training in the Architecture Department," *Bauhaus–Junge Menschen kommt aus*

Bauhaus, advertising pamphlet, published by Bauhaus, Dessau, 1929; in Wingler, *Bauhaus,* 151.

69 Ibid.

70 Hannes Meyer, "Bauen," *Bauhaus Journal* 2, no. 4 (1928): 12–13; in Wingler, *Bauhaus,* 153–54.

71 Meyer, "Bauen," 153.

72 Bauhaus student Arieh Sharon related the following story about his work on the ADGB building: "Basically we were even not allowed to draw elevations, which were supposed to be only a logical sequel of the windows' functional sizes and relationships. But nevertheless, I drew on the drawing edges some elevation sketches and always suspected Hannes Meyer of peeking with at least one eye." In Sharon, *Kibbutz + Bauhaus* (Tel Aviv and Stuttgart: Karl Krämer Verlag, 1976), 31; in K. Michael Hays, *Modernism and the Posthumanist Subject: The Architecture of Hannes Meyer and Ludwig Hilberseimer* (Cambridge, MA: MIT Press, 1992), 310, n. 29.

73 Wingler, *Bauhaus,* 489. For example, student Siegfried Giesenschlag analyzed neighbor relations: a visual analysis of the sounds, smells, views, and relationships of neighbors relative to the location of the units. See Kieren, "From the Bauhaus to Housebuilding," in Fiedler and Feierabend, *Bauhaus,* 564–65.

74 Tolziner, "Mit Hannes Meyer," 237.

75 Sharon, *Kibbutz + Bauhaus,* 31; in Hays, *Modernism and the Posthumanist Subject,* 310, n. 29.

76 "Semesterplan" (ca. 1928); Wingler, *Bauhaus,* 121.

77 Tolziner, "Mit Hannes Meyer," 241–43, and Wingler, *Bauhaus,* 495.

78 Wick, *Teaching at the Bauhaus,* 83.

79 When Meyer was the Bauhaus director, students had already demanded the elimination of the preliminary course because they felt that it aestheticized the use of materials. Mies eliminated it because it was not directly related to architecture. See Marty Bax, *Bauhaus Lecture Notes* (Amsterdam: Architektur and Natura Press, 1991), 56.

80 Droste, *Bauhaus,* 208–12, and Wingler, *Bauhaus,* 182–83.

81 Christian Wolsdorff, "Ende Gut–Alles Gut: Mies van der Rohe und das Bauhaus," *Mehr als der blosse Zweck: Mies van der Rohe am Bauhaus 1930–1933* (Berlin: Bauhaus-Archiv, 2001), 10.

82 Dearstyne, *Inside the Bauhaus,* 226.

83 Kieren, "From the Bauhaus to Housebuilding," in Fiedler and Feierabend, *Bauhaus,* 573.

84 Wingler repeatedly emphasizes Mies and Hilberseimer's complementary relationship. See Wingler, *Bauhaus,* 539.

85 According to Wolsdorff, this is most often true in the English-language texts. See "Ende Gut–Alles Gut," in *Mehr als der blosse Zweck,* 7.

86 Pius Pahl, "Experiences of an Architectural Student," in Neumann, *Bauhaus and Bauhaus People,* 229.

87 Wolsdorff, "Ende Gut–Alles Gut," in *Mehr als der blosse Zweck,* 15–16.

88 Ibid., 13–14.

5. BAUHAUS THEATER OF HUMAN DOLLS

Translations are my own except where otherwise noted; I thank Marc Katz and Steven Lindberg for checking them. For facilitating my research, I am grateful to the staff in Special Collections at the Getty Research Institute, Los Angeles, and to those at the Kunstbibliothek and at the Bauhaus Archive in Berlin. Material from this essay was presented at the Los Angeles County Museum of Art in April 2002; thanks are due to my audience there and to the students in my seminar "Human Dolls" at Scripps College that spring. For their comments on earlier drafts, I thank Perry Chapman, Lory Frankel, Maria Gough, Kathleen James-Chakraborty, David Joselit, Wallis Miller, Sarah Whiting, and the two anonymous readers for the *Art Bulletin.* My research has been funded by fellowships from the Getty Research Institute, Los Angeles; Scripps College, Claremont; and the Humboldt Foundation, Bonn, for all of which I am deeply grateful.

1 Walter Gropius, introduction to Oskar Schlemmer, *The Theater of the Bauhaus,* ed. Walter Gropius, trans. Arthur S. Wensinger (Middletown, CT: Wesleyan University Press, 1961), 7.

2 Walter Gropius, "Program for the Staatliche Bauhaus in Weimar" (April 1919), in Hans M. Wingler, *Bauhaus: Weimar, Dessau, Berlin, Chicago,* trans. Wolfgang Jabs and Basil Gilbert (Cambridge, MA: MIT Press, 1969), 31. By contrast, Gropius called for instruction in a range of other subjects that he considered necessary for a complete education in the arts. These included anatomy, garden design, contract negotiation, bookkeeping, and art history—this last, he enjoined, "not presented in the sense of a history of styles, but rather to further active understanding of historical working methods and techniques" (32). The "Statutes of the Staatliche Bauhaus in Weimar" published in January 1921, which includes a section on the curriculum, likewise makes no mention of theater. See Wingler, *Bauhaus,* 44–48.

3 Schlemmer had been hired in 1922 as master of form in charge of woodworking and stone sculpture but was already overseeing theater work when Schreyer quit in early 1923, during rehearsals for performances that summer during Bauhaus week. See Wingler, *Bauhaus,* 360, as well as Karl Toepfer, *Empire of Ecstasy: Nudity and Movement in German Body Culture 1910–1935* (Berkeley and Los Angeles: University of California Press, 1994), 136–38.

4 Oskar Schlemmer, László Moholy-Nagy, and Farkas Molnár, *Die Bühne im Bauhaus* (Munich: Albert Langen, 1925). Copies of the book are dated 1924, when it was put together in Weimar; secondary literature on the Bauhaus generally gives a publication date of 1925, when the book was edited in Dessau. The book contained essays by Molnár, Moholy-Nagy, and Schlemmer himself, with additional images by Marcel Breuer, Kurt Schmidt, and Alexander (Xanti) Schawinsky. It gained an introduction by Gropius when it was published in 1961 in English translation as *The Theater of the Bauhaus.*

5 Schlemmer, "Mensch und Kunstfigur," in Schlemmer, Moholy-Nagy, and Molnár, *Die Bühne im Bauhaus,* 7.

6 On the contemporaneous relation of theater and sports (and boxing in particular), see Bertolt Brecht, "More Good Sports" (1926), in *The Weimar Republic Sourcebook,* ed. Anton Kaes, Martin Jay, and Edward Dimendberg (Berkeley and Los Angeles: University of California Press, 1994), 536–38; and Hans Ulrich Gumbrecht, *In 1926: Living at the Edge of Time* (Cambridge, MA: Harvard University Press, 1997), 42–52.

7 Johann Joachim Winckelmann, *Gedanken über die Nachahmung der griechischen Werke in der Malerei und Bildhauerkunst* (Dresden: Im Verlag der Waltherischen Handlung, 1756), 21.

8 Schlemmer, "Mensch und Kunstfigur," 18–19.

9 Oskar Schlemmer in *Oskar Schlemmer: Idealist der Form; Briefe, Tagebücher, Schriften,* ed. Andreas Hüneke (Leipzig: Reclam, 1989), 230–31. He continued: "In all *early* cultures that were also *high* cultures— the Egyptians, the early Greeks, early Indian art—the human form is far from the naturalistic image, but thus closer to the *lapidary* symbolic form: the *idol,* the *totem,* the *doll. . . ."* The modernist emphasis on theatricality, Rainer Nägele has argued, "radicalizes exteriority to the point where the living actors are replaced by the puppet," a creature that "radically refuses dialogue," its silence enforced by the impossibility of discerning the creature's source of speech. Nägele, *Theater, Theory, Speculation: Walter Benjamin and the Scenes of Modernity* (Baltimore: The Johns Hopkins University Press, 1991), 27.

10 See, for example, Brigid Doherty, "'See We Are All Neurasthenics!'; or, The Trauma of Dada Montage," *Critical Inquiry* 24 (Autumn 1997): 82–132; Doherty, "Figures of the Pseudorevolution," *October* 84 (Spring 1998): 65–89; Mia Fineman, "Ecce Homo Prostheticus," *New German Critique* 76 (Winter 1999): 85–114; Maud Lavin, *Cut with a Kitchen Knife: The Weimar Photomontages of Hannah Höch* (New Haven, CT: Yale University Press, 1993); and Matthew Teitelbaum, ed., *Montage and Modern Life: 1919– 1942,* exhibit catalog, Institute for Contemporary Art, Boston (Cambridge, MA: MIT Press, 1992). Matthew Biro discusses Raoul Haussmann's photomontages of 1920 through the insistent anachronism of the "Weimar cyborg" in "The New Man as Cyborg: Figures of Technology in Weimar Visual Culture," *New German Critique* 62 (Spring–Summer 1994): 71–110. On the contemporaneous technophilic creations of Wyndham Lewis and F. T. Marinetti, see Hal Foster, "Prosthetic Gods," *Modernism / modernity* 4, no. 2 (1997): 5–38.

11 "For much of the first half of this [the twentieth] century," Christopher Phillips has written, "montage served not only as an innovative artistic technique but functioned, too, as a kind of symbolic form, providing a shared visual idiom that more than any other expressed the tumultuous arrival of a fully urbanized, industrialized culture." Phillips, introduction to Teitelbaum, *Montage and Modern Life,* 22. An anonymous text in the Soviet journal *Lef,* probably by Gustav Klutsis, advocates the technique for its effectiveness: "A combination of snapshots takes the place of the composition in a graphic depiction. . . . [The] precision and documentary character of the snapshot have an impact on the viewer that a graphic depiction can never attain." [Klutsis], "Photomontage," *Lef,* no. 4 (1924): 43–44, trans. John E. Bowlt, in Phillips, ed., *Photography in the Modern Era* (New York: Metropolitan Museum of Art, 1989), 211–12; see also Sergei Tretyakov, "From the Editor," *Novyi Lef* 11 (1928): 41–42, in Phillips, 270–72; as well as Peter Bürger, *Theory of the Avant-Garde* (1979), trans. Michael Shaw (Minneapolis: University of Minnesota Press, 1999), passim.

12 For an extended analysis of this image, see Lavin, *Cut with a Kitchen Knife,* 193–94.

13 On this "return to order," see Benjamin H. D. Buchloh, "Figures of Authority, Ciphers of Regression: Notes on the Return of Representation in European Painting," in *Art After Modernism: Rethinking Representation,* ed. Brian Wallis (Boston: Godine, 1984), 106–35.

14 "Results of the Investigation Concerning the Staatliche Bauhaus in Weimar," in Wingler, *Bauhaus,* 42.

15 Under the directorship of Hannes Meyer (1928–30), the Bauhaus in fact encouraged leftist politics, inspiring an engagement with collective production as much as with communism.

16 See, for example, Winfried Nerdinger, ed., *Bauhaus-Moderne im Nationalsozialismus: Zwischen Anbiederung und Verfolgung* (Munich: Prestel, 1993), especially Magdalena Droste, "Bauhaus-Maler im Nationalsozialismus: Anpassung, Selbstentfremdung, Verweigerung," 113–41.

17 Schlemmer to Gunta Stötzl, 16 June 1933, quoted in Nerdinger, "Modernisierung, Bauhaus, Nationalsozialismus," in Nerdinger, *Bauhaus-Moderne im Nationalsozialismus,* 19. "Schlemmer, who in 1934 submitted to a competition for a mosaic in the Deutsches Museum a design depicting a group marching and giving the Hitler salute to a luminous image of the Führer, wrestled for years with his position toward and within National Socialism, as his diaries (in the Bauhaus Archive) suggest." Ibid., 23, n. 52. Wingler, *Bauhaus,* 257, told a different story in 1969: "Following his dismissal from the teaching profession, which had been decreed by the National Socialists [in 1933], he was forced to take odd jobs in order to manage."

18 Following World War II, such diametrically opposed arguments were indeed made in East and West Germany about the Bauhaus. See Nerdinger, *Bauhaus-Moderne im Nationalsozialismus,* 17–18. For a critique of retrospective allegations of protofascism, see Koss, "Allegorical Procedures, Apocalyptic Threats: Early Weimar Cultural Positions," in *Issues of Performance in Politics and the Arts: Proceedings of the Third Annual German Studies Conference at Berkeley* (Berkeley: Berkeley Academic Press, 1997), 101–15. Relevant here is Jeffrey Herf, *Reactionary Modernism: Technology, Culture, and Politics in Weimar and the Third Reich* (Cambridge: Cambridge University Press, 1984).

19 Siegfried Kracauer, "Those Who Wait" (1922), in *The Mass Ornament: Weimar Essays,* ed. and trans. Thomas Y. Levin (Cambridge, MA: Harvard University Press, 1995), 138.

20 Franz Roh, *Nachexpressionismus, Magischer Realismus: Probleme der neuesten europäischen Malerei* (Leipzig: Klinkhardt & Biermann, 1925), 45–46.

21 Heinrich von Kleist, "On the Marionette Theater" (1810), trans. Roman Paska, in *Fragments for a History of the Human Body,* ed. Michael Feher, pt. 1 (Cambridge, MA: Zone Books, 1989), 420. His essay inspired the theater impresario Edward Gordon Craig, whose own "The Actor and the Über-Marionette" appeared in 1908. Notably, Sigmund Freud wrote several pages about the Sandman tale by Hoffmann, whom he termed "the unrivalled master of the uncanny in literature." Freud, "The Uncanny" (1919), in *Writings on Art and Literature* (Stanford, CA: Stanford University Press, 1997), 209 and passim.

22 Walter Benjamin, "Convolute Z," *The Arcades Project,* trans. Howard Eiland and Kevin McLaughlin (Cambridge, MA: Harvard University Press, 1999), 694. See also Benjamin, "Lob der Puppe," *Literarische Welt* (10 January 1930), reprinted in *Gesammelte Schriften,* vol. 3, ed. Hell Tiedemann-Bartels (Frankfurt: Suhrkamp, 1989), 213–18; as well as Benjamin, "Old Toys: The Toy Exhibition at the Märkisches Museum," 98–102, "The Cultural History of Toys," 113–16, and "Toys and Play: Marginal Notes on a Monumental Work," 117–21, all in *Walter Benjamin: Selected Writings,* vol. 2, *1927–1934,* ed. Michael W. Jennings, Howard Eiland, and Gary Smith, trans. Rodney Livingstone (Cambridge, MA: Harvard University Press, 1999). For an overview and bibliography of writings on dolls, see John Bell, "Puppets, Masks, and Performing Objects at the End of the Century," *Drama Review* 43, no. 3 (Fall 1999): 15–27. An excellent compendium of essays on and images of twentieth-century dolls is Pia Müller-Tamm and Katharina Sykora, eds., *Puppen Körper Automaten: Phantasmen der Moderne,* Düsseldorf Kunstsammlung Nordrhein-Westfalen, exhibition catalog (Cologne: Oktagon, 1999); see especially Horst Bredekamp, "Überlegungen zur Unausweichlichkeit der Automaten," 94–105, and Karoline Hille, "'. . . über den Grenzen, mitten in Nüchternheit': Prothesenkörper, Maschinenherzen, Automatenhirne," 140–59. The literature on surrealist doll figures (in this volume and elsewhere) is extensive; see, for example, Hal Foster, *Compulsive Beauty* (Cambridge, MA: MIT Press, 1993); Therese Lichtenstein, *Behind Closed Doors: The Art of Hans Bellmer* (Berkeley and Los Angeles: University of California Press, 2001); and Sue Taylor, *Hans Bellmer: The Anatomy of Anxiety* (Cambridge, MA: MIT Press, 2002).

23 Small wooden figures made in the stage workshop after designs by Eberhard Schrammen (1923–25) may be found in Dirk Scheper, *Oskar Schlemmer, "Das Triadische Ballett" und die Bauhausbühne* (Berlin: Schriftenreihe der Akademie der Künste, 1988), 92–93; photographs of three marionettes by Hilde Rantzsch appeared in *Bauhaus* 1, no. 3 (1927). Moholy-Nagy, whose photograph *Puppen* was made in 1925, also worked with dolls; "out of his theoretical laboratory experiments at the Bauhaus," Gropius, introduction to Oskar Schlemmer, *The Theater of the Bauhaus,* 10, recalled in 1961, "Moholy later developed original stage settings for the Kroll Opera House in Berlin for the *Tales of Hoffmann* and for other operatic and theatrical performances."

24 Felix Klee, introduction to *Paul Klee: Puppen, Plastiken, Reliefs, Masken, Theater* (Neuchâtel: Éditions Galerie Suisse de Paris, 1979), 21. My thanks to Stefan Jonsson for bringing these creatures to my attention.

25 Schlemmer, "Mensch und Kunstfigur," 19.

26 So, too, did cinema: Ernst Lubitsch based *Die Puppe* (1919) on Hoffmann's tales, for example; Walther Ruttmann's *Berlin, Symphonie der Großstadt* (1927) is permeated by mannequins. James Whale's

1931 film *Frankenstein,* based on Mary Shelley's book of 1817, assigned the inventor's name to his creation, conflating creator and creation precisely as had the ballet *Coppélia,* which reassigned to the doll the name of its inventor, Coppelius, in Hoffmann's tale "The Sandman" of 1815.

27 László Moholy-Nagy, "Theater, Zirkus, Varieté," in Schlemmer, Moholy-Nagy, and Molnár, *Die Bühne im Bauhaus,* 50.

28 Kleist, "On the Marionette Theater," 416 (emphasis in the original).

29 The most famous automata, however, often proved to be elaborate hoaxes. See, for example, Mark Sussman, "Performing the Intelligent Machine: Deception and Enchantment in the Life of the Automaton Chess Player," in *Puppets, Masks, and Performing Objects,* ed. John Bell (Cambridge, MA: MIT Press, 2001), 71–84; as well as Tom Standage, *The Turk: The Life and Times of the Famous Eighteenth-Century Chess-Playing Machine* (New York: Walker, 2002).

30 Julien Offray de La Mettrie, "Machine Man" (1747), in *Machine Man and Other Writings,* ed. and trans. Ann Thomson (Cambridge: Cambridge University Press, 1996), 9.

31 Jean-Claude Beaune, "The Classical Age of Automata: An Impressionistic Survey from the Sixteenth to the Nineteenth Century," trans. Ian Patterson, in Feher, *Fragments for a History of the Human Body,* 432. For a history of playful automata in the context of the *Kunstkammer,* see Horst Bredekamp, *The Lure of Antiquity and the Cult of the Machine,* trans. Allison Brown (Princeton, NJ: Markus Wiener, 1995); see also Bruce Mazlish, *The Fourth Discontinuity: The Co-Evolution of Humans and Machines* (New Haven, CT: Yale University Press, 1993), 31–58; and Victoria Nelson, *The Secret Life of Puppets* (Cambridge, MA: Harvard University Press, 2001), 47–73.

32 Beaune, "The Classical Age of Automata," 436. According to André Pieyre de Mandiargues, "The word automaton contains a contradiction, because it applies both to spontaneity of movement and to the mechanization of it. Thus we come back to the idea of ambiguity and the light it casts on the strange spell automata exercise over us." Pieyre de Mandiargues, "Les rouages de l'automate," preface to Jean Prasteau, *Les* *automates* (Paris: Gründ, 1968), quoted in Beaune, "The Classical Age of Automata," 475.

33 On the "disenchantment with language and the growing appeal of nonverbal expression" characteristic of European theatrical modernism, see Howard B. Segal, *Body Ascendant: Modernism and the Physical Imperative* (Baltimore: The Johns Hopkins University Press, 1998), 32 and passim. For Segal, this tendency is epitomized in the work of Hugo von Hofmannsthal, whose "Letter to Lord Chandos" captured the crisis of narrative and language in 1900 and who in 1911 wrote, "Words evoke a keener sympathy, but it is at the same time figurative, intellectualized, and generalized. Music, on the other hand, evokes a fiercer sympathy, but it is vague, longingly extravagant. But the sympathy summoned by gestures is clearly all-embracing, contemporary, gratifying." Notably, the purpose of each art form here is the evocation of sympathy. Hofmannsthal, quoted in Segal, *Body Ascendant,* 43.

34 For an analysis of abstraction in Schlemmer's choreography, see Toepfer, *Empire of Ecstasy,* 138–45; on the antipsychologist impulse, see Martin Jay, "Modernism and the Specter of Psychologism," *Modernism / Modernity* 3, no. 2 (May 1996): 93–111. Related (but not identical) to the emphasis on to physical gestures is Brecht's theory of *Gestus,* or gest, first articulated in print in 1930 in "The Modern Theatre Is the Epic Theatre," reprinted in *Brecht on Theatre: The Development of an Aesthetic,* ed. and trans. John Willett (New York: Hill and Wang, 1994), 33–42. More directly linked is the development of biomechanics by the Soviet director Vsevolod Meyerhol'd, inspired partly by the German development of theatrical modernist abstraction.

35 Schlemmer, diary entry of September 1922, in Tut Schlemmer, ed., *The Letters and Diaries of Oskar Schlemmer,* trans. Krishna Winston (Middletown, CT: Wesleyan University Press, 1972), 126.

36 Moholy-Nagy, "Theater, Zirkus, Varieté," 49.

37 Ibid.

38 On the concept of *Sachlichkeit,* see Stanford Anderson, introduction to Hermann Muthesius, *Style-Architecture and Building Art* (Santa Monica, CA: Getty Research Center for the History of Art and the Humanities, 1994), especially 14–19; and Frederic J. Schwartz, "Form Follows Fetish: Adolf Behne and

the Problem of *Sachlichkeit*," *Oxford Art Journal* 21, no. 2 (1998): 45–77. Wilhelm Worringer's *Abstraktion und Einfühlung: Ein Beitrag zur Stilpsychologie* (1908; repr., Amsterdam: Verlag der Kunst, 1996) is available in a poor English translation as *Abstraction and Empathy: A Contribution to the Psychology of Style,* trans. Michael Bullock (Chicago: Elephant Paperbacks, 1997).

39 "Posthumanism is the conscious response, whether with applause or regret, to the dissolution of psychological autonomy and individualism brought by technological modernization. It is a mobilization of aesthetic practices to effect a shift away from the humanist concept of subjectivity and its presumptions about originality, universality, and authority." K. Michael Hays, *Modernism and the Posthumanist Subject: The Architecture of Hannes Meyer and Ludwig Hilberseimer* (Cambridge, MA: MIT Press, 1992), 6. See also Brecht, "Neue Sachlichkeit," in *Schriften zum Theater,* vol. 1, *1918–33* (Frankfurt: Suhrkamp, 1963), 129–30. On *neue Sachlichkeit* and subjectivity, see Helmut Lethen, *Cool Conduct: The Culture of Distance in Weimar Germany* (Berkeley and Los Angeles: University of California Press, 2001); and Richard W. McCormick, *Gender and Sexuality in Weimar Modernity: Film, Literature, and "New Objectivity"* (New York: Palgrave, 2001), especially 39–58.

40 Schlemmer, "Mensch und Kunstfigur," 7. The two other signs of the age were, according to Schlemmer, mechanization and "the new possibilities given by technology and invention."

41 Schlemmer, wall text written in 1930 for the Folkwang Museum, Essen, in Hüneke, *Schlemmer,* 231, emphasis in the original.

42 See the caption for plate 1 in Wulf Herzogenrath and Stefan Kraus, eds., *Erich Consemüller: Fotografien Bauhaus Dessau* (Munich: Schirmer/Mosel, 1989), 19. Another version of the dress, designed by Lis Beyer for Dora Fieger in 1927, is in the collection of the Stiftung Bauhaus, Dessau.

43 In this context, see Anja Baumhoff, "Die 'moderne Frau' und ihre Stellung in der Bauhaus Avant-Garde," 83–94, and Katharina Sykora, "Die neue Frau: Ein Alltagsmythos der Zwanziger Jahre," 9–24, both in *Die neue Frau: Herausforderung für die Bildmedien der Zwanziger Jahre,* ed. Sykora et al. (Marburg: Jonas, 1993); as well as Katerina Rüedi Ray, "Bauhaus

Hausfraus: Gender Formation in Design Education,"
Journal of Architectural Education 55, no. 2 (November 2001): 73–80.

44 Kracauer, *The Mass Ornament,* 76. "The hands in the factory," he noted, "correspond to the legs of the Tiller Girls" (79). On Weimar chorus lines, see Kirsten Beuth, "Die wilde Zeit der Schönen Beine: Die inszenierte Frau als Körper-Masse," in Sykora et al., *Die neue Frau,* 95–106; Terri Gordon, "*Girls Girls Girls:* Re-Membering the Body," in *Rhine Crossings: France and Germany in Love and War,* ed. Peter Schulman and Aminia Brueggemann (Albany: State University of New York Press, 2004); and Janet Ward, *Weimar Surfaces: Urban Visual Culture in 1920s Germany* (Berkeley and Los Angeles: University of California Press, 2001), especially 228–33. If the doll is the inanimate embodiment of empathy and estrangement, its animate equivalent is the prostitute, a creature of infinite fascination in Weimar culture. Chorus lines contain liminal creatures, somewhere between hired women and stage dolls.

45 Kracauer, *The Mass Ornament,* 76.

46 Ibid.

47 See Nicole Bronowski Plett, "The Performance Photographs of Oskar Schlemmer's Bauhaus Theater Workshop, 1923–29" (M.A. thesis, University of New Mexico, 1989), 20–21; as well as Gisela Barche, "The Photographic Staging of the Image—On Stage Photography at the Bauhaus," trans. Michael Robinson, in *Photography at the Bauhaus,* ed. Jeannine Fiedler (Cambridge, MA: MIT Press, 1990), 238–53. The sculpted head reappears in the anonymous image reprinted in Schlemmer et al., *The Theater of the Bauhaus,* 104.

48 Rainer Maria Rilke, "Puppen," in *Schriften,* vol. 4, ed. Horst Nalewski (Frankfurt: Insel, 1996), 689. A discussion of similar themes in Rilke's writings on Auguste Rodin is found in Alex Potts, "Dolls and Things: The Reification and Disintegration of Sculpture in Rodin and Rilke," in *Sight and Insight: Essays on Art and Culture in Honor of E. H. Gombrich at 85,* ed. John Onians (London: Phaidon, 1994), 355–78. Schlemmer's last diary entry consists entirely of a quotation from Rilke: "To consider art not as a microcosm of the world, but rather as the world's complete transformation into magnificence." Schlemmer, diary entry of 1 April 1943, quoted in Hüneke, *Schlemmer,* 348.

49 Robert Vischer, preface to "On the Optical Sense of Form: A Contribution to Aesthetics" (1873), in *Empathy, Form and Space: Problems in German Aesthetics, 1873–1893,* ed. and trans. Harry Francis Mallgrave and Eleftherios Ikonomou (Santa Monica, CA: Getty Center Publications, 1994), 92. The introduction to this indispensable anthology provides a historical overview of the development of the concept of empathy in the nineteenth century, treating the work of Conrad Fiedler, August Schmarsow, Vischer, Heinrich Wölfflin, and others.

50 Gropius, *The Theater of the Bauhaus,* 8, 9–10. Acknowledging the importance of theater in the autumn of 1922, Gropius emphasized "the power of its effect on the soul of the spectator and the auditor," an effectiveness that was, in turn, "dependent on the success of the transformation of the idea into (visually and acoustically) perceivable space." Gropius, "The Work of the Bauhaus Stage," in Wingler, *Bauhaus,* 58.

51 Walter Benjamin, "The Work of Art in the Age of Mechanical Reproduction," in *Illuminations,* ed. Hannah Arendt, trans. Harry Zohn (New York: Schocken Books, 1968), 239 (translation modified).

52 After many years' work with the concept, Brecht named the technique of *Verfremdung* in 1936 in response to a performance he had attended in Moscow the previous year. See Brecht, "Alienation Effects in Chinese Acting," in Willett, *Brecht on Theatre,* 91–99. The background historical narrative provided here extends from 1914, when the Russian formalist writer and critic Viktor Shklovsky proclaimed *ostranenie,* or estrangement, as the defining concept of art, through the Soviet theorists in the Lef group to Brecht's articulation in 1936 of the *Verfremdungseffekt.* See Stanley Mitchell, "From Shklovsky to Brecht: Some Preliminary Remarks Towards a History of the Politicisation of Russian Formalism," 74–81, and Ben Brewster, "From Shklovsky to Brecht: A Reply," 82–102, both in *Screen* 15, no. 2 (Summer 1974); Peter Demetz, introduction to *Brecht: A Collection of Critical Essays* (Englewood Cliffs, NJ: Prentice-Hall, 1962), 1–15; Juliet Koss, "Brecht and Russian Estrangement," paper presented at the International Brecht Society Annual Symposium, San Diego, May 1998; and Koss, "Playing Politics with Estranged and Empathetic Audiences: Bertolt Brecht and Georg Fuchs," *South Atlantic Quarterly* 96, no. 4 (1998): 809–20.

53 Worringer had used empathy as a foil for his discussion of abstraction in 1908; the concept also operated as an ambiguous foil for *Zerstreuung,* or distraction, in Kracauer's work. See Koss, "Embodied Vision: Empathy Theory and the Modernist Spectator" and "Empathy Resurgent," papers presented at the College Art Association annual conferences in New York in 2000 and 2003.

54 Bertolt Brecht, entry for 21 July 1944, in *Journals 1934–1955,* ed. John Willett, trans. Hugh Rorrison (New York: Routledge, 1996), 321.

55 Brecht, entry for 1 February 1941, in ibid., 131.

56 Moholy-Nagy, "Theater, Zirkus, Varieté," 47.

57 Walter Benjamin, *The Origin of German Tragic Drama* (1928), quoted in Nägele, *Theater, Theory, Speculation,* 111.

58 Kracauer, "Cult of Distraction: On Berlin's Picture Palaces" (1926), in Levin, *Mass Ornament,* 326. "Nobody would notice the figure at all if the crowd of spectators, who have an aesthetic relation to the ornament and do not represent anyone, were not sitting in front of it." Kracauer, "The Mass Ornament," in ibid., 77. Notably, Paul de Man associated Kleist and Kracauer via the theme of distraction. "When, in the concluding lines of Kleist's text ["On the Marionette Theater"], K is said to be 'ein wenig zerstreut,' then we are to read, on the strength of all that goes before, *zerstreut* not only as distracted but also as dispersed, scattered, and dismembered." De Man, "Aesthetic Formalization in Kleist," in *The Rhetoric of Romanticism* (New York: Columbia University Press, 1984), 289.

59 "Ever since capitalism has existed, of course, within its defined boundaries rationalization has always occurred. Yet the rationalization period from 1925 to 1928 represents a particularly important chapter, which has produced the irruption of the machine and 'assembly-line' methods into the clerical departments of big firms." Siegfried Kracauer, *The Salaried Masses: Duty and Distraction in Weimar Germany,* trans. Quintin Hoare (1929; repr., New York: Verso, 1998), 29–30.

60 Kracauer, "The Little Shopgirls Go to the Movies" (1927), in Levin, *Mass Ornament,* 76. On the relation of gender and attention among Weimar cinema audiences and the theorists who described them, see Patrice Petro, "Perceptions of Difference: Woman as Spectator and Spectacle," in *Women in the Metropo-*

lis: Gender and Modernity in Weimar Culture, ed. Katherina von Ankum (Berkeley and Los Angeles: University of California Press, 1997), 41–66.

61 On this tendency, see Andreas Huyssen, "Mass Culture as Woman: Modernism's Other," in *After the Great Divide: Modernism, Mass Culture, Postmodernism* (Bloomington: Indiana University Press, 1986), 44–62.

62 By 1926, as Toepfer writes in *Empire of Ecstasy,* "the dance was famous enough to spawn a gallery exhibit in Central European cities. As the piece grew older, it became shorter; once an evening-long event, it wound up featured on a program of modernist works. Finally, in 1932 the piece went to Paris as part of an international dance competition promoting the restoration of elite, high cultural glory to ballet" (140). For more on the history and significance of the *Triadic Ballet,* see Karin von Maur, *Oskar Schlemmer,* exhibit catalog, Staatsgalerie, Stuttgart, 1977, 197–212; Scheper, *Schlemmer*; Nancy Troy, "An Art of Reconciliation: Oskar Schlemmer's Work for the Theater," 127–47, and Debra McCall, "Reconstructing Schlemmer's Bauhaus Dances: A Personal Narrative," 149–59, both in *Oskar Schlemmer,* ed. Arnold L. Lehman and Brenda Richardson, exhibit catalog, Baltimore Museum of Art, 1986; and *Oskar Schlemmer–Tanz–Theater–Bühne,* exhibit catalog, Kunsthalle Vienna, 1997.

63 "The surprising success of the debut of the Bauhaus theater in Berlin," Schlemmer proudly noted in May 1929, "created the pleasant circumstance that theoretical defences and speculations are justified by the facts of practice and may be detached from these." Schlemmer, diary entry, in Hüneke, *Schlemmer,* 209–210. "'Why is the public so enthusiastic? From primitivism, opposition, the emotion of contemporary culture? From a misunderstanding of the humor, from a desire for Variety shows?' So asks the well-known expert dance scholar Professor Oskar Bie." Ibid., 209.

64 Schlemmer, "The Mathematics of the Dance," *Vivos Voco* 5, nos. 8–9 (August–September 1926); trans. Wingler, 119.

65 Ibid.

66 Foreshadowing the exuberance of this final figure, the two men in the second-act finale ("Turkish dancers") brandish batons beyond their own rectangular frames; the hand of one man is also cut off by the column's left edge.

67 Freud, "The Uncanny," 195. See also Anthony Vidler, *The Architectural Uncanny: Essays in the Modern Unhomely* (Cambridge, MA: MIT Press, 1992), especially 3–14, 21–26. On the link between *Unheimlichkeit,* Martin Heidegger, and the Bauhaus, see Peter Sloterdijk, *Critique of Cynical Reason,* trans. Michael Eldred (Minneapolis: University of Minnesota Press, 1987), 203–4.

68 Kracauer, "The Mass Ornament," in Levin, *Mass Ornament,* 78. While the prevalence of isolated body parts in Weimar cultural representation is often attributed to the German experience of World War I, the presence of severed limbs across a spectrum of works, both before and after the war, demands a larger treatment of the relationship between cultural production, industrial society, and the evolving discussion of modern subjectivity. Such a project would accommodate Kracauer's association of the limbs of alienated labor with those performing cultural estrangement ("the hands in the factory correspond to the legs of the Tiller Girls"; ibid., 79); it would also engage further the thematic of gender among the androgynous Weimar dolls.

69 The two paragraphs of text read as follows: "'Triadic,' derived from triad = mathematical and musical. There are 3 dancers (one female and two male, who dance individually, in pairs, or all three together); three main colors on the stage: lemon yellow, white, and black; there are 12 dances and 18 costumes altogether.

"The ballet had already begun prior to 1914. Parts of it were performed in 1916. Premiere of full ballet in 1922 in the Landestheater in Stuttgart. Repeated in Weimar and Dresden. Later (with music for mechanical organ by Paul Hindemith) in Donauschingen and in a revue in Berlin."

70 Schlemmer, diary entry of September 1922, in Hüneke, *Schlemmer,* 96.

71 Gropius, *The Theater of the Bauhaus,* 31.

72 Richard Wagner, *Das Kunstwerk der Zukunft* (Leipzig: Otto Wiegand, 1850), 186–87 (emphasis in the original). On the Wagner cult in late-nineteenth- and early-twentieth-century Germany, see Uta Grund, *Zwischen den Künsten: Edward Gordon Craig und*

das Bildertheater um 1900 (Berlin: Akademie Verlag, 2002), especially 152ff.

73 That Gropius and others embraced this cultural lineage with renewed zeal in early 1919 is also unremarkable; Wagner's cultural politics, developed in the context of the 1848–49 revolution, would have appealed strongly to those of Nietzschean bent during the revolutionary early Weimar era, when socialist leanings were easily expressed as a demand for cultural unity achieved by means of revolutionary creativity.

74 Gropius, *The Theater of the Bauhaus,* 31. The notion of the theater of the future and that of theater as the highest cultural symbol had recently been formulated in Germany by Peter Behrens in *Feste des Lebens und der Kunst: Eine Betrachtung des Theaters als höchsten Kultursymbols* (Darmstadt: C. F. Winter'schen, 1900) and by Georg Fuchs in *Die Schaubühne der Zukunft* (Leipzig: Georg Müller, 1905).

75 Count Harry Kessler, quoted in Steven Aschheim, *The Nietzsche Legacy in Germany* (Berkeley and Los Angeles: University of California Press, 1992), 23. "For the post-1890 literate public, some sort of confrontation with Nietzsche—the man, the image, and his works—was becoming virtually obligatory" (18).

76 Gropius, *The Theater of the Bauhaus,* 32. Schlemmer even created his own Nietzschean aphorisms. "The world belongs to the dancer, as Nietzsche would say." Schlemmer, letter to Otto Meyer-Amden, 28 December 1919, in Hüneke, *Schlemmer,* 58. Hüneke, *Schlemmer,* 374 n. 34, wryly notes: "Unfortunately I have not yet been able to verify such a statement."

77 Felix Klee, "On the Urge for Renewal and Parties at the Bauhaus," in *Bauhaus,* ed. Jeannine Fiedler and Peter Feierabend, trans. Translate-A-Book, Oxford (Cologne: Könemann, 1999), 172.

78 The spontaneous festivities of the Weimar years became more organized in Dessau; gaining infamy as financial burdens increased, they operated as fundraisers in the school's final year, in Berlin. See Ute Ackermann, "Bauhaus Parties—Histrionics between Eccentric Dancing and Animal Drama," in Fiedler and Feierabend, *Bauhaus,* 126–39.

79 One figure is Casca Schlemmer, older brother of

Oskar; the other is Georg Hartmann. I am grateful to C. Raman Schlemmer for this information.

80 Nägele, *Theater, Theory, Speculation,* 3, has described the foregrounding of the body in the performances of the 1920s; citing "Brecht's gestural and epic theater, the theater of cruelty and the absurd, a theater where a clown appears and stumbles ostentatiously," he states that after the "increasing interiorization" that characterized bourgeois drama, "the body becomes visible as an obstacle; it speaks through irritation." Likewise relevant is the growing popularity of cabaret performance and theatrical revues in the 1920s; see Peter Jelavich, *Munich and Theatrical Modernism: Politics, Playwriting, and Performance, 1890–1914* (Cambridge, MA: Harvard University Press, 1985), 139–84.

81 "Something Metallic," *Anhalter Anzeiger,* Dessau, 12 February 1929, trans. Wingler, *Bauhaus,* 157.

82 Ibid. A related discussion of the contemporaneous productions of Erwin Piscator, beyond the scope of the present essay, might explore the shared effort to render the spectator a participant by combining such elements as film and slide projections into a larger theatrical event. Bauhaus performances avoided Piscator's political orientation (and Brecht's attempt to "refunction" spectators politically). Schlemmer called Piscator "very politically tendentious, but strong in this approach. Doesn't understand our thing—for him it's just play. Nevertheless he intends—said this in passing—eventually to collaborate on creating a theater school in Berlin, but very politically leftist." Schlemmer to Tut Schlemmer, 11 April 1927, in Hüneke, *Schlemmer,* 170. John Willett has described Piscator, whose Berlin home was outfitted by the Bauhaus furniture workshop, as "providing the Bauhaus with its main link to the Berlin stage"; in addition to the Total Theater, he also commissioned theater settings from Moholy-Nagy in 1928. Willett, introduction to *Erwin Piscator, 1893–1966* (Berlin: Archiv der Akademie der Künste, 1979), 1.

83 Karl Friedrich Schinkel to Carl Friedrich Zelter, 22 October 1821, quoted in Jochen Meyer, *Theaterbautheorien zwischen Kunst und Wissenschaft: Die Diskussion über Theaterbau im deutschsprächigen Raum in der ersten Hälfte des 19. Jahrhunderts* (Berlin: Grebrüder Mann, 1998), 191.

84 Moholy-Nagy, "Theater, Zirkus, Varieté," 54.

85 Molnár presented his U-Theater in Schlemmer, Moholy-Nagy, and Molnár, *Die Bühne im Bauhaus,* 57–62; Schlemmer included Weininger's Spherical Theater in his lecture "Bühne," presented on 16 March 1927, and published in *Bauhaus* 1, no. 3 (July 10, 1927), and reprinted in the same volume; and Gropius inserted a discussion and several illustrations of his Total Theater in the introduction to the book's English-language edition, Schlemmer et al., *The Theater of the Bauhaus,* 10–14. On the link between Gropius's theater design and Italian fascism, see Jeffrey T. Schnapp, "Border Crossings: Italian/German Peregrinations of the *Theater of Totality,*" *Critical Inquiry* 21 (1994): 80–123.

86 See Schlemmer, "Bühne"; an English translation appears in Schlemmer et al., *The Theater of the Bauhaus,* 81–101. For further description of the auditorium, see Scheper, *Schlemmer,* 137–38.

87 On the link between the birth of abstraction, auditorium design, the unified audience, and cinema spectatorship, see Koss, "Empathy and Abstraction in Munich," in *The Built Surface,* vol. 2, *Architecture and the Pictorial Arts from Romanticism to the Twenty-First Century,* ed. Karen Koehler (London: Ashgate, 2002), 98–119.

88 Wagner, *Das Kunstwerk der Zukunft,* 188–89.

89 Schlemmer, "Mensch und Kunstfigur," 20.

6. UTOPIA FOR SALE

1 The expression "cathedral of socialism" was first used by Oskar Schlemmer in a controversial pamphlet of 1923. See Schlemmer, "The Staatliche Bauhaus in Weimar," in Hans M. Wingler, *Bauhaus: Weimar, Dessau, Berlin, Chicago,* trans. Wolfgang Jabs and Basil Gilbert (Cambridge, MA: MIT Press, 1978), 65–70.

2 "Art and Technics: A New Unity" was the title of a lecture given by Gropius during the "Bauhaus Week" in Weimar, August 1923.

3 Konrad Wünsche's fine formulation: Wünsche, *Versuche, das Leben zu ordnen* (Berlin: Wagenbach, 1989).

4 The title of Elaine S. Hochman, *Bauhaus: Crucible of Modernism* (New York: Fromm, 1999).

5 Walter Gropius, "Bauhaus Dessau—Principles of Bauhaus Production," in Wingler, *Bauhaus,* 109.

6 Ibid., 110.

7 Marcel Breuer, "Metallmöbel und moderne Räumlichkeit," *Das neue Frankfurt,* 1928, no. 1, reprinted in *Neues Bauen, neues Gestalten. Das neue Frankfurt/Die neue Stadt: Eine Zeitschrift zwischen 1926 und 1933,* ed. Heinz Hirdina (Dresden: Verlag der Kunst, 1985), 210 (original set entirely in lowercase).

8 Ernst Kállai, "Zehn Jahre Bauhaus," originally published in *Die Weltbühne* 26 (1930), reprinted in Kállai, *Vision und Formgesetz: Aufsätze über Kunst und Künstler, 1921–1933* (Leipzig/Weimar: Kiepenheuer, 1986), 133. An abridged translation, which I follow here, appears as "Ten Years of Bauhaus," in Wingler, *Bauhaus,* 161.

9 Kállai, "Zehn Jahre Bauhaus," 133; "Ten Years of Bauhaus," 161 (translation modified).

10 Kállai, "Zehn Jahre Bauhaus," 133; "Ten Years of Bauhaus," 161–62.

11 "aus 'die frauenwelt', wien," *bauhaus* 2, no. 4 (1928): 23.

12 From notes for a lecture held in Vienna and Basel, reprinted in Hannes Meyer, *Bauen und Gesellschaft: Schriften, Briefe, Projekte,* ed. Lena Meyer-Bergner (Dresden: Verlag der Kunst, 1980), 54.

13 Kállai, "Zehn Jahre Bauhaus," 133; "Ten Years of Bauhaus," 161–62 (translation modified).

14 Kállai, "Zehn Jahre Bauhaus," 134; "Ten Years of Bauhaus," 162.

15 "The Culture Industry: Enlightenment as Mass Deception," in Max Horkheimer and Theodor W. Adorno, *Dialectic of Enlightenment,* trans. J. Cumming (New York: Continuum, 1987).

16 Magdalena Droste, "Herbert Bayers künstlerische Entwicklung 1918–1938," in *Herbert Bayer: Das künstlerische Werk 1918–1938,* ed. Magdalena Droste (Berlin: Bauhaus-Archiv, 1982), 36 (Droste illustrates a similarly monumental lead pencil erected as a pavilion for a pencil factory).

17 Erich Kästner, *Fabian: Die Geschichte eines Moralisten* (Stuttgart: Deutsche Verlags-Anstalt, 1931), 51.

18 Reg. Baumeister Dr. Poser, "Der Geschmackvolle Messestand: Ein vornehmes Werbemittel," *Gebrauchsgraphik* 3, no. 2 (1926): 45, where four of Bayer's designs for "advertising buildings" are illustrated.

19 The evolution of the advertising workshop is outlined in *Das A und O des Bauhauses. Bauhauswerbung: Schriftbilder, Drucksachen, Ausstellungsdesign,* ed. Ute Brüning (Berlin: Bauhaus-Archiv, 1995); Brüning, "Die Druck- und Reklamewerkstatt," in *Experiment Bauhaus* (Berlin: Bauhaus-Archiv, 1988), 154–98; Wulf Herzogenrath, "Typographie in der Reklamewerkstatt," in *Bauhaus Utopien–Arbeiten auf Papier,* ed. Herzogenrath (Cologne: Kölnischer Kunstverein, 1988), 103–15; and Gerd Fleischmann, ed., *Bauhaus: Drucksachen, Typographie, Reklame* (Düsseldorf: Marzona, 1984). Herzogenrath writes of this workshop as "without doubt the most effective and perhaps also the most popular" (103).

20 See the semester plan of 1927 reproduced in Wingler, *Bauhaus,* 121 (here imprecisely dated "about 1928").

21 Examples of Moholy-Nagy's graphic design and translations of his texts on the topic appear in Krisztina Passuth, *Moholy-Nagy* (London: Thames and Hudson, 1985). On Bayer, see Droste, *Herbert Bayer,* and Arthur A. Cohen, *Herbert Bayer: The Complete Work* (Cambridge, MA: MIT Press, 1984).

22 See Brüning, *Das A und O des Bauhauses,* 89.

23 On the "New Typography" in Germany, see Robin Kinross, *Modern Typography: An Essay in Critical History* (London: Hyphen Press, 1992), Chapter 8; Kinross's introduction to Jan Tschichold, *The New Typography,* trans. Ruari McLean (Berkeley and Los Angeles: University of California Press, 1987); and Maud Lavin, "Photomontage, Mass Culture, and Modernity: Utopianism in the Circle of New Advertising Designers," in *Montage and Modern Life, 1919–1942,* ed. M. Teitelbaum (Cambridge, MA: MIT Press, 1992), 36–59.

24 Josef Albers, "Zur Ökonomie der Schriftform," *Offset: Buch- und Werbekunst,* no. 10 (1926); repr. in Fleischmann, *Bauhaus: Drucksachen, Typographie, Reklame,* 23.

25 László Moholy-Nagy, "Contemporary Typography–Aims, Practice, Criticism" (1925), in Passuth, *Moholy-Nagy,* 294.

26 Ibid.

27 Hannes Meyer, "Mein Hinauswurf aus dem Bauhaus" (1930), reprinted in Hans M. Wingler, ed., *Das Bauhaus,* 3rd ed. (Bramsche: Gebr. Rasch, 1975), 170; and in English edition in Wingler, *Bauhaus,* 164 (translation modified).

28 Gropius, "Bauhaus Dessau–Principles of Bauhaus Production," in Wingler, *Bauhaus*, 110.

29 See the invaluable research in Anna Rowland, "Business Management at the Weimar Bauhaus," *Journal of Design History* 1 (1988): 153–75, on which I rely here.

30 Ibid., 153.

31 Quoted in ibid., 174, n. 81.

32 The best-known example is Josef Hartwig's chess set. See Wingler, *Bauhaus*, 86.

33 Rowland, "Business Management at the Weimar Bauhaus," 159.

34 Ibid., 163.

35 See the documents in Wingler, *Bauhaus*, 111.

36 On Breuer's tubular steel furniture and the controversies over it, see Magdalena Droste and Manfred Ludewig, *Marcel Breuer* (Cologne: Taschen, 1992); Werner Möller and Otakar Mácel, *Ein Stuhl macht Geschichte* (Munich: Prestel, 1992); and Mácel, "Avant-garde Design and the Law: Litigation over the Cantilever Chair," *Journal of Design History* 3 (1990): 125–43.

37 Droste and Ludewig, *Marcel Breuer*, 15.

38 On the laws regarding ownership of artistic form, see Molly Nesbit, "What Was an Author?" *Yale French Studies*, no. 73 (1987): 229–57; Frederic J. Schwartz, *The Werkbund: Design Theory and Mass Culture before the First World War* (New Haven, CT: Yale University Press, 1996), 151–63, 192–203; and Schwartz, "Commodity Signs: Peter Behrens, the AEG, and the Trademark," *Journal of Design History* 9 (1996): 153–84.

39 See Peter Hahn et al., *Bauhaustapete: Advertising and Success of a Brand Name* (Cologne: DuMont, 1995); and Herzogenrath, *Bauhaus Utopien*, 181–85.

40 Hahn, *Bauhaustapete*, 26.

41 The contract is reproduced in Hahn, *Bauhaustapete*, 23; and reprinted in Herzogenrath, *Bauhaus Utopien*, 184.

42 A look at a popular commercial manual of 1936 shows us how the market dealt with the Bauhaus. The author discusses diversifying production by superficial cosmetic difference, referring to a factory that produced furniture "in all the common styles (Baroque, Rococo, Empire, Biedermeier, Chippendale, Bauhaus, etc.)." E. A. Bauer, *Von der Idee zum Erfolg,* 2nd ed. (Berlin: Spaeth & Linde, 1936), 18.

43 The literature on the signifying role of consumer commodities is extensive. One classic account is Jean Baudrillard, *The System of Objects,* trans. J. Benedict (London: Verso, 1996). In the context of design in Germany, see Schwartz, *The Werkbund,* esp. Chapter 1.

44 See Hans-Ernst Mittig, "Die Reklame als Wegbereiterin der nationalsozialistischen Kunst," in *Die Dekoration der Gewalt: Kunst und Medien im Faschismus,* ed. Berthold Hinz (Giessen: Anabas, 1979).

45 Most effectively, perhaps, in the work of Adolf Behne. See Behne, *The Modern Functional Building,* trans. M. Robinson (Santa Monica, CA: The Getty Research Institute for the History of Art and the Humanities, 1996), and the introduction to this translation by Rosemarie Haag Bletter; and Frederic J. Schwartz, "Form Follows Fetish: Adolf Behne and the Problem of Sachlichkeit," *Oxford Art Journal* 21 (1998): 45–77.

46 Technocracy, Americanism, and the New Objectivity are discussed in Helmut Lethen, *Neue Sachlichkeit 1924–1932: Studien zur Literatur des "Weissen Sozialismus,"* 2nd ed. (Stuttgart: Metzler, 1975); and Mary Nolan, *Visions of Modernity: American Business and the Modernization of Germany* (Oxford: Oxford University Press, 1994); as well as Charles Maier's classic essay "Between Taylorism and Technocracy: European Ideologies and the Vision of Industrial Productivity in the 1920s," *Journal of Contemporary History* 5, no. 2 (1970): 27–61. But the political ambiguity of the technocratic position is clear: it was described as a "white" (as opposed to "red") socialism; see Lethen, *Neue Sachlichkeit.*

47 The best account remains Barbara Miller Lane, *Architecture and Politics in Germany, 1918–1945* (1968; repr., Cambridge, MA: Harvard University Press, 1985).

48 On social housing in Weimar Germany, see the special issue of *Architectural Association Quarterly* 11, no. 1 (1979); and Lane, *Architecture and Politics in Germany,* Chapters 4 and 5.

49 Especially the conservative Swiss architect and critic Alexander von Senger. See Lane, *Architecture and Politics in Germany,* 140–45; and Norbert Huse, *Neues Bauen 1918 bis 1933: Moderne Architektur* *in der Weimarer Republik,* 2nd ed. (Berlin: Ernst & Sohn, 1985), 125.

50 One striking example is a Social Democratic election campaign flyer from 1929 showing an aerial view of the GEHAG Hufeisensiedlung (Horseshoe Settlement) in Berlin-Britz by Bruno Taut and Martin Wagner (1925–33), accompanied by the following text: "The lucky inhabitants of the settlements in Britz naturally vote for the Social Democrats, whom they have to thank for their beautiful homes! You too should vote SPD–if you want things to improve for you!" See Norbert Huse, ed., *Vier Berliner Siedlungen der Weimarer Republik* (Berlin: Bauhaus-Archiv, 1984), 124.

51 Adelheid von Saldern, "Neues Wohnen: Wohlverhältnisse und Wohnverhalten in Grossanlagen der 20er Jahre," in *Massenwohnung und Eigenheim: Wohnungsbau und Wohnen in der Großstadt seit dem Ersten Weltkrieg,* ed. Axel Schildt and Arnold Sywottek (Frankfurt: Campus, 1988), 211–12.

52 Alexander Schwab, *Das Buch vom Bauen* (1930; repr., Düsseldorf: Bertelsmann, 1973), 67.

53 See the information on prices in Möller and Mácel, *Ein Stuhl macht Geschichte,* 332–33.

54 Kállai, "Zehn Jahre Bauhaus," 134.

55 Erwin Piscator, *The Political Theatre* (1929), ed. and trans. Hugh Rorrison (London: Eyre Methuen, 1980), 327. The photographs from Sasha Stone's photoessay "Das Heim Piscators (Möbel von Marcel Breuer)" (*Die Dame,* no. 14 [1928]) are still commonly reproduced. See Droste and Ludewig, *Marcel Breuer,* 74, 76–77 (a–c). In 1927, Bertolt Brecht wrote a fascinating satire on the fashionability of the New Objectivity, perhaps based partially on the Piscator flat, which he would have known: "Nordseekrabben oder Die moderne Bauhauswohnung" (North Sea Prawns; or, The Modern Bauhaus Apartment), in Brecht, *Über die bildenden Künste,* ed. J. Hermand (Frankfurt: Suhrkamp, 1983), 50–58. Brecht's text is discussed in Helmut Lethen, *Verhaltenslehren der Kälte: Lebensversuche zwischen den Kriegen* (Frankfurt: Suhrkamp, 1994), 164–70; and Schwartz, "Form Follows Fetish," 62–63.

56 Joseph Roth, "Architektur," *Münchner Illustrierte Presse,* 27 October 1929, repr., in Roth, *Berliner Saisonbericht: Reportagen und journalistische Arbeiten, 1920–1939* (Cologne: Kiepenheuer & Witsch, 1984), 341.

57 Ibid.

58 Siegfried Kracauer, *The Salaried Masses: Duty and Distraction in Weimar Germany,* trans. Quintin Hoare (London: Verso, 1998), 91.

59 Ibid., 92.

60 Ibid.

61 Hans Fallada, *Kleiner Mann–was nun?* (Berlin: Rowohlt, 1932), 147. This scene is discussed in Janet Ward Lungstrum, "The Display Window: Designs and Desires of Weimar Consumerism," *New German Critique,* no. 76 (1999): 148–49.

62 Fallada, *Kleiner Mann–was nun?,* 148.

63 On Waldsiedlung Zehlendorf and the "battle of the roofs," see Annemarie Jaeggi, "Waldsiedlung Zehlendorf 'Onkel Toms Hütte,'" in Huse, *Vier Berliner Siedlungen der Weimarer Republik,* 137–58, and Richard Pommer, "The Flat Roof: A Modernist Controversy in Germany," *Art Journal* 43 (1983): 158–69.

64 Jaeggi, "Waldsiedlung Zehlendorf," 143. (GEHAG stands for Gemeinnützige Heimstätten-, Spar- und Bau-Aktiengesellschaft; GAGFAH, Gemeinnützige Aktien-Gesellschaft für Angestellten-Heimstätten.)

65 Kurt Junghanns, *Bruno Taut, 1880–1938,* 2nd ed. (Berlin: Henschelverlag, 1983), 87.

66 Jaeggi, "Waldsiedlung Zehlendorf," 143.

67 The exhibition was organized and funded by the building society GAGFAH together with the AHAG (Allgemeine Häuserbau Aktiengesellschaft), a large building concern headed by Adolf Sommerfeld, a longtime patron of Gropius's. The two pavilions were clearly distinguished, but Gropius and Moholy-Nagy designed both, in a similar society; the café was shared by the two exhibitors. See Winfried Nerdinger, *Walter Gropius* (Berlin: Gebr. Mann, 1985), 108–9; Hartmut Probst and Christian Schädlich, eds., *Walter Gropius* (Berlin: Verlag für Bauwesen, 1986), vol. 2, 148–49; and Brüning, *Das A und O des Bauhauses,* 313–14.

68 Wilhelm Lotz, "Die Gagfah-Siedlung," *Die Form* 3, no. 10 (1928): 297.

7. BAUHAUS ARCHITECTURE IN THE THIRD REICH

1 Ernst Göhl, letter to Walter Gropius, 23 July 1935, Bauhaus-Archiv, Berlin. See also the relevant letter from Hans Volger of 20 July 1935. Göhl was principally active as a builder of hospitals.

2 Alfred Arndt, letter to W. J. Hess, 4 April 1940, Bauhaus-Archiv.

3 Letter of 25 August 1934, Bauhaus-Archiv, Gropius Papers 14/205, as cited in *Bauhaus Berlin,* ed. Peter Hahn (Weingarten: Kunstverlag Weingarten, 1985), 147. On the background and the subsequent quarrel between Rosenberg and Goebbels, see Ralf G. Reuth, *Goebbels* (Munich and Zurich: Piper, 1990), 321ff. As for the rest, following Germany's withdrawal from the League of Nations on 14 November 1933, the former Bauhaus master Lothar Schreyer, together with eighty-eight prominent artists and writers, signed a manifesto as the "Promise of True Followers" for Hitler. See H.-J. Eitner, *Hitlers Deutsche* (Gernsbach: Katz, 1991), 116.

4 Martin Wagner, letter to Gropius, Bauhaus-Archiv, Gropius Papers 5/374.

5 Kósa Zoltan, letter to Gropius, Bauhaus-Archiv, Gropius Papers 49/12. See also the letter from Gropius to Albert Hadda of 20 October 1946: "Never have I received news from Dustmann, Otto [Otto Meyer-Ottens] and Neufert. All three, as far as I hear, have discovered swastikas in their hearts, which diminishes my interest in them" (Gropius Papers 42/205).

6 Waldemar Alder, letter to Hannes Meyer, 16 June 1947; also for the following quotation the Meyer Archive in the German Architectural Museum, Frankfurt am Main.

7 Emanuel Lindner (b. 1905), a student of Mies's, would become known for his X-ray institute in Osnabrück of 1949/50 in the style of his teacher; all information about Bauhauslers comes, when there is no other source, from the assembly of biographies in the Bauhaus-Archiv. I thank Magdalena Droste, who made this material available to me and helped me with many pointers and inquiries.

8 See the biographical collection in the Bauhaus-Archiv.

9 The mostly self-written biographies in the Bauhaus-Archiv are exemplary examples of suppression, often simply of lies, as becomes apparent if one reads the archives of the Berlin Document Center. For instance, Gustav Hassenpflug, to cite only one example, says: "1933–45: independent architect and industrial de-

signer in Berlin and Switzerland." Hubert Hoffmann supplied a downright grotesque self-representation, "The Friday Group" (typewritten copy, Bauhaus-Archiv).

10 *Die zwanziger Jahre des Deutschen Werkbunds,* ed. Wolfgang Abramowski (Giessen: Anabas, 1982), 282.

11 Letter to Hönig, 27 March 1934, Gropius Papers 13/77–80; to Lörcher, 20 February 1934, Gropius Papers 13/58–62; see also Walter Scheiffele, "Das neue Bauen unter dem Faschismus," in *Kunst Hochschule Faschismus* (Berlin: Verlag für Ausbildung und Studium in der Elefanten Press, 1984), 226–44.

12 For a discussion of the "nationalization of modern art" that largely took place in the alleged argumentation given by Wilhelm Pinder in the journal *Der Kunst der Nation,* see Winfried Nerdinger, "Theodor Fischer und die deutsche Architektur der dreißiger Jahre," in *Kunst und Kunstkritik der dreißiger Jahre,* ed. Maria Rüger (Dresden: Verlag der Kunst, 1990), 141–47, in which the shelving of Fischer mentioned by the author is made more precise: his negative opinion of Troost's planning of Munich's Königsplatz brought him disgrace.

13 See Winfried Nerdinger, "Versuchung und Dilemma der Avantgarde im Spiegel der Architekturwettbewerbe 1933/1935," in *Faschistische Architekturen,* ed. Hartmut Frank (Hamburg: Christians, 1985), 65–87.

14 Competition documents in the Bauhaus-Archiv, Berlin. Ernst Hegel worked from 1934 to 1936 with Werner March on the planning of the Berlin Olympics, then as an independently practicing architect. See Berlin Document Center Reichskulturkammer (subsequently BDC RKK).

15 See Winfried Nerdinger, *Walter Gropius* (Berlin: Gebr. Mann Verlag, 1985), 184ff.

16 Copy of the report in Bauhaus-Archive, Gropius Papers 13/42–54.

17 Fieger's application for admission to the Reichskulturkammer would in 1933 be refused; only in 1936 would he be accepted upon reapplying (BDC RKK, Fieger). He eked out a wretched existence and during the war had to draw air-raid defense installations and temporary dwellings. Thanks for information from M. Rumler and I. Hildebrand from the Bauhaus Dessau.

18 *Ferdinand Kramer Architektur und Design,* exhibition catalog (Berlin: Bauhaus-Archiv, 1982), 9.

19 Letter from Hönig to Gropius of 4 October 1934, Bauhaus-Archiv, Gropius Papers 5/92.

20 Letter from Alexander Dorner to Gropius in (unordered) papers in the Busch-Reisinger Museum, Cambridge, Massachusetts.

21 Letter to Hönig with refusal of this confirmation, 5 August 1936, Gropius Papers 9/150.

22 Gropius to the *News Chronicle,* 9 November 1936, Gropius Papers 8/37, and to the *Listener,* 6 May 1936, Gropius Papers 9/30.

23 Gropius to Hönig, 17 December 1936, Gropius Papers 8/271; for the reference see Otto Thomae, *Die Propagandamaschinerie, Bildkunst und Öffentlichkeit im Dritten Reich* (Berlin: Mann, 1978), 77.

24 Gropius to Hönig, 31 December 1936, Bauhaus-Archiv, Gropius Papers 8/269. After his emigration Gropius thanked Hönig: "It is for me very valuable that I must not feel cut off from my homeland. That would be a terrible thought for me, if barriers were built between me and Germany."

25 Gropius to Frank, letter of 13 March 1938, Bauhaus-Archiv, Gropius Papers 41/338.

26 Klaus Briegleib, "Das freie Wort, Berlin 1933, München 1953," in Thomas Koebner, Wulf Köbke, et al., eds., *Exilforschung: Ein internationales Jahrbuch* 1 (Munich: Text und Kritik, 1983).

27 See the exchange of letters between Gropius, Hugh Simon, and Thomas Mann, Bauhaus-Archiv, Gropius Papers 40/460ff. and 40/304, 49/30ff.

28 Ise Gropius to Alexander/Xanti Schawinsky, undated letter in the Bauhaus-Archiv: "Both—that is the point—will have nothing against Walter."

29 Gropius, "Data for Design," *Architectural Review* 479 (1936): 172ff.; see also the letter from Neufert to Gropius of 1936, Gropius Papers 7/132.

30 Gropius, "A Mechanistic and Technocratic Attitude, Derived from Nazi Mentality," Gropius Papers 53/158: after an appeal from Hillebrecht. Gropius withdrew the objection to Neufert contained in his report to L. D. Clay, Gropius Papers 45/153ff.

31 File with title handwritten by Gropius in Bauhaus-Archiv, Gropius Papers 13/1ff.

32 Hanns Dustmann, "Vom Bauen der Hitlerjugend," in *Der deutsche Baumeister* 1 (1939).

33 For the dispute over the appointment of Meyer-Ottens as building director of Hamburg in 1948, see the letters between Gropius and Hillebrecht, Gropius Papers 44/196 and 45/299.

34 Walter Tralau (1904–75) became in 1946 building director and in 1962 head building director in Cologne. Bauhaus-Archiv biography.

35 Eduard Ludwig (1906–60), *Neue deutsche Biographie,* vol. 15, 1987, 425ff.

36 Siegfried Giesenschlag, BDC RKK.

37 Johann F. Geist and Klaus Küvers, *Das Berliner Mietshaus 1945–1989* (Munich: Prestel, 1989), 109 (thanks to Christian Wolsdorff for this reference).

38 Letter from Walther to Mies of 10 June 1947, Mies Collection, Library of Congress, Washington, DC, Box 60, Walther file, which contains a grotesque explanation for his entry into the SS.

39 Mies Collection, ibid.

40 Martin Mächler, *Weltstadt Berlin,* ed. Ilse Balg (Berlin: Galerie Wannsee Verlag, 1986), 368.

41 The Reichsluftschutzbund and Nationalsozialistische Volkswohlfahrt; Mies Collection, Private R and N.

42 For the letter from Hönig with the invitation of 8 June 1934, see Richard Pommer, "Mies van der Rohe and the Political Ideology of the Modern Movement," in *Mies van der Rohe: Critical Essays,* ed. Franz Schulze (New York: Museum of Modern Art, 1989), note 183.

43 Arthur Drexler, *An Illustrated Catalogue of the Mies van der Rohe Drawings in the Museum of Modern Art,* vol. 1 (New York: Garland, 1986), 84.

44 Pommer, "Mies van der Rohe," note 198.

45 Sonja Günther, *Lilly Reich 1885–1947* (Stuttgart: Deutsche Verlag-Anstalt, 1988), 58ff.

46 Pommer, "Mies van der Rohe," 97. Pommer's contribution is indeed carefully researched (in contrast to the useless and sensational Elaine S. Hochman, *Architects of Fortune: Mies van de Rohe and the Third Reich* [New York: Grove, 1989]), but unfortunately one finds in his essay several serious errors that stem from a misreading of some German texts.

47 Sibly Moholy-Nagy, in *Journal of the Society of Architectural Historians* 24 (1966): 80ff.

48 See the list of work and projects in Drexler, *Illustrated Catalogue;* for Mies's gas stations, see the letter from Carl Bauer on the Bauhaus of 5 September 1978.

49 BDC RKK Mies, explanation of the setting of fees for the Reichskulturkammer. Hans Thiemann wrote to P. M. Naeff on 10 February 1937: "I don't know what really is going on with and around Mies; some say he has hardly any income—but how can this be with his big commission?! (and why he then does not take the American position!?) (perhaps he is more German than his opponents believe him to be . . .)"; card in Bauhaus-Archiv.

50 According to Hahn, *Bauhaus Berlin,* 143.

51 Richard Pommer, David Spaeth, and Kevin Harrington, *In the Shadow of Mies: Ludwig Hilberseimer, Architect, Educator, and Urban Planner* (Chicago: Art Institute of Chicago, 1986), 122–27.

52 See the list of works compiled by Christine Mengin in "Ludwig Hilberseimer," *Rassegna* 27 (1986).

53 Rudolf Ortner to author, October 1991; Ortner was a party member in 1940, according to BDC Party Correspondence (PK) and the biography in the Bauhaus-Archiv; for his competition success in two school buildings see *Eisenacher Zeitung* from 5 September 1936 with illustrations.

54 Helmuth Weber (1911–77) became a party member 1 May 1933, BDC PK; for detailed data on Weber's work in Jena, I thank Anka Zinserling, who has worked with Weber's daughter and in the Jena city archives.

55 Hermann Bunzel (1901–85), biography, Bauhaus-Archiv.

56 Hans Vogler (1904–73), biography, Bauhaus-Archiv; for his Nazi activity see letter in Gropius Papers 42/501.

57 Waldemar Husing (1909–79) became a party member in 1937 and joined the Waffen SS in 1939, according to BDC PK; information from F. Fischer in Hamburg indicates that Husing hardly left Lübeck after the war.

58 Rudolf Sander (1902–67), biography in the Bauhaus-Archiv. Sander worked, among other projects, on the Rasthof Hermsdorf and a hotel in Thorn.

59 Ernst Kanow (b. 1906), manuscript, "Bauhaus-Erinnerungen," Bauhaus-Archiv, according to BDC RKK.

60 Gerhard Weber (1909–87); detailed information on his life and work can be found in the personnel papers of the Technical University in Munich, where Weber taught from 1955 to 1975.

61 Lothar Lang (1907–74), party member, according to BDC RKK.

62 Herbert Hoffmann (b. 1904), biography, Bauhaus-Archiv and BDC RKK.

63 About Erich Brendel (1898–1987), see the biography in the Bauhaus-Archiv and Ulrich Hölms, "Wiederaufbau in der Westmark," in *Deutsch-französische Beziehungen 1940–1950 und ihre Auswirkung auf Architektur und Stadtgestalt,* ed. Jean-Louis Cohen and Hartmut Frank, research project 1986–89 of the Volkswagen Foundation, Hannover, vol. 3, 59.

64 Carl Bauer (b. 1909), biography, Bauhaus-Archiv; Carl Bauer, "Aus der niedersächischen Baupflege," in *Heimatpflege–Heimatgestaltung,* no. 7 (1939): 83ff.; "Carl Bauer 75: Ein Leben für Gestaltung, Architektur, Sport," 8 May 1984 (privately published); a list of trustworthy architects is included in Anatol von Hübbenet, *Das Taschenbuch Schönheit der Arbeit* (Berlin, 1938), 263–66.

65 The "Einfa," i.e., the Berliner Gesellschaft zur Förderung des Einfamilienhauses Gemeinschaft GmbH was the successor to the GEHAG. In its newspaper *Gross-Siedlung* (friendly thanks to Christian Wolsdorff), one finds countless examples of modern buildings with hip roofs; old housing settlements such as Bruno Taut's Britz also were unproblematically advertised.

66 Christian Grohn, *Gustav Hassenpflug* (Dusseldorf: Marzona, 1985), 41–52, about the work for Junkers, thanks to information from H. Erfurth, Museum für Stadtgeschichte Dessau, letter of 27 September 1991.

67 According to Ernst Hegel (see note 14).

68 See the countless examples in the journal *Moderne Bauformen.*

69 Rodolf Lodders in the yearbook of the Freien Akademie der Künste in Hamburg (1960), 160.

70 Ulrich Höhns, "Fritz Schleifer," in *Deutsches Architektenblatt* 6 (1987): 81–87; on the path of the Schneider student following Wolfgang Voigt, "Fortsetzung oder Ende der Moderne," in *Deutsches Architektenblatt* 12 (1987): 173–77, and 1 (1988): 6–11; see also the publication of his modern country houses in Elmshorn in *Bauwelt* 50 (1935): 7, which Schleifer sent to Gropius in a letter of 22 December 1935 and inscribed that it had been approved "with the help of a sensible Building Department."

71 See Karl-Heinz Ludwig, *Technik und Ingenieure in Dritten Reich* (Königstein: Athenäum, 1979); Joan Campbell, *Joy in Work, German Work: The National Debate, 1800–1945* (Princeton, NJ: Princeton University Press, 1989), 312ff. The idea had been in place since the time of the Werkbund, according to Franz Kollmann, *Schönheit der Technik* (Munich: Langen, 1927); the "technological buildings" were depicted in all official Nazi architecture publications as equal to the huge monumental buildings.

72 Josef Goebbels, speech of 1 May 1939 to the Reichskulturkammer, in *Der deutsche Baumeister* (1939), 54.

73 "Der Führer eröffnet die 'Grosse deutsche Kunstausstellung 1937,'" in *Die Kunst im Dritten Reich* (1937), 54.

74 Albert Speer, *Spandauer Tagebücher* (Frankfurt am Main: Propyläen, 1975), 261ff.

75 Egon Eiermann, "Erweiterung und Umbau der Total-Werke Foerstner & Co," *Moderne Bauformen* 41 (1939): 561–68.

76 *Bauwelt* 3 (1935): 3–6; for Kremmer and Schupp see, for example, *Bauwelt* 9 (1935): 1–6.

77 Wolf Tegethoff, "Industriearchitektur und Neues Bauen, Mies van der Rohes Verseidag Fabrik in Krefeld," in *Archithese* 3 (1983): 33–38. Holthoff worked from 1933 to 1969 for Verseidag, according to his biography in the Bauhaus-Archiv.

78 "Eine Fabrikanlage," in *Bauwelt*, no. 35/36 (1942): 1–4; Heinrich Sigfrid Bormann stated that he was chief architect in the Braunschweig steelworks in Salzgitter and led under others the general planning of the iron works in Teschen; for Fritz Pfeil (1909–65), see the biography in the Bauhaus-Archiv.

79 Neufert's new Lausatz factory building is programmatically a copy of the composition of Fritz Rauda; see "Neues Bauen, Neue Architektur: Die neue Baukunst ist das Spiegelbild des deutschen Volkes," in *Die sächsische Wirtschaft*, no. 10 (11 March 1938); also Ernst Neufert, *Industriebauten* (Wiesbaden/Berlin, 1973), 16–20.

80 Heinrich Kölling, BDC RKK, according to Dr. Adler, "Technische Fette und Futtermittel aus Tierkör-

pern," in *Der Vierjahresplan: Zeitschrift für nationalsozialistische Wirtschaftspolitik* 14 (1939): 83ff.

81 Wils Ebert (1909–79), biography, Bauhaus-Archiv.

82 Matthias Riedel, "Gründung und Entwicklung der Reichswerke 'Hermann Göring' und deren Position in der Wirtschaftspolitik des Dritten Reiches 1935–1945," in *Salzgitter: Geschichte und Gegenwart einer deutscher Stadt 1942–1992*, ed. Wolfgang Benz (Munich; Bech, 1992), 41–77, for the following citations.

83 Gerd Balzer (1909–86), "Entwurfsarchitekt in Orianenburg und im Salzgittergebiet," biography, Bauhaus-Archiv.

84 For H. S. Bormann, see note 78.

85 For Gerhard Weber, see note 60.

86 Rudolf Lodders, *Industriebau und Architekt und ihre gegenseitige Beeinflussung* (Hamburg: Phönix-Verlag, 1946), 30; "That this hard school [i.e., Nazi industry] is one born in troubles and has been developed in a generation of architects steeled in terror has led to a new discipline" (33). The same author, "Zuflucht im Industriebau," in *Baukunst und Werkform* 1 (1947): 39: "and finally we plunge in where Hitler had left a vent: in industrial building." For the denazification of Rimpl, see *Die neue Zeitung* of 10 March 1950.

87 Alfons Leitl, "Anmerkungen zur Zeit," in *Baukunst und Werkform* (January 1947): 3–11.

88 Gottfried Benn, "Doppelleben," in his *Prosa und Autobiographie,* vol. 4 of the complete works (Frankfurt am Main: Fischer Verlag, 1984), 415; following Peter de Mendelssohn, *Die Geist in der Despotie* (Frankfurt am Main: Fischer-Taschenbuch, 1987), 243, Mendelssohn calls this sentence "a dressed-up abomination."

89 Herbert Rimpl, *Ein deutsches Flugzeugwerk* (Berlin: Wiking Verlag, 1938), also his "Ein deutsches Flugzeugwerk," in *Moderne Bauformen* 41 (1942): 1–13.

90 This definition of "fascist" art is a paraphrase of Wolfgang Fritz Haug, "Ästhetik der Normalität—Vorstellung und Vorbild," in *Inszenierung der Macht: Ästhetische Faszination im Faschismus* (Berlin: Nishen, 1987), 79–102.

8. FROM ISOLATIONISM
TO INTERNATIONALISM

I am enormously grateful to Greg Castillo for his rigorous critique of an earlier draft of this essay.

1 See, for instance, Franz Schulze, "The Bauhaus Architects and the Rise of Modernism in the United States," in *Exiles and Emigrés: The Flight of European Artists from Hitler,* ed. Stephanie Barron (Los Angeles: Los Angeles County Museum of Art, 1997), 224–34. For the exhibit itself see Terrence Riley, *The International Style: Exhibition 14 and the Museum of Modern Art* (New York: Rizzoli, 1992). For a critique of the operative criticism on which it is based, see Beatriz Colomina, *Privacy and Publicity: Modern Architecture as Mass Media* (Cambridge, MA: MIT Press, 1994), 195–212.

2 This thesis is based upon a thorough survey of the leading American architectural periodicals, *Architectural Forum, Architectural Record,* and *Pencil Points* (later *Progressive Architecture*), from 1930 to 1955.

3 Most notoriously, Tom Wolfe, *From Bauhaus to Our House* (New York: Farrar, Straus and Giroux, 1981). Elaine Hochman, *Bauhaus: Crucible of Modernism* (New York: Fromm, 1997), is a more recent example.

4 Donald Albrecht, ed., *World War II and the American Dream* (Washington, DC: National Building Museum, 1995). See also Andrew M. Shanken, "From Total War to Total Living: American Architecture and the Culture of Planning, 1939–194X" (Ph.D. diss., Princeton University, 1999).

5 Even elite patrons like Harvard University no longer wished to pay for the degree of finish that had dignified their buildings for generations. The Graduate Center that Gropius and his new firm, The Architects Collaborative, designed there in 1948–49 cost half of the amount per square foot, even before factoring in increases in the cost of both labor and materials, that the university had spent during the 1930s on its undergraduate counterparts. See "Harvard Builds a Graduate Yard," *Architectural Forum* 93 (December 1950): 61–72.

6 Greg Castillo, "Thermonuclear Family Values: Cold War Architecture," *Design Book Review* 27 (Winter 1993): 61–67.

7 Paul Betts, "The Bauhaus as Cold War Legend: West German Modernism Revisited," *German Politics and Society* 14, no. 2 (1996): 75–100. See also

Herbert Bayer, Walter Gropius, and Ise Gropius, *Bauhaus, 1919–1928* (New York: Museum of Modern Art, 1938); Walter Gropius, *Apollo in der Demokratie* (Mainz: Florian Kupferberg, 1967); and Karen Koehler, "The Bauhaus, 1919–1928: Gropius in Exile and the Museum of Modern Art, N.Y. 1938," in *Art, Culture, and Media under the Third Reich,* ed. Richard Etlin (Chicago: University of Chicago Press, 2002), 287–315.

8 The first important corrective to this account was Marcel Franciscono, *Walter Gropius and the Creation of the Bauhaus in Weimar* (Chicago: University of Illinois Press, 1971).

9 Barron, *Exiles and Emigrés*; Gabriele Diana Grewe, *Call for Action: Mitglieder des Bauhauses in Nordamerika* (Weimar: Verlag und Dantenbank für Geisteswissenschaft, 2002); William Jordy, "The Aftermath of the Bauhaus in America: Gropius, Mies, and Breuer," in *The Intellectual Migration: Europe and America, 1930–1960,* ed. Donald Fleming and Bernard Bailyn (Cambridge, MA: Harvard University Press, 1969), 485–543; and Georg-W. Költzsch and Margarita Tupitsyn, eds., *Bauhaus: Dessau, Chicago, New York* (Cologne: DuMont, 2000), provide general overviews of the activities of the émigrés.

10 For a thoughtful analysis of a parallel case see Mardges Bacon, *Le Corbusier in America: Travels in the Land of the Timid* (Cambridge, MA: MIT Press, 2001).

11 Franz Schultz, *Philip Johnson: Life and Work* (New York: Knopf, 1994), 104–46.

12 See William Littmann, "Assault on the Ecole: Student Campaigns against the Beaux-Arts," *Journal of Architectural Education* 53, no. 3 (February 2000): 159–66, for an important account of the impact of grassroots political activism.

13 Margaret Kentgens-Craig, *The Bauhaus and America: First Contacts, 1919–1936* (Cambridge, MA: MIT Press, 1999). Hitchcock's own *Modern Architecture: Romanticism and Reintegration* (New York: Payson and Clark, 1929) was an important text in this regard, as was Sheldon Cheney, *The New World Architecture* (London: Longmans, Green, 1929). Cheney's contribution has been almost totally ignored by historians, probably because it is so at odds with Hitchcock's canonical work.

14 Katherine Solomonson, *The Chicago Tribune*

Tower Competition: Skyscraper Design and Cultural Change in the 1920s (Cambridge: Cambridge University Press, 2001), offers a compelling analysis of American taste during this period in relation to an awareness of European modernism.

15 James Ford and Katherine Morrow Ford, *The Modern House in America* (New York: Architectural Book Publishing, 1940), and Elizabeth Mock, *Built in the USA 1932–44* (New York: Museum of Modern Art, 1944).

16 The literature on Wright during the thirties is enormous. See in particular Donald Leslie Johnson, *Frank Lloyd Wright versus America: The 1930s* (Cambridge, MA: MIT Press, 1990). For Wurster, see Marc Trieb, ed., *An Everyday Modernism: The Houses of William Wurster* (San Francisco: San Francisco Museum of Modern Art, 1995).

17 The two had been published side by side in Catherine Bauer, *Modern Housing* (Boston: Houghton Mifflin, 1934).

18 Alfred Barr, "Preface," Henry-Russell Hitchcock and Philip Johnson, *The International Style* (1932; repr., New York: Norton, 1966), 12, 15.

19 Mock, *Built in the USA*. Interestingly, this was one of the first American books on architecture to be translated into German following the end of World War II.

20 Philip Godwin, "Introduction," Mock, *Built in the USA*, 5.

21 Mock, *Built in the USA*, 13–14.

22 Walter Gropius to Marcel Breuer, letter of 17 April 1937, quoted in Isabelle Hyman, *Marcel Breuer, Architect: The Career and the Buildings* (New York: Abrams, 2001), 89.

23 Marcel Breuer, 1934 typescript, quoted in Joachim Driller, *Breuer Houses* (London: Phaidon, 2000), 40.

24 I am indebted to Joachim Driller, ibid., for identifying the ways in which this house was indebted to the Gropius House in Dessau. I disagree, however, with his minimizing of the degree to which its architects were inspired by their new context.

25 "Aluminum City Terrace Housing," *Architectural Forum* 81 (July 1944): 65–76.

26 Most famously in the case of the Levittowns erected in New York, Pennsylvania, and New Jersey.

27 Although this argument runs counter to that proposed by Cammie McAtee in "Alien #5044325," in *Mies in America,* ed. Phyllis Lambert (Montreal: Canadian Centre for Architecture, 2001), 132–91, I am indebted to her excellent research.

28 This was recognized at the time. See Russell Lynes, *The Tastemakers* (New York: Harper, 1954).

29 In addition to the crucial example provided by Serge Guilbaut, *How New York Stole the Idea of Modern Art: Abstract Expressionism, Freedom, and the Cold War* (Chicago: University of Chicago Press, 1983), see Frances Stonor Saunders, *The Cultural Cold War: The CIA and the World of Arts and Letters* (New York: New Press, 1999).

30 Philip Johnson, *Mies van der Rohe* (New York: Museum of Modern Art, 1947). See also Terence Riley, "Making History: Mies van der Rohe and the Museum of Modern Art," in *Mies in Berlin,* ed. Terence Riley and Barry Bergdoll (New York: Museum of Modern Art, 2001), 11–25.

31 See Barbara Miller Lane, *Architecture and Politics in Germany 1918–1945* (Cambridge, MA: Harvard University Press, 1968), 147–84, and Richard Pommer, "Mies van der Rohe and the Political Ideology of the Modern Movement in Architecture," in *Mies van de Rohe: Critical Essays,* ed. Franz Schultze (New York: Museum of Modern Art, 1989), 96–145.

32 For the best discussion of the earlier skyscraper projects, see Wolf Tegethoff, "From Obscurity to Maturity: Mies van der Rohe's Breakthrough to Modernism," in Schultze, *Mies van de Rohe: Critical Essays,* 28–74. The classic account of Lake Shore Drive remains William Jordy, *American Buildings and their Architects,* vol. 5, *The Impact of European Modernism in the Mid-Twentieth Century* (Garden City, NY: Doubleday, 1972), 221–27.

33 More difficult to integrate into this narrative of triumph, but extremely important at the time was Pietro Belluschi's Equitable Building in Portland, Oregon, of 1948. See Meredith Clausen, *Pietro Belluschi* (Cambridge, MA: MIT Press, 1994), 162–97.

34 "Glass and Brick in a Concrete Frame," *Architectural Forum* 92 (January 1950): 70; "Mies van der Rohe," *Architectural Forum* 97 (November 1952): 96, 100, 102; and Henry-Russell Hitchcock, "The International Style Twenty Years After," *Architectural Record* 110 (August 1951): 96.

35 Fritz Neumeyer, *The Artless Word: Mies van der Rohe on the Building Art,* trans. Mark Jarzombek (Cambridge, MA: MIT Press, 1991), and Detlef Mertins, ed., *In the Presence of Mies* (New York: Princeton Architectural Press, 1994), for both Mies's own theory and the way in which it has been deployed by contemporary advocates of a critical architecture.

36 For an interpretation of the impact of American affluence upon modern architecture, see Greg Castillo, "Triumph and Transformation: American Modernism, 1952–1969," in *Helmut Jacoby: Master of Architectural Drawing,* ed. Helge Bofinger and Wolfgang Voigt (Berlin: Ernst Wasmuth Verlag, 2001), 34–45.

37 Alice T. Friedman, *Women and the Making of the Modern House* (New York: Abbeville, 1999), 126–59. I am also much indebted to Kathleen Corbett's unpublished paper "'The Pretty Lady on the Soapbox' Takes on 'The Cult of Austerity': *House Beautiful*'s Editorial War on the International Style" for my understanding of this fracas.

38 See Friedman, *Women and the Making,* 147–54, for an apt comparison with Philip Johnson's Glass House, as well as "This Is the First House Built by Ludwig Mies van der Rohe," *Architectural Forum* 95 (1951): 157.

39 Lewis Mumford, "The Skyline," *New Yorker,* 11 October 1947, 106, 109, as republished in *The Museum of Modern Art Bulletin* 15, no. 3 (Spring 1948): 2. See also Robert Wojtowicz, *Lewis Mumford and American Modernism: Eutopian Themes for Architecture and Urban Planning* (Cambridge: Cambridge University Press, 1996), 109.

40 Jean Murray Bangs, "Greene and Greene," *Architectural Forum* 89 (October 1948): 81–88, and "Bernard Ralph Maybeck, Architect Comes into His Own," *Architectural Record* 100 (January 1948): 138–39. See also Lisa Germany, *Harwell Hamilton Harris* (Austin: University of Texas Press, 1991).

41 The proceedings were published in *The Museum of Modern Art Bulletin* 15, no. 3 (Spring 1948): 3–21. See also Gail Fenske, "Lewis Mumford, Henry-Russell Hitchcock and Bay Regional Style," in *The Education of the Architect: Historiography, Urbanism, and the Growth of Architectural Knowledge,* ed. Martha Pollak (Cambridge, MA: MIT Press, 1997), 37–85.

42 *The Museum of Modern Art Bulletin* 15, no. 3 (Spring 1948): 14.

43 Ibid., 8–10.

44 Ibid., 7.

45 Peter Blake, "The House in the Museum Garden," *The Museum of Modern Art Bulletin* 17, no. 3 (Spring 1950): 3.

46 Henry-Russell Hitchcock and Arthur Drexler, *Built in USA: Post-war Architecture* (New York: Simon and Schuster, 1952).

47 Hitchcock, "Introduction," in *Built in USA,* by Mock, 10.

48 Important accounts of the education they received there can be found in Anthony Alofsin, *The Struggle for Modernism: Architecture, Landscape Architecture, and City Planning at Harvard* (New York: Norton, 2002), and Klaus Herdeg, *The Decorated Diagram: Harvard Architecture and the Failure of the Bauhaus Legacy* (Cambridge, MA: MIT Press, 1983).

49 Sigfried Giedion, *Space Time and Architecture: The Growth of a New Tradition* (Cambridge, MA: Harvard University Press, 1953), 495–508, 541–64.

50 Henry-Russell Hitchcock, *Architecture: Nineteenth and Twentieth Centuries* (1958; repr., Hammondsworth: Penguin, 1977), especially 517, 556.

51 Jane C. Loeffler, *The Architecture of Diplomacy: Building America's Embassies* (New York: Princeton Architectural Press, 1998).

52 Annabel Jane Wharton, *Building the Cold War: Hilton International Hotels and Modern Architecture* (Chicago: University of Chicago Press, 2001), and Hyman, *Marcel Breuer.*

53 See, for instance, the controversy that erupted over the design of the Air Force Academy, as detailed in Robert Bruegmann, ed., *Modernism at Mid-Century: The Architecture of the United States Air Force Academy* (Chicago: University of Chicago Press, 1994).

54 For a description of the way that these forces played out in residential and commercial architecture in Los Angeles, see Greg Hise, *Magnetic Los Angeles: Planning the Twentieth-Century Metropolis* (Baltimore: The Johns Hopkins University Press, 1997), and Richard Longstreth, *City Center to Regional Mall: Architecture, the Automobile, and Retailing in Los Angeles, 1920–1950* (Cambridge, MA: MIT Press, 1997).

55 Kate Bristol, "The Pruitt Igoe Myth," *Journal of Architectural Education* 44 (1991): 163–71.

56 Sandy Isenstadt, "Richard Neutra and the Psychology of Architectural Consumption," in *Anxious Modernisms: Experimentation in Postwar Architectural Culture,* ed. Sarah Williams Goldhagen and Réjean Legault (Montreal: Canadian Centre for Architecture, 2000), 102.

57 Maud Lavin, "Anni Albers: Issues of Gender and Design, Eine moderne Frau und ihr Lebenswerk," in Költzsche and Tupitsyn, *Bauhaus: Dessau, Chicago, New York,* 46–57; Nicholas Fox Weber and Pandora Tabatabai Asbaghi, *Anni Albers* (New York: Guggenheim Museum, 1999); and Sigrid Wortmann Weltge, *Women's Work: Textile Art from the Bauhaus* (San Francisco: Chronicle Books, 1994).

58 David De Long and Craig Miller, eds., *Design in America: The Cranbrook Vision, 1925–1950* (New York: Harry N. Abrams, 1983), 276.

59 Mary Emmy Harris, *The Arts of Black Mountain College* (Cambridge, MA: MIT Press, 1987), and Weltge, *Women's Work,* 163–70.

60 De Long and Miller, *Design in America.*

61 Barbara Miller Lane, *National Romanticism and Modern Architecture in Germany and the Scandinavian Countries* (Cambridge: Cambridge University Press, 2000).

62 De Long and Miller, *Design in America,* 270.

63 Pat Kirkham, *Charles and Ray Eames: Designers of the Twentieth Century* (Cambridge, MA: MIT Press, 1995).

64 David De Long, "Eliel Saarinen and the Cranbrook Tradition in Architecture and Urban Design," in De Long and Miller, *Design in America,* 47–89.

65 Christa C. Mayer Thompson, "Textiles," in De Long and Miller, *Design in America,* 174–92.

66 Ibid., 193–201.

67 For an example see Peter Blake, *No Place like Utopia: Modern Architecture and the Company We Kept* (New York: Knopf, 1993).

9. THE BAUHAUS IN COLD WAR GERMANY

1 Paul Betts, "The Bauhaus as Cold War Legend: West German Modernism Revisited," *German Politics and Society* 14, no. 2 (1996): 82–83. Triumphalist narratives focusing on U.S. preeminence in modernist culture were not limited to America, but echoed in the writings of Eastern Europe's anti-American propaganda and Western Europe's pro-American propaganda.

2 Katherine Verdery, *What Was Socialism and What Comes Next?* (Princeton, NJ: Princeton University Press, 1996), 7.

3 This idea was articulated by Otto Bartning, an early postwar president of the Deutsche Werkbund. See Otto Bartning, "Werkbund und Staat," *Baukunst und Werkform* (1950); cited in Paul Betts, "The Pathos of Everyday Objects: West German Industrial Design Culture, 1945–1965" (Ph.D. diss., University of Chicago, 1995), 55.

4 On the topic of Bauhaus alumni participation in Third Reich architecture, see the essay by Winfried Nerdinger in this collection.

5 Ralf Körner, "Uses of the Bauhaus Building, 1926–1989," in *The Dessau Bauhaus Building 1926–1989,* ed. Bauhaus Dessau Foundation and Margret Kengens-Craig, trans. Michael Robinson (Basel: Birkhäuser, 1998), 142–59.

6 Henry Cohen to William Wurster, 27 April 1945, Box 6, Reginald Isaacs Papers, Smithsonian Institution, Archives of American Art.

7 Ibid.

8 Hoffmann's candid autobiographical account can be found in Hubert Hoffmann, "die freitagsgruppe" (undated unpublished manuscript), Spende Hubert Hoffmann, Bauhaus-Archiv, Berlin.

9 Dessau's mayor was not the only Soviet-zone administrator to dream of reviving the Bauhaus. Hermann Henselmann, the director of Weimar's Academy of Architecture and Fine Arts (the successor institution to Gropius's Weimar Bauhaus), hoped to reorganize his school "along the lines of the Bauhaus as it was before the Nazi period." Hermann Henselmann, cited in Christian Schädlich, "Der Neubeginn an der Staatlichen Hochschule für Baukunst und bildende Künste Weimar im Jahre 1946," *Wissenschaftliche Zeitschrift der Hochschule für Architectur und Bauwesen Weimar* 13 (1996): 508, 513. A local newspaper report that the Bauhaus was about to resurface in Weimar drew a complaint from Mayor Hesse, who informed Henselmann that alumni in Dessau were resurrecting the school. Henselmann courteously withdrew his competing claim. Svenja Simon, "Der Versuch der Wiedereröffnung des Bauhauses in Dessau nach 1945," in *das Bauhaus zerstört, 1945–1947, das Bauhaus stört,* ed. Stiftung Bauhaus Dessau (Dessau: Anhaltische Verlagsgesellschaft, 1996), 10.

10 Hubert Hoffmann, "die wiederlebung des Bauhauses nach 1945," in *Bauhaus und Bauhäusler,* ed. Eckhard Neumann (Bern and Stuttgart: Hallwag, 1971), 208, 206.

11 Dirk Manzke and Svenja Simon, "Das nach 1945 enstandene Lehrkonzept im Kontext des historischen Bauhauses," in Stiftung Bauhaus Dessau, *das Bauhaus zerstört,* 34–51.

12 Simon, "Der Versuch der Wiedereröffnung des Bauhauses," 18.

13 Hoffmann, "die wiederlebung des Bauhauses nach 1945," 206.

14 Simon, "Der Versuch der Wiedereröffnung des Bauhauses," 16–17.

15 Hubert Hoffmann to Walter Gropius, 20 June 1947, 81M–84 bMS Ger 208 (900), Gropius Archive, Houghton Library, Harvard University.

16 Hubert Hoffmann, opening remarks at the exhibition hubert hoffmann–annäherung an einen heyerschüler, 2 July 1989, published in *Hubert Hoffmann: Festschrift zum 90. Geburtstag,* ed. Dirk Manzke (Dessau: bauhaus, 1994); Questionnaire for Reginald Isaacs, 17 May 1965, Box 6, Isaacs Papers.

17 Hubert Hoffmann to Walter Gropius, 20 June 1947, 81M–84 bMS Ger 208 (900), Gropius Archive.

18 Gerhard Strauss, "Mart Stam und sein früher Versuch: Traditionen des Bauhauses in der DDR schöpferisch aufzunehmen," in *Wissenschaftliche Zeitschrift der Hochschule für Architektur und Bauwesen* 23 (1976): 540–42.

19 Hiltrud Ebert, "Von der 'Kunstschule des Nordens' zur sozialistischen Hochschule: Das erste Jarzent der Kunsthochschule Berlin-Weißensee," in Günther Feist, Eckhardt Gillen, and Batrice Vierneisel, *Kunstdokumentatin SBZ/DDR 1945–1990: Aufsätze, Berichte, Materialien* (Berlin: Dumont, 1996), 169, 167.

20 Strauss, "Mart Stam," 540.

21 Simone Hain, "ABC und DDR: Drei Versuche, Avantgarde mit Sozialismus in Deutschland zu verbinden," in Feist et al., *Kunstdokumentation SBZ/DDR 1945–1990,* 436.

22 Ibid., 438.

23 Stam, quoted in Ebert, "Von der 'Kunstschule des Nordens,'" 173.

24 Ibid.

25 For a review of the emigration of Weimar-era modernists to the USSR during Stalin's first Five-Year Plan, see Christian Borngräber, "Foreign Architects in the USSR: Bruno Taut and the Brigades of Ernst May, Hannes Meyer, Hans Schmidt," *AAQ* (Architectural Association Quarterly) 2, no. 1 (1979): 50–62.

26 The original decree that launched the *Zhdanovshchina* is reproduced in *The Central Committee Resolution and Zhdanov's Speech on the Journals Zvezda and Leningrad,* bilingual edition, English trans. Felicity Ashbee and Irina Tidmarsh (Royal Oak, MI: Strathcone, 1978). For a survey of the *Zhdanovshchina*'s impact on Moscow's cultural scene, see Alexander Werth, *Russia: The Post-War Years* (New York: Taplinger, 1971), 197–216, 349–79.

27 Stam's comments on postwar industrial design were publicized through newspaper interviews published in *Neues Deutschland* (20 October 1949) and *National-Zeitung* (6 June 1952); both cited in Ebert, "Von der 'Kunstschule des Nordens,'" 177.

28 Stam's Palace of Culture was rejected by its intended beneficiaries, the workers at Böhlen, as a "glass box with stilts." Simone Hain, "Kultur und Kohle: Das Böhlen-Projekt" (typescript; Berlin: Institut für Regionalentwickung und Strukturplanung, n.d.). An alternative interpretation of this unbuilt project as essentially modernist, rather than neoclassical, is advanced by Simone Rümmle in *Mart Stam* (Zurich and Munich: Artemis+Winkler, 1991), 128.

29 Ebert, "Von der 'Kunstschule des Nordens,'" 174. This episode of the school's history is documented in detail in Hildtreud Ebert, ed., *Drei Kapitel Weißensee: Dokumente zur Geschichte der Kunsthochschule Berlin-Weißensee, 1946 bis 1957* (Berlin: Kunsthochschule Berlin-Weißensee, 1996).

30 Ebert, "Von der 'Kunstschule des Nordens,'" 174–75.

31 Ibid., 175, 176, n. 83.

32 Kurt Liebknecht, "Im Kampf um eine neue deutsche Architektur," *Neues Deutschland,* 13 February 1951.

33 Kurt Liebknecht, in *Der Kampf gegen den For-*

malismus in Kunst und Literatur, für eine fortschritt-liche deutsche Kultur. Referat von Hans Lauter, dis-kussion und Entschließung von der 5. Tagung des Zentralkomittees der Sozialistischen Einheitspartei Deutschlands vom 15. bis 17. März 1951 [The Battle against Formalism in Art and Literature, for a Progres-sive German Culture. Report by Hans Lauter, Discus-sion and Resolution of the SED Fifth Congress, 15–17 March 1951] (Berlin: Dietz Verlag, 1951), 94, 96.

34 Walter Ulbricht, *Das nationale Aufbauwerk und die Aufgaben der deutschen Architektur* (Berlin: Amt für Information der Regierung der DDR, 1952), 8.

35 Ebert, "Von der 'Kunstschule des Nordens,'" 177.

36 Hain, "ABC und DDR," 440.

37 Walter Gropius to Donald Drew Egbert, 14 Octo-ber 1948, Box 7, Isaacs Papers.

38 Hubert Hoffmann to Walter Gropius, 12 Octo-ber 1946, 81M–84 bMS Ger 208 (900), Gropius Archive.

39 Walter Gropius to Wilhelm Jakob Hess, 9 January 1948, 81M–84 bMS Ger 208 (874), Gropius Archive.

40 Walter Gropius to Hans Scharoun, 12 July 1946, 81M–84 bMS Ger 208 (1472), Gropius Archive; form letter from Harvard Committee on Military Government and International Administration, 27 November 1942, UAIII 10,196.10, Harvard Archives.

41 C. J. Friedrich to Chester D'Arms, 22 July 1947, Box 7, Isaacs Papers.

42 Many of these images are reproduced in "'Inter-national sind die Säulen . . .': Bilder und Gedanken zu Walter Gropius' Vortrag," *Neue Bauwelt,* no. 36 (1947): 567–69.

43 Hans Scharoun, "Gropius als Gast der Tech-nischen Universität Berlin," *Neue Bauwelt,* no. 37 (1947): 583.

44 "Russian Propaganda Regarding American Way of Life," 10 October 1947. Records of the Army Staff, Assistant Chief of Staff (G–2) Intelligence Administra-tive Division, Document Library Branch Publications Files, 1946–51, RG 319 270/9/23/7, Box 2900, Na-tional Archives.

45 On the history of these U.S. propaganda efforts, see Serge Guilbaut, *How New York Stole the Idea of Modern Art: Abstract Statement, Freedom, and the Cold War,* trans. Arthur Goldhammer (Chicago: University of Chicago Press, 1983); Robert Burstow,

"The Limits of Modernist Art as a 'Weapon of the Cold War': Reassessing the Unknown Patron of the Monu-ment to the Unknown Political Prisoner," *Oxford Art Journal* 20, no. 1 (1997): 68–80; and Frances Stonor Saunders, *The Cultural Cold War: The CIA and the World of Letters* (New York: New Press, 1999).

46 Walter Gropius, "Proposed Planning Procedure for Frankfurt am Main to Be the Capital of Western Germany," OMGUS Records of the Civil Administra-tion Division, Executive Branch, Central Files 1945–1949. RG 260/390/42/24/32, Box 93, National Ar-chives. New York City planning chief Robert Moses was an alternative for Gropius's consulting position in occupied Germany. According to Carl J. Friedrich, Gropius had "a great deal more to contribute to the re-construction of German cities than Bob Moses." Fried-rich to Chester D'Arms, 22 July 1947, Box 7, Isaacs Papers. That the U.S. military government considered Moses as a contender suggests that its primary con-cern was planning a new western capital, and not German-American cultural relations.

47 "U.S. Is Reported Ready to Build New Frankfurt," *Herald Tribune,* 17 December 1947. The story also appeared in the *New York Times, Washington Post,* the *Boston Globe,* and in newspapers throughout Germany. In Berlin's Soviet sector, the SED newspa-per *Neues Deutschland* reported that plans for the new western capital had been approved by the British and American negotiators after they had sabotaged the quadripartite conference on Germany's future; "48 Stunden nach London: Architekt Gropius über amerikanische Baupläne für Frankfurt," 18 December 1947. Other interpretations of the Frankfurt scandal can be found in Friedhelm Fischer, "German Recon-struction as an International Activity," in *Rebuilding Europe's Bombed Cities,* ed. Jeffry M. Diefendorf (Houndmills: Macmillan Press, 1990), 140–41; and Reginald Isaacs, *Gropius: An Illustrated Biography of the Creator of the Bauhaus* (Boston: Bulfinch, 1991), 260–61.

48 Walter Gropius to Hans Scharoun, 12 July 1946, 81M–84 bMS Ger 208 (1472), Gropius Archive.

49 Hubert Hoffmann to Walter Gropius, 20 June 1947, 81M–84 bMS Ger 208 (1472), Gropius Ar-chive.

50 David E. Murphy, Sergei A. Kondrashev, and George Bailey, *Battleground Berlin: CIA vs. KGB in*

the Cold War (New Haven, CT: Yale University Press, 1997).

51 Precisely what use was made of Gropius's matchmaking efforts between Scharoun and Durand will only be known when CIA archival sources are declassified. However, East German archives have revealed that Scharoun's Institut für Bauwesen (IfB) was seething with political intrigues and espionage scares just as Durand's CIA headquarters came of age in the late 1940s (as documented in IfB correspondence of November 1948, DH2 DBA A/39, in the Bundesarchiv SAMPO).

52 Gustav Kilian Ringel, "Bemühungen um die Rückkehr Schmitthenners an die T.H. Stuttgart," in *Schönheit Ruht in der Ordnung: Paul Schmitthenner zum 100. Geburtstag,* ed. Gerhard Müller-Menckens (Bremen: Wolfdruck, 1984), 114, 117; HICOG Office of the Executive Secretary, General Records 1947–52, RG 466/250/83/24/3, Box 49, National Archives. For a discussion of the Schmitthenner affair, see Hartmut Frank, "Trümmer: Traditionelle und moderne Architekturen in Nachkriegsdeutschland," in *Grauzonen. Kunst und Zeitbilder: Farbwelte 1945–1955,* ed. Bernard Schutz (Berlin: NGBK Medusa, 1983).

53 Inge Scholl, quoted in Eva von Seckendorff, *Die Hochschule für Gestaltung in Ulm: Gründung (1949–1953) und Ära Max Bill (1953–1957)* (Marburg: Jonas Verlag, 1989), 18–19.

54 Ibid., 33–34.

55 Ibid., 30.

56 Otl Aicher to Max Bill, 25 March 1950, quoted in Seckendorff, *Die Hochschule für Gestaltung in Ulm,* 31.

57 John P. Steiner to Inge Scholl, 27 April 1950, quoted in Seckendorff, *Die Hochschule für Gestaltung in Ulm,* 31.

58 Seckendorff, *Die Hochschule für Gestaltung in Ulm,* 34.

59 "Geschwister-Scholl-Hochschule/Ulm Graduate School of Design Instruction Method and Programme," Max Bill to Walter Gropius, 2 May 1950, 81M–84 bMS Ger 208 (464), Gropius Archive.

60 John J. McCloy, quoted in Betts, "The Bauhaus as Cold War Legend," 94, n. 30.

61 Max Bill to Walter Gropius, 2 May 1950, 81M–84 bMS Ger 208 (464), Gropius Archive.

62 Walter Gropius to Max Bill, 28 May 1950, 81M–84 bMS Ger 208 (464), Gropius Archive.

63 Seckendorff, *Die Hochschule für Gestaltung in Ulm,* 31.

64 Max Bill to John J. McCloy, 15 April 1952, quoted in Seckendorff, *Die Hochschule für Gestaltung in Ulm,* 31–32.

65 Walter Gropius to John J. McCloy, 23 April 1952, Box 1 (Bill file), Isaacs Papers.

66 John J. McCloy, quoted in Thomas Alan Schwartz, *America's Germany: John J. McCloy and the Federal Republic of Germany* (Cambridge, MA: Harvard University Press, 1991), 28.

67 On the strategies deployed by the U.S. Marshall Plan to promote international-style modernist household furnishings as a medium for the creation of a transnational consumer culture, see my essay "Building Culture in East and West Berlin: Two Cold War Globalization Projects," in *Hybrid Urbanism: On Identity and Tradition in the Built Environment,* ed. Nezar Alsayyad (London: Praeger, 2001).

68 Richard Biedrzynski, quoted in Seckendorff, *Die Hochschule für Gestaltung in Ulm,* 82.

69 Robin Kinross, "Hochschule für Gestaltung Ulm: Recent Literature," *Journal of Design History* 1 (1988): 253.

70 On the multiple directions of Ulm HfG pedagogy in its "post-Bill" era, see Paul Betts, "The Pathos of Everyday Objects," 119–206, and "Science, Semiotics and Society: The Ulm Hochschule für Gestaltung in Retrospect," *Design Issues* 14, no. 2 (Summer 1998): 67–82; Robin Kinross, "Hochschule für Gestaltung Ulm"; Kenneth Frampton, "Apropos Ulm: Curriculum and Critical Theory," *Oppositions* 3 (May 1974): 17–36; and Herbert Lindinger, ed. (Trans. David Britt) *Ulm Design: The Morality of Objects* (Cambridge, MA: MIT Press, 1990).

71 Tomás Maldonado, "New Developments in Industry and the Training of Designers," *Architects' Yearbook* 9 (1960): 174–80.

72 Tomás Maldonado and Gui Bonsiepe, "Science and Design," *Ulm* 10/11 (May 1964): 8–9.

73 Claude Schnaidt, *Hannes Meyer: Bauten, Projekte und Schriften. Buildings, Projects and Writings,* trans. D. Q. Stephenson (New York: Architectural Book Publishing, 1965).

74 Reyner Banham, untitled review of Hans Wingler's book *Bauhaus, Art Quarterly* 34, no. 1 (Spring 1971): 113.

75 Maldonado, "New Developments," 175.

76 Tomás Maldonado, "Design Education," in *Education of Vision*, ed. Gyorgy Kepes (New York: George Braziller, 1965), 132.

77 Claude Schnaidt, "Architecture and Political Commitment," *Ulm* 19/20 (August 1967): 30–32; quoted in Kenneth Frampton, *Modern Architecture: A Critical History* (New York: Thames and Hudson, 1992), 287.

78 Hans M. Wingler, *Bauhaus* (Cambridge, MA: MIT Press, 1969), 575.

79 Paul Reilly, "German Enterprise in Wallpaper Design," *Design* 55 (July 1953): 16–19, quoted in Paul Betts, "The Pathos of Everyday Objects," 181, n. 196.

80 This phenomenon is compellingly documented in Paul Betts, "The Bauhaus as Cold-War Legend," 75–100.

81 Rudolf Schwarz, "Bilde Künstler, Rede Nicht," *Baukunst und Werkform* 6, no. 1 (January 1953): 9–17.

82 Hermann Mäckler, "Praeceptor Germaniae et Europas?" *Baukunst und Werkform* 6, no. 2 (February/March 1953); reproduced in Ulrich Conrads et al., eds., *Die Bauhaus Debatte 1953* (Braunschweig: Vieweg, 1994), 71 (emphasis in the original).

83 Ibid., 80, 77.

84 CIAM-Gruppe Hamburg. Gustav Hassenpflug, Werner Hebebrand, Bernard Hermkes, Rudolf Hilebrecht, et. al., "Siehe auch die Verurtielung von anderer Seite . . ." *Die Neue Zeitung*, 11/12 April 1953. Reproduced in Conrads et al., *Die Bauhaus Debatte*, 121.

85 Richard Döcker to Walter Gropius, 5 March 1953, in Conrads et al., *Die Bauhaus Debatte*, 55–56.

86 Paul Betts, "The Bauhaus as Cold War Legend," 76.

87 For example, as of 1951 in Leningrad (considered one of the best-housed cities in Russia), on average three to four entire families shared an apartment unit designed for a single household. Blair A. Ruble, "From Khrushcheby to Korobki," in *Russian Housing in the Modern Age: Design and Social History*, ed. William Craft Brumfield and Blair A. Ruble (Cambridge: Cambridge University Press, 1993), 255.

88 Successive volleys in this debate, which pitted reformists and traditionalists within East Germany's state-managed design establishment against each other, appeared in the professional journal *Deutsche Architektur* in 1959. They include Herbert Letsch, "Das Bauhaus—Wegweiser zur sozialistischen Architektur?" (no. 8, 459–60); and Lothar Kühne, "Der Revisionismus in Architekturtheorie," (no. 10, 575–77).

89 L. Pazitnov, *Das schöpferische Erbe des Bauhauses, 1919–1933* (Berlin: Institut für angewandte Kunst, 1963). The last East German denunciation of the Bauhaus as a degenerate aesthetic was Herbert Letsch, "Die konstruktivistische Ästhetik und das Problem der künstlerischen Widerspieglung der Wirklichkeit" [The Constructivist Aesthetic and the Problem of Artistic Reflection of Reality], *Deutsche Zeitschrift für Philosophie* 9, no. 2 (1961): 1102–18.

90 Karl-Heinz Hüter submitted his manuscript "Das Bauhaus in Weimar. Studie zur Sozialgeschichte einer deutschen Kunstschule" [The Weimar Bauhaus: Towards a Social History of a German Art Academy] for publication by the Bauakademie in 1968 and received assurances that it would be published. Three years later he was still writing exasperated letters attempting to solve the mystery of why the Bauakademie had suddenly reversed itself and deemed the manuscript unpublishable (letter attached to Hüter's uncataloged manuscript, archive of the Institut für Regionalentwicklung und Strukturplanung, Berlin-Erkner). Hüter's study was finally published in 1976, timed to coincide with the restoration of the Dessau Bauhaus building. On East Germany's retrieval of the Hannes Meyer Bauhaus as a beacon of socialist design, see Winfried Nerdinger, "Anstösiges Rot: Hannes Meyer und der linke Baufunktionalismus—ein verdängtes Kapitel der Architekturgeschichte," in *Hannes Meyer, 1886–1954*, ed. Peter Hahn (Berlin: Ernst & Sohn, 1989), 12–29.

91 Leonardo Benevolo, *The Modern Movement*, Vol. 2 of *History of Modern Architecture*, trans. H. D. Landry (Cambridge, MA: MIT Press, 1971), 425. This case was of special concern to the party, given Benevolo's international standing as a "[socially] progressive Italian art historian" ("Beschluß des Sekretariats des ZK der SED," 7 April 1976, DH2 A/499, SAMPO, 5).

92 "Beschluß des Sekretariats des ZK der SED," 7 April 1976, 5–6. It is interesting to note that, in making its decision to proceed with the renovation project, for historical information about the Bauhaus the SED relied on a translation of a Russian work on the school, published in 1962 by Leonid Pazitnov, rather than any of the more recent East German studies that had appeared since then.

93 Ibid.

94 Gerhard Strauss, "Mart Stam und sein früher Versuch: Traditionen des Bauhauses in der DDR schöpferisch aufzunehmen," 542.

95 "Origins of Socialist Countries' Architecture: Bulgaria, Czechoslovakia, GDR, Hungary, Poland, USSR," in a theme issue of *Architecture and Society* 4/5 (1985/1986): 50.

96 As proposed in the theme issue of *Architecture*

and Society dedicated to "Origins of Socialist Countries' Architecture," the imagined tradition of Soviet bloc architecture also spanned stylistic boundaries to include everything from expressionism to socialist realism, both defined as expressions of "revolutionary romanticism."

97 See Simone Hain, "Zwischen Arkonaplatz und Nikolaiviertel. Stadt als soziale Form versus Inszenierung. Konflikte bei der Rückkehr in die Stadt," in *Stadt der Architektur, Architektur der Stadt: Berlin 1900–2000,* ed. Thorsten Scheer et al. (Berlin: Nikolai, 2000), 336–47.

98 Gert Selle, *Design-Geschichte in Deutschland von 1870 bis heute* (Cologne: Dumont, 1990).

99 Peter Blake, *Form Follows Fiasco: Why Modern Architecture Hasn't Worked* (Boston: Little, Brown, 1977), 123.

100 Tom Wolfe, *From Bauhaus to Our House* (New York: Farrar, Straus and Giroux, 1981), 20–26.

SELECT BIBLIOGRAPHY

Albers, Anni. *On Weaving*. Middletown, CT: Wesleyan University Press, 1963.

Alofsin, Anthony. *The Struggle for Modernism: Architecture, Landscape Architecture and City Planning at Harvard*. New York: W. W. Norton, 2002.

Anderson, Stanford. *Peter Behrens*. Cambridge, MA: MIT Press, 1999.

Bartram, Alan, *Bauhaus, Modernism and the Illustrated Book*. New Haven, CT: Yale University Press, 2004.

Baumhoff, Anje. *The Gendered World of the Bauhaus: The Politics of Power at the Weimar Republic's Premier Art Institute, 1919–1932*. Frankfurt am Main: Peter Lang, 2001.

Bax, Marty. *Bauhaus Lecture Notes, 1930–1933*. Amsterdam: Architectura and Natura Press, 1991.

Bayer, Herbert, Walter Gropius, and Ise Gropius. *Bauhaus, 1919–1928*. New York: Museum of Modern Art, 1938.

Benton, Tim, Charlotte Benton, and Aaron Scharf. *Design 1920s: German Design and the Bauhaus 1925–32; Modernism in the Decorative Arts: Paris, 1910–1930*. Bletchley: Open University Press, 1975.

Betts, Paul. *The Authority of Everyday Objects: A Cultural History of West German Industrial Design*. Berkeley and Los Angeles: University of California Press, 2004.

———. "The Bauhaus as Cold War Legend: West German Modernism Revisited." *German Politics and Society* 14, no. 2 (1996): 75–100.

Blaser, Werner. *After Mies: Mies van der Rohe, Teachings and Principles*. New York: Von Nostrand Reinhold, 1977.

Buddensieg, Tilmann. *Industriekultur: Peter Behrens and the AEG, 1907–1914*. Translated by Mark Jarzombek. Cambridge, MA: MIT Press, 1981.

Campbell, Joan. *The German Werkbund: The Politics of Reform in the Applied Arts*. Princeton, NJ: Princeton University Press, 1978.

Cohen, Arthur A. *Herbert Bayer: The Complete Work*. Cambridge, MA: MIT Press, 1984.

Dearstyne, Howard. *Inside the Bauhaus*. New York: Rizzoli, 1986.

Driller, Joachim. *Breuer Houses*. London: Phaidon, 2000.

Droste, Magdalena. *Bauhaus, 1919–1933*. Berlin: Bauhaus-Archiv Museum für Gestaltung, 1990.

———. *Marcel Breuer, Design*. Cologne: Taschen, 1990.

Fiedler, Jeannine. *Laszlo Moholy-Nagy*. London: Phaidon, 2001.

———, ed. *Photography at the Bauhaus*. Cambridge, MA: MIT Press, 1990.

Fiedler, Jeannine, and Peter Feierabend, eds. *Bauhaus*. Cologne: Könemann, 1999.

Forgács, Éva. *The Bauhaus Idea and Bauhaus Politics*. Budapest: Central European University Press, 1995.

Franciscono, Marcel. *Walter Gropius and the Creation of the Bauhaus in Weimar: The Ideals and Artistic Theories of Its Founding Years*. Urbana: University of Illinois Press, 1971.

Geelhaar, Christian. *Paul Klee and the Bauhaus*. Bath: Adams and Dart, 1973.

Gropius, Walter. *The New Architecture and the Bauhaus*. New York: Museum of Modern Art, 1936.

Guilbaut, Serge. *How New York Stole the Idea of Modern Art: Abstract Expression, Freedom, and the Cold War*. Translated by Arthur Goldhammer. Chicago: University of Chicago Press, 1983.

Hays, K. Michael. *Modernism and the Posthumanist Subject: The Architecture of Hannes Meyer and Ludwig Hilberseimer*. Cambridge, MA: MIT Press, 1992.

Herdeg, Klaus. *The Decorated Diagram: Harvard Architecture and the Failure of the Bauhaus Legacy*. Cambridge, MA: MIT Press, 1983.

Heskett, John. *German Design, 1870–1918*. New York: Taplinger, 1985.

Hight, Eleanor M. *Picturing Modernism: Moholy-Nagy and Photography in Weimar Germany*. Cambridge, MA: MIT Press, 1995.

Hochman, Elaine. *Bauhaus: Crucible of Modernism*. New York: Fromm, 1997.

Hyman, Isabelle. *Marcel Breuer, Architect: The Career and the Buildings*. New York: Harry N. Abrams, 2001.

Isaacs, Reginald. *Walter Gropius: An Illustrated Biography of the Creator of the Bauhaus*. Boston: Bulfinch, 1991.

Itten, Johannes. *Design and Form: The Basic Course at the Bauhaus*. New York: Reinhold, 1963.

Jeffries, Matthew. *Politics and Culture in Wilhelmine Germany: The Case of Industrial Architecture*. Oxford: Berg, 1995.

Kandinsky, Wassily. *Kandinsky: Complete Writings on Art*. Edited by Kenneth C. Lindsaz and Peter Vergo. Boston: G. K. Hall, 1982.

Kaplan, Louis. *Laszlo Moholy-Nagy: Biographical Writings*. Durham, NC: Duke University Press, 1995.

Kaplan, Wendy, ed. *Designing Modernity: The Arts of Reform and Persuasion, 1885–1945*. New York: Thames and Hudson, 1995.

Kentgens-Craig, Margret. *The Bauhaus and America: First Contacts 1919–1936*. Cambridge, MA: MIT Press, 1999.

———, ed. *The Dessau Bauhaus Building 1926–1989*. Translated by Michael Robinson. Basel: Birkhäuser, 1998.

Kinross, Robin. *Modern Typography: An Essay in Critical History*. London: Hyphen Press, 1992.

Kracauer, Siegfried. *The Mass Ornament: Weimar Essays*. Edited and translated by Thomas Y. Levein. Cambridge, MA: Harvard University Press, 1995.

Lambert, Phyllis, ed. *Mies in America*. New York: Harry N. Abrams, 2001.

Lane, Barbara Miller. *Architecture and Politics in Germany, 1918–1945*. Cambridge, MA: Harvard University Press, 1968.

Lehman, Arnold L., and Brenda Richardson, eds. *Oskar Schlemmer*. Baltimore: Baltimore Museum of Art, 1986.

Long, Rose-Carol Washton. *Kandinsky: The Development of an Abstract Style*. Oxford: Clarendon Press, 1980.

———, ed. *German Expressionism: Documents from the End of the Wilhelmine Era to the Rise of National Socialism*. Berkeley and Los Angeles: University of California Press, 1995.

Lupton, Ellen, and J. Abbott Miller, eds. *The ABC's of [triangle square circle]: The Bauhaus and Design Theory*. New York: Herb Lubalin Study Center of Design and Typography, Cooper Union for the Advancement of Science and Art, 1991.

Maciuika, John V. *Before the Bauhaus: Architecture, Politics and the German State, 1890–1920*. Cambridge: Cambridge University Press, 2005.

Moholy-Nagy, László. *Painting, Photography, Film*. Translated by Janet Seligman. Cambridge, MA: MIT Press, 1987.

Muthesius, Hermann. *The English House*. Translated by Janet Seligman. Introduction by Dennis Sharp. New York: Rizzoli, 1979.

———. *Style-Architecture and Building Art*. Translated by Stanford Anderson. Santa Monica, CA: Getty Center for the History of Art and Humanities, 1995.

Naylor, Gillian. *The Bauhaus Reassessed: Sources and Design Theory*. New York: E. P. Dutton, 1985.

Nerdinger, Winfried. *Walter Gropius*. Berlin: Gebr. Mann Verlag, 1985.

Neumann, Eckhard, ed. *Bauhaus and Bauhaus People*. New York: Van Nostrand Reinhold, 1970.

Passuth, Krisztina. *Moholy-Nagy*. New York: Thames and Hudson, 1985.

Pevsner, Nikolaus. *Pioneers of the Modern Movement from William Morris to Walter Gropius*. London: Faber and Faber, 1936.

Poling, Clark V. *Kandinsky: Russian and Bauhaus Years*. New York: Solomon R. Guggenheim Museum, 1983.

———. *Kandinsky's Teaching at the Bauhaus: Color Theory and Analytical Drawing*. New York: Rizzoli, 1986.

Pommer, Richard, and Christian F. Otto. *Weissenhof 1927 and the Modern Movement in Architecture*. Chicago: University of Chicago Press, 1991.

Pommer, Richard, David Spaeth, and Kevin Harrington. *In the Shadow of Mies: Ludwig Hilberseimer, Architect, Educator, and Urban Planner*. Chicago: Art Institute of Chicago, 1986.

Posener, Julius. *From Schinkel to the Bauhaus: Five Lectures on the Growth of Modern German Architecture*. Preface by Dennis Sharp. London: Architectural Association, 1972.

Riley, Terence, and Barry Bergdoll, eds. *Mies in Berlin*. New York: Museum of Modern Art, 2001.

Roters, Eberhard. *Painters of the Bauhaus*. New York: Praeger, 1969.

Schlemmer, Oskar. *The Letters and Diaries of Oskar Schlemmer*. Edited by Tut Schlemmer. Translated by Krishna Winston. Middletown, CT: Wesleyan University Press, 1972.

Schlemmer, Oskar, László Moholy-Nagy, and Farkas Molnár. *The Theater of the Bauhaus*. Introduction by Walter Gropius. Middletown, CT: Wesleyan University Press, 1961.

Schulze, Franz. *Mies van der Rohe: A Critical Biography*. Chicago: University of Chicago Press, 1985.

———, ed. *Mies van der Rohe: Critical Essays*. New York: Museum of Modern Art, 1989.

Schwartz, Frederic J. *The Werkbund: Design Theory and Mass Culture before the First World War*. New Haven, CT: Yale University Press, 1996.

Sembach, Klaus-Jürgen. *Henry van de Velde*. New York: Rizzoli, 1989.

Siebenbrodt, Michael, ed. *Bauhaus Weimar—Designs for the Future*. Ostfildern-Ruit: Hatje-Cantz, 2000.

Weltge, Sigrid Wortmann. *Women's Work: Textile Art from the Bauhaus*. San Francisco: Chronicle Books, 1993.

Whitford, Frank. *Bauhaus*. London: Thames and Hudson, 1984.

———, ed. *The Bauhaus: Masters and Students by Themselves*. With additional research by Julia Engelhardt. London: Conran Octopus, 1992.

Wick, Rainer K. *Teaching at the Bauhaus*. Ostfildern-Ruit: Hatje Cantz, 2000.

Wingler, Hans M. *Bauhaus: Weimar, Dessau, Berlin, Chicago*. Translated by Wolfgang Jabs and Basil Gilbert. Cambridge, MA: MIT Press, 1978.

Wolfe, Tom. *From Bauhaus to Our House*. New York: Farrar, Straus and Giroux, 1981.

CONTRIBUTORS

GREG CASTILLO is senior lecturer in architecture at the University of Sydney, Australia. His essay "Design Pedagogy Enters the Cold War: The Reeducation of Eleven West German Architects" was named the best article published in 2004 in *Journal of Architectural Education.* He collaborated with Spiro Kostof on *The City Assembled: The Elements of Urban Form through History.*

KATHLEEN JAMES-CHAKRABORTY is professor of architecture at the University of California, Berkeley. She is the author of *Erich Mendelsohn and the Architecture of German Modernism, German Architecture for a Mass Audience,* and *"In the Spirit of Our Age": Erich Mendelsohn's B'nai Amoona Synagogue.*

JULIET KOSS is assistant professor of art history at Scripps College in Claremont, California. She is the author, most recently, of "On the Limits of Empathy" (*Art Bulletin,* March 2006) and is currently completing *The Total Work of Art: Modernism, Spectatorship, and the Gesamtkunstwerk.*

ROSE-CAROL WASHTON LONG is professor of art history at the Graduate Center, City University of New York. Her many publications include *German Expressionism: Documents from the End of the Wilhelmine Empire to the Rise of National Socialism* and *Kandinsky: The Development of an Abstract Style.*

JOHN V. MACIUIKA is assistant professor of art and architectural history at Baruch College of the City University of New York. He is the author of *Before the Bauhaus: Architecture, Politics, and the German State, 1890–1920,* and has published essays on Adolf Loos and on the architecture of Lithuania.

WALLIS MILLER is associate professor of architecture at the University of Kentucky in Lexington. Her essay on Berlin's 1987 International Building Exhibition was named the best article published in 1993 in the *Journal of Architectural Education.* She also contributed to the catalog of the exhibition Mies in Berlin held at the Museum of Modern Art, New York, in 2001.

WINFRIED NERDINGER is professor of architectural history and director of the architecture museum at the Technical University in Munich. His many books on a variety of nineteenth- and twentieth-century German topics include *Bauhaus-Moderne im Nationalsozialismus: Zwischen Anbiederung und Verfolgung* and *Walter Gropius.*

FREDERIC J. SCHWARTZ is a reader in the history of art at University College London. He has written numerous articles on German critical theory and is the author of *The Werkbund: Design Theory and Mass Culture before the First World War* and *Blind Spots: Critical Theory and the History of Art in Twentieth-Century Germany.*

INDEX

German Werkbund. *See* Werkbund, German